POLICY COMMUNITIES AND PUBLIC POLICY IN CANADA:

A Structural Approach

William D. Coleman, McMaster University
Grace Skogstad, University of Toronto

Copp Clark Pitman Ltd.
A Longman Company

ISBN 0-7730-4982-7

Executive Editor: Brian Henderson
Editing: Brenda Clews
Design: Bill Laughton
Typesetting: Andrea Weiler
Printing and binding: Alger Press

Canadian Cataloguing in Publication Data

Main entry under title:

Policy Communities and Public Policy in Canada

Proceedings of a conference held at the University of Toronto, May 1989.
Includes bibliographical references.
ISBN 0-7730-4982-7

1.Political planning–Canada–Congresses.
2.Policy sciences–Congresses. I. Coleman,
William D. (William Donald), 1950– .II. Skogstad,
Grace Darlene, 1948– .

JL75.P65   1990320'.6'0971   C89-090747-1

Copp Clark Pitman Ltd.
2775 Matheson Blvd. East
Mississauga, Ontario
L4W 4P7

Associated Companies:
  Longman Group Ltd., London
  Longman Group Inc., New York
  Longman Cheshire Pty., Melbourne
  Longman Paul Pty., Auckland
Printed and bound in Canada

CONTENTS

ACKNOWLEDGEMENTS

The chapters which comprise this collection were first presented at a conference at the University of Toronto in May 1989. The idea for the conference was one we shared with Paul Pross; we thank him for agreeing to join our endeavour. The success of the conference, and the revision of papers for subsequent publication, was expedited by the helpful comments of the following individuals who served as discussants: Michael Atkinson, Sylvia Bashevkin, Grant Jordan, Klaus Schubert, Hugh Thorburn, and Robert Young. Marsha Chandler, Henry Jacek, and Ronald Manzer also made important contributions to the conference's success.

The financial assistance of the Social Sciences and Humanities Research Council of Canada (through grant 443-89-0014) was crucial in funding the conference and preparing the papers for publication. The project has also been funded by the British Council, the Premier's Office of the Government of Ontario, the Departments of Political Science at McMaster University and the University of Toronto, and by Peter George, Dean of Social Science at McMaster University.

No edited collection can proceed without the cooperation of all contributors. The editors have been especially fortunate in this regard. We would like to thank all contributors for meeting our deadlines and for their enthusiasm and support for the project. It has been most enjoyable to work with them.

A number of individuals in the departments of Political Science at McMaster University and the University of Toronto have lent important support. At the University of Toronto, we would like to thank Vera Melnyk, for ensuring the success of the May Conference; Ilone Eurchuk, for her word processing expertise; and Yvonne Rose for secretarial support. At McMaster University, Mara Minini and Lori Ewing have provided much appreciated assistance. We would like to thank Brenda Clews for her invaluable editorial contribution. Our last word of thanks is to two individuals who do not appear in this volume but who have done much to help us clarify our thoughts: Michael Atkinson and Richard Stubbs.

T he late 1980s in Canadian political science have seen a growing
convergence in research focus of two previously distinct sub-
fields: interest group studies and public policy analysis. The
focus of interest group research has expanded beyond traditional
concerns with political influence to include the different roles groups
might assume in the policy process and the implications these differences might have on group structure.[1] And, recent studies of public policy
have given particular prominence to organized interests in the policy
formation process and the politics of policy implementation. These
studies have begun to address themes related to state autonomy and
bureaucratic capacity.

The role of organized interests and their relations with particular
bureaus emerge as a crucial component in policy studies where researchers have integrated some of the insights of the interest group
subfield. We see this approach in studies of agricultural policy
(Skogstad, 1987a, 1987b), unemployment insurance (Pal, 1987),

textiles restructuring (Mahon, 1984), industrial policy (Atkinson and Coleman, 1985, 1989a), native peoples (Weaver, 1981), transportation policy (Schultz, 1980; Kaplan, 1989), fisheries (Pross and Mc-Corquodale, 1987), health policy (Tuohy, 1988) and defence procurement (Atkinson and Nossal, 1981), to name but a few. Such policy studies have furthered our theoretical understanding both of the state and of organized interests in policy-making.

These investigations of the role of organized interests in the Canadian public policy process, when linked to broader theoretical debates surrounding the concepts of corporatism and the relative autonomy of the state, share several common themes. First, they have forced a reconsideration of the long-dominant pluralist model of interest intermediation. They have done so not only by demonstrating the variety of roles organized interests play in policy-making, but also by highlighting the role of the state in structuring sectoral demands and influencing the organization and strategies of interest associations. Moreover, while pluralists point to a number of resources that affect organized interests' political influence, the debates over corporatism have revealed the utility of paying closer attention to the internal structural characteristics of interest groups and to the structure of the *associational systems* to which groups belong. The involvement of groups in the implementation of policy, for example, often rests upon how comprehensively they represent their domains, their ability to discipline and control their members' behaviour, and their policy and administrative expertise. Similarly, if groups are to participate directly in the formulation of policy, these same properties again become relevant for assessing the likelihood of success and hence the utility of the policy that eventually emerges (Berry, 1974; Coleman and Jacek, 1983; Coleman, 1988; Fulton and Stanbury, 1986; Goldstein, 1979; Toner and Doern, 1986; Tuohy, 1976).

Second, it has proven fruitful to concentrate studies at the sectoral or meso level. Following Arthur Wassenberg (1982), we distinguish three levels at which an analysis can be carried out. The *macro* level refers to the organizing principles of the political regime—federalism, parliamentary government, the Charter of Rights and Freedoms, for example—and to societal-wide phenomena such as social classes and overall economic performance. The *micro* level includes localized, very specialized and limited activities such as the behaviour of individual persons, the activity of single firms, voting behaviour in one constituency, or a strike at a single plant. Between these two levels falls a third level of analysis, the *sectoral* or *meso* level. Included at this level are the activities of particular sectors or regions of the economy, the behaviour of one part of the labour movement such as the Autoworkers or Steelworkers, and the decision-making of a limited set of state agencies and politicians.

Wassenberg gave an initial impetus to this focus on sectors when he argued that the sectoral level is often the site for productive negotiations between state agencies and societal actors while symbolic posturing takes place at the macro level and more bitter class conflict occurs at the micro level. This observation became a working hypothesis in a series of books that have emerged during the 1980s (Atkinson and Coleman, 1989a; Cawson, 1985, 1986; Wilks and Wright, 1987; Grant, 1985, 1987a, 1987b; Grant, Paterson and Whitson, 1988; Streeck and Schmitter, 1985).

Third, consistent with an interest in the meso level of analysis is a growing dissatisfaction with global characterizations of the "state." Conceptions of the state developed in comparative political economy that have drawn contrasts between strong and weak states have been of limited use at the sectoral level. Inconsistencies have occurred frequently; supposedly strong states have been found to harbour sectors dominated by classical pressure group politics and so-called weak states to possess sectors where state capacity and autonomy were surprisingly strong. Similarly, views offered by radical political economy on the essential unity of the capitalist state, or on the posited domination of a particular coalition of interests of the business class by one of its members (a hegemonic fraction) have provided less assistance when it comes to sectoral level politics. The assumed correspondence between state structures and class organization postulated by radical political economy theory has offered little in the way of explanations for the variations in state capacity and autonomy across sectors of the state.

The apparent importance of sectoral organizations in civil society and the benefits obtained from disaggregating the state reflect, we suspect, both changes in Canadian political institutions and ongoing changes in the global economy. Thus, a structural approach that stresses the analysis of sectors and a disaggregated state, and that allows for variations in state capacity, state autonomy and the organizational development of interests across sectors, appears to accommodate better these domestic political and global economic changes.

Specifically, on the domestic front, since the promulgation of the Charter of Rights and Freedoms in 1982, various Supreme Court decisions relating to national defence, minority language rights, abortion, and trade union activity suggest the courts will have an expanded role in defining the contours of public policy. Morton (1987) noted that this enhanced role provided organized interests with new targets and may call into question long-standing hypotheses about the greater effectiveness of institutionalized groups as opposed to single issue groups.

Changes in national and provincial decision-making processes also have altered the environment for organized interests by reshaping the autonomy and policy processes of the state. Some argue (Gillies, 1981; Pross, 1985) that the emergence of central agencies complicates the task of interest groups by diminishing the role of traditional clientele departments and their ministers. So in the bureaucratic forum, in contrast to the courts, the advantage goes to the most institutionalized and best-resourced groups. Also, changes in parliamentary procedures, which enhance the roles of standing committees and private members, have created new opportunities for alliances between groups and elected officials. The diffusion of policy-making authority at the national level, Pross argues, alters the strategies of organized interests by making Parliament a more important target for group activity. Moreover, he claims that such structural changes diffuse state authority and change the role of associations in the policy process. Competing with one another for resources and influence, bureaucratic agencies try "to give all who are most affected by specific policies an opportunity to influence them" and they grope "towards more comprehensive representation of interests" (Pross, 1985: 74).

Dupré believes that the transition from the departmentalized to the institutionalized cabinet of collegial decision-making "means that departmental ministers and officials are less effective conduits for the claims of client interest groups than was once the case" (1985: 25). Special interests are now subject to "greater scrutiny and increased competition" than happened previously (1985: 4). The scrutinizing agency has varied depending on the government (Aucoin, 1986), but the institutionalization of cabinet decision-making appears to be firmly entrenched.

Changes in the character of international relations also reinforce the need for a particular focus on sectors. The process of trade liberalization initiated after the Second World War and the stabilization of the economies of Western Europe and Japan following reconstruction have been followed by gradual restrictions on the amplitude of national sovereignty. Individual states have felt increased pressure to coordinate internationally each of macro-economic, fiscal, financial and monetary policy. Attempts among capitalist states to harmonize economic policy-making resulting from the movement toward open markets in Europe and from attempts to build more elaborate free trade areas in North America and in East and South-East Asia constrain the operation of "national differences" in the policy sphere. The European Community example indicates that efforts to harmonize economic policy bring in their wake an interest in coordinating policies affecting the environment, product quality standards, and vocational training.

Ironically, perhaps, the movement of policy deliberations on such issues as environmental quality or the regulation of financial markets from the national to the supra-national plane reinforces the importance of sectoral level analysis in the domestic national context. Invariably policy negotiations at the international level take place among *sector-specific* state agencies and draw less frequently on broader political input. The internationalization of policy-making thus reinforces the importance of sectoral actors in individual states. The development of a national approach to these international discussions will often evolve out of intensive negotiations between the relevant state agencies and sector-specific interest associations.

Awareness of these domestic political and global economic changes, in addition to the theoretical concerns that have emerged from the convergence of interest group studies and policy analysis, represented the primary reasons for the convening of a conference on organized interests and public policy in May 1989. The editors drafted a paper that outlined an analytic framework that focussed on the capabilities of both state and societal actors in the given sector and on the relationships that exist among them. The concepts of policy community and policy network sought to incorporate these very capabilities and relationships. Participants at the conference prepared their papers reacting to the framework and suggesting changes and adaptations. The revised theoretical approach constitutes Chapter One of this book. In addition, the individual chapters were all revised based on discussions at the conference and the comments of the editors. The book begins with an introductory chapter that highlights the arguments and findings of the eleven sectoral chapters. Due to the large number of organizations referenced throughout the book, an acronym glossary is provided at the end of the book to assist the reader.

References

Atkinson, M.M. and William Coleman (1985). "Corporatism and Industrial Policy." In Alan Cawson, ed. *Organized Interests and the State: Studies in Meso-Corporatism.* London: Sage: 22-44.

_____ (1989a). *The State, Business and Industrial Change in Canada.* Toronto: University of Toronto Press.

Atkinson, M.M. and Kim Richard Nossal (1981). "Bureaucratic Politics and the New Fighter Aircraft Decisions." *Canadian Public Administration*, 24: 531-62.

Aucoin, Peter (1986). "Organizational Change in the Machinery of Canadian Government: From Rational Management to Brokerage Politics." *Canadian Journal of Political Science*, 19: 3-28.

Berry, Glyn R. (1974). "The Oil Lobby and the Energy Crisis." *Canadian Public Administration*, 17: 600-35.

Cawson, Alan, ed. (1985). *Organized Interests and the State: Studies in Meso-Corporatism*. London: Sage.

_____ (1986). *Corporatism and Political Theory*. Oxford: Basil Blackwell.

Coleman, William D. (1985). "Analysing the Associative Action of Business: Policy Advocacy and Policy Participation." *Canadian Public Administration*, 28: 413-33.

_____ (1988). *Business and Politics: A Study in Collective Action*. Montreal: McGill-Queen's University Press.

Coleman, William D. and Henry J. Jacek (1983). "The Roles and Activities of Business Interest Associations in Canada." *Canadian Journal of Political Science*, 16: 257-80.

Dupré, J. Stefan (1985). "Reflections on the Workability of Executive Federalism." In R. Simeon, eds. *Intergovernmental Relations*. Toronto: University of Toronto Press: 1-32.

Fleck, James and Isiah Litvak (1984). *Business Can Succeed*. Toronto: Gage.

Fulton, Jane and W.T. Stanbury (1985). "Comparative Lobbying Strategies in Influencing Health Care Policy." *Canadian Public Administration*, 28: 269-300.

Gillies, James (1981). *Where Business Fails*. Montreal: Institute for Research on Public Policy.

Goldstein, Jonah (1979). "Public Interest Groups and Public Policy: The Case of the Consumers Association of Canada." *Canadian Journal of Political Science*, 12: 137-55.

Grant, Wyn P., ed. (1985). *The Political Economy of Corporatism*. London: Macmillan.

_____ (1987a). *Business and Politics in Britain*. London: Macmillan.

_____ ed. (1987b). *Business Interests, Organizational Development and Private Interest Government: A Study of the Food Processing Industry*. Berlin: de Gruyter.

Grant, Wyn P., William Paterson and Colin Whitson (1988). *Government-Industry Relations in the Chemical Industry: An Anglo-German Comparison*. Oxford: Oxford University Press.

Kaplan, Harald (1989). *Policy and Rationality: The Regulation of Canadian Trucking*. Toronto: University of Toronto Press.

Mahon, Rianne (1984). *The Politics of Industrial Restructuring: Canadian Textiles*. Toronto: University of Toronto Press.

Morton, F.L. (1987). "The Political Impact of the Canadian Charter of Rights and Freedoms." *Canadian Journal of Political Science*, 20: 31-56.

Murray, V.V., ed. (1985). *Theories of Business-Government Relations*. Toronto: TransCanada Press.

Pal, Leslie A. (1987). *State, Class and Bureaucracy: Canadian Unemployment Insurance and Public Policy*. Montreal: McGill-Queen's University Press.

Pross, A.P. (1975). *Pressure Group Behaviour in Canadian Politics*. Toronto: McGraw-Hill.

Pross, A.P. (1985). "Parliamentary Influence and the Diffusion of Power." *Canadian Journal of Political Science*, 18: 235-66.

_____ (1986). *Group Politics and Public Policy*. Toronto: Oxford University Press.

Pross, A. P. and Susan McCorquodale (1987). *Economic Resurgence and the Constitutional Agenda: The Case of the East Coast Fisheries*. Kingston: Institute of Intergovernmental Relations.

Schultz, Richard (1980). *Federalism, Bureaucracy, and Public Policy*. Montreal: McGill-Queen's University Press.

Skogstad, Grace (1987a). "State Autonomy and Provincial Policy-Making: Potato Marketing in New Brunswick and Prince Edward Island." *Canadian Journal of Political Science, 20: 501-524.*

_____ **(1987b).** *The Politics of Agricultural Policy.* Toronto: University of Toronto Press.

Stanbury, W.T. (1986). *Business-Government Relations in Canada.* Toronto: Methuen.

Streeck, Wolfgang and P. C. Schmitter, eds. (1985). *Private Interest Government.* London: Sage.

Toner, Glen and G.B. Doern (1986). "The Two Energy Crises and Canadian Oil and Gas Interest Groups: A Re-examination of Berry's Propositions." *Canadian Journal of Political Science, 19: 467-93.*

Tuohy, Carolyn (1976). "Private Government, Property and Professionalism." *Canadian Journal of Political Science, 9: 668-81.*

_____ **(1988).** "Medicine and the State in Canada: The Extra-Billing Issue in Perspective." *Canadian Journal of Political Science, 21: 267-96.*

Wassenberg, Arthur F. (1982). "Neo-Corporatism and the Quest for Control: the Cuckoo Game." In P. Schmitter and G. Lehmbruch, eds. *Patterns of Corporatist Policy-Making.* London: Sage.

Weaver, Sally (1981). *Making Canadian Indian Policy.* Toronto: University of Toronto Press.

Wilks, Stephen and Maurice Wright, eds. (1987). *Comparative Government-Industry Relations.* Oxford: Oxford University Press.

Endnotes

1. These questions were posed first by Pross (1975, 1986) when he elaborated and extended his distinction between issue-oriented versus institutionalized groups. They have been further addressed by Coleman (1985, 1988) in the distinction between policy advocacy and policy participation and in frameworks elaborated by those in business administration interested in questions related to issues management (Fleck and Litvak, 1984; Murray, 1985; Stanbury, 1986).

INTRODUCTION

T he studies in this volume reflect the diversity and range of policy-making processes that prevail across provincial and federal governments in Canada. Together, these studies pose questions to students of public policy both about methodologies that can be used in policy studies and about the very nature of the policy process in Canada. All the chapters in this volume, except for those by Yates *(Chapter 11)* and Landry *(Chapter 12)*, draw heavily on a structural approach utilizing the concepts of policy community and policy network that are outlined in Chapter One. Yates' chapter on labour and lobbying, which falls more directly within the radical political economy tradition than any of the others, departs somewhat from the overall framework. Landry in his chapter, "Biases in the Supply of Public Policies to Organized Interests," uses a public choice approach to the study of organized interests that diverges radically from the remaining chapters. Underlying the divergence between Landry's chapter and the rest are differences over whether political institutions should be viewed as historical entities that have an independent impact on political behaviour and events. These differences translate into distinct approaches to conducting research on organized interests and public policy.

This chapter begins with a review of methodological issues. It then summarizes the major hypotheses related to the public policy process in Canada that emerge from this book. Specifically, we argue that the Canadian state must be disaggregated and that attention be paid to variations in the strength of the Canadian state across sectors. The increase in concern with the character of organized interests noted in the preface must be reflected, in our view, in more research on the level of organizational development of these groups. Certainly, this book indicates clearly that variations in organizational development have an important bearing on a group's ability to influence policy outcomes. The book stresses as well that the structural characteristics of the relationships between state actors and societal groups vary widely across sectors and that these differences greatly affect democratic access to the policy process and the likelihood of policy change. Finally, a structural approach that focusses on policy communities and policy networks highlights how the character of the policy process has evolved in the postwar period from relationships that are relatively informal and usually cooperative (Presthus, 1973) to ones that are highly formal, more frequently adversarial, and increasingly technocratic in character.

Methodological Issues: Institutionalism versus Public Choice

The structural or institutional approach used in most chapters holds, first, that the preferences and values of policy actors are shaped fundamentally by their structural position. Institutions are conceived as structuring political reality and as defining the terms and nature of political discourse (March and Olsen, 1986). Political institutions, accordingly, take on a life of their own; as autonomous political actors, they promote certain ideologies and constrain the choices of individuals. When referring to political institutions, the authors in these chapters look at formal rules of operation, intra-organizational structures, and various operating practices. Where these are not clearly defined, these authors tend to examine with care the expressed values and norms offered by those working in the institutions.

Second, all of the chapters have a relational component (Hall, 1986: 19). They seek to characterize patterns of relationships among societal actors—interest associations, firms, individual persons—and state agencies. In mapping these relationships, the authors pay particularly close attention to the internal organization of the actors and agencies in play. The net cast over these kinds of relationships tends to be wide. Not only do the authors examine the patterns of interaction between multiple societal actors and a plurality of state actors, but also, in most cases, they consider market structures as well. Whether this consideration refers to the internationalization of finance *(Chapter 4)*, international competition in forest products *(Chapters 5, 6)*, the changing role of women in the economy *(Chapter 8)*, or the organization of labour markets *(Chapter 11)*, economic variables are seen to affect political-institutional relationships. Yates, reflecting the assumptions of radical political economy, finds these variables to be of overriding importance for understanding the political action of autoworkers; they assume less importance in other chapters. None the less, the emphasis on institutional relationships that occurs in most chapters is found in Yates's chapter as well.

Underlying these assumptions is a normative question about who possesses political power in a given policy area. The most powerful, it is believed, are those who will have the greatest impact on the outcomes of policy. All institutional chapters, including that by Yates, seek to identify differences in political power and endeavour to use these differences to evaluate particular policy outcomes. It is evident that this approach to research is fraught with difficulties and often no clear answers can be given. Thus, although progress has been made, the contribution of the chapters collectively has been to raise hypotheses rather than present generalizations about the relationships between the structures of policy communities and policy networks and the outcomes of public policy-making.

Following institutionalist assumptions also appears to favour a particular methodology. Chapters utilizing a structural approach first looked at institutions historically. As autonomous, relatively fixed actors, institutions are seen as developing over time. Hence several authors found it important to search out archives of information on the historical development of institutions. Archival evidence also furnishes information about the ideas, values, and norms shared by those working within institutions. In many cases, authors supplemented these archival sources with interviews of key persons currently working in state institutions in order to determine further the contours of these value systems. Interviews were also crucial for mapping out the important relationships within a policy community and determining their frequency, the degree of interdependence between actors, and ultimately the relative capacity for action of each member of a policy network. Techniques of elite interviewing and the collection of qualitative information took precedence over mass public interviews and quantitative data.

This institutionalist approach differs significantly from the public choice approach favoured by Landry in Chapter 12. It must be recognized that Landry's minority status in this volume by no means reflects the relative unimportance of the public choice approach to the study of organized interests; on the contrary, his approach is likely the dominant one in US political science. Perhaps the most important difference between the public choice and the institutionalist or structuralist approaches lies in their respective conceptions of institutions. In the public choice approach, institutions provide the rules of the game. They do not, however, determine the values and preferences of political actors. Values and preferences are exogenously (or externally) determined, based on economic position, social class or technology. Hence Landry tends to speak about broad groups of economic actors— owners of production factors, consumers, entrepreneurs, workers— and assumes that their wants and demands arise from their economic position.

Because preferences that are exogenously determined form the theoretical starting point for their analysis, public choice theorists pay less attention to the internal workings of institutions and to the differences among specific policy communities. Where the institutionalist chapters took great pains to sketch out the internal organizational properties of societal and state actors and to map out policy networks, Landry's starting point is policy outputs across all policy areas over a significant historical period. Each of the three theoretical hypotheses he examines empirically, whether related to market failure, vote maximization or party ideology, is based on definitions of preferences. These are again exogenously given, and not endogenously (or internally) determined by the structures of policy communities and policy networks. Since the same basic rationality prevails throughout the given political system, the public choice theorist is less concerned with differences at the sectoral level. The macro institutional rules of the game are seen to affect all policy arenas, allowing the social scientist to define a wide data base for analysis. Landry's chapter thus focusses system-wide on an analysis of all outputs of Québec's National Assembly over a 20 year period.

Drawn from the discipline of economics, the public choice approach has elaborated a more formal theory linking the preferences of political actors and public policy outcomes. Landry is able to use this theory in postulating several hypotheses that are rather formal in character and give his chapter a scientific emphasis not found in the other chapters. His analysis of data is rather distinct as well; rather than a qualitative sifting of idiographic information, he uses a quantitative assessment of literally thousands of policy outputs. At the end of his chapter, he is able to reach rather firm conclusions about the strengths and weaknesses of each hypothesis examined.

Underlying these differences may be distinctive normative positions. Landry appears to be committed to the development of a formal, scientific theory of politics. He also assumes that the avenue to such a theory flows out of neo-classical economics and its assumptions about individual rationality.[1] The other authors in the collection appear less committed to this goal. Although they too are empirical in their approach and interested in policy outcomes, the question of the distribution of power takes precedence over a formal theory of politics. The double focus on individual behaviour and institutional dynamics requires a level of complexity of analysis that does not lend itself at this stage to quantification.

The Canadian State

The studies in this collection suggest caution when seeking to speak of the Canadian state in aggregate terms. Thus, at the provincial level, Québec, for instance, shows strength across a range of policy areas which include agriculture, labour, occupational health and safety, and financial institutions. In other provinces, the strength of the state shows more variance across policy sectors. Thus, Newfoundland authorities have considerable capacity to devise fisheries policy *(Chapter 2)*, while the remaining Atlantic provinces are much weaker. Similar interprovincial differences occur in banking policy *(Chapter 4)*, and in forestry policy *(Chapters 5, 6)* where the strength of the BC state is not paralleled in other provinces.

Nor is the federal state uniformly strong. It has been shown to have considerable strength when dealing with policies for banking *(Chapter 4)*, social welfare *(Chapter 9)*, and official language minority groups *(Chapter 7)*, but appears weaker when treating forestry *(Chapters 5, 6)* and fisheries issues *(Chapter 2)*. The institutional base upon which to build a policy-making capacity for addressing forestry issues, primarily a matter of provincial jurisdiction, has been virtually absent until very recently. Even in the fisheries arena, a sphere over which the federal government exercises predominant jurisdiction and responsibility, the fragmentation of policy-making authority away from the lead department, the Department of Fisheries and Oceans, weakens state capacity. Finally, the combination of strong capabilities at both the federal and provincial levels may create the possibility for a stalemate in the formulation of policy. This problem was identified in banking *(Chapter 4)* and, to a lesser extent, in agriculture *(Chapter 3)*.

If the studies reported here demonstrate the merits of caution when speaking of the state as a whole and of disaggregating the state, they also help us to refine our conceptualization of state strength. First, they underline the importance of distinguishing between state autonomy and capacity, a point that we elaborate further in Chapter One. An autonomous state is not necessarily a policy-capable state. For example, although the weakness of organized interests leaves the state with considerable independence when formulating day care policy *(Chapter 8)*, the dispersion of authority across a number of government agencies and departments seriously weakens its capacity to devise a coherent policy. Nor is a state with considerable financial, jurisdictional, and bureaucratic capability to execute its own goals and programmes, necessarily willing to do so. Instances have been cited in both banking and farm policy where state authorities have been reluctant to act autonomously and prefer to proceed only with the support of the client community. This gap between state actors' willingness to act on their own goals and their ability to devise their own agenda suggests that perceptions of autonomy vis-à-vis societal interests are important in determining state strength.

The ability of state actors to control access to the policy network and thereby control the policy agenda (Wilks and Wright, 1987: 304) emerges as an important indicator of state autonomy. Wilson *(Chapter 6)* points to the skillfulness of officials in British Columbia's Ministry of Forests in keeping issues of environmental land use at the margins of the forestry policy agenda. Network access and agenda control are also a gauge of sectoral state actors' autonomy from trans-sectoral actors such as departments of finance. For example, indicative of the decline in the independence of officials in the federal Department of Health and Welfare is their inability to prevent officials from other departments (Finance) from entering the social welfare policy network and seizing control of its agenda *(Chapter 9)*.

The focus on network access and agenda control as indicators of sectoral state autonomy highlights the close relationship between the strength of the state and the strength of organized interests. Sectoral state actors appear to be more able to control the policy agenda—from interference by private interests and other public actors—when they enjoy the support of well organized client interests. Close state-societal relations may augment the state's ability to proceed with its state-societal agenda. Tuohy *(Chapter 10)* suggests that the PQ government succeeded in implementing its corporatist proposals for occupational health and safety regulation with the help of its alliance with organized labour. The ministries of agriculture in Québec and Ontario retain a pre-eminent role on interdepartmental committees examining international trade policy issues not only because of their considerable policy capacity, but also because of the legitimacy they derive from their close links to farm groups *(Chapter 3)*. Conversely, the ineffectiveness of the Women's Bureau in pursuing maternity leave pay in the 1950s and 1960s probably owed much to the absence of an organizationally well developed women's lobby *(Chapter 8)*.

But the line between state-societal interdependence and state autonomy is a fine one. In policy sectors where societal-state relations are embedded and politicized, state autonomy may be sufficiently attenuated to exist "only at the margins" (Cairns, 1986). Thus, official language minority groups' dependence upon the state for funding would seemingly give state officials considerable scope to act on their own goals; however, Pal *(Chapter 7)* suggests that state and society are so interpenetrated in this area that state authorities cannot act independently.

The studies shed light on other instruments that state authorities draw upon to enhance and preserve their strength. Autonomy may be increased by the state's exploiting its jurisdictional base, defining its legislative mandate so as to leave extensive pools of discretionary power in the hands of cabinet ministers and their officials, and making symbolic and minor substantive concessions that do not threaten agenda control. Trans-sectoral events that threaten to destabilize the state economically or politically can provide the incentive and rationale for growth in the state's capacity. Illustrative examples are the buildup of state capacity on forestry issues following recognition of a "crisis" facing the industry *(Chapter 5)*; the increase in the capacity of the state to supervise the behaviour of individual banks, following deregulation of banking and greater international competition *(Chapter 4)*; and the growth in the capacity of the Secretary of State on matters of official language minority policy in the wake of the threat to national unity posed by Québécois nationalism *(Chapter 7)*.

To summarize, the institutional parameters of the Canadian state favour considerable variation in state capacity across policy sectors and territorial jurisdictions. Similarly, these parameters invite different degrees of interdependence between societal actors and state agencies which lead again to different levels of state autonomy across sectors. To the extent that these findings can be generalized, they cast doubt on attempts to speak of the Canadian state in holistic or global terms: for example, by referring to the "relative autonomy" of the Canadian state, by saying that the Canadian state is "embedded" in society, or by suggesting that the state organizes the hegemony of a single class fraction of the capitalist class. Future theoretical reflection on the nature of the Canadian state must try to specify better the institutional properties that foster such a disaggregated entity.

Organizational Development of Societal Interests

Variations in the strength of the state across sectors are accompanied by significant differences in the level of organizational development of societal interests. We develop in some detail the meaning of this concept in Chapter One. Well developed associational systems represent the interests of Newfoundland fishermen, Québec farmers, Canadian bankers, and forestry companies. By contrast, groups that articulate the interests of social welfare recipients, day care clients, labour, BC forest environmentalists, and Maritime fishermen are fragmented, competitive, and generally undeveloped. Between these two ends of the continuum, displaying medium and variable levels of organizational development are groups representing Ontario farmers, Québec businessmen, and fish processors.

Affecting the degree of organizational development of societal interests are both logic of influence (environmental) and logic of membership (internal characteristics of the industry or social group which affect the interests and motives of individuals) factors. Logic of membership factors are clearly important. As the examples of the Maritime fishery *(Chapter 2)*, Ontario agriculture *(Chapter 3)*, and BC forest environmentalists *(Chapter 6)* attest, organizational development is variously impeded by economic, cultural, and ideological diversity; geographic dispersion; and an ideology of individualism and independence. It is furthered by shared communal traits (such as a common language and collectivist ideology among Québec farmers), and vertical integration (such as exists in the forest industry).

Perhaps more surprising is the impact of environmental factors on organizational development. A number of state policies and goals have acted as catalysts to the mobilization and growth of organized interests. The studies in this volume indicate that the state in Canada has often assisted the organizational development of groups representing the disadvantaged. Although women's groups had existed for close to a century before the Royal Commission on the Status of Women, the implementation of that commission's report gave rise to a funding programme for status of women groups *(see Chapter 8)*. By the late 1980s, much of the network formed around the National Action Committee for the Status of Women was drawing heavily on these state funds. Similar programmes assisted the poor and official language minorities. Pal *(Chapter 7)* attributes the emergence of the Fédération des francophones hors Québec, the umbrella group for provincial official language minority associations, to sustained financial support in order to improve consultative structures between them and the

Secretary of State. Pross and McCorquodale (Chapter 2) note that state funding was drawn upon by the Nova Scotia Fishermen's Association, an organization representing the "small folk" in the fishery sector.

Yet the pursuit of organizational development through state support has obvious limits. The groups involved feel rather constrained when their agenda challenges the orientation of governments and of the corporate sector. If they take their challenge too far, they risk losing their funds and perhaps their capacity to act. If they back down from the agenda established by their members, the group faces factionalism and eventual disintegration. To varying degrees, all of the groups accepting state support have experienced these tensions during the 1980s. State sponsorship of interest associations appears to be as much a method for controlling dissent as it is for assisting the disadvantaged. The possibilities for state-supported groups to initiate policy innovations are clearly limited.

The state may also promote organizational development directly by legislating corporatist structures or by supporting the development of monopolies of representation. Tuohy *(Chapter 10)* describes how the Parti québécois government developed a corporatist-like structure for the administration of occupational health and safety legislation in Québec. The new structure offered labour a stronger voice in this policy arena than it had had under the previous system of employer-controlled safety associations. Tuohy shows that participation in these structures has resulted in greater integration of organized labour, as "organizational and strategic bonds among rival labour federations and unions" are forged. Yet these arrangements remain fragile because of the weak level of organizational development of labour in the province and, to a lesser extent, of business.

Yates *(Chapter 11)* demonstrates the creation of more informal tripartite structures in Ontario that incorporated labour representation. These arrangements did not prove to be particularly useful to labour. In fact, the Ontario example reverses the procedures found in European corporatism. In Europe, the structural arrangements for the organization and representation of class interests are highly formalized while discussions within these structures tend to be informal and free-wheeling (Marin, 1985). In Ontario, structural arrangements are very informal with the bargaining then tending to be much more formalized, stylized, and empty of real significance.

Skogstad *(Chapter 3)* and, to a lesser extent, Coleman *(Chapter 4)*, document the value of state support for representational monopolies. The Union des producteurs agricoles in Québec received such a monopoly through state legislation and the association has used this asset to develop the most highly integrated and cohesive farmers' organization in Canada. This monopoly position, coupled with the high degree of integration of the associational system has increased significantly the effectiveness of Québec's farmers in the policy process, and probably within the national peak association, the Canadian Federation of Agriculture. Coleman notes that the Canadian Bankers' Association received a state-sanctioned monopoly when it was incorporated by Parliament in 1900. This asset has been used well by bankers as they have fashioned one of the most effective business interest associations in Canada.

Conversely, state policies can also handicap the growth of strong associational systems. We see this in the Ontario state's promotion of sub-sectoral (commodity) interests, which, combined with other factors, mitigate sector-wide mobilization and thwart the emergence of a strong provincial agricultural producer associational system *(see Chapter 3)*. The fragmentation of the BC forest environmental movement *(Chapter 6)* has undoubtedly been furthered by the province's adoption of a piecemeal rather than comprehensive approach to forest land use issues.

Whether the state advances or hinders the organizational development of societal interests, these studies certainly offer support for a more general point made in discussions of corporatism. Systems of interest intermediation are not simply given and completely divorced from the state; the state intervenes to structure these systems in ways that attempt to advance its own interests (Offe, 1981; Schmitter, 1982).

Events and institutions outside the sector can clearly affect incentives for interest mobilization and organizational growth. Changes in the international economy that threaten to destabilize the sector may have a catalytic effect on organizational development. One example is the trade disputes with the United States, which spurred the development of the Canadian Forest Industries Council *(Chapter 5)*. Another is the threat posed to the job security and incomes of Ontario labour by the growing competitive edge of Asian auto manufacturers in the late 1970s *(Chapter 11)*; the latter had the dual effect of making Ontario labour more cohesive and the state more inclined to grant legitimacy to union leadership. Certainly, rapid changes in communications technology that furthered the globalization of capital markets were crucial to the formation of the Canadian Payments Association in the banking sector *(Chapter 4)*.

Trans-sectoral institutions may also, directly or indirectly, impede interest associational strength. The competitive party system in the Maritimes, argue Pross and McCorquodale *(Chapter 2)*, has directly thwarted the growth of fishermen's unions by dividing fishermen on partisan grounds. Further, because the government is also efficient at ensuring that the interests of fishermen are heeded in the party caucus and governing cabinet, it has indirectly undermined the perceived need for a strong and united fishermen's lobby. Regarding the impact of federalism on organizational development, the limited evidence here tends to reinforce Coleman and Grant's (1985:26) finding that "association structures tend to be very sensitive to ... the actual distribution of power in a policy area." As Grant notes *(Chapter 5)*, because provinces exercise most, although not all, jurisdiction for forests, the impetus has been to organize at the provincial level. This has slowed the development of a national umbrella association representing the forest industry. The investigation of agricultural producers *(Chapter 3)* indicates that strong associational systems at the provincial level (as in Québec) may be nourished by perceptions of federal neglect and discrimination, the effects of which can only be mitigated by a responsive provincial state and provincial state-farmer solidarity before federal officials. Where federal policies and officials are perceived as more attentive (as in Ontario), the incentives to integrate producers within one provincial peak association are weaker.

Business Interests: A Special Case?

Charles Lindblom (1977) has argued persuasively that business interest associations possess a "privileged" position in the policy process. Such a position is implicit as well in much of the radical political economy literature. The comprehensive survey of policy arenas found in this volume provides some support for Lindblom's position. Pross and McCorquodale *(Chapter 2)* report that the "Big Boys" emerged the relative winners following the restructuring of the fishery during the 1970s and 1980s. The "small folk" and supportive agents in the state (fisheries biologists, Newfoundland's fishery department) were not as successful at seeing their aims implemented. Coleman *(Chapter 4)* describes how the most powerful financial institutions and banking regulators in the state maintained control over the policy process in the face of increased consumer discontent following bank and trust company failures in the 1970s and 1980s. Together Grant *(Chapter 5)* and Wilson *(Chapter 6)* detail the resilience of a concertation network composed of big forestry companies and the Ministry of Forests in British Columbia despite a sustained challenge by environmental groups. Burt *(Chapter 8)* and Haddow *(Chapter 9)* demonstrate the fragility of organized interests representing women and the poor in the face of business interests and the Department of Finance. Yates *(Chapter 11)* provides ample evidence of the subsidiary policy role played throughout the postwar period by one of the strongest trade unions in Canada, the Canadian Autoworkers Union. The bottom line of careful empirical analysis of the Québec National Assembly shows business groups to be further in the black than any other organized interest.

Yet business does not always win. From time to time, the state acts autonomously in favour of other interests; interests opposed to business may develop organizational structures that give them additional leverage in policy conflicts. Skogstad *(Chapter 3)* reflects on the strength of farmers in the policy process and describes, in particular, how greater organizational development in the Québec associational system has assisted farmers in their struggles. Coleman *(Chapter 4)* notes that a two decade long battle by financial cooperatives finally resulted in their incorporation into the policy network managing the payments system. Wilson *(Chapter 6)* describes the concertation policy network in the BC forest sector as "contested," suggesting that the forestry companies' opponents have succeeded in some of their battles to preserve forest areas. Tuohy *(Chapter 10)* shows that the institutionalization of tripartite structures, with parity for capital and labour, has improved the access of workers to decisions affecting the safety of their workplaces. Somewhat less formalized tripartism developed in the auto sector in Ontario, enabling a strong trade union to have greater input into longer term assessments of the future of the industry *(Chapter 11)*. Both the women's groups described by Burt *(Chapter 8)* and the anti-poverty organizations analyzed by Haddow *(Chapter 9)* developed policy agendas and articulated policy positions that challenged the arguments of the corporate establishment. These studies indicate that there is nothing inevitable about business victories and that challenges to business dominance by other social categories appear to be more common at the start of the 1990s than they were 30 years previously.

These examples notwithstanding, the studies in this book allow for several tentative conclusions about the role of business in the policy process. First, concertation policy networks, those where societal interests have the greatest influence over policy outcomes, virtually always include business as the societal partner. The only exception we found is that of agricultural interests in Québec *(Chapter 3)*. It is possible that other sectoral studies will furnish examples of other social categories participating in concertation networks, but we suspect that the majority of these will involve business interests. Second, even when the state intervenes on behalf of non-business interests and financially supports their organizations, as occurred with the poor *(Chapter 9)* and women's groups *(Chapter 8)*, such interests are vulnerable to challenge by other state agencies or business interest groups. Thus, it is important to note that even within pressure pluralist policy networks, all interests are not at the same level of organizational development. Again, business interest associations appear more likely to have reached a higher level of development than other societal groups.

The authors of the studies in this book have reached these conclusions after a close consideration of the structural characteristics of policy communities and policy networks. Their work reflects, as well, particular attention to the concepts of state capacity, state autonomy, and the organizational development of societal interests. Before proceeding to these studies, the book begins with a theoretical chapter that sets out the structural approach that has informed most of the research that follows.

References

Cairns, Alan (1986). "The Embedded State: State-Society Relations in Canada." In Keith Banting, ed. *State and Society: Canada in Comparative Perspective.* Toronto: University of Toronto Press.

Coleman, W.D. and Wyn Grant (1985). "Regional Differentiation of Business Interest Associations." *Canadian Journal of Political Science,* 18: 3-29.

Hall, Peter A. (1986). *Governing the Economy.* New York: Oxford University Press.

Lindblom, Charles (1977). *Politics and Markets.* New York: Basic Books.

March, James and Johan Olsen (1986). "Popular Sovereignty and the Search for Appropriate Institutions." *Journal of Public Policy,* 6: 345–65.

Marin, Bernd (1985). "Austria: The Paradigm Case of Liberal Corporatism." In Wyn Grant, ed. *The Political Economy of Corporatism.* London: Macmillan.

Offe, Claus (1981). "The Attribution of Public Status to Interest Groups: Observations on the West German Case." In S. Berger, ed. *Organizing Interests in Western Europe.* Cambridge: Cambridge University Press.

Presthus, Robert (1973). *Elite Accommodation in Canadian Politics.* Toronto: Macmillan.

Schmitter, P.C. (1982). "Reflections on Where the Theory of Neo-Corporatism Has Gone and Where the Praxis of Neo-Corporatism May Be Going." In Gerhard Lehmbruch and P.C. Schmitter, eds. *Patterns of Corporatist Policy-Making.* London: Sage.

Wilks, Stephen and Maurice Wright (1987). "Conclusion: Comparing Government-Industry Relations: States, Sectors and Networks." In Wilks and Wright, eds. *Comparative Government-Industry Relations.* Oxford: Oxford University Press: 274-313.

Endnotes

1. Tracing its origins ultimately to Adam Smith, but perhaps more significantly to Alfred Marshall, neo-classical economics includes a theory of individual economic behaviour based on assumptions about preferences and the maximization of self-interest. It posits a model of the competitive marketplace in which the laws of supply and demand dictate price.

CHAPTER ONE

POLICY COMMUNITIES AND POLICY NETWORKS:
A STRUCTURAL APPROACH

William D. Coleman and Grace Skogstad

T his chapter is organized into four sections, with each yielding some of the conceptual tools needed for public policy analysis. The first examines the issue of disaggregating the state, notes the theoretical developments that have led to this position, and suggests how the concepts of state autonomy and state capacity might be defined for empirical study. Second, we argue that although the focus in public policy studies has shifted to the sectoral level, theoretical room must be left for examining the relationship between sectoral policy-making and the more general institutional context, including state structures and traditions, at the macro level. The attention of the chapter then shifts to the specific problems of conceptualizing organized interests, including both associational systems and the properties of individual associations. Here the concept of organizational development is offered as a tool for empirical analysis. The chapter concludes with a consideration of conceptual tools available for studying the *structural relations* between groups and the state, emphasizing the opportunities provided by a policy network/policy community approach.

Thus we are proposing an approach that emphasizes the importance of structures at both the meso and macro levels. The structural characteristics of sectoral-level organizations, whether these be state agencies or societal actors, constrain the options available to policy-makers and reinforce particular values and beliefs in the policy process. The enduring character of these institutions over time must be included explicitly in the analysis of public policy. In focussing on policy communities (a term that we define more explicitly below), we stress three sets of structures: the autonomy and capacity of state agencies, the organizational development of sectoral interests, and the relationships or networks that develop between state and societal actors.

Disaggregating the State

An interest in moving toward a more disaggregated conception of the state arises out of increasing dissatisfaction with the integrated, holistic characterizations that have dominated theory in international political economy and in radical political economy. Successive studies have demonstrated that significant variations occur across sectors in the degree to which states can direct market activity and that these variations are not easily explained by broad conceptions of the "strength" of the state or, following radical political economy, by the identification of the characteristics of a particular hegemonic fraction of the capitalist class. Such broader macro-level theories of the state do not account adequately for the rich variety of state-society relations being uncovered at the meso or sectoral level of analysis.

The disaggregated study of the state as a structural variable begins with two general concepts, state *autonomy* and state *capacity*. State autonomy refers to the degree of independence from societal groups possessed by state actors when they formulate policy objectives. The goals of an autonomous state, including its diagnosis of societal problems and the formulation of policy alternatives to deal with these, are internally generated and not simply reflective of societal interests or demands. Atkinson and Coleman (1989b) suggest several characteristics of bureaucratic agencies and their staff that may enhance state autonomy.

- The bureaus involved should have a clear conception of their role and a value system consistent with and supportive of that mandate. Political support for the bureau's role should be strong.

- Where officials are charged with conveying and interpreting the demands of clientele groups, they should possess a professional ethos distinct from that prevailing among professionals in society at large. If a bureau has a functional rather than a clientele mandate (Lowi, 1979: 79-91), autonomy becomes more easily realized.

- Individual bureaus will be more autonomous when they administer a corpus of law and regulations that explicitly define their responsibilities and those of societal groups. The less these rules are subject to negotiation the greater the autonomy of the agency.

- State agencies will gain autonomy if they generate internally the information, particularly if it has a technical character, that is required for the pursuit of their mandate. An autonomous bureau will possess an in-house capacity to evaluate and employ other information collected from firms and associations.

The degree of state autonomy may vary across different agencies within the same state. In Canada, for example, decisions on energy policy in the early 1980s (Doern and Toner, 1985), on unemployment insurance in the 1960s and 1970s (Pal, 1987) and on satellite development in the 1970s (Atkinson and Coleman, 1989a) were developed by highly autonomous agencies; policies on pharmaceuticals (Campbell and Pal, 1989; Atkinson and Coleman, 1989a) and on securities regulation (Coleman, 1989) by contrast appear to have been devised by somewhat penetrated state bureaus. Based on her work with Kenneth Finegold, Theda Skocpol (1985: 14) adds that autonomy is not fixed—it varies in strength over time. Such variation may result from crises that precipitate an intensive mobilization of resources by state officials. Or they may arise "as the organizations of coercion and administration undergo transformations, both internally and in their relations to societal groups and to representative parts of government" (Skocpol, 1985: 14).

State capacity refers to the ability of the state to draw on sufficient institutional resources both to design policies that will realize its policy objectives and to implement these policies. Like state autonomy, state capacity is affected significantly by the skill of bureaucratic officials; plentiful resources are also important (Skocpol, 1985), and so is the ability to coordinate or concentrate the actions of participants in the policy process (Atkinson and Coleman, 1989b). Normally, the capacity to coordinate policy-making is enhanced when a single agency or bureau dominates relations in a given sector. Inter-departmental committees, when fully staffed, may also have the same effect. The absence of such structures can seriously undermine the state's capacity for effective policy design and implementation (Tennant, 1977).

It must be recognized that state capacity and autonomy may not occur together. Moreover, they are structural characteristics defined relative to the organizational development of societal actors and the strength of other nation-states. For example, a state agency may have sufficient autonomy to define its own policy goals, but lack capacity, that is, adequate administrative or financial resources to design policy instruments or implement policies in the face of determined societal opposition or international constraints. Similarly, capable state actors may devise policy initiatives whose successful implementation necessitates accommodating sectoral interests. Such webs of interdependence, in turn, may constrain the autonomy of state officials.

Investigations of specific policy areas and particular sectors reveal that state capacity and autonomy thus defined vary significantly across agencies within the same state. In fact, the particular mix of capacities across sectors becomes one of the key properties of any given state (Skocpol, 1985; Cawson et al., 1987). Skocpol (1985: 17-18) adds that overall assessments of the capacity and autonomy of a given state "are perhaps best built up from sectorally specific investigations, for one of the most important facts about the power of a state may be its *unevenness* across policy areas. And the most telling result, even of a far-reaching revolution or reform from above, may be the *disparate* transformations produced across sociopolitical sectors."

Sectoral Analysis and Macropolitical Institutions

The capacity, autonomy and actions of the state at the meso level will be more or less influenced by broader institutional macropolitical variables. In other words, *the relationship between the meso and macro levels of analysis is itself a variable.* In their preliminary overview of the comparative study of government-industry relations, Stephen Wilks and Maurice Wright (1987: 305-6) note some of the kinds of macropolitical institutions that may have a bearing upon sectoral policy-making: the relative preference for informal as opposed to formal procedures, rules about the acceptable mode and language for the articulation of policy issues, and informal understandings about the limits of application of state authority.

The most systematic discussion of the possible impact of macropolitical institutions on sectoral politics occurs in the work of Kenneth Dyson (1980). He (1980: 50) argues that " 'political world pictures', in terms of which political conduct is defined, and attitudes towards the accommodation of interests typical of different polities are closely related to an experience of authority . . . exercised through both public institutions and a particular set of social relations." Dyson (1980: 57) adds that the "mode of interest-group politics" depends not so much on conditions in civil society and the structure of the economy, but on "frameworks of ideas and historical experiences of authority."

Central to Dyson's analysis is the notion of a state tradition. The presence or absence of such a tradition, he suggests, is crucial to the nature of state-society relations. Societies with a state tradition have evolved a notion of an abstract, impersonal state above and distinct from the government and the governed. Such societies prefer bureaucratic and legalistic methods of conflict resolution, deny that the public interest is simply the sum of private interests, stress the distinctiveness of state and society and the unitary character of public power, and promote strongly collectivist and regulatory attitudes. Societies without such a tradition, in contrast, emphasize the role of governments in representing society. They prefer private resolution of disputes and pragmatic episodic definitions of a public interest. They function on the basis of an interpenetration of state and society and stress the diffusion of power.

Utilizing this concept in combination with several others, Dyson defines a number of ideal typical polities including a dual polity model (France under the Fifth Republic[1]), an accommodative/liberal corporatist model[2], (West Germany) and an adversarial polity (United Kingdom). Adversarial polities promote the role of public debate, are hostile to inter-party coalitions and power sharing, and discourage the effective functioning of investigative machinery within Parliament. Without an abstract concept of the state, power is easily diffused away from the centre to a host of autonomous centres of decision-making. Accompanying political world views are "not informed by a deep institutional consciousness or constitutional awareness but rather by the notion of politics as a game in which the rules, which are often vague and subject to various interpretations, are mainly the result of mutual understandings between contestants who compete for the favour of the spectators" (Dyson, 1980: 67).

The Canadian polity conforms most closely to Dyson's adversarial model. Parliament tends to be even more partisan than its British counterpart; party discipline is more strict; and the smaller size of the legislature prevents the emergence of a body of MPs who can make use of parliamentary investigative committees in a non-partisan way. With very few safe seats, members of Parliament tend to have short terms in office and thus remain "amateurs" (Franks, 1987) and fail to develop careers independent of the party organizations. Provincial legislatures do not differ significantly from the federal Parliament in these respects. In spite of the larger number of safe seats at the provincial level, the smaller size of the legislature contributes to party dominance over members.

The federal constitution sometimes accentuates these adversarial characteristics. The actual impact of federalism in any given polity, it must be noted, depends, in part, on the strength of a state tradition. Here the contrast between Canada and the Federal Republic of Germany is instructive. Dyson (1980: 218) notes that, in Germany, where the state tradition is strong, federal organs like the *Bundesrat,* the upper house composed of members appointed by the states or *Länder,* acts as an integrating force. Conceiving its institutional purpose as defending the idea of a *Bundesstaat* (federal state), this house does not act as a narrow defender of the rights of the *Länder,* but as a means for integrating regional concerns into the larger, coherent whole. In the absence of such a state tradition, however, Dyson (1980: 218) notes that federal arrangements are likely to generate zero-sum, conflictual relationships rather than cooperative political strategies. Certainly, the Canadian experience tends to heighten the visibility and political salience of intergovernmental conflict. But appearances aside, there may well be differences in the extent of cooperation and conflict across sectors, depending upon whether jurisdiction is exclusive to one level, shared, or divided between levels.

In short, the overall institutional configuration of the polity will affect the policy process at the meso level, but in an indirect fashion. Hayward (1986: 19) reminds us that the prescriptive values and culture of those who make and implement policy must be distinguished from the actual conduct of actors. The institutional and normative framework in a given polity sets the limits within which state and societal actors take initiatives, defines the extent to which policy planning can be longer term, and circumscribes the degree to which state actors can impose their will. We hypothesize that policy-making at the sectoral level will reflect these macropolitical constraints. For example, in accommodative polities, formal structures promoting negotiation among societal producer groups and the state (what we term below concertation and corporatism) will be the normal policy networks; in adversarial polities, societal groups will compete with each other rather than negotiate (what we define as pressure pluralism) yielding quite a different mode of governance. If Canada is an adversarial polity, conventional pressure group politics becomes the normal mode of state-society relations. Certainly this expectation is consistent with Alan Cairns's (1986) analysis of the "politicized society" and the "embedded state" in Canada. He (1986: 58) writes, because "both state and society are multiple, it is common for one state actor to involve segments of society in competition primarily directed against another state actor. It is equally common for private socio-economic actors to involve the state to their own advantage relative to other private actors." Nevertheless, empirical research on state-society relations in Canada and in other adversarial polities like Britain, the

United States, and Australia reveals that other modes of state-society relations occur. For example, in the prototypical pluralist, adversarial polity, the United States, Skocpol and Finegold (1982) find agencies responsible for agricultural policy-making to be highly autonomous and to have engaged in longer term planning during the New Deal era. Donald Brand (1988: 20) coins the term "administrative corporatism" for his analysis of the National Recovery Administration during the same period. Leslie Pal (1987) stresses state capacity and autonomy in the face of organized interests in explaining the character of unemployment insurance policy in Canada. In contrast, in what many have argued is the most "statist" society in Western Europe, France, Hayward (1986: 63) describes industrial policy to be the subject of a "bipartite corporatist relationship." Cawson, Holmes and Stevens (1987) describe policy-making in the French consumer electronics sector in terms of "agency capture."

The need to coin hybrid terms like "bipartite" or "administrative" corporatism, the existence of agency capture in the supposedly strong French state, or of long-term planning in the diffused and weak US state, reinforce the need for a nuanced analysis of the relationship between macro and meso level structures. Explaining departures from ad hoc, special interest group deals in adversarial polities, or from strong state direction in France, requires that explicit attention be given to sectoral level variables. The characterization of the policy process and the explanation of policy outcomes at the sectoral level will normally draw explicitly on the specific economic and social properties of the firms or individuals comprising the sector, the manner in which they organize their interests, and the relative capacity and autonomy of state agencies making policy for the sector. Such organizational attributes will often vary significantly from sector to sector and from class to class. We suspect that they become an important means for accounting for differences between the patterns of policy-making found in a given sector and those that might be expected given the broader institutional characteristics of a given policy.

Conceptualizing Organized Interests

The organizational development of interests within a sector differs depending upon the roles that sectoral associations play in policy-making. *Policy advocacy* is the first of these roles. Groups approach the state as lobbyists, outside the decision-making circles, seeking to influence the nature and content of public policy. Successful advocacy depends on the group's capacity to develop a knowledge of the policy-making process, to generate information about specific policies, to mobilize support for its policy proposals, and to maintain internal member cohesion. A second possible role, *policy participation*, requires that an association not only develop these capacities, but also formalize its internal structures and cultivate a distinct identity as an organization. Schmitter and Streeck (1981: 124) capture these requirements in their concept of organizational development. Organizational structures are said to be the more developed "the more encompassing they are in scope and purpose...; the more specialized and coordinated they are internally; the more safely their supply of strategic resources is institutionalized; and the greater their autonomous capacity to act and to pursue long-term strategies regardless of short-term environmental constraints and fluctuations."

The organizational development required for policy participation refers to two properties in particular. First, the interest organization must be able to order and coordinate a range of complex information and activity so as to arrive at positions on relatively sophisticated policy questions. Second, as an organization, the group must be sufficiently autonomous from members to be able to transcend their short-term interests and to take a longer term perspective on policy while still guaranteeing members' compliance (Coleman, 1987: 153).

The assumption of one of these roles partially depends on the structure of the *associational system* to which the individual association belongs. The associational system refers to the collection of associations within a given domain. Normally a sector will be populated by several associations with narrow, specialized domains that represent only particular structural subsectors, sub-national territories, or that restrict their activities to a limited set of functions. These contrast with more encompassing associations that possess broad domains—domains that are comprehensive in their representation of all relevant product, territorial and functional interests in a sector.

Policy participation and the capacity to order and manage complex information, to be successful, require an associational system with members who possess both narrow and broad domains. Hence the system is highly differentiated. A well-differentiated system contains sub-units that represent each of the structural sub-sectors, territorial divisions or functional tasks, and hence is capable of furnishing specialized information pertinent to particular, highly technical, policy issues. A poorly differentiated system, by contrast, does not provide the organizational means for articulating well the specific structural, territorial, or functional interests of members. It is thus handicapped when it comes to providing the specialized knowledge often requisite to effective policy participation.

Associations that participate effectively in public policy forums must also be able to coordinate and rise above very specialized interests. Hence an associational system must be able to integrate diverse and narrow interests, whether structural, territorial or functional. At the sectoral level, integration may be achieved in one of two ways. A single association may do the job, utilizing an encompassing domain and a highly differentiated internal system of subsectoral branches and regional divisions, supported by an expert staff and executive structures capable of coordinating diverse concerns. Or there may develop a sectoral peak association (an association whose members are other associations) that, by virtue of the breadth of its member organizations, is sufficiently differentiated to speak for the range of interests in its domain and that also possesses the organizational means (through executive councils and boards of directors) to integrate and find a consensus among its member associations.

The second aspect of organizational development relevant to policy participation—the autonomy of the association from the state and its members—depends on the source and diversity of the association's resources and the development of a kind of monopoly status as an intermediary between the sector and the state. The distinction is between associations that rely mainly upon members for resources and usually, therefore, have a limited and unstable supply and those which have diverse sources of institutionalized resources. In the latter case, group leaders are better able to realize the necessary autonomy from members and from the state to participate in policy-making. This independence may be facilitated by a publicly conferred legitimacy that comes from official recognition of a right to be a party to decision-making. The attainment of such a public status becomes more likely when associations lack competitors for the representation of the interests of a sector or sub-sector.

If organizational development, then, is understood to refer to a logical continuum, two extreme types of associational systems can be identified. In a weakly developed system, there is an unlimited number of specialized groups whose domains overlap and that compete with one another for members. Groups are weakly, if at all, linked together and there usually is no one encompassing association able to coordinate the diverse interests of the sector. Some interests within the domain may even remain unorganized and hence outside the associational system. Such a weakly developed system lends itself to policy advocacy. Groups with narrow, specialized domains can maintain internal cohesion more easily than those with broad domains whose members are more likely to have conflicting objectives. But as policy participants, such a system poses a problem for the state which will have to consult and seek accommodations among several, possibly competing groups. Even then, it will be difficult for state officials to know who speaks for what interest and which association is most representative of the sector.

In a strongly developed system, by contrast, associations are linked in ways to make the system encompassing in scope and purpose. They are specialized and coordinated internally, balanced and secure in their supply of resources, and autonomous in their actions and capacity to plan for the longer term (Grant and Coleman, 1987: 219). Such systems are more likely to survive in the face of unpredictable environmental pressures and are more able to engage in strategic planning for the sector. These properties, plus the opportunity they present to the state to bargain with and seek consensus among a limited number of organizations, render such a strong associational system an attractive prospective participant in policy-making.

In this way, the level of organizational development and the policy role of the association appear to be reciprocally related. Well-developed associational systems are better equipped to move beyond policy advocacy to policy participation and the incentives to increase the level of organizational development should rise as a system becomes involved in policy-making. Still the reciprocity here appears to be finely balanced. Sally Weaver's (1981) analysis of the joint Cabinet-Indian Brotherhood experiment in the early 1970s reveals that participation in policy formulation in the absence of a well-developed associational system is doomed to failure, particularly where there are no shared norms on secrecy and the language of decision-making.

Schmitter and Streeck (1981) identify two broad sets of factors that affect the level of organizational development of an associational system: the *logic of membership* and the *logic of influence (see Figure 1)*. The logic of membership refers to the interests and motivations of individuals and firms that bring them to join a group. These, in turn, will be governed by deeper values held by the individuals concerned, their sense of collective identity, and by such factors as the size of the potential membership domain, the geographical distribution of members, their resource base, and the nature of primary, informal social relations. The logic of influence includes the structures of significant institutions in the environment of the associational system, particularly the state.

Figure 1

Factors Explaining the Policy Role of Associations

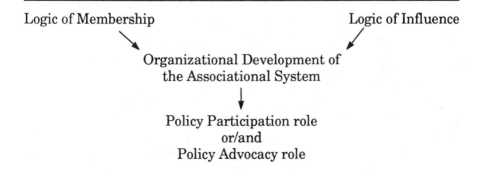

Logic of Membership   Logic of Influence

Organizational Development of
the Associational System

Policy Participation role
or/and
Policy Advocacy role

To date, analysis of these two logics has been confined largely to their impact on business interest associations. For business associations, logic of membership factors refer to industry structure. For example, the more competitive firms in a sector are with one another, the greater the differences among firms, and the larger the number of firms, the more difficult it will be to reach a higher level of organizational development. Intra-sectoral divisions between domestic- and export-oriented industries such as in agriculture are another example of a structural property likely to constrain associative action on a national plane (Skogstad, 1987b). The impact of these factors is often compounded when firms are geographically dispersed and their interests differ depending on their spatial location. In contrast, organizational development becomes easier where firms are oriented to the domestic market and hence may need the protection of the state, where oligopoly prevails, or where sectoral and territorial interests coincide at the provincial level.

The most prominent component of the logic of influence is the structure of the state itself at the sectoral level. We have already noted the properties of state capacity and autonomy. What is not always recognized is that these characteristics of the state may, in turn, shape the organization of interests. For example, decentralized state structures that vest responsibility in sub-national governments may discourage organizational development by strengthening strong and autonomous regional associations. Alternatively, where supra-national state structures (such as the European Economic Community or EEC) become important, national associational systems may receive an impetus to greater organizational development.

State policies themselves may also have an impact on organizational development. The more the government intervenes in the market to determine price and supply, the more associations may have incentives to coodinate and integrate their activities through monopolistic associations. State policies may also have contradictory effects upon organizational development. Specific agencies may encourage associational involvement in the formulation and implementation of policies thereby promoting further organizational development. Yet they may also devise different policies for different commodity groups thereby dividing the association's membership. When market structures underpinning the logic of membership are themselves influenced by state action (Grant, 1987c: 14), the effects of the two logics become difficult to disentangle.

The studies that follow in this collection demonstrate that this approach to the study of organizational development and the role of interest associations in the policy process, summarized in Figure 1, has relevance for the study of organized interests beyond those in the business community. The structural characteristics of associational systems play a significant role in shaping policy in the areas of the environment, women's issues, labour relations and occupational health, and the disadvantaged. The diversity in membership and the structures of the state shape the parameters of the roles associations are able to assume. In this respect, the chapters in this volume provide a broader empirical foundation for the organizational development framework.

Policy Communities and Policy Networks

What is perhaps most striking about the findings of studies of organized interests in recent years is the diversity in arrangements between civil society and the state. Scholars such as Katzenstein (1978) have stressed the differences in macropolitical "policy networks" in discussing variations in international economic behaviour among nation states. In his discussion of domestic influences on international policy, Katzenstein noted differences in national policy networks between the US and Britain on the one side and Japan and France on the other. Similarly, the literature on neo-corporatism that emerged in the 1970s outlined differences in societal relationships involving the state, business and labour and argued that these differences had an impact on a given nation-state's ability to manage economic crises.[3] More recent research has taken these models developed for characterizing state-society relations on the macro plane and examined their applicability on the sectoral or meso plane.[4] This research has already demonstrated that diversity in state-society relations is common across sectors within the same nation-state. At times, the differences between such relationships at the sectoral level and those at the macro level are very large indeed.

These kinds of findings have led to increased interest in disaggregating the state and to a search for concepts that would help understand better the diversity of arrangements at the sectoral level. Two concepts of particular interest are those of policy community and policy network. Following Wilks and Wright (1987b), we define *a policy community to include all actors or potential actors with a direct or indirect interest in a policy area or function who share a common "policy focus," and who, with varying degrees of influence shape policy outcomes over the long run.* For example, within the health policy universe, one could identify the policy community whose focus is the licensing and training of health care professionals.

A policy community, in turn, subdivides into two segments: the *sub-government* and the *attentive public* (Pross, 1986: 98). The sub-government, normally composed of government agencies, interest associations, and other societal organizations such as business firms, makes policy in the given field. The attentive public, whose composition varies depending on the policy field, but which is likely to contain relevant media and interested and expert individuals, is less tightly knit and more loosely defined. It follows and attempts to influence policy, but does not participate in policy-making on a regular basis.

Policy network then is a concept reserved for describing *the properties that characterize the relationships among the particular set of actors that forms around an issue of importance to the policy community*. For example, in the policy community concerned with licensing health care professions, a network might form around the question of whether chiropractors or naturopaths should be officially recognized as professionals. Two different approaches to the characterization of such policy networks, one based on power dependence and the other on structural properties of the actors involved, may be distinguished. First, Wilks and Wright (1987) following Rhodes (1985, 1986) draw on power dependence and network theory in sociology to focus on the *integration* of a policy network. A highly integrated network is characterized by stable relationships among members of the network, continuity of a highly restrictive membership, high interdependence and shared responsibility for policy implementation, and insulation from other networks (Wilks and Wright, 1987b: 301-2). By contrast, then, a weakly integrated network tends to have a less restricted and more unstable membership, a lower degree of organizational interdependence, and is more open to influences from outside the network. This continuum based on the notion of integration is then used to compare and contrast policy networks in different sectors within the same state or in the same sector but in different states. Thus, to continue our example, Wilks and Wright would examine the kinds of power dependencies existing between health care state officials and chiropractors or naturopaths and compare these with the relations maintained with other health care professionals.

Second, following Cawson, Holmes and Stevens (1987) and Atkinson and Coleman (1985, 1989b), we propose a different approach to that outlined by Wilks and Wright. We prefer to reserve the variables associated with integration in the Wilks and Wright approach for analyzing differences among policy communities. When it comes to policy networks, we find it more useful to focus upon the structural properties of state agencies and organizational interests. The key state properties are state autonomy and coordinating capacity, the ability of the state to concentrate its resources and expertise in making decisions *(see pp. 15-16)*. The relative centralization of state actors or the presence of effective inter-departmental committees are seen to be useful indicators of coordinating capacity. Organizational development, as defined above *(pp. 20-23)*, is the crucial property of sectoral interests. Differences across these variables yield six different patterns of group-state relations or policy networks that we present as ideal types. In the real political world, networks can be expected to deviate somewhat from the following models, perhaps including aspects of more than one network.

Table 1

Groupings of Policy Networks

Pluralist	Closed	State-Directed
pressure pluralism	corporatism	
clientele pluralism	concertation	
parentela pluralism		

The six different networks may be grouped loosely into three families: pluralist, closed and state-directed networks *(see Table 1)*. Pluralist networks tend to arise in sectors where state authority is fragmented and the organized interests are at a low level of organizational development. This combination of dispersed state authority and a weak associational system unable to coordinate the multiple, narrow, specialized groups competing with one another, gives rise to a mode of group-state relations where groups approach the state independently, often competing for the ear of the state. When these groups assume primarily a policy advocacy role and state agencies remain autonomous, the network that emerges is termed *pressure pluralism*. The combination of dispersed state authority and low organizational development may give rise to a second pluralist network, *clientele pluralism*, when state officials are unable to differentiate themselves from organized interests. They become dependent on interest associations to supply information and expertise and to ensure member compliance and offer them an opportunity to *participate* in the policy process in exchange. Clientele pluralism appears to have developed in Canada in the pharmaceutical sector (Atkinson and Coleman, 1985, 1989a), some components of the financial services sector (Coleman, 1988: Chapter 9), and in the delivery of health services (Tuohy, 1976; Boase, 1982).

A third pluralist network, *parentela pluralism*, arises when organized interests gain a dominant place within a governing political party that, in turn, has members in prominent bureaucratic positions. State authority tends to be diffused to party/state officials who operate at the regional level. The growth of bureaucratic pluralism, the decline of political parties, and the reduced relevance of legislatures in Canada reduce the likelihood of this network at the national level. However, the coincidence of one party dominance and dependence on only one or two industries in some provinces (Richards and Pratt, 1979; Skogstad,

1987a) may provide conditions rather conducive to parentela pluralism.

Associations may thus assume either a policy advocacy (pressure, parentela) or a policy participation (clientele) role in pluralist networks. But all pluralist networks involve bilateral relations between the state and groups with weak associational systems. In situations where state agencies have the capacity to be autonomous from the sectoral interests, pressure pluralism is more likely; where autonomy is less developed and officials are dependent on sectoral groups, clientele pluralism may arise.

Pluralist networks stand in considerable contrast with a second family of group-state relations that we term *closed* policy networks. In a closed policy network, state decision-making capacity is concentrated and well-coordinated, normally through the offices of a single agency that has persisted for some time. Organized interests play a prominent role, tending to draw on highly developed associational systems that guarantee a virtual monopoly relationship with the dominant agency. Two different types of closed networks have been identified.

Corporatist networks are multilateral in composition: two or more organized interests representing conflicting producer or consumer groups participate with the state in the formulation and implementation of policy. Such a network usually arises when a particular group finds its very viability threatened by impending economic or social change and responds by developing a highly integrated associational system to defend its interests against perceived economic or social opponents. In such situations of real or apprehended societal conflict, the state seeks to draw the conflicting interests inside the policy arena to formulate a policy compromise. It then delegates sufficient authority so that the respective associational systems can enforce the compromise on their members. Grant (1987c: 16) summarizes well the trade-offs involved: "organised interests involved in corporatist arrangements are necessarily drawn closer to the state; the price of partnership is some loss of autonomy." Both the multilateral character of the network and the stronger position of the state differentiate corporatism from clientele pluralism. Tuohy's *(Chapter 10)* discussion of occupational health and safety in Québec provides a useful illustration of a corporatist network.

Concertation refers to a second closed network: a single association represents a sector and participates with a corresponding state agency in the formulation and implementation of policy. The state agency has considerable capacity in its own right, being autonomous and able to concentrate power for coordinated decision-making. Sectoral interests match the state's strength by drawing on an inclusive, hierarchical associational system capable of engaging in longer term policy deliberations while maintaining member support. Concertation networks occur frequently in Japan (Samuels, 1987) and to some extent in France (Zysman, 1983). They will be more likely at the sectoral level in Canada when business associations are strong and labour, consumer, or other public interest groups are weak. Their bilateral character distinguishes them from corporatism; the strength of the state differentiates them from clientele pluralism. Wilson *(Chapter 6)* and Grant *(Chapter 5)* describe a concertation network in the forest sector; Coleman *(Chapter 4)* notes the development of this kind of network in the banking sector.

The third general category of policy networks, *state-directed* networks, include highly autonomous, coordinated state agencies and sectoral interests with a very weak associational system, possibly at a nascent stage. As such, organized interests play neither an important advocacy nor participant role in the policy process. State officials dominate policy-making and are able to impose their solutions, often without even consulting organized interests. Evidence in Canada suggests that these networks arise in three kinds of circumstances. First, the state may be able to set directions for a sector autonomously from organized interests in times of crisis (Berry, 1974). Such state direction, however, tends to be short-lived because it encourages sectoral interests to reorganize so as to strengthen their position in the policy network. Second, the state may take a lead role in fostering the development of an industry from an infant stage (Atkinson and Coleman 1989a) or even of more developed organized interests. Haddow's *(Chapter 9)* analysis of the poor, Pal *(Chapter 7)* of official language minorities, and Burt *(Chapter 8)* of women's issues all illustrate this phenomenon. In such circumstances, the network is likely to persist until the sector reaches a more mature stage of development and has built up an associational system capable of policy advocacy or participation. Third, where policies tend to be horizontal, thus affecting a broad spectrum of interests, the state can take advantage of weak encompassing organizations to impose its own point of view. Pal's (1987) analysis of unemployment insurance policy illustrates well this scenario.

In reflecting further upon the concepts of policy community and policy network, these definitions must not be allowed to overshadow the dynamics of the policy process involved. First, policy communities are institutions in themselves and become integrated to greater or lesser degrees by developing a set of shared values, norms and beliefs which shape the policy networks that emerge and, ultimately, the policy outcomes in the given sector. Attention must be given to understanding the rules of the game and the strength of the belief systems that predominate in a policy community. Second, different types of policy networks may exist within the same policy community. Several types of networks may emerge because different issues will affect the interests of members of the community to varying degrees shaping, in turn, the particular constellation of actors involved in resolving the issue. For example, Skogstad *(Chapter 3)* shows that in Ontario agriculture, corporatist policy networks prevail in regulated marketing while pressure pluralist networks predominate in most other issue areas. Similarly in the forestry sector, Wilson *(Chapter 6)* demonstrates that concertation networks predominate in issues relating to resource management while Grant *(Chapter 5)* reveals that pressure pluralism has characterized policy settlement in the area of international trade.

Third, the studies in this collection indicate that some types of policy networks are more susceptible to change over time. Wilson's *(Chapter 6)* analysis of environmental groups in British Columbia demonstrates well the resilience and staying power of concertation networks. By contrast, Tuohy's *(Chapter 10)* study of occupational health and safety emphasizes the fragility of corporatist networks in the absence of a supportive macro-level associational system. Related to this point is the fact that over time the type of policy network used for addressing an issue may itself change. The analyses of the disadvantaged by Haddow *(Chapter 9)*, of women's issues by Burt *(Chapter 8)*, and of banking by Coleman *(Chapter 4)* all illustrate these kinds of changes.

The case studies that follow were chosen to provide a broad empirical base for further theoretical development in the area of organized interests and public policy. Sectors were chosen to facilitate cross-sectoral comparisons by maximizing variations in the degree of organizational development of sectoral interests (banking versus the disadvantaged), and in the degree of state autonomy (fishing versus official language minorities) and capacity (agriculture versus the environment). Studies were selected also to allow an examination of group-state relations at two levels, the federal and the provincial, and to explore the differential impact of the courts and parliamentary committees on the structure of policy networks and on policy outcomes. As noted in the Introduction, to a significant extent, most of the chapters have drawn on the theoretical framework developed in this chapter. In this respect, the book shows the promise of this structural approach and also raises some questions to be resolved in future research. The book does include two chapters that depart to some extent from the framework presented in this chapter. Charlotte Yates' *(Chapter 11)* study of organized labour contains a broad theoretical explanation for pluralist politics that has its roots in radical political economy and the French *régulation* school. Within this framework, however, Yates does find it useful to distinguish policy networks in a manner analogous to the approach we have proposed. Similarly, her methodology—archival research coupled with elite interviews—does not differ significantly from that used in the other chapters.

A more important theoretical exception is the study by Réjean Landry *(Chapter 12).* As discussed in the Introduction, his chapter presents the most sophisticated, theoretical alternative to our structural approach, one based on public choice theory. In order to illustrate the differences in assumptions between the two approaches, Landry has provided detailed information on his research techniques and strategy. We hope that the inclusion of this chapter will indicate clearly to students of organized interests and public policy some of the key theoretical and methodological questions that will need to be addressed further in the 1990s.

References

Atkinson, M.M. and William Coleman (1985). "Corporatism and Industrial Policy." In Alan Cawson, ed. *Organized Interests and the State: Studies in Meso-Corporatism.* London: Sage: 22-44.

_____ (1989a). *The State, Business and Industrial Change in Canada.* Toronto: University of Toronto Press.

_____ (1989b). "Strong States and Weak States: Sectoral Policy Networks in Advanced Capitalist Economies." *British Journal of Political Science,* 19: 47-67.

Berry, Glyn R. (1974). "The Oil Lobby and the Energy Crisis." *Canadian Public Administration,* 17: 600-35.

Boase, Joan (1982). "Regulation and the paramedical professions: an interest group study." *Canadian Public Administration,* 25: 339-341.

Brand, Donald R. (1988). *Corporatism and the Rule of Law: A Study of the National Recovery Administration.* Ithaca: Cornell University Press.

Cairns, Alan (1986). "The Embedded State: State-Society Relations in Canada." In Keith Banting, ed. *State and Society: Canada in Comparative Perspective.* Toronto: University of Toronto Press.

Campbell, Robert M. and Leslie A. Pal (1989). *The Real Worlds of Canadian Politics: Cases in Process and Policy.* Peterborough: Broadview Press.

Cawson, Alan, ed. (1985). *Organized Interests and the State: Studies in Meso-Corporatism.* London: Sage.

Cawson, Alan, Peter Holmes, and Anne Stevens (1987). "The Interaction between Firms and the State in France: The Telecommunications and Consumer Electronics Sectors." In Stephen Wilks and Maurice Wright, eds. *Comparative Government-Industry Relations.* Oxford: Oxford University Press: 10-34.

Coleman, William D. (1985). "Analysing the Associative Action of Business: Policy Advocacy and Policy Participation." *Canadian Public Administration,* 28: 413-33.

_____ (1988). *Business and Politics: A Study in Collective Action.* Montreal: McGill-Queen's University Press.

_____ (1989). "Self-Regulation in the Canadian Securities Industry: A Case Study of the Investment Dealers Association of Canada." *Canadian Public Administration,* 32: 503-523.

Doern, G. Bruce and Glen Toner (1985). *The Politics of Energy: The Development and Implementation of the NEP.* Toronto: Methuen.

Dyson, Kenneth P. (1980). *The State Tradition in Western Europe.* Oxford: Basil Blackwell.

Franks, C.E.S. (1987). *The Parliament of Canada.* Toronto: University of Toronto Press.

Grant, Wyn P. (1987a). *Business and Politics in Britain.* London: Macmillan.

_____ ed. **(1987b).** *Business Interests, Organizational Development and Private Interest Government: A Study of the Food Processing Industry.* Berlin: de Gruyter.

_____ **(1987c).** "Introduction." In Grant (1987b).

Grant, Wyn P. and William D. Coleman (1987). "Conclusions." In Grant (1987b).

Hayward, Jack (1986). *The State and the Market Economy: Industrial Patriotism and Economic Intervention in France.* Brighton: Wheatsheaf.

Katzenstein, Peter (1978). "Conclusion: Domestic Structures and Strategies of Foreign Economic Policy." In Katzenstein, ed. *Between Power and Plenty.* Madison: University of Wisconsin Press.

Lehmbruch, Gerhard and Philippe Schmitter, eds. (1982). *Patterns of Corportist Policy-Making.* London: Sage.

Lowi, Theodore (1979). *The End of Liberalism.* Second Edition. New York: Norton.

Pal, Leslie A. (1987). *State, Class and Bureaucracy: Canadian Unemployment Insurance and Public Policy.* Montreal: McGill-Queen's University Press.

Pross, A.P. (1975). *Pressure Group Behaviour in Canadian Politics.* Toronto: McGraw-Hill.

_____ **(1986).** *Group Politics and Public Policy.* Toronto: Oxford University Press.

Rhodes, R.A.W. (1985). "Power-Dependence, Policy Communities and Inter-governmental Networks." *Public Administration,* 49: 4-31.

_____ **(1986).** *The National World of Local Government.* London: Macmillan.

Richards, John and Larry Pratt (1979). *Prairie Capitalism.* Toronto: McClelland and Stewart.

Samuels, Richard (1987). *The Business of the Japanese State.* Ithaca: Cornell University Press.

Schmitter, Philippe C. and Gerhard Lehmbruch, eds. (1979). *Trends Toward Corporatist Intermediation.* London: Sage.

Schmitter, Philippe C. and Wolfgang Streeck (1981). "The Organization of Business Interests." Discussion Paper IIM/LMP 81-13. Berlin: Wissenschaftszentrum Berlin.

Skocpol, Theda (1985). "Bringing the State Back In: Strategies of Analysis in Current Research." In Peter B. Evans, Dietrich Rueschmeyer and Theda Skocpol, eds. *Bringing the State Back In.* New York: Cambridge University Press.

Skocpol, Theda and Kenneth Finegold (1982). "State Capacity and Economic Intervention in the Early New Deal." *Political Quarterly,* 97: 255-78.

Skogstad, Grace (1985). "Interest Groups, Representation and Conflict Management in the Standing Committees of the House of Commons." *Canadian Journal of Political Science,* 18: 739-72.

_____ **(1987a).** "State Autonomy and Provincial Policy-Making: Potato Marketing in New Brunswick and Prince Edward Island." *Canadian Journal of Political Science,* 20: 501-524.

_____ **(1987b).** *The Politics of Agricultural Policy.* Toronto: University of Toronto Press.

Streeck, Wolfgang and P. C. Schmitter, eds. (1985). *Private Interest Government.* London: Sage.

Tennant, Paul. (1977). "The NDP Government of British Columbia: Unaided Politicians in an Unaided Cabinet." *Canadian Public Policy*, 3: 489-503.

Tuohy, Carolyn (1976). "Private Government, Property and Professionalism." *Canadian Journal of Political Science*, 9: 668-81.

Weaver, Sally (1981). *Making Canadian Indian Policy.* Toronto: University of Toronto Press.

Wilks, Stephen and Maurice Wright, eds. (1987). *Comparative Government-Industry Relations.* Oxford: Oxford University Press.

_____ **(1987b).** "Conclusion: Comparing Government-Industry Relations: States, Sectors, and Networks." In Wilks and Wright. *Comparative Government-Industry Relations.* Oxford: Oxford University Press: 274-313.

Zysman, John (1983). *Governments, Markets, and Growth: Financial Systems and the Politics of Industrial Change.* Ithaca: Cornell University Press.

Endnotes

1. The Fifth Republic refers to the new constitutional regime put in place in France in 1958 in response to the parliamentary instability of the previous or Fourth Republic (1945-1958). The new constitution strengthened considerably the position of the President.

2. We define below the concept of corporatism. In the West German state, Dyson is referring to the systematic opportunities for discussion and cooperation between business and labour that exist from the shop floor to the highest levels of policy-making.

3. Many of the important articles of this first phase of the corporatist literature are collected together in Schmitter and Lehmbruch (1979) and Lehmbruch and Schmitter (1982).

4. See, for example, the essays in Cawson (1985), Streeck and Schmitter (1985), Grant (1987b) and Wilks and Wright (1987).

CHAPTER TWO

THE STATE, INTERESTS, AND POLICY MAKING IN THE EAST COAST FISHERY

A. Paul Pross and Susan McCorquodale

An examination of the East Coast fishery offers a fascinating perspective on the sectoral character of Canadian policy-making. It forces us to question the extent of sectoral influence on the industry, and teaches us caution in conceptualizing the organization of the policy process within the sector. Although policy relating to the sector is significantly influenced by the fishing industry, the industry is so crucial to the region that, on many important issues, sectoral interests are over-ruled on regional and national grounds. In some respects highly organized, its participants are notoriously individualistic. Much of the organization that does exist in the fishery has been achieved through the efforts of the state, rather than of the interests involved. Yet the sector cannot be described as corporatist. Even within the sector, a strong element of regionalism divides the industry and the policy process.

These themes are explored in this chapter by reviewing developments in the East Coast fishery over the last 15 years. The particular focus is the period 1977 to 1983, a time of major change in the industry. In an attempt to understand the nature of policy organization within the sector, it is useful to think in terms of policy in the field being organized through policy communities, a concept that combines the traditional idea of network communication with the influence of broader social forces in determining the processes and frameworks of policy formation (Pross, 1986; Pross and McCorquodale, 1987).

The discussion will proceed as follows: first, we look briefly at the industry, noting its socio-economic significance, its history and political importance and its recent history. Second, we describe the leading institutional actors in fisheries policy: government agencies; industry associations in business and labour; specific corporations, other interests and individuals. Finally, we consider the general question of policy-making in the fisheries sector and the implications of our findings for the concept of sectoralism. We stress the importance of linkages between macropolitical institutions and sectoral policy-making.

The Significance of the Fishery to the Atlantic Region

Fishing contributed about 10 per cent to the economies of Newfoundland, Prince Edward Island and Nova Scotia during the period under discussion. The economies of New Brunswick and Québec derived less than three per cent of provincial product from the industry.[1] In the 1970s about 19,000 person-years of employment were created annually in Newfoundland by the fishery (Newfoundland and Labrador, 1980: 5). In Nova Scotia, in 1984, 15,000 were directly employed in the industry which was the third most valuable in the province, generating $460 million in revenue. About 75 per cent of all communities in Atlantic Canada take part in commercial fishing, and of these, some 20 per cent (roughly 250,000 people) have no other economic base (Department of the Environment [DOE], 1976: 7). The Canadian fishery is highly dependent on exports. During the early 1970s, Canada ranked second or third in terms of the value of fish products exported, and since 1977, partly as a result of the declaration of the 200 mile economic zone, has headed the list. The value of Canadian fish exports in 1980 was US $1,073 million and in 1986 had reached US $2,418 (Canada, 1988: Table 3.2).

Historically the geographic dispersal of the industry has given it immense political significance. Fisheries' concerns are important in many electoral ridings, dominant in a number. Consequently, governments are solicitous of the fortunes of the fishery, more often the cause of concern than of jubilation. A weak staple, Canadian fish products were easily replaced in the markets as fresh/frozen products succeeded salt cod and as mass produced poultry products gained popularity. The industry suffered accordingly. Although less true of the offshore fishery since the 1950s, the fishery has traditionally been labour intensive, as well as an employer of last resort, or the occupation to which those with no other employment opportunities turned. Consequently, incentives to modernize were few and even those few were sometimes resisted through public policy.

After the Second World War, when Japan, the USSR, and West Germany joined the nations fishing the East Coast banks, the Canadian fishery began a very difficult period of major change. With the introduction of the large freezer trawler in the late 1950s, the fishing effort intensified continuously. The total catch rose from 500,000 to 4,500,000 metric tons [2] by 1973, but Canada's share of the annual "groundfish" catch[3] dropped during this period from well over one-third to a little more than a quarter (DOE, 1976: Appendix II, Table 17). Canada's attempts to secure supply management through international cooperation were as unproductive as its efforts to maintain its share of the catch. By the mid-1970s, Canada faced a double-edged problem. On the one hand, Canada added considerably to the catching capacity of the nations fishing the banks, and so to the over-exploitation of the stocks. On the other, Canada contributed to the over-supply of fish on the market. A major crisis emerged in 1974 as the industry faced simultaneously a collapse of both the stock and prices. Government responded by assuming a supply management role by establishing a 200-mile economic zone encompassing most of the banks. On the domestic side, a new system of enterprise allocations was developed; these have assigned fishing enterprises property rights in the resource and are intended to encourage a conservationist ethic in the industry.

Unfortunately, declaration of the 200-mile limit released a spate of over-optimistic investment which, on being overtaken by the interest-rate surge of the early 1980s, led to an acute financial crisis. This was resolved through government intervention and a restructuring of the major companies. The measures taken in the last 15 years have done much to restore stability to the industry, but it is not yet on an even footing. Uncertainty, ranging from the recovery of fish stocks to the impact of free trade, a measure that the industry generally supported, characterizes the industry.

The Policy Community

Participants in the fishing industry generally divide themselves into three categories: government; the "Big Boys"; and the "smaller folk":

the fishermen, plant workers and the owners of small processing plants.

The State: The Federal Government

The federal Department of Fisheries and Oceans (DFO) exercises the jurisdictional authority for the fishery that was granted to the federal government by section 91(12) of the Constitution Act, 1867. Together with its spending power—generally ten times that of its provincial counterparts—this provision makes DFO the key government actor in fisheries policy formation. It is not, however, the sole federal actor and at times its capacity to influence federal fisheries policy is limited by the policy bureaucracy surrounding the cabinet, and the need to work with, or at least consult, other federal agencies, notably Transport, External Affairs and regional development agencies. The Department's role is also moderated by the authority of provincial agencies. While responsibility for the resource itself lies with the federal government, once fish are caught their handling and processing are subject to provincial regulation under section 92(13) and 92(16). Provincial programmes for fleet development and plant expansion may also affect the way in which the resource is exploited. They, too, of course, may be checked in turn by the federal government's ability to finance development and to regulate interprovincial and international trade. Finally, two other levels of government may have intermittent influence on fisheries policy. The government of the United States, through its ability to impose countervailing duties, has from time to time discouraged government assistance to the Canadian industry and has persistently called into question social programmes that benefit fishermen. The governments of the European countries, France in particular, have also influenced Canadian fisheries policy. At the other extreme, local development organizations are occasionally active, promoting plant location and frequently, beseeching government to keep open plants facing closure.

In spite of these complexities on matters of stock management and the general regulation of the fishery, the Department of Fisheries and Oceans has the most to do with initiating, reviewing and analyzing fisheries policies; regulating the industry; and delivering programmes. Consequently, DFO is a focal point for most other actors attempting to influence fisheries policy.

Despite its significance to Atlantic Canada, the Department prior to 1977 rarely afforded its minister an opportunity to command national attention, or even to build a useful power base. There are several reasons for this. First, much of fisheries administration is highly technical, depending on the advice and calculations of fisheries biologists and industry specialists. Second, for many years the Department's scope for action was constrained by anterior policies established by the Department of External Affairs. Even the patronage possibilities of the portfolio were limited, given that, until the 1970s, the Department of Public Works was responsible for small craft harbours. Thus constrained, few ministers took major initiatives in what they considered to be a technically oriented ministry best run by the experts who staffed it.[4] This historic tendency of ministers to leave the Department in the hands of officials augmented the significance of previous policy as a constraint and guiding influence, which, in turn, affected the power relations of professional groups within the Department.

Until 1977 the East Coast fishing grounds were international common property and as such open to general exploitation. Despite industry concern, Canada hesitated to challenge the prevailing international convention limiting territorial waters to 12 miles. Hence, it neither claimed the Banks for itself nor attempted to regulate their use. Instead, Ottawa responded to the invasion of the Banks in two ways. First, it promoted the technological development of the industry so that the Canadian offshore fleet could compete with the international fleet (DFO, 1956; Pepper, 1977; Alexander 1977). These policies gave some prominence to the professional engineers in the department and encouraged their association with the capital-intensive sectors of the industry.

Second, the federal government endorsed a conservationist approach to fisheries management. It argued that in order to harvest at a biologically sustainable level and to ensure that the fishery would yield a sustainable economic "rent" to those engaged in the industry, it was necessary either to limit both the total allowable catch and entry, or to limit access to the fishery (Munro, 1980: Chapter 2). As a result, Canada was one of the principal proponents of an international treaty setting up the International Commission on the North Atlantic Fishery (ICNAF) to manage the fishery on scientific grounds. On the basis of expert advice, ICNAF would determine how much exploitation fish stocks could sustain in any given year, apportion this total allowable catch (TAC) among the participating nations, and prescribe a regulatory regime intended to ensure that these allotments, or quotas, were not exceeded.

The ICNAF arrangements were intended to substitute a technical process of decision-making for an intensely political conflict. Unfortunately ICNAF lacked the conditions needed to achieve that goal—a strong incentive to conform and a consensus on the basic issues at play — and the exercise only politicized issues formerly the sole concern of competing enterprises.

Canada had very little leverage in ICNAF (Finkle, 1974: 2). It was difficult for a middle power to win in the negotiations that established quotas, and Canada could not effectively police the fishery. Its most potent weapon was science. By showing what was increasingly obvious, that fishing pressure was jeopardizing the stocks, the international fleet could be persuaded to accept more moderate TACs and even to respect regulations. Thus Canada sought to persuade ICNAF countries to harvest no more than the maximum sustainable yield (MSY), an amount equal to the quantity of new fish added to the stock each year, less the number of fish killed by natural rather than man-made causes. Though depletion of the stock attested to the fact that an MSY oriented regulatory regime was more a policy goal than a reality, the approach was nevertheless an important part of federal thinking about the fishery. It also reflected the prominence of fisheries biologists in fisheries policy development. Their information often served as the base for what little management ICNAF either endorsed or enforced.

Science, then, became one of the twin pillars of Canadian fisheries policy. The other was diplomacy. At ICNAF, scientific information had to be combined with negotiating skill. The well-being of the Canadian industry depended on international recognition of Canadian claims and, in making those claims,the Department of External Affairs became the chief agent for achieving the goals of the fishing community. In the eyes of the community, however, the Department of External Affairs was an unsatisfactory protector because it had to balance the concerns of the fishing industry with the many other interests of Canadians, from time to time trading off the interests of the fishery against the benefits that could be acquired for other groups (Mitchell, 1978: 179).

These realities fostered a centralist trend. In an effort to influence favourably the views of External Affairs, fisheries officials tried to develop close working relations with that Department. The whole fisheries policy analysis apparatus consequently had to be located near the Department of External Affairs in Ottawa. This change reinforced the tendency inherent in the cabinet system of government to place policy mechanisms as well as a lot of supporting apparatus, as close as possible to the ministerial level, which, of course, was Ottawa. As well, the highly technical nature of ICNAF regulations placed a premium on scientific information, much of the apparatus for which tended to be located in Ottawa as well. Furthermore, as the Canadian fishery became increasingly subject to regulation (following ICNAF), the policy centre insisted on maintaining closer, direct control over activities on the periphery. This meant that the field administration became highly fragmented with little local coordination. Thus, centralized policy and administrative machinery developed as a functional response to the regulatory regime governing the resource base, even though they were remote from the east coast industry and apparently unresponsive to it.

The ICNAF period, then, made necessary a policy process that was centralist in orientation and dominated by scientists, most of them biologists or oceanographers. The entrenchment of fisheries biologists and their paradigms in ICNAF's management system was a logical concomitant of Canada's policy—recommended by the Department of External Affairs—of accepting the view that the offshore fishery resource was international common property. The only other significant professional influence in the Service came from the engineers who, from the early 1950s onwards, promoted the installation of new fishing technologies in boats, gears, and technique. This role, however, was secondary to that of the scientists and their colleagues, the diplomats.

The 1977 declaration of the 200-mile limit signalled Ottawa's recognition that its policies of international stock management had failed and precipitated a major change in the power structure of the Department. The declaration of the 200-mile limit not only meant the introduction of a long-term radical change in the resource base and in the market structure, but also removed the rationale for the highly centralized policy/administrative machine that had been functional for so long. In other words, it was no longer necessary to make international arrangements the touchstone of fisheries policy.[5] As well, science and technology ceased to be a necessity for international negotiation and, becoming a management tool, declined in policy significance. The roles of two key actors were seriously affected. The Department of External Affairs still plays a role in boundary disputes, but this role is no longer central. Similarly, the scientific community has become much less significant, though it continues to be important.

As the influence of diplomats and scientists declined, other actors became more important within the federal fisheries administration. The administration itself became more significant. No longer a service within the Department of the Environment, it became a full-fledged Department of Fisheries and Oceans with a budget of $300,000,000. The minister responsible for fisheries, Romeo LeBlanc, also became more important. As the powerful regional minister for New Brunswick, LeBlanc's mission was to preserve the community structure of Atlantic Canada by rescuing the inshore fishery from the depredations, on the one hand, of international exploitation of the Banks, and on the other, from a development policy that favoured the major operators. Winning control of the 200-mile limit meant that the Minister of Fisheries and Oceans ceased to be merely the fishermen's advocate in Ottawa; he became a major arbiter of policy.

Unfortunately the Department lacked the capacity to respond to LeBlanc's policy objectives. Its professional leadership had been provided by biologists who, now that the ICNAF system had been discarded, were not able to address the issues at the top of the

Minister's agenda. The Department's engineers, who were more familiar with the industry, though not self-consciously in favour of a capital intensive fishery, tended to relate most easily to the larger firms and their pressure group, the Fisheries Council of Canada. Economists, however, and to a lesser extent, sociologists, were able to address LeBlanc's concern for the inshore fishery (McCracken and MacDonald, 1976; Anderson, 1978). By 1976, the publication of the *Policy for Canada's Commercial Fisheries* (DOE, 1976), signalled their growing influence by bringing to the fore arguments that fisheries economists had urged for some years. In it, the government argued that although it was necessary to preserve and replenish stocks, much more attention had to be paid to what would be in the best interests of the people who depended on the industry.[6] The desire to attain the "best use" of society's resources—defined as "the sum of net social benefits, personal income, occupational opportunity, and consumer satisfaction" would be the touchstone of policy, not the need to negotiate quota allocations and regulatory regimes. The open-access, free-for-all fishery prevalent in the ICNAF years had brought too many fishermen, too many boats, and too many under-utilized processing plants into the industry. The immediate need was therefore to "curtail" open access and to "apply systems of entry control" (DOE, 1976: 53-5).

As part of his attempt to develop policies that would restore the inshore fishery, LeBlanc also initiated a trend toward administrative decentralization. Within the new Department of Fisheries and Oceans a good deal of power and influence was shifted from the centre to the peripheral industrial area in which the fishery is prosecuted.

During the 1980s the structure of power within federal fisheries administration has evolved in two different but not necessarily incompatible directions. First, the decentralization of fisheries management operations encouraged by LeBlanc has continued. Second, the Department of Fisheries and Oceans has been integrated into the general framework for economic management of the Atlantic region and the machinery of federal policy-making. LeBlanc himself, as a regional minister and member of the Cabinet Committee on Priorities and Planning, was more likely to influence the fisheries-related activities of other departments, as, for example, in his intercession in negotiations over General Development Agreements. LeBlanc's power, however, was compromised by the 1981-84 crisis in the fishery precipitated by the financial difficulties of several leading companies. His antipathy to the companies was considered a barrier to resolution of the crisis and he was replaced by Pierre de Bané. In effect, the crisis could not be contained by DFO, and was ultimately resolved through senior intergovernmental negotiations, following the Kirby task force inquiry (Task Force on Atlantic Fisheries, 1983; Pross, 1984). In addition to the change in ministers, the crisis also provided the opportunity for important changes in senior personnel. The fisheries scientists and other officials who had spent their entire careers in the fisheries service were gradually replaced by officials out of the new central agencies mould: men and women expert in the processes of policy-making and programme management, rather than in the substantive areas of administration. Such officials are more inclined to synchronize fisheries policy with national objectives.

In summary, the DFO has changed remarkably in the last two decades. In 1970, it was highly centralized and remote, dominated by its scientific staff and preoccupied with imposing the regulatory framework necessitated by Canada's participation in ICNAF. Today its policies are more appropriately shaped by domestic concerns and by officials who represent the social as well as the natural sciences and who are attuned to the broader considerations of federal policy. Perhaps most important, the shift in mandate brought about by declaration of the 200-mile limit has made possible a more decentralized management approach that incorporates active industry participation.

The State: Provincial Governments

In contrast to the federal department, provincial fisheries agencies—with the exception of the Newfoundland Department of Fisheries—have had very limited influence on fisheries policy. Forced to the sidelines by the nature of fisheries policy-making in the ICNAF period, scarcely consulted even when provinces undertook major fish plant development projects, and treated as little more than a part of their Ottawa lobbying organization by the processors, the provincial departments were seldom able to muster the expertise to deal with the broad questions that emerged in the mid-1970s. Even Newfoundland, with its determination to call the shots in "its" fishery started far behind the federal agency and could not hope to equal the breadth of its resources. Consequently, provincial fisheries positions have not always been clearly defined or consistently taken.

Newfoundland's fisheries department possesses the greatest state capacity among those in Atlantic Canada. Historically, the fishery has dominated the economic, social and political life of Newfoundland to a greater extent than elsewhere in the Atlantic provinces. It is, therefore, not surprising that the province should have established a fisheries department as early as 1899, more than 60 years before the Maritime provinces, and that it should display legal and historical differences which influence present day concerns. Thus, from the beginning the Newfoundland department was concerned with the quality of fish products and the modernization of gear (Alexander, 1976; 1977; King, 1938). During the period of Commission Government (1934-49), all aspects of the catching, processing and marketing of fish were made subject to regulation by the highly competent officials of the

Newfoundland Fisheries Board. By means of export inspection, grading and licensing, buyer confidence in the quality of Newfoundland fish was improved. The Newfoundland exporters were compelled to participate in compulsory export groups. In 1947 these groups were merged into the Newfoundland Association of Fish Exporters Limited (NAFEL), a company with an exclusive license to export salt fish, which in marketing power and skill, was the equal of any of its competitors and far surpassed that of the fragmented exporters of the Maritimes.

The legislative and financial support thus created provided the basis for what was to become, relative to its size and resources, the best fisheries service in North America. The system which had evolved by 1947 offered Newfoundland a regulatory base and organization "far superior to anything available to Canada's east coast industry" (Alexander, 1977: 37). With Confederation it soon became clear that this approach was not compatible with the federal government's pan-Canadian policies. Ottawa was opposed to public sector involvement in marketing, favouring instead assistance to the industry at the catching and processing stages, in order to develop a modern, fresh/frozen industry able to tap the new markets emerging for these products. Newfoundland's market-oriented policies were therefore discouraged (Alexander, 1977: 145). By thus setting aside provincial priorities, federal officials created a legacy of distrust in Newfoundland which—together with a regard for the significance of the fishery—has led the province to maintain a stronger fisheries policy capacity than its sister provinces in the Maritimes.

Between 1922 and 1984, Québec acquired shared control of its coastal and inshore fisheries. The Québec Department of Fisheries was established in 1942 and has three regional bureaus and research laboratories. This level of development occurs despite the fact that overall, the fisheries of Québec contribute less than 1 per cent in value added to the commodity producing industries of the province, and is attributable to the fact that the industry is the backbone of the economy of the Magdalen Islands and the lower North Shore and is a major activity in the Gaspé Peninsula.

In contrast to Newfoundland's longstanding concern for, and active involvement in, fisheries administration, in the Maritime provinces of Nova Scotia, New Brunswick and Prince Edward Island, provincial policy-making and jurisdiction have been confined to playing a supportive role to the dominant federal authorities. The diversity of fishing interests in the region inhibited the development of a consensus. Moreover, as long as international fleets could fish within a few miles of Canada's coast, fisheries regulation—to the extent that it was possible at all—was best left in the hands of the federal government which could use its status as an international actor to negotiate a regulatory regime recognized by the various countries exploiting the North Atlantic. As a consequence, the Maritime provinces concerned themselves with ensuring that Ottawa understood their interests and with securing federal development funds to make their industry more internationally competitive. In these circumstances, it is not surprising that Nova Scotia, generally considered the regional leader in the field, waited until 1943 to establish a departmental division concerned with the fishery, and did not upgrade it to departmental status until 1964 (Watt, 1967; Fownes, 1980). New Brunswick's record was similar. For many years the province devoted less than one per cent of its total budget to supporting the fishery. Similarly, fisheries in Prince Edward Island did not loom large in provincial spending. Nearly 15 years after the Second World War, the administrative costs of the department were $32,525 and the staff numbered one deputy minister, one inspector, one investigator, one accountant and two secretaries (PEI, 1960).

None the less, the weakness of the provincial fisheries departments is deceptive. The fishery is extremely significant in certain locations in Atlantic Canada—the Gaspé Peninsula, the New Brunswick Gulf shore, south-west Nova Scotia, and most of coastal Newfoundland—and consequently excites concern at senior provincial levels. Provincial policy communities tend to be overseen by central agencies and senior ministers and not by sectoral departments. The fact that provincial power can be used to challenge—or augment— federal policies, ensures that provincial fisheries agencies often attract clusters of interests who wish either to complement their federal representations, or use their provincial influence to counteract federal policies. Thus, in Newfoundland, the Department of Intergovernmental Affairs takes an active part in developing fisheries policy. In Nova Scotia, the provincial agency seems to be a means of maintaining a presence in the field; when crises arise, the government tries to influence Ottawa through political bargaining. In extreme cases it pulls together competent and effective negotiating teams, largely drawn from the private sector (Pross, 1984). At the time of the constitutional debate, Newfoundland too had a constellation of groups and interests whose activities focussed on the provincial as well as the federal fisheries department.[7]

Sectoral Interests: Level of Organizational Development

The "Big Boys"

Nothing illustrates the volatility of the fisheries sector more eloquently than the changes that have occurred amongst the major corporations in the industry over the last decade. Of the group of companies known in the late 1970s as the "Big Five"—National Sea Products (NSP), H.B.

Nickerson and Sons, B.C. Packers (owners of Connors Brothers), Fisheries Products and the Lake Group—two, Nickersons and the Lake Group—were absorbed by Fisheries Products International (FPI) and NSP during the industry restructuring of the early 1980s. A company that did not exist in the mid-1970s, Clearwater, is now one of the giants of the industry. The influence of two major cooperatives, Pêcheurs Unis du Québec which dominated the Québec industry and the United Maritime Fishermen (UMF), declined. The UMF fell into bankruptcy in 1988; Pêcheurs Unis had to be restructured as Pêcheries Cartier in 1984.

The major vertically integrated fish processors enjoy regular and easy access to the minister and senior officials of all the departments of fisheries under discussion. Day to day consultations are routine and discussion of policy occurs frequently, not only with senior officials of fisheries agencies, but with federal regional ministers, premiers and even the Prime Minister.[8] The extent of their influence is unclear.[9] During the 1970s, the corporate sector was generally thought to be by far the most influential interest group in the fishery, inciting government reaction to foreign overfishing, for example (MacDonald, 1979). Later it was the shaky financial condition of several of the "Big Five"— and in particular, their indebtedness to one bank—which persuaded the federal government to establish the Kirby Task Force on the Atlantic Fisheries. A key advisor to the Task Force was Peter John Nicholson, who was seconded to it from his position as Vice-President of H.B. Nickerson. The Task Force (1983: Chaps. 5, 10) addressed particularly a central concern of the processors, security of supply, recommending the system of enterprise allocations which is today a fundamental element of offshore fisheries management policy.

Although the large corporations maintain their own direct links with government at both political and bureaucratic levels, they conduct a good deal of business with government through the Fisheries Council of Canada. Established in 1945, the Council is a federation of provincial associations of seafood producers—the Seafood Producers' Association of Nova Scotia (SPANS) and the Fisheries Association, of Newfoundland, for example—with the bulk of its members coming from the East Coast. Though the Association and its affiliates have at times attempted to speak for the industry as a whole, they are generally considered to be spokespersons for the processors. The Council and its affiliates can be categorized as institutionalized groups. They have offices in Ottawa and the provincial capitals from which they maintain regular contact with federal and provincial bureaucrats and politicians.

Business interests are very closely integrated. The chief of these are the processors groups which are federated in the Fisheries Council of Canada. The manager of the Atlantic Fisheries By-Products

Association in 1977 was Roger Stirling, President of what is now the Seafood Producers Association of Nova Scotia. He also managed the Atlantic Queen Crab Association. These business organizations, however, are not always successful in integrating members' interests. The FCC represents the industry on those issues where consensus can be achieved. ("To stay in existence you concentrate on those issues where you can get consensus and avoid issues where there is conflict."[10]) When its members' interests are too divergent—as in resource allocation issues—the Council leaves them to make representations to government either individually or through their provincial associations. As well, the major companies make regular representations to government on their own behalf, [11] and Interview with M. O'Connor, Chief, Resource Utilization Branch, DFO, Ottawa. Feb. 8, 1989. (Pross)assigning executive resources to the government liaison function.

Individual processors have enhanced their policy-making capability in the past decade. In the late 1970s, H.B. Nickerson and Sons and National Sea recruited vigorously from the federal bureaucracy and created a joint research and management oriented subsidiary, Inter-Ocean Limited, in which a group of highly trained economists, corporate planners, industry experts and communication specialists carried out advanced planning and presented the companies' views to government and, if necessary, the public at large. Today the leadership of National Sea, Fisheries Products and Clearwater is made up predominantly of individuals who have pursued careers in marketing, finance and business-government relations.

The creation of this "technostructure" (Galbraith, 1971; 1973) gives the "Big Boys" a level of expertise concerned with long-term corporate planning, research and development, relations with government, and a host of related issues. This level of management can seldom be afforded by small concerns, but it is essential to large-scale corporations whose survival may depend on their relations with government. Government's concern with resource management, its involvement in the supply of labour and raw materials, its role in managing the economy, and even its ability to ease entry into the market place all dictate that the modern large corporation must be close to government. Furthermore, the corporation must be equally close to the administrative and political arms of government given that the traditional politically oriented nature of the relationship is giving way to a complex, continuing and technocratic one.

The long-accepted view that the industry is dominated by large companies working in concert with government is deceptive. Not only did the coop movement create two influential firms, United Maritime Fishermen and Pêcheurs Unis du Québec, but also the labour movement has developed a powerful voice in one province, Newfoundland, in the form of the Newfoundland Fish, Food and Allied Workers' Union (NFFAWU). As its name implies, the NFFAWU is a vertically integrated union, bargaining for independent fishermen, plant workers and trawlermen. Led by the prominent Liberal politician, Richard Cashin, the emergence of the NFFAWU in the early 1970s radically changed the structure of power in the Newfoundland fishing industry and had a considerable impact on Canadian fisheries policy in general. It challenged the established power of local plant owners and that of the major fish companies and for the first time gave Newfoundland fishermen a concerted voice in the fisheries policy community.

Its size—23,000 members by 1980 (Clement, 1986: 160-63; 173-75) —and its representativeness of fishermen and plant workers across the province gave the NFFAWU legitimacy in the eyes of federal officials. Legitimacy was reinforced by policy capacity. A federal observer writing in the late 1970s noted that fishermen in Newfoundland were "planning their future in much the same manner as the processors," and that in contrast to fishermen's organizations in the Maritimes, the NFFAWU was putting forward sophisticated statements on fishery policy.[12] As the sole truly representative fishermen's organization in the four Atlantic provinces, and one with a genuine policy capacity, the NFFAWU exerted considerable influence in Ottawa during the LeBlanc years and still carries weight.

Unionization has been less successful in the Maritimes and still tends to be bitterly resisted (Barrett, 1979; Williams, 1979; Calhoun, 1984; Clement, 1986). Where it did occur, fisherman's organization tended to take place first in the most highly capitalized sections of the industry, and second, in the most depressed parts of the inshore fishery. Participants in the more affluent segments of the inshore fishery cherished their individualism and independence with a vigour that still has an impact on fisheries policy. Among plant workers, four unions have been most active, though only one of them has been associated strictly with the region and with seafood production, the Canadian Seafood and Allied Workers Union (CSAWU). In 1978, the CSAWU claimed some 2,000 to 3,000 members during the summer season at plants in Louisbourg, North Sydney, Pictou, Halifax, Lunenburg and Lockeport. The other three unions—the Canadian Food and Allied Workers Union (CFAWU), the Canadian Brotherhood of Railway, Transport and General Workers (CBRT and GW) and the Retail, Wholesale, Department Store Union (RWDSU)—counted fewer plant workers as members and were not concerned exclusively with the fishing industry (Melanson, 1978: 15-16).

Unionization was also widespread in the capital intensive, offshore segments. The CBRT and GW claimed 85 per cent of Nova Scotia's trawlermen in 1978, but had no industry members outside Nova Scotia and even there some membership discontent was evident. With some

40,000 members in a variety of occupations it was often accused of paying little attention to the fishery (Melanson, 1978: 15-16). The same kind of charge was also directed at the CFAWU which represented some trawlermen in Nova Scotia and in Prince Edward Island. During the 1980s the NFFAWU has drawn support away from these unions (Clement, 1986: 160–63; 173-75).

Amongst inshore fishermen, the standard-bearer for unionization has been the Maritime Fishermen's Union (MFU). Originating in southeastern New Brunswick, by March 1978, the MFU had about 1,000 members in New Brunswick and northeastern Nova Scotia. Affiliated with the Canadian Labour Congress (CLC), the union was granted exclusive jurisdiction to organize fishermen in the three Maritime provinces. This last represented a major concession, for not only had two other CLC affiliates, the CFAWU and the CBRT and GW, expressed interest in organizing the inshore fishermen, but the MFU had made clear its ambitions to emulate the NFFAWU and eventually represent trawlermen and plant workers as well as inshore fishermen (Melanson, 1978; MacDonald, 1979).

The Small Folk

The individualism that is characteristic of the fishery is attributed to historic, geographic and technical factors. The industry itself is highly diversified with interests clustering according to the species they fish and the technology they use. Different technologies are often incompatible, so that "gear conflicts" are frequent and foster tension between different sectors of the industry. Geographically, the industry varies immensely, generally in accordance with the richness of the fishing grounds exploited, their proximity and the physical conditions in which the fishermen have to work. Nature, technology and economic circumstances reinforce cultural distinctions created by the earliest patterns of settlement, so that the participants in the several distinct fisheries of the region distinguish themselves from one another by self-consciously subscribing to different ideologies, holding fiercely to their own particular philosophies of independence or collective action.

Individualism has affected communication patterns in the sector in several respects. First, traditional party affiliations are still strong, particularly where the fishery dominates. Second, individualism and the mythology of entrepreneurship have discouraged unionization. Third, that same ethos has led to the development of alternatives to unionization, notably the coops and the fishermen's associations, which eschew collective bargaining and attempt simply to represent fishermen's interests in discussions with government.

The dispersed nature of the fishing industry and its dominance of a number of East Coast ridings—particularly in Newfoundland, the Gulf coast of New Brunswick and southwest Nova Scotia[13]—means that local groups can still challenge the politics of sectoralism through the more traditional party politics of localism and regionalism. This avenue, in combination with the ideology of independence, has carried a great deal of weight with the Nova Scotia government which, regardless of its party colouration, tends to define the provincial fishery in terms of either the capital-intensive off-shore sector or the vigorous and productive inshore and near-shore fishery of southwestern Nova Scotia. It has been less useful in the more bureaucratic, politically diverse milieu of Ottawa.

The individualistic distrust of organization found in various parts of the fishery has proved so intense that the debate over forms of organization has assumed ideological proportions. In southwest Nova Scotia where the rich, diverse inshore fishery bred strident individualism, resistance to any form of collective action was intense. There, the federal and provincial governments seem to have hoped that the Nova Scotia Fishermen's Association (NSFA) would win broad support. The NSFA had evolved from the Atlantic Fishermen's Association (AFA), an association whose broad aspirations exceeded its support and which ultimately dissolved into a series of sub-regional and sectoral groups (Munroe and Stewart, 1981: 82). As the largest of these, the NSFA had some potential for representing inshore fishing interests, a potential both levels of government sought to reinforce through financial assistance and positional policies.

In contrast to the Official Language minority groups discussed in Chapter Seven and the poverty organizations described in Chapter Nine, government efforts to provide the NSFA with a strong functional base proved difficult for it to manage. Neither the membership nor the association's small professional staff and executive could easily assimilate, develop a consensus on, and respond to the diverse issues suddenly put before it. Nor was the membership sympathetic to the idea of supporting an organization capable of exerting influence as an actor in the increasingly bureaucratic setting of policy-making. Instead of manoeuvring the NSFA into a position of influence these efforts precipitated membership desertions, reorganization and staff resignations. Ultimately the NSFA was replaced by the Eastern Fishermen's Federation which also flourished for several years, with considerable federal government encouragement, but is now thought to be in decline (Clement, 1986: 152).

In retrospect, the individualism which was the foundation for these associations, and to a lesser extent, the coops, undermined the ability of Nova Scotia's independent fishermen to participate in the critical debates that have vitally affected their interests in recent years. Their representative base, despite federal and provincial government support, was too narrow and unstable to give them lasting legitimacy and their constant preoccupation with individualism inhibited their ability to respond collectively to the policy initiatives of others. Their belief in the traditional virtues of political channels of communication, was often rewarded provincially but was of limited help at the federal level. In fact, as Macdonald (1979: 171-89) has suggested, the immense political power of fishermen has been "exercised through a brokerage system, which was more effective in exerting leverage on the subsidy and social security system, and the surges of public spending (especially on construction of roads, wharves, community stages, etc.) just prior to elections, rather than on positive fishery policy formation." Today, associations and coops seem to be in decline, unionization is becoming more pervasive, and fishermen seem to have accepted a government created process of consultation as the most likely vehicle for influencing fisheries decisions.

Interpreting the Policy Process: Do We Have Sectoralism in the Fishery?

In reflecting upon the policy process in a given sector, we can speak of various degrees of "sectoralism." Sectoralism refers to the tendency for policy-making in a sector to be dominated by state and societal actors that are dedicated to and identified with the given sector. In a highly sectoralized policy arena such as banking discussed in Chapter Four, policy-making is concentrated in state agencies and interest groups whose prime, if not only, concern is the growth and solvency of financial institutions. In a less sectoralized policy arena, one might expect to find sectoral agencies sharing decision-making responsibility with central agencies or other line departments and sectoral interests lobbying in tandem with or against broader spatial or economic interest groups. What is striking about the fishery sector is that the degree of sectoralization varies widely depending on the issue area. Hence the fisheries sector features a number of dedicated sectoral agencies and interest groups, but these always act in conjunction with other state organizations for whom fisheries is a minor area of concern.

In other words, in describing fisheries-related policy, we have to be careful not to describe a static, narrowly-defined and closed system of communication. The linkages between macro and meso levels of organization are highly developed. Specifically, three points can be made:

1. *Fisheries policy is set within the framework of anterior policies developed to meet national objectives and, only to a minor degree, reflecting fisheries concerns (for example, foreign and constitutional policy).*

Table 1 Participation in Fisheries-Related Public Policies

Policy Actors	Resource Allocation	Fisheries Science	Resource Utilization	Fleet Development	Plant Development	Work Force Training & Development	Labour Force Income Maintenance	Market Development
Federal Agencies								
DFO- Soc. sci.	X		X					X
Science	X	X	X	X	X	X		X
PCO	X			X			X	X
DEA							X	X
International Trade								X
DIST.				X	X			X
ACOA				X	X	X		X
CEIC						X	X	X
Soc. Assistance						X	X	
Health						X	X	X
Provincial Agencies								
Central Agencies	X		X	X	X	X	X	X
Fisheries	X	X	X	X	X	X		X
Development				X	X	X		X
Social Services							X	
Interest Groups								
FCC			X	X		X	X	X
Provincial Affiliates of FCC			X	X		X	X	X
Can. Assoc. of Fish Exporters								X
Sector Committees	X		X	X	X	X		
Unions	X		X	X	X	X	X	X
Coops	X		X	X	X	X		X
Associations	X		X	X	X		X	
Other Actors								
University Scientists	X			X				
Consultants	X		X	X	X	X	X	X
Local Dev. Groups				X	X			
Boat Builders Assoc.				X		X		
Foreign Governments	X			X	X		X	

ACOA: Atlantic Canada Opportunites Agency
CEIC: Canadian Employment & Immigration Commission
DIST: Department of Industry, Science and Technology
DEA: Department of External Affairs
DFO: Department of Fisheries & Oceans
FCC: Fisheries Council of Canada
PCO: Privy Council Office

Other agencies often articulate policies that set conditions within which fisheries officials must set their own policy. For example, the view of the Department of External Affairs on the limits of Canadian claims over international waters framed fisheries policies for decades. A crucial set of policies for the industry—income maintenance—are not addressed at all by DFO but by Employment and Immigration and by Health and Welfare Canada.

2. *Fisheries policy is also affected by policies set within other sectors where, again, the concerns of the fishery have only limited currency.*

Key examples here include the search and rescue policies of Transport Canada, regulations on the handling and preparation of food and, perhaps most important of all, regional development policies. Our discussions with individual actors in the fishery, together with our previous research in the field, make it evident that the issues of fisheries management are treated as regional issues and thus as issues beyond the compass of any one department. The recent crisis over scientific estimates of the TAC illustrates this point. It was John Crosby, regional minister for Atlantic Canada, who told industry representatives the government's decision on the size of the quota that would be authorized.[14] An official of the Fisheries Council of Canada reported that it does a great deal of its lobbying at the cabinet level— particularly with regional ministers—because many of the issues facing the East coast fishery are regional in scope. Issues which cut across departmental boundaries and require central agency coordination and cabinet decisions have included the Free Trade and the General Agreement on Tariffs and Trade (GATT) negotiations, discussions related to St-Pierre and Miquelon, the northern cod problem, and even such apparently localized issues as the 1988 P.E.I. mussel scare.[15]

3. *Even regular participants in the fisheries sector vary their involvement in the setting of different fisheries policies.*

This being said, it should be noted that there remains a core of actors whose primary concerns are with the fishery and who devote a great deal of time and energy, generally in interaction with one another, to build and maintain policies that support the fishery. Table 1 illustrates these points. It selects a group of policies that are significant to the fishery and indicates which actors might be expected to participate in their formation and modification. The table is constructed from a general knowledge of the sector, and, in the interests of simplicity, lumps together policies that might be further differentiated. A more sophisticated presentation would differentiate the services within Fisheries and Oceans participating in each policy debate; we have contented ourselves with distinguishing between the social science divisions and those oriented to natural science. The matrix itself gives an estimation of the extent of actor involvement in policy areas. It may exaggerate the interest of certain actors in particular policies while underestimating that of others. Federal central agencies, for example, may be only sporadically interested in labour force income maintenance policies, whereas scientists in DFO may be more interested than we have suggested in fleet development. Nevertheless, a little exaggeration on the one hand seemed useful since central agency interventions when they do occur, often have momentous consequences. Underestimating scientific interest on fleet development, on the other hand, seemed to be a reasonable reflection of the fact that that intervention would have limited impact.

The table, however, does help us to clarify our thoughts about participation in the sector, perhaps its most important contribution being to demonstrate the variable nature of participation in fisheries related policies. Development agencies and interests, for example, are likely to be found in plant and fleet development discussions and in projects for labour force training. Their knowledge of resource allocation and utilization policies would be sufficient to guide investment decisions, and would be obtained second-hand, not through policy participation. External Affairs, as we have noted, is a key actor in certain aspects of resource allocation and sometimes in gaining access to foreign markets, but it has very limited contact with other aspects of the industry. Provincial agencies participate differently in specific policy sub-fields. Fisheries departments, and often central agencies, will maintain a watching brief in many fields but will expect other agencies to take the lead in a number. Similarly some interest groups will engage in only a few policy arenas while maintaining a pro forma interest in many. The principal unions, for example, will be allotted places on regional stock management advisory committees but may not attend regularly. Other interests may appear infrequently in only one or two arenas. Oceanographers and fisheries biologists are not prominent outside resource determination and fisheries science, though they are extremely influential in those spheres.

What is less evident from the table is that the kinds of policy networks that form around these various groups differ. As we have already indicated, the networks formed on issues related to development, whether of the fleet, plants, or work force training, tend to take a pressure pluralist form. Lobbying is important and ongoing; politicians are involved at the highest levels. In contrast, for issues related to resource allocation, the policy network shares many of the characteristics of sectoral corporatism as outlined in the first chapter. Today 100 committees in the Atlantic region are actively involved in the management of the major fisheries. The most significant is the Atlantic Groundfish Advisory Committee (AGAC) which, with its regional sub-committees, prepares an annual fishing plan for the offshore groundfishery and serves as a vehicle for the continuous administration of the plan. The plan itself has to divide the TAC—recommended by the fisheries biologists and determined in the final analysis by the minister—amongst the various participants in the fishery, taking into account legal, managerial and enforcement constraints and prescribing regulations designed to avoid gear conflict and resource wastage (DFO, 1989). The committees are made up of fishermen's representatives; DFO staff, one of whom chairs meetings; provincial government and fish company representatives. In local committees fishermen are either elected by license holders in the area or appointed by their organizations; DFO does not impose a procedure. On the major regional committees fishermen will be represented by organizations but major processors will be accorded seats of their own.

The committees provide a vehicle through which day-to-day adjustments can be made in the fishing plan; conflicts between sectors can be addressed; trade-offs between enterprises negotiated and the rate of catch monitored. In a session of the Scotia-Fundy Groundfish Advisory Committee, a sub-committee of AGAC, which one of the authors attended in 1984, it was quite clear that the members of the committee were accustomed to working together and found it a useful occasion for doing business with one another as well as with DFO. Although there were—and still are—deepseated antagonisms between segments of the industry, it was clear, at this meeting at least, that the members had established a relationship with one another that facilitated inter-company and inter-sector negotiations. It is probable that the working relationships created through these committees have eased tensions between segments of the industry; this has, for example, permitted the transfer, albeit temporary, of allocations between the offshore and inshore fisheries. The net effect of the committee system appears to be a sense in the industry of engagement in the day-to-day management of the fishery.

Finally, the table illustrates that certain actors are consistently involved in fisheries-related policy discussions. Not surprisingly those actors are the federal and provincial departments of fisheries, provincial central agencies and key fisheries interest groups. The DFO is the most prominent of these, even though its role tends to be confined to the more technical aspects of resource allocation and utilization. It is the most persistent and probably the most knowledgeable. We can call it the lead agency, although that does not mean that it dominates policy formation in the field. Nevertheless, the fact that DFO, its provincial counterparts and certain interest groups maintain a broad and consistent involvement in fisheries policy formation justifies the contention that there is a clearly definable fisheries sector. We describe a "sector" as the collectivity of actors and insitutions whose interaction produces a common understanding. As these institutions have addressed the successive issues that have challenged the fishery, they have pieced together a shared understanding of its character—its strengths, weaknesses and potential. That understanding is the intellectual basis for fisheries policy—its conventional wisdom—and it is drawn upon whenever governments focus attention specifically on fisheries issues.

Conclusion

If the system of policy communication prevalent within the fishery sector involves only in a limited way corporatist networks, how can it be characterized? We would suggest that it is one of those combinations—not uncommon in Canada—of pluralist and state-directed policy networks that some students of our policy process find baffling. The combination is found in other studies in this volume where interests involved are those of the less advantaged: the poor, official language minority groups, and women. In the fisheries sector, we find clusters of interests whose behaviour, method of organization, style of policy discussion and implicit ideology is individualistic. The processors' groups, fishermen's associations, local development groups and some of the organizations representing fishery-related businesses fall into this category. Their assumptions about policy and political behaviour reflect the political culture of parts of the region, particularly southwest Nova Scotia. That culture is also to some extent reflected in provincial government attitudes. The resistance to unionization in the inshore fishery is a good example.

In other respects, however, autonomous and capable state actors are a significant force. The efforts of the DFO to impose order on a disorderly policy community have led to the creation of structured patterns of communications between the department and segments of the industry. In creating the advisory committee system for sector management the Department has used regulatory inducements and positional politics in tandem to convince fishermen of the virtues of collective action; succeeding, to a degree, where self-interest, rhetoric and financial support had not. Such success can be attributed to the fundamental realities of fisheries administration: the state controls resource allocation. At a time of resource scarcity the state can use conservationist policies—its ability to control access to the resource— to persuade members of the industry to organize along the lines preferred by its officials. State direction also has some roots in the past experience of the Atlantic provinces. Newfoundland's tradition of fisheries administration, in particular, endorsed a pattern of state involvement in the industry that was quite unlike—and a great deal more proactive than—the patterns that emerged in the other Atlantic provinces. Even in the Maritime provinces, however, government involvement in fisheries development and income maintenance programmes has created an environment where state support of fisheries interest groups has been vigorously encouraged in the name of free enterprise. Perhaps such developments are only to be expected in a political system where paradox is commonplace and which has produced a policy community that displays a wide combination of policy networks—pluralist, corporatist, and state-directed.

References

Alexander, David (1977). *The Decay of Trade: An Economic History of the Newfoundland Saltfish Trade, 1935-1965.* St. John's: Memorial University of Newfoundland, Newfoundland Social and Economic Studies, 19.

_____ **(1976).** "The Political Economy of Fishing in Newfoundland." *Journal of Canadian Studies,* XI:32-40.

Anderson, R. (1978). "The Need for Human Sciences Research in Atlantic Coast Fisheries." *Journal of the Fisheries Research Board of Canada,* 35: 1031-1049.

Barrett, L. Gene (1979). "Underdevelopment and Social Movements in the Nova Scotia Fishing Industry." In R.J. Brym and R. James Sacouman, eds. *Underdevelopment and Social Movements in Atlantic Canada.* Toronto: New Hogtown Press: 127-60.

Calhoun, Sue (1984). *The Lockeport Lockout.* Halifax: Formac Publishing.

Canada (1988). *The Canada-U.S. Free Trade Agreement and Fisheries.* Ottawa: Supply and Services Canada.

Clement, Wallace (1986). *The Struggle to Organize: Resistance in Canada's Fishery.* Toronto: McClelland and Stewart.

Cushing, D.H. (1977). "The Atlantic Fisheries Commissions." *Marine Policy,* July: 230-8.

Department of Fisheries and Fisheries Research Board (1956). *The Commercial Fisheries of Canada.* Ottawa: Queen's Printer.

Department of Fisheries and Oceans (1981). *Policy for Canada's Atlantic Fisheries in the 1980s.* Ottawa: DFO.

_____ **(1989).** "The Fisheries Management Consultative Process." *Backgrounder,* February 15.

Department of the Environment (DOE) (1976). *Policy for Canada's Commercial Fisheries.* Ottawa: DOE.

Finkle, Peter Z.R. (1974). "The International Commission for the Northwest Atlantic Fisheries: An Experiment in Conservation." *Dalhousie Law Journal,* 1:526-50.

Fownes, Allan (1980). "Changes in Federal and Provincial Fisheries Departments, 1965-1980." Unpublished student paper, Dalhousie University.

Galbraith, J.K. (1971). *The New Industrial State.* New York: Mentor.

_____ **(1973).** *Economics and the Public Purpose.* Boston: Houghton, Mifflin.

Gordon, H. Scott (1954). "The economic theory of a common property resource: the fishery." *Journal of Political Economy,* 62: 124-42.

King, Henry (1938). "Report of the Seafisheries of Newfoundland." *Canadian Journal of Economics and Political Science,* III: 219-22.

Leblanc, Michael (1984). "Fisheries Administration in Canada: A Synopsis." In Cynthia Lamson and Arthur J. Hanson, eds. *Atlantic Fisheries and Coastal Communities: Fisheries Decision-Making Case Studies.* Halifax: Dalhousie Institute of Resource and Environmental Studies.

Macdonald, R.D.S. (1979). "Inshore fishing interests on the Atlantic coast: Their response to extended jurisdiction by Canada." *Marine Policy,* July, 171-89.

McCracken, F.D. and R.D.S. Macdonald (1976). "Science for Canada's Inshore Seas Fisheries." *Journal of the Fisheries Research Board of Canada,* 33: 2097-2139.

Melanson, R. (1978). "A Rough Voyage: A Report for the Fishermen of Nova Scotia." Student Paper, St. Francis Xavier University.

Mitchell, C.L. (1978). "The 200-mile limit: New issues, old problems of Canada's East Coast fisheries." *Canadian Public Policy,* IV: 172-84.

Munro, Gordon R (1980). *A Promise of Abundance: Extended Jurisdiction and the Newfoundland Economy.* Ottawa: Economic Council of Canada.

Munroe, C. and J. Stewart (1981). *Fishermen's Organizations in Nova Scotia: The Potential for Unification.* Halifax: Dalhousie School of Public Administration.

Newfoundland and Labrador (1980). *Managing all our resources: A development plan for Newfoundland and Labrador, 1980-1985.* St. John's.

Osbaldeston, Gordon (1988). "Keeping Deputy Ministers Accountable." London: University of Western Ontario, National Centre for Management Research and Development.

Pepper, D. (1977). *Men, Boats and Fish in the Northwest Atlantic: A Case History of Fisheries Management.* Unpublished Ph.D. thesis, University of Wales.

Prince Edward Island, Department of Fisheries (1960). *Annual Report.* Charlottetown.

Pross, A. Paul (1986). *Group Politics and Public Policy.* Toronto: Oxford University Press.

_____ **(1984).** "The Fishery: Ali versus Frazier." In Barbara Jamieson, ed. *Governing Nova Scotia: Policies, Priorities and the 1984-85 Budget.* Halifax: Dalhousie University School of Public Administration.

Pross, A. Paul and S. McCorquodale (1987). *Economic Resurgence and the Constitutional Agenda: The Case of the East Coast Fisheries.* Kingston: Institute of Intergovernmental Relations, Queen's University.

Scott, Anthony (1955). "The fishery: objectives of sole ownership." *Journal of Political Economy,* 63: 116-24.

Scott, Anthony and Philip A. Neher, eds. (1981). *The Public Regulation of Commercial Fisheries in Canada.* Ottawa: Supply and Services Canada.

Task Force on Atlantic Fisheries (1983). *Navigating Troubled Waters: A New Policy for the Atlantic Fisheries.* Ottawa: Supply and Services Canada.

Watt, J.W. (1967). *A Brief History of the Fisheries of Nova Scotia.* Halifax: Department of Trade and Industry.

Weeks, Ernie and Leigh Mazany (1983). *The Future of the Atlantic Fisheries.* Montreal: Institute for Research in Public Policy.

Williams, Rick (1979). "Inshore Fishermen, Unionization and the Struggle against Underdevelopment Today." In R.J. Brym and R. James Sacouman, eds. *Underdevelopment and Social Movements in Atlantic Canada.* Toronto: New Hogtown Press: 161-75.

Endnotes

We wish to thank Bill Coleman and Grace Skogstad for major assistance in editing this piece.

1. Canada. Statistics Canada. Report No. 61.202 (1978) Table 1.

2. The Metric ton, or tonne (t), is equivalent to 2,204 pounds and is the standard unit of volume in fisheries statistics.

3. Fish such as cod, haddock and hake, which feed on the sea bottom.

4. Interview. L. Dickie, 18 July 1979 (Dunn, McCorquodale, Pross). See also Mike LeBlanc (1984).

5. To some extent, of course, international obligations are still important. For example, Canada is obliged to make stocks excess to Canadian needs available to other countries.

6. Or, as a later document put it: "Historically fisheries management has focussed primarily on the biological aspects of the fisheries, concerned primarily with the protection and conservation of fish stocks. It is now clear that if fisheries are to make their fullest contribution to society, social, economic, political and environmental factors must be incorporated into the management process" (DFO, 1981: 8).

7. These include the Newfoundland Fishermen, Food and Allied Workers Union; the Fisheries Association, representing large processors; the various independent processors; co-op organizations; the Newfoundland Boat Builders Association; the Salt Fish Processors Association; the Joint Council of Mayors of Burin Peninsula; the Bank of Nova Scotia, the banker for the industry; and various individuals, particularly academics connected with Memorial University.

8. Interview with M. O'Connor, DFO; and P. MacGuinness (FCC) by A.P. Pross.

9. At one point during the LeBlanc years their reported efforts to unseat the federal minister seem to have left the Prime Minister unmoved, and certainly did not attain their objective. On the other hand, during the constitutional debate their support of continued federal jurisdiction over the fishery influenced the Nova Scotia government and thus may have had a decisive effect on the debate.

10. Interview with P. MacGuiness. Feb. 7, 1989 (Pross)

11. Ibid. and Interview with M. O'Connor, Chief, Resource Utilization Branch, DFO, Ottawa. Feb. 8, 1989. (Pross)

12. Including a major statement in December 1977, that called for establishing an effective management regime; equitable access to the resource; the optimal combination of public and private investment; the management of Northern Cod in the interests of the inshore fishery; the establishment of a regional fisheries management council and the development of a licensing policy (MacDonald, 1979: 181-2).

13. The impact of the fishery is particularly noticeable in the constituency of South West Nova which regularly changes hands in response to developments in the fishery.

14. As reported to Pross by an industry representative attending the meeting.

15. Interview with P. MacGuinness, Feb. 7, 1989.

CHAPTER THREE

THE FARM POLICY COMMUNITY AND PUBLIC POLICY IN ONTARIO AND QUEBEC

Grace Skogstad

D
espite their dwindling numbers and diminished economic significance, agricultural producers in most industrialized countries have forged close and influential links with politicians and civil servants. Their ability to do so is often attributed to the effectiveness of their organizations, the latter the result of farmers' recognition that they have no option: "to exert influence, they have to associate" (Grant and Coleman, 1987:214). This theme is explored in Canada's two most industrialized provinces, Ontario and Québec. In both provinces agricultural producers constitute less than 5 per cent of the population and most of the contribution which agriculture makes to the economy comes in the form of value added to the product once it leaves the farm gate.[1]

The following discussion analyzes important interprovincial differences between the level of producers' organizational development, their role in the agricultural policy process, the autonomy and strength of provincial state agencies, and the resulting policy networks. Québec farmers are highly organizationally developed; Ontario farmers, by contrast, have a much weaker associational system. Across the two provinces, differences in the structure of the agricultural industry and the historic role of the state have combined to shape significantly the interests and motivations of farmers for collective organization. In Ontario, a highly diverse industry structure combined with a facilitative state to reinforce particularistic identities and undermine province-wide collective action. State direction in the 1960s reinforced this trend and gave rise to private interest governments in market regulation. Elsewhere, a fragmented producer associational system, in conjunction with strong state capacity, yield pluralist policy networks in most issue-areas. In Québec, a much less diverse agricultural industry, strong communitarian sentiments rooted in a common language and propagated by the parastatal Catholic Church, and a relatively passive state until the 1960s, produced a set of motivations and incentives that gave rise to a well developed associational system. The emergence of a strong state in the 1970s helped to create concertative policy networks. However, existing policy networks in both Ontario and Québec are being challenged by larger societal and international trends. New actors are being added to the policy community and the ability of the state and producer interests to demonstrate flexibility and durability is being tested.

The Policy Environment

Industry Structure

The organizational development of Ontario and Québec farmers has been significantly affected by both logic of membership and logic of influence factors (Schmitter and Streeck, 1981). In Ontario, the structure of the industry and the historic role of the state served to weaken the motivation for developing a strong associational system among farmers. The most significant structural characteristics that have hampered organizational development in Ontario were and continue to be the following: the wide diversity of commodities produced, the territorial concentration of specific commodities but the relative geographic dispersion of other key commodities, and the dependence of producers on domestic consumers and processing industries located within the province to purchase their product. By contrast, organizational development in Québec has been shaped by a less diverse agricultural industry and by a greater geographic contiguity of important agricultural products.

Table 1

Most Important Farm Cash Receipts (%)

	%	Québec Cumulative %	%	Ontario Cumulative%
Dairy Products	36.3	36.3	19.8	19.8
Cattle & Calves	9.6	45.9	19.5	39.3
Hogs	20.1	66.0	12.4	51.7
Poultry	8.3	74.3	6.5	58.2
Corn	3.0	77.3	5.5	63.7
Vegetables	3.8	81.1	6.5	70.2
Eggs	2.8	83.9	3.3	73.5
Soybeans & Oilseeds			4.7	78.2

Ontario agriculture is heterogeneous, the result of both the temperate climate and an easy access to large urban markets. *(See Table 1.)* Ontario farmers produce a wide range of commodities and no single commodity so predominates as does milk in Québec (where it accounts for over one-third of farm cash receipts).[2] The more heterogeneous commodity production in Ontario is accompanied by considerable territorial concentration of specific commodities. Fruit and vegetable production is especially concentrated, facilitating local organization along specialist commodity lines. But the geographic dispersion of producers of other significant commodities—milk, cattle —is a liability to mobilization of farmers within one organization in Ontario.[3] By contrast, in Québec, the most important commodity, milk, occurs in contiguous counties throughout the province. This creates a similarity of interest among producers that facilitates province-wide organizational development.

If farmers who produce for a domestic market have greater incentives for collective action—to pressure governments to protect them from lower priced imports (Atkinson and Coleman, 1985:29)—then the dependence of producers in both provinces upon the domestic market would seem not to handicap either in building strong farm organizations. Historically and especially today, Québec agriculture is domestically oriented: almost 50 per cent of farm cash receipts are earned by products that enjoy domestic protection.[4] A smaller proportion (30 per cent) of farm cash receipts in Ontario come from products produced for a protected domestic market. However, until recently, only a few Ontario commodities have relied on export markets, and then usually to dispose of surpluses (Rae, 1985:145). Today, as a larger proportion of production is exported and imports account for a greater proportion of consumption, some important sectors of Ontario agriculture (cattle and hogs) have become more exposed to international prices.

The reliance of over 80 per cent of Ontario farmers on their products being purchased by provincial food, beverage, and tobacco manufacturing industries puts the farmers in a position of dependency. That producers were dependent on certain buyers, and lacked clout in the market place, was a significant catalyst to specialist commodity organization and the formation of marketing boards from the 1930s to the 1960s. The government, however, stressed the interdependence of the relationship, a view which, in more recent years, producers have apparently been willing to adopt. A perception that the health of the food manufacturing industry is "vital to agriculture in the province" (Agricultural Council of Ontario, 1986: 6) tends to undermine the development of a "we/them" attitude which could foster general farm organizational development. Its absence contributes to fragmentation along commodity lines as commodity producers tend to see their well being linked more to that of those who buy their products than to that of those who also produce foodstuffs.

The acceleration of economic differences among farmers over the last two decades, between, for example, commercially viable and non viable farms, and part-time and full time farmers, has also posed a handicap to the organizational development of farmers. These cleavages appear to be greater in Ontario than in Québec.[5]

Such provincial differences in industry structure have had an important bearing upon the organization of farm interests in both provinces. The Ontario history is one of constant tension between the interests of specialized commodity producers and farmers sharing general interests (such as in tax, credit, and land protection policies). The incentives and motivations to organize as specialized commodity groups have proven to be stronger than those pushing for a peak farm organization and a strong associational system. While tensions of the same nature appeared in Québec in the 1960s and have periodically cropped up as an undercurrent in the 1980s, they are much less important and have not created the schism visible in Ontario. This contrast between Ontario and Québec, with its potent implications for organizational development, is a function of differences in both the historic role of the state, and the circumstances and goals of farm organizations in the two provinces.

Traditional State-Producer Relations
The parameters of agricultural policy are broad and may legitimately be construed as including the range of activities associated with the production and marketing of foodstuffs, including the provision of production inputs and supplies, and the distribution and processing of foodstuffs. From the perspective of the state, the Canadian and

provincial departments of agriculture concur that minimally the following activities fall within their mandate: farm income security and stability, assurance of nutritious and stable food supplies, domestic and export market development, and land stewardship (water and soil resource management). From the perspective of both governments and farmers in the western industrialized world in the twentieth century, the issue of farm income protection is at the core of farm policy. Moreover, much of the debate over agricultural policy has centred, and continues to centre, on, first, how best to protect farm incomes, whether through the market place or government intervention on behalf of farmers; and, second, in finding the appropriate balance between the interests of farmers in stable and adequate incomes, on the one hand, and the food and non-food concerns of non-farmers, on the other. Farm income protection is thus a central issue in state-producer relations in Ontario and Québec agriculture. The manner and degree of success with which Ontario and Québec farmers have pursued regulatory policies to enhance producers' bargaining power in the market place, and expenditure policies to augment and stabilize farm incomes bear significantly upon farm organizational development, current farm policy networks, and of course, policy outcomes.

Ontario

It is helpful to distinguish two phases in Ontario state-producer relations. The first, from 1930 to 1960, is characterized by specialist commodity organization, a facilitative state with respect to marketing legislation, and a growing cleavage between specialist commodity groups and the general farm organization. The second, from 1960 to the early 1970s, is a period of state direction and intervention in some areas leading to the creation of private interest governments, and the defeat of a proposed potential agricultural associational system. It is against this background that contemporary state relations, characterized by an absence of state planning and reactive measures, have evolved.

When Dominion legislation delegating producers authority to regulate and compel the marketing of agricultural commodities was declared *ultra vires* in 1937, Ontario moved quickly to facilitate producers' requests for enhanced bargaining power in a buyer-dominated market place. The Farm Products Marketing Act (FPMA)[6] enabled producers to control the marketing of their products by establishing two types of marketing boards. The first, negotiating boards, were able to negotiate with buyers the terms and conditions of the sale of their produce. The second, called agency type boards, could appoint a marketing agency, and were later empowered to establish production quotas and prices.

Throughout the 1930s and 1940s, a variety of marketing plans, unequalled in any other province, were created (MacLeod:379). The initiative came from growers of commodities produced within a geographically concentrated area. The provincial government, through its supervisory body, the Farm Products Marketing Board (FPMB), was supportive and exercised its powers to serve as a conduit between producers and buyers when buyer resistance to producer boards threatened to undermine the producer board or create societal discord. Thus, when tobacco buyers refused to cooperate with the newly created Tobacco Marketing Board in 1951, and to buy their tobacco from it under negotiated price contracts, the premier intervened personally to ensure the continuation of the tobacco board (Perkin, 1962:43).

While the state was willing to enhance the bargaining power of producers in the market place through the creation of private interest governments with limited powers, it was not willing to allow producers to use that power to create industrial conflict. In the 1950s, it intervened directly to dictate a new marketing scheme for the Hog Producers Board, and, in the process, to end industrial discord as well as to restore the Hog Board's public legitimacy (MacLeod, 1961:356-9; Perkin, 1962:52-65). These actions demonstrate the state's limited tolerance for private interest government in the face of prolonged sectoral discord (Coleman, 1985).

The state's promotion of marketing schemes as the main thrust of its agricultural policy in the immediate postwar period did little to address the major problem confronting producers throughout the 1950s and 1960s: the inadequate level and instability of farm incomes. Its response to repeated lobbying by farm organizations on this issue demonstrated an absence of state planning and a reliance on market forces to "rationalize" the industry and so weed out the inefficient farmers. Thus, while the provincial department of agriculture commissioned a major inquiry on farm income that paralleled the federal task force on agriculture (1967-69), it largely ignored its recommendations for greater government regulation in agriculture (Rae, 1985:146). Rae's (1985:250) characterization of economic policy-making in the province between 1935 and 1975 as lacking clearly defined sets of goals and priorities seems to hold true for agriculture.

But there were important exceptions. Agriculture Minister William Stewart (1961-75) exercised leadership in the 1960s to organize marketing plans for those commodities whose geographical dispersion undermined their bargaining power in the market place: milk, eggs, poultry, and turkeys. Such state direction came in the wake of industrial chaos in the sector and was spurred on by developments outside the province which compelled provincial and federal state leadership to restore order to the industry (Safarian, 1974; Skogstad,

1980). A case in point is the creation of a province-wide milk marketing plan after 1965 that enabled milk producers to become the first Ontario farmers to control production and determine prices, and to become subsequently part of a national supply management scheme for milk. In creating what was to develop into a corporatist policy network, without first giving producers the right to vote on it, the minister was acting on the report of a one-man commission. It had investigated the chaotic marketing conditions and discord in the milk industry and recommended such a board after wide consultation with the industry (Ontario Milk Industry Inquiry Committee, 1965). Still, by no means did a consensus exist in the industry and the Agriculture Minister was thus said to have "imposed" a marketing board on the milk sector.

Such state direction was rare, and did not extend beyond the corporatist arrangements for milk and eggs[7] which were implemented in concert with federal and extraprovincial state authorities. Pluralism was the norm. Thus, all farm groups were given ample opportunity to provide input into the second major programme of government support, the General Farm Income Act, introduced in 1975-76 to supplement the federal price stabilization programme (Skogstad, 1987:67-9).

The mixture of pluralism in general farm policy issues and private interest governments in commodity marketing reflects the fragmented farm lobby and the varying strength of commodity and general farm organizations. The priority which state officials, and the largest farm federation, the Ontario Federation of Agriculture (OFA)[8] placed on the development of marketing schemes obviously contributed to the growth and financial strength of commodity organizations through their ability to collect compulsory producer levies. But it intensified the tension between them and the OFA in terms of their respective roles in farm policy, especially marketing policy. This had become a significant issue by the early 1950s when the OFA found that its organizational members were reluctant to finance the federation adequately (MacLeod, 1961:351). At the same time, the OFA's sponsorship of commodity marketing plans created a perception that it was the voice of highly specialized cash crop growers in south-western Ontario and inattentive to the needs of lower-income family farmers. This fostered greater organizational disunity, helping to fuel support for a new farm organization, the Ontario Farmers Union (OFU).[9]

The increasingly obvious fragmentation of the farm community was singled out by the Ontario Farm Income Committee, in its 1969 report, "The Challenge of Abundance", as a factor contributing to farmers' lack of political influence in improving farm incomes. The result was a major effort in the late 1960s to unite the farm lobby under one umbrella organization. The provincial government supported the effort, passing legislation providing for a producer plebiscite on the formation of a General Farm Organization (GFO), authorized to require compulsory levies of commodity boards and associations marketing farm products. The vote failed to garner the necessary 60 per cent support of voting producers. The association proposed was too strong for the commodity boards—apprehensive of the loss of their marketing power and funding to the GFO—and too weak for the OFU.[10]The defeat of the GFO, even while it would have allowed multiple farm organizations and associations to continue to exist, ruled out the possibility of a peak association with assured funding that would have enabled a greater degree of organizational development of Ontario's farm producers.

Québec

Farmers' organizational development took a different course in Québec than it did in Ontario, largely because of a relatively passive state and the Catholic Church's institutional support for a general farm organization (Kesteman, 1984).

Québec farm organization began under the aegis of the Catholic Church in 1924 with the formation of local parish organizations of the Union des Cultivateurs Catholiques (UCC). From the beginning the emphasis was on building strong local organizations which served as educational vehicles. The common language and shared cultural norms, combined with a prevailing ideology which reified the rural agrarian society as the bulwark against English Protestant materialism, tended to create a sense of collective solidarity.

In spite of the high value accorded the occupation of agriculture, and the fact that the Ministry of Agriculture and Colonization was the largest government department during the Duplessis years, the state played a minimal role in important policy areas like agriculture (Heintzman, 1983). In sharp contrast to Ontario, the Duplessis government was very slow to respond to repeated requests from the UCC after 1944 for producer marketing legislation. It was caught between farmers to whom it owed its re-election and the private companies, processors, and local factories upon whom it relied for patronage. Only after repeated distress in the milk industry in the first half of the 1950s, and following the recommendation of the Héon Commission, did the Duplessis government pass legislation in 1956 enabling producer marketing boards to regulate marketing. Québec was the last Canadian province to pass such enabling legislation, and even then, it was not until 1965 that the Marketing Act was amended to give Québec producer marketing boards comparable powers to those existing in other Canadian provinces.

Like the OFA in Ontario, the UCC took the lead in pushing for strong marketing legislation, and drafting marketing plans and garnering producer support for them once they were legal. But the organization of commodity marketing plans did not drive a strong wedge between the specialized "syndicates" and the Union des Producteurs Agricoles (UPA). As early as 1952, and before the provincial government had passed legislation to enable the delegation of marketing powers to syndicates, the UCC Congress had approved the creation of a structure within the UCC for specialist syndicates. By 1972, almost 80 per cent of the specialized federations which were administering marketing plans were members of the UPA. Thus, after 1972, when the UPA, as the UCC was renamed, obtained official recognition as the representative of Québec farmers, it was able to take over the administration of the marketing plans through its administrative component, the specialist federations.

The emergence of a statist tradition that began with the Quiet Revolution continued in the 1970s when it had its greatest effect on agriculture. Agriculture assumed a place in the furthering of collective, nationalist goals, especially following the election of the PQ government in 1976. An agricultural development strategy was formulated to meet the goal of self-sufficiency in foodstuffs, viewed as requisite to the étapiste strategy of independence (Québec, 1978). While the agriculture minister in Ontario virtually always has a farm background, the two most recent agriculture ministers in Québec have been lawyers. This reflects the latter's need to have an understanding of the many laws which define the relations between the state and agricultural producers and groups. The agricultural programmes put in place to further that goal—the Farm Income Stabilization Act establishing cost-of-production formula, for example—were formulated and implemented in concert with the UPA.

The Farm Policy Community

The farm policy communities in Ontario and Québec, summarized in Figures 1 and 2 respectively, are readily identifiable. There is a core of state, quasi-state, and private officials who are in frequent and regular communication as they formulate and implement farm policies. These individuals can be fairly easily distinguished by their isolation from those who make policy in other settings and by members' perceived interdependence through shared responsibility for the delivery of programmes for farmers. Members within each policy community share a number of professional norms which relate to the substance of agricultural policy and the process by which it should be formulated; those (private interests) who do not share these norms remain at the periphery of the farm policy community. Shared substantive goals include a commitment to efficient production, for example, and the assumption that the state and the producer have mutual and particular obligations in the furtherance of efficient production. The state's duty is to provide the (scientific, transportation) infrastructure that promotes efficient production; whereas, the farmer is responsible for utilizing capital and technology to produce more and cheaper foodstuffs. Shared procedural norms include an expectation of producer consultation and the exchange of sensitive information, as well as an emphasis on personal interaction of private and public sub-government actors.

Figure 1

Ontario Farm Policy Community

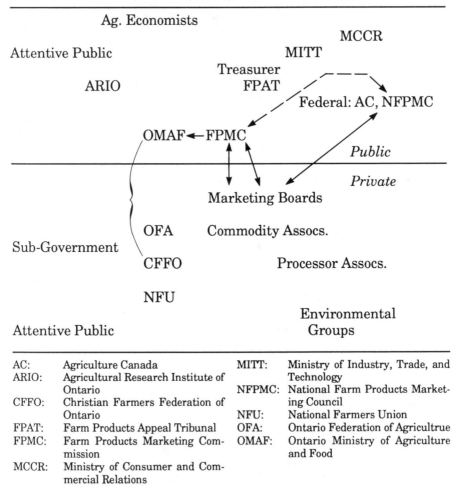

AC:	Agriculture Canada	MITT:	Ministry of Industry, Trade, and
ARIO:	Agricultural Research Institute of		Technology
	Ontario	NFPMC:	National Farm Products Market-
CFFO:	Christian Farmers Federation of		ing Council
	Ontario	NFU:	National Farmers Union
FPAT:	Farm Products Appeal Tribunal	OFA:	Ontario Federation of Agricultrue
FPMC:	Farm Products Marketing Com-	OMAF:	Ontario Ministry of Agriculture
	mission		and Food
MCCR:	Ministry of Consumer and Com-		
	mercial Relations		

Although the Ontario and Québec farm policy communities share a number of characteristics, including their considerable stability over time, they do differ. The Québec farm policy community is more integrated than Ontario's: its membership is characterized by greater closure, and restriction; members' real interdependence is greater; and they are more united in their view of the world. The emphasis on informality as an accepted rule of the game in the Ontario policy community does not prevail to the same extent in Québec, where there is a greater reliance on legal and formal relationships. More significant differences occur in the norms concerning what constitutes acceptable state intervention in agriculture, and rules regarding what is appropriate conduct by which to articulate positions.

Figure 2

Québec Farm Policy Community

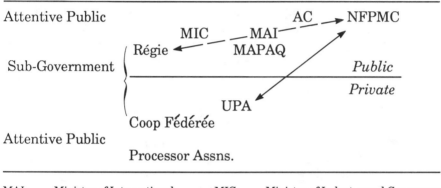

MAI:	Ministry of International Affairs	MIC:	Ministry of Industry and Commerce
MAPAQ:	Ministry of Agriculture, Fisheries and Food	UPA:	Union des Producteurs Agricoles

The primary actors in the Ontario agricultural policy community share a general view which includes a limited role for the state in agriculture. In keeping with the dominant political culture of pragmatism (Rae, 1985:252) and progressive conservatism (Wilson, 1980), it is believed that, rather than government goals and plans, the machinations of the market place should be the major determinant of the structure of agriculture. However, there is a recognized role for government assistance when the market fails. Another aspect of the shared view is a norm relating to the appropriateness of quiet diplomacy as the proper mode of government-industry conduct and interaction. Any differences that exist should be aired behind closed doors.

However, not all actors in the policy community share these norms, particularly that of the government maintaining a subsidiary role in agriculture. The neo-classical economic orientation of governmental officials is not as heartily endorsed by the OFA leadership. Some commodity producers, most notably the Ontario Cattlemen's Association (OCA), eschew any government intervention in the market place, while the National Farmers Union (NFU) advocates large scale regulation. The NFU does not share, as well, the norm of quiet diplomacy, opting for confrontationist lobbying tactics. These value differences keep it on the periphery of the sub-government. On the other hand, the Christian Farmer's Federation of Ontario's (CFFO) absention from public criticism of OMAF staff and policies has enhanced its perceived integrity and influence over public policy, despite its meagre membership of about 500 farm families. Also still on the periphery of the policy community are organizations committed to a pesticide/chemical-free agriculture, although the heightened public demand for "natural" food seems destined to augment their influence over time.

The operative norms in the Québec agricultural policy community include the goal of a competitive, efficient agricultural industry, augmented with and constrained by the belief that agriculture serves as an instrument of economic development of rural areas. Thus a more interventionist state is required to ensure farmers' livelihood and maintain rural communities. And second, norms concerning group-state modes of conduct go beyond peaceful negotiations to embrace more militant tactics.

These differing rules of the game reflect not only the impact of different historical traditions and industry structures, but, as well, variations in the composition of the two policy communities and the impact of various actors. Two in particular can be singled out. These are professional agricultural economists and the federal department of agriculture (Agriculture Canada). As state actors, within the Ontario Ministry of Agriculture and Food (OMAF), and private actors located principally at the University of Guelph, professional agricultural economists have had considerable success in having their market economy ideology hold sway in Ontario. In Québec, professional agricultural economists (based at Laval and McGill universities) appear to ascribe to norms that stress the importance of agriculture in maintaining a rural society and economy and the state's role in furthering this. These professional norms balance more evenly with those of private members (farm organizations) in Québec than is the case in Ontario.

Although Agriculture Canada is not consistently a part of the sub-government that makes policy in the Ontario and Québec farm policy communities, the prevailing professional norms within the two policy communities have been shaped by Agriculture Canada's relationship with farmers and governments in the two provinces. From Ontario's perspective, the federal state is an ally that shares Ontario's bias for a market economy and policy goals; moreover, Ontario applauds Ottawa for having generally accepted the primary responsibility for furthering those mutual interests. Hence, there has been no inducement for the provincial state to use available policy instruments to undertake distinct goals. Not so for Québec, where federal policies have been perceived as less supportive of Québec agriculture and federal authorities have been viewed as either irrelevant or hostile (McRoberts, 1988:426). This has led private actors to turn to Québec City to achieve collective goals, including the reversal of agricultural underdevelopment created by federal policies.

The dominant public actor in the sub-government of both policy communities is the provincial department of agriculture: in Ontario, OMAF, and, in Québec, the Ministry of Agriculture, Fisheries, and Food (MAPAQ). Other government departments have not been consistently part of the sub-government, but have moved in and out, depending on the issue. Thus, on expenditure matters, the Treasury Ministry/Board is an important actor whose salience was raised in the 1980s due to continuing depressed farm incomes and preoccupations with budget deficits. A 1986 Interministerial Task Force on Agricultural Finance to develop a long term approach to farm finance issues was jointly announced by the Ontario Minister of Agriculture and Food and the Treasurer and Minister of Economics. Other departments that are sporadically part of the sub-government depending, again, on the issue, include the ministries responsible for industry and commerce, trade, the environment, natural resources, labour, municipal affairs, and consumer and commercial relations.

An important part of the sub-government are the government agencies which supervise producer marketing boards in the two provinces. They occupy somewhat different positions in the sub-government. The Ontario Farm Products Marketing Commission includes both private and public actors who provide balanced representation of farmers, processors, and consumers. Its secretariat is located within the Farm Products Marketing Branch of the OMAF, whose senior bureaucrat is responsible for the Commission directly to the Minister of Agriculture. The Régie des marchés agricoles du Québec has greater independence of the MAPAQ. Its members are all technically "non-civil" servants who are appointed by the Cabinet for their expertise of marketing and not their sectoral representativeness.[11] (The Minister of Agriculture is responsible for it in the National Assembly and for its budget, but the Régie is otherwise autonomous.)

The significant societal actors which comprise the sub-government of the Ontario agricultural policy community are the general farm organizations. Of these the OFA is the most important, but also influential is the CFFO. The NFU (Ontario region) is more remote from the centre of the sub-government. Specialist commodity associations (the Ontario Cattlemen's Association, Ontario Corn Producers

Association) and various of the 25 marketing boards move in and out of the sub-government, depending upon the salience of issues to their sector and their expertise on more general farm matters. A subset of producer marketing boards, those which operate supply management plans, are a permanent part of the sub-government. Their operations bring federal and extra-provincial dairy, egg, hatching egg, and poultry regulatory authorities, as well as provincial processors of these commodities in from the peripheries of the policy community to the sub-government.

The UPA is the dominant private actor in the sub-government of the Québec policy community. The only other actor of significance is the Coopérative Fédérée du Québec which represents food processing cooperatives. As in Ontario, processors of supply managed commodities become part of the sub-government by virtue of their representation on national marketing agencies.

Other actors, including institutionally based agricultural economists and members of the processing, distribution, and retail sector have less consistent roles, although they are usually part of the attentive public. Environmental and consumer groups have traditionally only sporadically been a part of the attentive public, although this seems to be changing.

Capacity and Autonomy of State Agencies

The Ontario and Québec states have considerable capacity to make agricultural policy. In both, decision-making authority is concentrated and coordinated, and state officials have much independent expertise and information.[12]

The collegial process of decision-making in the Ontario government necessitates bureaucratic interdepartmental consultation and interministerial consensus in cabinet committees (Economic Policy in the case of Agriculture and Food). The shift from the departmental to the institutionalized cabinet (Dupré, 1985; Bell and Pascoe, 1988:65) requires the OMAF to be alert to the disparate interests of other departments. But OMAF's autonomy to devise agricultural policy relatively independently of other departments is not diminished in this process. OMAF has much expertise in agricultural policy matters[13] a coordinated internal decision-making process, and is invariably able to demonstrate clientele support. In addition, formalized inter-departmental consultation ensures coordinated decision-making within the government as a whole.

Despite their capacity to act autonomously, the state officials in the two policy communities, MAPAQ and OMAF, are not always willing to exercise that autonomy. Both are committed to consultation with farm organizations. The Québec policy community has been described as small, where everyone knows everyone else, and where there is easy and constant informal personal contact. MAPAQ and UPA form an alliance before federal and extraprovincial officials, and, within the province, before other departments, such as the Treasury Board. In Ontario, OMAF is extremely loathe to act without first building a consensus in the farm community. Its most frequent method of dealing with conflict and outstanding economic problems in the industry is to create industry-wide committees to find a consensus among competing interests and advise state officials.[14] Alternatively, state officials themselves broker interests, meeting farm and other interest organizations individually and collectively. The days are long gone, reflected a senior OMAF official in an interview with the author, when a minister of agriculture could impose a policy on the farm community.

Organizational Development of Interest Associations

Québec

The associational system of Québec agricultural producers is highly developed and well suited for policy advocacy and policy participation. Producers are represented by a single association, the UPA. The UPA is structured to generate policy specific and technical information, to mobilize members and public support for its policy proposals, and to maintain the internal cohesion that is necessary for effective lobbying. Moreover it possesses the organizational requirements needed to participate with the state in the formulation and implementation of public policy. First, it has a broad domain that is comprehensive in its representation of all territorial and commodity interests. Second, it is structurally organized so as to be able to generate highly differentiated and specialized information and to integrate and coordinate diverse and narrow interests. Third, its secure and ample strategic resources are institutionalized. And fourth, the UPA leadership is sufficiently autonomous from the state and its members to be able to engage in long-term strategies.

The UPA has a dual structure consisting of local and specialized syndicates. This structure provides for the representation of general producer interests that transcend commodity lines, as well as special-ized syndicate (commodity) interests. At the base of the organization are 180 local syndicates which provide province-wide territorial repre-sentation of general farm interests. These are aggregated to form 16 regional federations. Paralleling this structure are 150 specialized syndicates to which producers of a specific commodity may belong. Larger in size than the local syndicate, they are affiliated to the regional federation, as well as to a specialized federation. These 16 specialized federations operate the marketing plans of specific commodity sectors on a province-wide basis.

Along with the ability to focus on specialized areas, the UPA also has institutionalized ways of integrating the specialized and general interests of its members. The annual General Congress brings together 370 producer delegates, who represent fairly equitably the regional federations (57 per cent) and specialized federations (43 per cent). This policy ratification body adopts the general policy framework of the UPA and elects the executive officers, the president and two vice-presidents, for a two-year term. More important in policy-making terms is the General Council of the UPA which brings together the leaders of the specialized and regional federations. The General Council exercises full powers between the annual congresses of the UPA and adopts the budget. Since the members of the council possess both narrow and broad domains, they represent and harmonize specialized and general farm interests. An example of the General Council's ability to harmonize specific and sometimes conflicting interests of producers was its role in facilitating the integration in the late 1970s of the fluid and industrial milk plans (Kesteman, 1984:290-93).

The daily decision-making body of the UPA is the executive committee. Composed of the president, and two vice-presidents (elected at the annual meeting), plus four members elected from the General Council, it is assisted by a general secretariat. The executive committee provides a constant two-way flow of communication with local syndicates, regional federations, and the province-wide General Council. The activism of local general syndicates, in particular, fosters a two-way dialogue and makes democratic decision-making and leader responsiveness necessary. Proposals at the annual general congress often arise from the grass roots level at local annual meetings of the syndicates, which are often called to discuss policy resolutions. These, in turn, go to the regional federation and then to the general congress. Pre-congress deliberations between the General Council (presidents of the regional federations) and the Executive Council ensure that the UPA leadership is constantly aware of grass root concerns and policy positions.

While democratic decision-making is a priority within the UPA, the leaders do have considerable resources to be autonomous of their members and the state. The key here is the financial security and stability which the UPA enjoys as a result of the passage of the Farm Producers Act in 1972. Following a plebiscite endorsed by two-thirds of the producers, this law provided for the accreditation of a single professional association. The 1972 Act, itself the product of an intensive lobbying campaign by the UCC/UPA, requires all Québec producers to pay annual dues to the UPA, whether they are members or not. Farm producers as well as specialized federations (marketing boards) both pay annual dues, the level of which is approved by the annual general congress. The UPA is reported to have an annual budget of $33 million, the biggest of any farm union in North America.

This ample and secure financial footing funds a general secretariat of over 200 staff with considerable expertise and research capacity. The UPA secretariat is structurally differentiated to perform tasks necessary for both policy advocacy and policy participation. The two divisions entrusted with education and information and publication of the UPA's weekly periodical ensure membership cohesion and readiness for mobilization. A great deal of effort is put into providing farm leaders and members with an in-depth knowledge of current farm policy issues. This entails weekly meetings and colloquia organized by the UPA and MAPAQ throughout the winter months. Educational forums, such as the biennial orientation meeting for leaders of local syndicates and regional federations, are viewed as very important in educating producers about the traditions of the UPA and its democratic procedures. A frequent lobbying strategy is for regional federations to lobby the provincial Member of the National Assembly (MNA), or federal MP if the policy issue is a federal one. Also illustrative of the UPA's ability to mobilize members was the amassing of 1500 delegates in Québec City to argue successfully for farm income stabilization with a cost of production formula (the most generous in Canada). That rally was supported by spontaneous demonstrations in several regions that blocked roads and aroused considerable media attention. (See Kesteman, 1984:293-96). The policy research and development division enables participation in policy formulation and the producer controlled marketing section is responsible for implementation of marketing plans.

Ontario
In contrast to Québec, while the organizational pluralism of Ontario's agricultural producers facilitates policy advocacy and policy participation at the sub-sectoral or commodity level, it handicaps it on a province-wide, sectoral or cross-commodity basis. Interests are well organized at the commodity level: there are in excess of 30 associations which represent the interests of producers of one or a few specific commodities (such as fresh vegetables or tender fruits). The narrow domains of the organizations at the sub-sectoral level facilitate member mobilization and the internal cohesion necessary for successful lobbying. And the fact that many of these groups have been granted a legal right to collect compulsory levies for marketing and promotional purposes gives them the financial resources to acquire the specialized information requisite to successful lobbying.[15]

However, policy advocacy and participation at the province-wide cross-commodity level is handicapped by the absence of either a single peak association which represents and aggregates all important commodity and territorial interests, or an association which formally links and integrates the plurality of farm groups. Rather, there are three general farm organizations: the Ontario Federation of Agriculture, the National Farmers Union (Ontario Region), and the Christian Farmers Federation of Ontario. The OFA attempts to function as an integrative mechanism for commodity-specific and general farm interests.

The factors that handicap the OFA as a policy advocate also limit its ability to participate in the formulation and implementation of public policy. First, the OFA does not represent all territorial and commodity interests. The OFA has only 21,000 farm family members in a province of over 72,000 census farms. While it has 18 marketing boards and commodity associations as well as two cooperatives as affiliated members, the boards and associations which represent producers of milk, soybeans and wheat, and many vegetable growers are not members of the OFA. Together these non-members account for about 30 per cent of farm cash receipts.[16]

Second, neither of the two major policy-making bodies—the annual convention and the Board of Directors—nor the Executive Committee of the OFA is structured to allow a flow of communication between the groups that form the OFA as is the case in Québec. Because of the lack of institutionalized mechanisms that would facilitate communication, the OFA has been unable to develop specialized information to represent different particularistic interests, or to accommodate and seek a consensus between specialized (commodity) interests and the broader, cross-commodity matters of interest to farmers as a whole. Although the annual convention brings together delegates from each local OFA county organization as well as affiliated (commodity and cooperative) organizational members, the interests of farm family delegates tend to dominate. Delegates of farm families propose the majority of resolutions at the annual convention, and are the most active participants on the Board of Directors.

The Board of Directors is the second major policy-making body. The OFA's Constitution allows for up to 130 Board directors; in 1989-90, it was composed of 76 regional representatives, 27 representatives of the 27 member organizations, and 5 *ex officio* members. However, the capacity of the Board of Directors to represent particular interests and integrate them with general farm concerns is undermined by the way in which organizational members construe their role. They have not used their position on the Board to serve as representatives of their commodity group/association: their attendance at Board meetings tends to be poor and when present, they behave as observers rather than active participants attempting to influence OFA policy. It has been suggested that their role reflects the fact that many of these organizational delegates have no mandate from their own members to serve other than as a communication link.

Nor is there any formal mechanism to resolve commodity-farm conflicts in the seven member Executive Committee, composed of the elected president and two vice presidents, and the four members from the Board of Directors elected by the Board. Previous efforts to create a formal mechanism to represent commodity marketing concerns within the OFA (1970-74) and to bring together supply and non-supply management producer boards under the chairmanship of the OFA (1982-1984) failed (OFA, 1985:10-11). While insufficient resources of time and energy to sustain these structures are cited as reasons for their failure, an equally compelling explanation is the resistance of commodity groups to any efforts by the OFA to represent marketing interests. With their assured funding and substantial administrative structure, which enables them to branch out into policy areas beyond marketing, producer boards and the commodity associations which represent corn, wheat, milk, hogs, and cattle producers zealously guard their territory from OFA encroachment.[17] The consequence is that both the OFA and the commodity associations waste a lot of resources protecting their turf.

A third factor which detracts from the policy-making capacity of the OFA is the insecurity of its financial resources. It is unduly dependent upon a single, voluntary source of funds—family farm membership dues—for revenues. In 1988, 83 per cent of its $2.4 million revenues came from farm family membership fees. The OFA has no legislated right to compel dues of all farmers.[18] Nor is there a formula to determine what the amount of contributions from affiliated members should be; the contribution of each organizational member is dependent on what the member organization is able and willing to pay. In spite of this, and offsetting to some degree the OFA's handicaps in the areas of structure and resources—it has a secretariat of 32, of whom 15 are field representatives—are a number of factors that make it a more influential lobbyist than one might predict. The first is the credibility the OFA derives from its grass roots base. Like the UPA local syndicates, the 47 county federations which form the foundation of the OFA are a useful vehicle through which farmers can lobby local MPs and MPPs throughout the province, and gain the attention of the local media. In a province where a number of agrarian ridings are very competitive elected members are anxious to appear accessible and attentive to constituents. Face to face contact of OFA county federations with elected members represents another channel of policy advocacy. The second is the enhanced capability to generate policy-relevant information that the OFA derives by virtue of its affiliation with the Canadian Federation of Agriculture.[19] The CFA provides a forum within which the OFA can tap the information, research and policy analyses generated by other CFA-affiliates with more resources (UPA, Prairie Pools) than itself. The third is its success in forming links to the CFFO, a farm organization that shares many of the OFA's policy objectives and often supports its policy advocacy. These three factors, combined with the fact that the OFA comes closer than any of its rivals to serving as a voice of Ontario farmers, make it the predominant private actor in the Ontario sub-government on matters of general farm policy.

Finally, it must be noted that the absence of a formal associational system does not prohibit farm group alliances on single issues. This occurs particularly when the stakes are high, as for example during the negotiations of the Canada-US trade agreement.

Policy Networks

The policy network which describes most group-state relations in the Québec farm policy community is concertation. A single association, the UPA, represents the farm sector. It participates with a single state agency, the MAPAQ, in the formulation and implementation of policy.[20] The sectoral and state actors that are party to the bilateral relationship are both strong.

The policy network in Ontario is more difficult to label, as the level of producer organizational development suggests a pressure pluralist network, while the strengths of the state, more difficult to gauge, implies either state direction or concertation. Sectoral interests are fragmented and compete for the ear of the state. State authority is concentrated, but just how autonomous state actors are is difficult to determine. The unclarity of state autonomy suggests two possible policy networks. A concentrated state that lacks autonomy, in conjunctions with sectoral interests at a low level of organizational development, will promote pressure pluralist networks (Atkinson and Coleman, 1989: 54). Alternatively, autonomous state officials alongside a weak producer associational system gives rise to state-directed networks. But, with the temporary exception of the 1960s, state direction has not occurred, largely because state officials rule it out as unrealistic. On the contrary, state officials' emphasis on individual or collective consultation with the multiple groups, to achieve a consensus on issues that cross commodity interests, suggests that concertation may be a more appropriate label to describe policy networks that prevail on particular sub-issues. This point is illustrated by an analysis of the policy networks managing producer marketing boards and the formulation of an international trade policy. The latter example is helpful in illustrating the changing nature of the policy community in response to socio-economic changes in the domestic and international environment (Pross, 1986:107).

Producer Marketing Boards and Plans

The concept of "private interest governments" (Streeck and Schmitter, 1985:20,22) can be applied to the many producer boards which regulate the production and marketing of agricultural commodities in Ontario and Québec. They are self-regulatory groups that have been delegated a share (or all) of the state's authority to make and enforce binding decisions within one and the same organizational structure. The authority which such boards have been delegated varies enormously; the few boards able to control production and set prices (milk, eggs, chickens, turkeys, and broiler hatching eggs in both provinces, and tobacco in Ontario) clearly have much greater capacity to enhance their own self-interest than do the majority of boards which only negotiate prices.

If producer boards function in the self-interest of the producers who run them, can they be made to internalize the costs of their self-interested behaviour so that the general interest is upheld? Whether this occurs or not is a key to defining the policy network that prevails. Streeck and Schmitter suggest that the strength of the state is pivotal here. Having given up autonomy to make substantive policy, the state must retain sufficient procedural authority to "design, monitor, and keep in check" self-regulatory systems. It does this by maintaining "a credible threat of direct intervention" and retaining "the general capacity to resort to direct regulation if it so desires" (Streeck and Schmitter, 1985:26). If it is able to do so, concertation results; if it does not, clientele/sponsored pluralism ensues.

A comparison of the relationship of state authorities to producer-run marketing boards in Ontario and Québec suggests that, while the relationship differs in a number of significant respects, in both provinces there is a limited will and capacity to make credible "the Damocles sword of threatened direct state intervention" (Streeck and Schmitter, 1985:20). The relationships between state agencies and producer boards operate at a more formal level in Québec where they are defined by the legislated roles of each. In Ontario, by contrast, because there is a greater informality, considerable state-societal interpenetration prevails. This divergence stems from differences in the mandate and composition of the respective state supervisory agencies: the Ontario Farm Products Marketing Commission (FPMC) and the Québec Régie des marchés agricoles (Régie). The FPMC is composed of both OMAF civil servants and private actors representing farmers, processors and consumers. The inclusion of non-civil servants after 1986 was in response to criticism that the FPMC did not have a sufficient understanding of farmers and processors' problems. The latter is deemed important because of the FPMC's active involvement in the implementation of some marketing plans, including, for example, its chairmanship of some committees which negotiate annual contracts, as well as its retained authority to license vegetable processors. The involvement of the FPMC staff in the daily functioning of many producer boards, combined with the fact that the FPMC resides within a branch of the OMAF, means that senior officials within the ministry, including the Minister, occasionally become entwined in producer board affairs.

By contrast, the Régie operates at an arm's length from Québec producer boards and MAPAQ. Its members are non-civil servants appointed by and responsible to the Cabinet, rather than to the Minister of Agriculture, Fisheries and Food. In addition, its relationship to producer boards differs from that of the Ontario FPMC in that Québec producer boards are delegated powers directly in the legislation which creates their marketing plan, rather than via the FPMC as in Ontario. This distance from both the MAPAQ and producer boards allows the Régie to operate more as an independent tribunal, removed from the daily administration of marketing plans and hence more able to arbitrate industry conflicts. Its supervisory role includes approving all regulations passed by the producer boards in order to implement marketing plans. Most Ontario producer boards, by contrast, are authorized at the time of the passage of their marketing plan to implement a range of regulations. This restricts the FPMC's pre-audit regulatory authority to a few negotiated pricing agreements.

The Ontario Minister of Agriculture and Food and the FPMC have the legal authority to "design, monitor, and keep in check" producer boards. Although producer boards are generally only created following a favourable producer plebiscite, the Cabinet can circumvent this practice and create a marketing plan itself. It can also dissolve a producer board. Both have been done, but only following substantial consultation with the affected interests, and with their consensus. In addition, the FPMC can amend and revoke regulations and orders. In practice, it rarely does so, using persuasion to get boards to propose regulations that it will be able to approve.

Québec state authorities have some constraints, as well, on their ability to maintain "a credible threat of direct intervention." As in Ontario, the Cabinet can create a marketing plan—and did on one occasion—without the normal producer plebiscite and after public hearings. But it cannot amend a marketing plan once it has approved it without a petition from the board/producer association. And while the Régie must approve or disapprove all regulations, it can do only that; it cannot amend them.

These are not serious limitations on state agencies' authority to ensure that the interest of the public and not that of the self-regulatory group prevails. A greater constraint appears to be the limited resources of the supervisory agencies: insufficient bureaucratic support to ensure that boards are performing efficiently, and inadequate legal and economic expertise to develop independent analyses (OMAF,1985). To some extent, the Régie's practice of holding public hearings helps to compensate for the latter by making available to the Régie information other than that provided by the producer boards. By requiring the producer board to demonstrate the support of regulated members for major changes in marketing plans, it also guards against board administrators acting in their own self-interest. However, the extensive resources of time and energy expended on supervising and coordinating the provincial marketing plans which are part of national supply management plans, and the almost instinctive inclination to assume a parochial attitude toward these boards in the face of extraprovincial threats (Skogstad, 1987:100-02), undermines the capacity and the autonomy of the provincial supervisory agencies. It thus seems likely that at times concertation policy networks give way to clientele pluralism.

Agricultural Trade Policy
National and provincial agricultural policy has always been greatly shaped by macro economic and political goals—so much so that one could say that agriculture has received financial and legislative benefits only to the extent it contributes to broader goals (Fowke, 1946: 9, 272). Policies and appropriate policy instruments within the sector are guided by extra-sectoral factors, including provincial and national policies of fiscal restraint, government trading and diplomatic goals, and international trading regimes. The negotiations surrounding the Canada—US Free Trade Agreement (FTA) and the Uruguay Round of the GATT provide an opportunity to examine the impact of such macro factors on sectoral policy-making and reveal how the relatively closed farm policy communities in Ontario and Québec respond to external challenges and the entry of new, powerful actors.

In the area of international trade policy, the autonomy of the provincial state to devise an agricultural policy in the interests of the province as a whole is diminished. The federal government enjoys exclusive jurisdiction to negotiate and sign international trade agreements. Moreover, it controls a number of policy instruments from which Ontario and Québec producers benefit, including tariffs and import quotas. Within the provincial state, the dominant role that officials in the department of agriculture play is lessened and that of others heightened during international trade negotiations. In particular, the ministries of Industry, Trade and Technology, and Consumer and Commercial Relations in Ontario, and the ministries of Industry and Commerce and International Affairs in Québec become part of the sub-government. In addition, because trade policy provides opportunities for groups to be partly excluded from a public good (Ikenberry, 1988:237), there is a heightened mobilization of sectoral interests. In the absence of a strong associational system in Ontario, OFA's traditional assumption of prime responsibility to lobby on general farm issues is lost as commodity groups champion their own interests. Groups representing vegetable and food processors move into the sub-government, as do agricultural economists with an expertise in international trade.

To use an example to illustrate the scenario we have just described, provincial state policy on the FTA was determined outside the Ontario and Québec farm policy communities. In both provinces, the provincial position was set in the premier's office. Premier Bourassa supported the agreement, although UPA and MAPAQ opposed it. Premier Peterson rejected the FTA and found allies for his opposition in the Ontario farm community (the OFA, CFFO, and NFU) and the OMAF. While this example is not very instructive concerning policy efficacy at the *provincial* level of well developed organizations or particular networks, it does, however, shed light on how policy communities evolve and sectoral state actors respond to the entry of trans-sectoral state actors.

An examination of the process by which Ontario state officials formulated the province's position on the FTA reveals a policy network with considerable state capacity. This is demonstrated in the detailed analyses of the FTA that were developed and coordinated by interdepartmental committees.[21] To overcome the fragmentation in the farm community, exacerbated by the cleavages between the commodity associations who supported the FTA—representing cattle, hogs, and corn producers—and those opposed to it—the supply management marketing boards, horticultural producers, the OFA, the NFU, the CFFO—officials in the Economics and Policy Coordination Branch of the OMAF held industry-wide and individual group consultations with sectoral groups. These served to brief the groups on the issues and progress of the negotiations. As well, along with the expert advice offered by agricultural economists at the University of Guelph, the Economics and Policy Coordination Branch provided data for the OMAF's detailed analysis of the impact of the FTA on agriculture. Under the leadership of the Ministry of Industry, Trade and Technology, the OMAF analyses were coordinated with those of other departments in interdepartmental committees to yield a consistent government position that supported the Premier's opposition to the FTA.

In Québec, the sub-government widened to include other ministries but not, of course, other sectoral groups. The policy network continued to be characterized by concertation. The position of MAPAQ was arrived at after regular meetings with the UPA and the Coop Fédérée. MAPAQ officials along with those from International Affairs (the lead ministry), Industry and Commerce, Intergovernmental Affairs, and Energy and Resources comprised the interministerial committee mandated to derive a position consistent with the Premier's support for bilateral free trade. (The vice-premier and minister of Cultural Affairs also sat on this interministerial committee on planning and economic development.)

Examining the rationale of the sub-government public actors' positions on free trade is instructive in demonstrating the differing philosophical norms which prevail in the farm policy communities of Québec and Ontario. Ikenberry (1988:237-8) notes that the public character of political goods "is not an inherent and immutable characteristic of a policy area" but is subjectively defined and shaped by "political elites and prevailing institutional structures." In Québec, the UPA argued persuasively to MAPAQ that the collective farm interest in retaining programmes to support and ensure adequate farm incomes was a public good. MAPAQ officials, of course, were not able to persuade other members of the sub-government. In Ontario, in the absence of one collective farm group interest, the government had more freedom to determine the content of the public good on freer bilateral trade. By stressing the interrelatedness of producers and processors, public actors defined the public good to be that which benefitted both equally. Thus, it was the interest of warding off the predicted damage to the grape and wine, vegetable, poultry and dairy processing industries that constituted the OMAF's opposition to free trade.

Neither state nor societal actors in the farm policy community appreciably influenced the final outcome of the FTA debate in the two provinces. Broader political and economic goals prevailed. However, even with these constraints, the closed concertation network in Quebéc proved more efficacious than the more open, pressure pluralist network in Ontario. Unsuccessful in persuading their premier to reject the FTA because of its agricultural provisions, the UPA, in alliance with the provincial minister of agriculture, mounted a lobby of federal MPs that secured the amendments to the FTA coveted by the UPA as necessary to protect supply management in the dairy sector. The combined pressure of the Ontario government and the OFA-CFFO-NFU alliance to protect the horticultural sector and to ward off higher poultry import quotas was not similarly successful. The conclusion would seem to be that a well organized lobby can always benefit from the two "kicks at the can" that federalism affords.

Conclusion

The analytical framework which guides this chapter and the collection as a whole premises the utility, for understanding public policies, of a focus upon the structural characteristics of private interests and public actors within a sector, and the policy communities and networks through which they are related. While emphasizing the sectoral level of analysis, it cautions that macro-political variables may also be important.

This examination of Ontario and Québec farm policy communities does show, firstly, that the same sector may process public policies in different ways; and, secondly, that, across provinces, the structural organization of private interests is important in explaining the ensuing differences in policy networks. But, while structural characteristics of private and public actors clearly shape policy networks, this cross-provincial comparison highlights the contributory effect of other variables on contemporary policy communities and networks.

Foremost among these variables is the legacy of history. Ontario and Québec offer an interesting contrast in how the historical organizational strategies of private interests, combined with the past goals and policies of state actors, bear upon the contemporary organizational development of farm interests. History exercises an impact as well on the current structural characteristics of the state, particularly that of state actors' autonomy. The policies of yesterday's state actors, in particular those which established private interest governments, have effectively diminished the autonomy of today's state authorities either by locking them into webs of interdependence from which it is difficult— if not impossible—for them to extract themselves, or by excluding them from some matters of decision-making.

Current policy networks are rooted in the past in yet another sense. Norms, beliefs and traditions of policy-making that originated when agriculture was a much more significant economic sector than it is today continue to have an impact. The close communication links established between farmers and government in nineteenth and early twentieth century Ontario, as governments undertook to educate farmers and assist their communal societies, continue to manifest in the way consultation is practiced today. In Québec, the pre-Quiet Revolution belief in the rural community as the backbone of the French society and the later, 1960s perception of agriculture as an endangered species, constitute the philosophical framework within which policy networks devise agricultural policy. Cultural norms like these which encapsulate historical experiences thus emerge as another variable that shapes the development and functioning of policy networks. They help to explain, for example, why the relatively greater cohesiveness and policy capability of Ontario state officials vis-à-vis the fragmented farm interests has not been fully exploited. It has been noted that, rather than acting autonomously in the face of sectoral discord, Ontario state officials have traditionally assumed responsibility for building the consensus that the divided farm community cannot. Although the reluctance of OMAF officials to act autonomously may reflect their perception that their own intragovernmental clout is best furthered by a united department-clientele front, it more probably is an artifact of historically rooted values and norms that place a premium on sectoral consultation.

Recognizing the importance of mutual rules of the game as possible constraints on state actors' autonomy suggests that the latters' perceptions of their autonomy may not always coincide with what an "objective" appraisal based on the structural characteristics of the state would imply. This is likely to be especially true of those policy sectors where state-societal relations are "embedded" (Cairns, 1986). To the extent that sectoral "clients" lobby vociferously to prevent discontinuation of policies from which they benefit, especially in a sector like agriculture where the policies that link citizens and state are myriad, state officials may well have little room to manoeuvre. Accordingly, where state-society relations are embedded by the weight of past policies and norms, one might well witness more pressure pluralistic networks—even in the face of organized interests' fragmentation—than one might expect, given the state's structural organization and resources.

Today's policy networks cannot be understood in isolation from their past, nor can they be extracted from the broader, macro context. Federalism (both by virtue of divided jurisdiction over marketing and the mechanism of executive federalism) was a direct catalyst to the creation of private interest governments in commodity marketing; indirectly, policies of the government of Canada have contributed to the goals of state actors and the motivations for organizational development of sectoral interests. And, as Chapter 2 indicates for fisheries policy, the example of the free trade agreement demonstrates that macro considerations frequently prevail over sectoral interests—even in the face of strong sectoral actors.

Finally, it is important to raise the question of the connection, if any, between policy networks and policy outcomes. There is some evidence to indicate that organized interests are better able to maximize their self-interest in closed networks, such as the concertation that typifies Québec agricultural policy-making, than in the pressure pluralism that predominates in Ontario. Data, for example, suggest that, compared to Ontario framers, Québec farmers not only feel but are more financially secure, at least in terms of the proportion of farmers whose incomes are protected, the amount of debt per farm, and the proportion of farmers in serious financial difficulty (Agriculture Canada, 1987: 214-15). Such data must, however, be treated with caution, since they reflect not only the efficacy of organizational development and concertation networks, but, differences in commodity production and the greater philosophical commitment to an interventionist state in Québec.

To apply a final criterion in our analysis, that of flexibility in responding to crises and challenges facing the industry, there appear to be few differences between the two policy communities. The Québec farm associational system is well positioned to respond to the emergence of new consumer and environmental concerns and changes in the international agricultural trading regime. It has reached out to forge links with consumers, environmental groups, and international farm organizations. Although the pluralistic and competitive farm organizational system in Ontario is less well equipped, the task will be performed by state officials who subscribe to a notion of the public good consistent with the interests of food processors, consumers, and environmentalists.[22] The latter will likely mean a diminution of the influence of the farm community, but not necessarily of OMAF state officials.

References

Agricultural Council of Ontario (1986). *The Incomes of Farmers and Their Families in Ontario.* Toronto.

Agriculture Canada (1988). *Proceedings: Canadian Agricultural Outlook Conference December 1987.* Ottawa: Minister of Supply and Services.

Atkinson, M.M. and William Coleman (1985). "Corporatism and Industrial Policy". In Cawson: 22-44.

_____ **(1989).** "Strong States and Weak States: Sectoral Policy Networks in Advanced Capitalist Economies." *British Journal of Political Science,* 19: 47-67.

Bell, George G. and Andrew D. Pascoe (1988). *The System of Government in Ontario.* Toronto: Wall and Thompson.

Cairns, Alan C. (1986). "The Embedded State: State-Society Relations in Canada." In Keith Banting, ed. *State and Society: Canada in Comparative Perspective.* Toronto: University of Toronto Press.

Cawson, Alan, ed. (1985). *Organized Interests and the State: Studies in Meso-Corporatism.* London: Sage.

Coleman, William D. (1985). "State corporatism as a sectoral phenomenon: The case of the Québec construction industry." In Cawson: 106-24.

Dupré, Stefan J. (1985). "Reflections on the Workability of Executive Federalism." In Richard Simeon, ed. *Intergovernmental Relations.* Toronto: University of Toronto Press: 1-32.

Fowke, Vernon C. (1946). *Canadian Agricultural Policy.* Toronto: University of Toronto Press.

Grant, Wyn and William Coleman (1987). "Conclusions." In Grant, Wyn P., ed. *Business Interests, Organizational Development and Private Interest Government: A Study of the Food Processing Industry.* Berlin: de Gruyter.

Heintzman, Ralph (1983). "The Political Culture of Québec, 1840-1960." *Canadian Journal of Political Science,* 16: 3-60.

Ikenberry, G. John (1988). "Conclusion." *International Organization,* 42: 219-243.

Kesteman, Jean-Pierre (1984). *Histoire du Syndicalisme agricole au Québec: UCC-UPA 1924-1984.* Montreal: Boréal Express.

MacLeod, Marion Jean (1961). Agriculture and Politics in Ontario Since 1867. Unpublished Ph.D. Dissertation, University of London.

McRoberts, Kenneth (1988). *Québec: Social Change and Political Crisis,* Third edition. Toronto: McClelland and Stewart.

Ontario Farm Income Committee (1969). "The Challenge of Abundance." Toronto.

Ontario Report of the Ontario Milk Industry Inquiry Committee (1965). Toronto.

Ontario Federation of Agriculture (OFA) (1985). *Overview of the OFA Relationship with Marketing Boards.* Toronto.

Ontario. Ministry of Agriculture and Food (OMAF) (1985). "Review of the Farm Products Marketing Branch, the Farm Products Marketing Board, and the Milk Commission of Ontario." Toronto.

Perkin, G.F. (1962). *Marketing Milestones in Ontario 1935-1960.* Toronto: Ontario Department of Agriculture.

Pross, A. Paul (1986). *Group Politics and Public Policy.* Toronto: Oxford University Press.

Québec. (1978). *L'Agro-Alimentaire pour une stratégie de développement.* Québec.

Rae, K.J. (1985). *The Prosperous Years: The Economic History of Ontario: 1939-75.* Toronto: University of Toronto Press.

Safarian, A.E. (1974). *Canadian Federalism and Economic Integration.* Ottawa: Information Canada: 48-57.

Schmitter, Philippe C. and Wolfgang Streeck (1981). "The Organization of Business Interests." Discussion Paper IIM/LMP 81-13. Berlin: Wissenschaftszentrum Berlin.

Skogstad, Grace (1980). "The Farm Products Marketing Agencies Act," *Canadian Public Policy,* 6: 89-100.

_____ **(1987).** *The Politics of Agricultural Policy-Making in Canada.* Toronto: University of Toronto Press.

Streeck, Wolfgang and P.C. Schmitter (1985). "Community, Market, State— and Associations? The Prospective Contribution of Interest Governance to Social Order." In Streeck, W. and P.C. Schmitter, eds. *Private Interest Government: Beyond Market and State.* London: Sage: 1-29.

Wilks, Stephen and Maurice Wright (1987). "Conclusion: Comparing Government-Industry Relations: States, Sectors and Networks." In Stephen Wilks and Maurice Wright, eds. *Comparative Government-Industry Relations.* Oxford: Clarendon Press.

Wilson, John (1980). "The Red Tory Province: Reflections on the Character of the Ontario Political Culture." In Donald C. MacDonald, ed. *The Government and Politics of Ontario.* Toronto: Van Nostrand Reinhold: 208-226.

Endnotes

1. The agri-food sector accounts for 12 per cent of Ontario's labour force and 7 per cent of its gross domestic product, making agriculture the second most important manufacturing industry (after transportation equipment). Agriculture accounts for 2 per cent of Québec's GDP. See Ontario Ministry of Agriculture

and Food, *Facts and Figures on the Agri-Food Sector*, January 1989, Issue No. 3.

2. As many as eight commodities are tallied to yield three quarters of Ontario farm cash receipts; only four (dairy, hogs, cattle and calves, and poultry) account for three quarters of Québec farm cash receipts.

3. 93 per cent of grape production and over 50 per cent of asparagus production takes place in one county. The production of hogs, the third most important commodity in terms of cash receipts, is concentrated in contiguous counties in southern Ontario; winter wheat and small grains in southern Ontario, and soybeans in three adjoining counties in south-western Ontario. On the other hand, milk production is spread throughout the province; the largest production areas are western and eastern Ontario, a geographic distance that is compounded by a language barrier. Cattle production is also spread between western and northern Ontario, and poultry production occurs throughout the province. See OMAF, *Agricultural Statistics for Ontario 1941-1978*, 1979, 59, 66-7.

4. Hogs are the only significant Québec commodity that is exported and a price-taker on international markets. Ontario tobacco, cheese, and white beans relied on export markets in the postwar years; cheese no longer does.

5. Especially in the cattle and small grains sectors in Ontario, there is a large amount of non-farm employment and fully 80 per cent of cattle producers are described as non-or quasi-commercial. In the mid-1980s, off-farm employment, wages, and salaries contributed more than half the income of rural farm people. But even among farmers who rely on farm production for their entire income, there are large disparities in income. See Agricultural Council of Ontario, *The Incomes of Farmers and Their Families in Ontario*, June 1986, xix.

6. The original act passed in 1937 was called the Ontario Farm Products Control Act. It was amended and renamed the Farm Products Marketing Act in 1946.

7. The Ontario Egg Marketing Board was also created by Minister Stewart without a producer vote, although one was subsequently held.

8. The OFA dates from 1936, when representatives of the United Farmers of Ontario joined with a number of specific commodity associations and the United Farmers Cooperative Company to form the Ontario Agricultural Conference as a branch of the Canadian Chamber of Agriculture. This federation was renamed the Ontario Federation of Agriculture in 1940. The OFA joined commodity associations in pressing for marketing boards (for hogs, wheat, poultry, tobacco) apparently out of the belief that "commodity groups could be induced to give greater support and financial contribution to the Federation if their overriding concern with marketing was recognized and emphasized." (MacLeod:351)

9. Based on individual farm family members and with a program in support of the family farm, the OFU gathered strength in the 1950s and 1960s in marginal areas like eastern Ontario, and mixed farming regions.

10. The OFU was committed to a direct farm membership organization and withdrew its support for the GFO on the grounds that marketing boards could continue to exist independently of it, leaving the GFO with no control over marketing.

11. Members of the Régie who come from the civil service are absorbed back in to the civil service once their term expires but while serving on the Régie they are under contract for a specified period and subject to the terms of that contract rather than to legislation applying to civil servants.

12. MAPAQ has about 4000 employees; OMAF, 1700. This makes OMAF the ninth largest of 33 Ontario ministries and central agencies in terms of personnel and eighth largest in terms of expenditures. See Bell and Pascoe:65.

13. Within the OMAF, policy expertise is lodged in the Economics and Policy Coordination Branch. Since 1962 the Agricultural Research Institute of Ontario has been charged with spending OMAF research funds for agriculture, veterinary medicine, and consumer studies. Eight institutions receive funding, including the University of Guelph (which receives the largest amount) and the Economics and Policy Coordination Branch of OMAF. See *Agricultural Research Institute of Ontario, April 1, 1987-March 31, 1988.*

14. A recent example includes the handling of prolonged economic distress in the cattle industry. The government appointed an industry-wide task force to advise it and recommend solutions. See OMAF, *Beef Marketing Task Force Report*, October 1988. When this task force was unable to agree on a cattle marketing method, the ministry pursued its recommendation to allow producers to decide in a plebiscite.

15. The Ontario Cattlemen's Association has a non-refundable checkoff. The Ontario Milk Marketing Board collected $3.9 million in license fees in 1986 and reported a net income of $5.6 million. See Ontario Milk Marketing Board, *21st Annual Report*, 1986, 22.

16. The Ontario Milk Marketing and Wheat Producers' boards make voluntary contributions to the OFA. The Ontario Fruit and Vegetable Growers and the Ontario Green House Vegetable Producers' Marketing Board are members of the OFA, allowing it to provide some representation of vegetable growers.

17. An illustrative example is the fate of a resolution passed at the 1986 OFA Annual Convention which called for the OFA to demand that the government have a referendum allowing red meat producers the option of establishing a marketing board for the red meat sector. The motion was very controversial. It passed by a narrow margin and a motion to overturn it at the 1987 convention was narrowly defeated. The representative of the hog producers board on the Board of Directors opposed it. The Board subsequently decided to exclude pork and sheep from the resolution (a sheep agency had been put in place), leaving the provincial government to act on the resolution of the Beef Task Force to hold a plebiscite on a cattle marketing board.

18. The OFA and CFFO are currently lobbying the provincial government for legislation enabling a producer vote on an automatic refundable checkoff that all agricultural producers would make to a general farm organization of their choice.

19. The OFA accounts for 22.3 per cent of CFA funding and is represented on its national executive.

20. Examples of concertation in implementing programs include the monthly meeting between the General Manager of the UPA and the Deputy Minister of Agriculture on a committee concerned with administering existing programs.

The UPA is represented on all advisory committees of the National Assembly that are concerned with agriculture and environmental matters.

21. Among analyses prepared by the Economics and Policy Coordination Branch were: "Canada-US Trade Negotiations: Implications for Ontario's Agriculture, Food and Beverage Sector", February 6, 1987, and "Assessment of the Impacts of the Canada-U.S. Free Trade Agreement on the Ontario Agriculture and Food Sector", January 1988. A monthly circular, "Agricultural Trade Update", published since January 1986 has furnished detailed information about bilateral and multilateral trade negotiations and developments.

22. A 1987 OMAF strategy paper reveals OMAF's recognition of the altered environment and the shift to the politics of consumption. It identified four components of a strategy for agriculture: competitiveness in domestic and foreign markets; financial stability for farmers; education and training to ensure competition and appropriate resource management; and soil and water management. See OMAF, *Annual Report 1987/88*, 5. The growing impact of other departments on OMAF is suggested by the striking in January 1989 of an interdepartmental Advisory Committee on Food Processing, co-chaired by the ministers of Agriculture and Food, and Industry, Trade and Technology. It includes representatives of producer marketing boards, processors, and consumers.

CHAPTER FOUR

THE BANKING POLICY COMMUNITY AND FINANCIAL CHANGE

William D. Coleman

F
inancial firms in Canada engage in a broad range of activities
that have traditionally been grouped under four pillars: the
taking of deposits and the making of third party loans, the
management of estates and trusts, the provision of insurance, and the
underwriting and distribution of securities. Until the end of the Second
World War, each of these four activities was associated with one type
of institution only: chartered banks, trust companies, insurance companies, and investment dealers respectively. None the less, even prior
to the war, the correspondence between institution and activity was
never perfect, banks underwrote some kinds of securities, sales finance
companies made loans, insurance companies offered mortgages, for
example. Since 1945 these institutional pillars have crumbled almost
completely with governments often recognizing changes post facto in
legislation and in new regulations. Consequently, competition has
increased among domestic financial institutions, particularly in the
sale of mortgages and of consumer and business loans. In addition,

over the past two decades, some of the largest Canadian financial institutions have sought to expand their business in international markets. This expansion brought pressures on Canadian governments to allow foreign institutions reciprocal access to Canadian financial markets, which, in turn, has resulted in policy changes that have enabled foreign firms to increase their business in Canada during the 1980s.

These changes in competitive conditions over the last few decades have been driven by advances in technology, the breakdown of the international financial regime centred on fixed exchange rates, and the rapid expansion of international financial or Euro-markets that are largely beyond the control of individual nation-states.[1] In all advanced capitalist societies, the state has greeted these shifts in the marketplace with mixed emotions. Increased competition tends to benefit consumers (including governments) who pay less for financial services. Governments have thus agreed to change regulations governing the activities of financial firms in order to encourage market activity. Yet more competition among financial firms also invites more risk-taking and with it a higher probability of insolvencies. Participation in international markets is particularly risky and individual nation-states often have very little knowledge of transactions in these markets.[2] Hence capitalist states have found themselves faced with higher rates of failures in the financial sector and, to the extent that the institutions that fail are large, with higher probabilities of instability within the whole financial system.

Not surprisingly, then, market deregulation has been followed by a strengthening of the state's capacity to supervise financial firms. The buttressing of the state in Canada has reinforced bureaucratic pluralism within the federal government and hardened the divisions between the federal and the provincial governments. These changes in the Canadian state, coupled with the breakdown of market compartmentalization in the financial sector, have led to a significant growth in the number of actors in the banking policy community and have begun to foster changes in the policy networks in this community. The number of issues decided in pressure pluralist rather than clientele pluralist networks has expanded.[3] In other instances, clientele networks have changed over to concertation and, in some instances, to sectoral corporatist networks. The expansion in the policy community and the changes in policy networks have not altered greatly the accessibility of financial policy-making to the citizenry at large. It is also questionable whether the consumer of financial services is more secure as a result of these changes. A larger policy community brings a greater probability of a hiatus in policy-making because of federal-provincial conflict and because of competing value systems possessed by professionals speaking for community actors.

This chapter, focussing primarily on the function of deposit-taking, begins with a brief analysis of the changes in the policy environment. Next, the chapter outlines the structure of what will be called the banking policy community. It reviews the organization of business interests in the sector, and describes the organization of the Canadian state as it bears upon financial firms, highlighting recent changes that have reinforced the state's pluralist character. The resulting changes in policy networks are then illustrated by two examples: the restructuring of the Canadian payments system leading to the substitution of a corporatist network for a clientele pluralist one and Canadian participation in the negotiation of an international agreement on capital adequacy utilizing a concertation network. The conclusion analyzes the impact of the changes in the policy community and in policy networks on democratic accessibility and consumer protection.

The Policy Environment

During the postwar period the financial sector evolved away from a regulatory structure based on restricting the activities of a financial firm to one main activity. Subsequent changes in regulation have gradually opened a number of activities to financial firms, although restrictions usually remain on which activity can be offered by which subsidiary of the firm. This deregulation of the marketplace has led the state, in turn, to increase its capacity to supervise the behaviour of individual firms. Consequently, by the end of the 1980s, competition had increased in a number of financial markets and the state was more visible as a supervisor of those markets.

Market Deregulation
The chartered banks in Canada benefit from a tradition not available to any other financial firm—their legislation, the Bank Act, is reviewed and updated every ten years. In anticipation of this decennial review due in 1964, the federal government appointed a Royal Commission on Banking and Finance (the Porter Report) in 1961 and asked it to review the structure of the financial system and to make recommendations for its improvement. The Commission's report, tabled in 1964, gave the first decided impetus to market deregulation in the postwar period and highlighted emerging problems of supervision.

Until the 1940s, the chartered banks had not been allowed to enter the mortgage loan field. The banks had seen themselves as commercial banks, making short-term loans in order to keep their assets very liquid and thus to ensure the safety of their deposit liabilities (Porter Report, 1964: 115). Mortgages represented a long-term asset and thus were more properly administered by institutions like trust and loan companies that managed much less liquid estates and trusts liabilities. The 1944 revision of the Bank Act marked the first change in this practice when it permitted banks to take land mortgage security against loans made to farmers under the new Farm Improvement Loans Act (Neufeld, 1972: 110). The door was opened further in the 1954 revision to the Act when the banks began to make government-guaranteed mortgage loans under the National Housing Act and were permitted to take chattel mortgages as security for bank loans (Neufeld: 111). In their submission to the Porter Commission in 1962, the banks asked that all remaining prohibitions on mortgage lending be removed. The Commission agreed and the 1967 Bank Act instituted this change. Table 1 indicates that the banks have emerged as strong competitors to the trust and loan companies in the mortgage loan field.

Table 1

Distribution of Loans - Financial Institutions

	Mortgage	Personal	Business
1967			
Banks	1.7	89.5	
Trust Cos.	43.5	0.9	
Loan Cos.	37.3	0.2	
Credit Unions	17.6	9.8	
1977			
Banks	25.1	79.5	97.0
Trust Cos.	37.7	1.4	1.1
Loan Cos.	17.5	0.1	0.4
Credit Unions	19.7	19.0	1.6
1987			
A Banks	45.5	69.1	75.6
B Banks	0.7	2.5	16.5
Trust Cos.	20.3	8.9	1.7
Loan Cos.	23.4	6.1	1.5
Credit Unions	10.2	13.5	4.6

Sources: Statistics Canada, Financial Institutions, various years

Similarly, governments had initially sought to restrict the ability of trust and loan companies to take deposits and to offer unsecured loans. Both of these restrictions have not stood the test of time. Trust companies were given the right to receive funds on deposit, providing they were "held in trust" and gradually allowed to set up branches and to offer chequing privileges. Finally, they were empowered to make personal loans under a basket clause—the loans could not exceed a certain portion of their assets. Even here trust companies have proven inventive in defining what is and what is not in the basket. Revisions to legislation on trust and loan companies introduced by Ontario and by Québec in 1988, and by British Columbia in 1989, accordingly expanded the business powers of these companies, recognizing de facto what had already taken place. Recent changes to federal legislation move in similar directions. Markets for deposits and for consumer and business loans now join those of mortgages in becoming even more open to competition.

The pillar of securities underwriting has also fallen. Traditionally, this market had been reserved for investment banking or investment dealer firms, companies that accept monies for the purchase of the debt or equity of another corporate entity. These firms facilitate direct financing, the immediate transaction of business between borrower and lender. In primary markets, they design financial instruments that are attractive to users of capital and investors, and engineer their sale from users to investors (Securities Industry Capital Markets Committee (SICMC), 1985: 2-3). They participate in secondary markets by facilitating the sale of financial instruments between investors. The essential difference then between market (investment dealers) and financial (chartered banks, trust and loan companies, credit unions) intermediaries is that the actions of the former enable investors to emerge with a direct investment in the business, government or other user of capital. Investment dealer firms are used primarily by governments and large corporations who seek to issue securities stocks, bonds, short-term money market instruments—and a host of new financial innovations (Dept. of Finance, 1985: 51).

During the 1970s, interest rates became more volatile and banks began to shorten the term of the loans they were willing to make to corporate customers. The corporate sector responded by raising more funds in capital markets, whether through debt (bonds) or equity (stocks) issues. Commercial banks in Canada, like those in Britain and the United States, wished to play a greater part in the securities business, but legislation prevented them from taking a direct underwriting role in the issuance of corporate securities. They responded to this situation by pushing beyond the limits of legislation, thereby forcing governments to respond. The first step in this direction came when the Toronto Dominion Bank established a discount brokerage service in 1985. After an intensive investigation, and the setting of some conditions, the Ontario Securities Commission approved this step. In 1986, the Commission des valeurs mobilières du Québec (Québec Securities Commission) gave the Bank of Nova Scotia permission to set up a securities dealer subsidiary, directly contravening in the process the federal Bank Act. Late in 1986, the bankers initiated discussions with the Ontario Securities Commission to develop more general rules for securities subsidiaries prior to deregulation in that province.[4] Its hand forced, the federal government entered into negotiations with Ontario resulting in an agreement in April 1987 that permitted the chartered banks to set up securities subsidiaries that would be regulated by provincial securities commissions. Following implementation of the agreement in June 1987, all of the larger banks, with the exception of the Toronto Dominion, purchased a major investment dealer firm.[5] The wall between the banks and securities underwriting had crumbled.

A final set of changes added to competition in both domestic lending and securities markets. Most Western countries had traditionally protected domestic financial markets from foreign competition; restrictions existed on the foreign ownership of financial firms and on the activities of foreign firms in domestic markets.6 In Canada, foreign banks were allowed only to operate representative offices or non-bank subsidiaries.7 Individual foreign participation in a chartered bank was limited to 10 per cent and aggregate foreign participation to 25 per cent. Analogous restrictions existed for securities dealers. These restrictions became an increasing anomaly throughout the 1970s as Canadian chartered banks and life insurance companies expanded their operations abroad in pace with the general internationalization of the industry.

Following publication of a white paper in 1976 (Canada. Dept. of Finance, 1976), the 1980 Bank Act introduced several changes. The new act created a new category of bank, Schedule B (as opposed to the widely-held, domestic chartered or Schedule A banks), and permitted foreign banks to establish wholly-owned subsidiaries under this category, providing they could demonstrate that they were contributing to competitive banking in Canada and that reciprocity for Canadian banks existed in their home country. Restrictions were imposed on the size of the subsidiary and the aggregate domestic assets of all foreign bank subsidiaries were not to exceed 16 per cent of all banks' domestic assets (Pecchioli, 1983: 184). Beginning in 1989, US banks gained additional access to the Canadian market with the implementation of the US-Canada free trade agreement and the "national treatment" principle. Finally, provincial securities commissions removed all remaining restrictions on foreign companies' access to domestic capital markets and on foreign ownership of Canadian securities firms.

Tightening Supervision

Increased competition among deposit-taking institutions often jeopardizes the solvency of some set of those firms in the marketplace. An insolvent financial firm makes governments and other firms uneasy. Depending on their kinds of investments, depositors may lose funds and put pressure on politicians for repayment. Depending on the size of the firm, its failure may raise questions about the overall viability of the financial system, prompting a run on deposits and the possible collapse of the system. For these reasons, all governments seek to encourage prudential behaviour by financial firms through the creation of a supervisory authority that seeks to ensure behaviour is proper and that can identify, in advance, solvency problems. The degree to which such a supervisor intervenes in the affairs of financial enterprises has varied across nation-states and over time.

The Canadian tradition has been one of minimal state supervision coupled to significant self-regulation by financial firms themselves. For example, since 1923, the Bank Act has required chartered banks to engage two firms of accountants to act as the shareholders' auditors. The auditors report to the shareholders on whether the annual financial statements prepared by management reflect accurately the financial position of the firm. These auditors, in turn, provide certified financial statements to the banking supervisor; they also meet annually with the supervisor to discuss the accounting practices of the bank. In short, the auditors act as the eyes and ears of the supervisor.[8] In addition, legislation for the banks and for other financial institutions specifies certain responsibilities for the members of the board of directors and for internal inspection departments. This substantial measure of self-regulation rested on the belief that the industry possessed a knowledge of its own workings and problems that no outside agency could hope to equal. It was also thought that self-discipline would encourage firms to develop a broader sense of public responsibility (Porter Report, 1964: 347).

A series of insolvencies in the 1980s raised questions about the viability of this approach to supervision. Alberta, British Columbia, and Ontario experienced a dramatic series of failures of provincially-regulated financial firms. In 1984 and 1985, the Canadian Commercial Bank and the Northland Bank collapsed, the first chartered bank failures since 1923. In the aftermath of the failures, three other smaller banks were merged into larger entities.[9] The bankruptcy of the securities firm, Osler, left the Canadian Co-operative Credit Society, a liquidity facility for English-language provincial credit union centrals, with a debt of close to 30 million dollars to recoup. By the end of 1985, the Standing Committee on Finance, Trade and Economic Affairs (1985: 5) noted that five insurance companies and 14 trust and loan companies, plus the two banks had failed since 1981. Early in 1986, the commercial conglomerate, Imasco, took over Canada Trust, the country's largest (and only widely held) trust company. This takeover revived longstanding concerns about self-dealing between financial firms and their non-financial owners.

Both the federal government and the provincial governments responded to these events by increasing their supervisory capacity. The federal government merged the Office of the Inspector General of Banks and the Department of Insurance into a new Office of the Superintendent of Financial Institutions (OSFI) and approved a significant expansion of staff. The mandate of the Canada Deposit Insurance Corporation (CDIC) was also reviewed10 and new legislation strengthened its supervisory capability. At the provincial level, in Ontario, a white paper (Ontario, 1983) proposed a significant strengthening of the government's regulatory authority. This document was followed by a task force on financial institutions chaired by Stefan Dupré that recommended further changes to government operations (Ontario, 1985). By 1988, financial institutions had been lifted out of the relatively obscure bailiwick of the Ministry of Consumer and Commercial Relations, given their own minister, and ultimately their own government department. Québec revamped its Securities Act in 1982, created a new supervisory office, the Inspector General of Financial Institutions in 1983, and then undertook an even larger scale review of its financial legislation culminating in new laws for insurance firms, trust and loan companies, credit unions, and "intermediary organizations". BC introduced changes in 1989 creating a new Financial Institutions Commissioner with expanded powers. The words of the Ontario White Paper (1983: 4) summarized a key conclusion behind many of these changes: "It is obvious that the so-called 'gentlemen's agreement' approach to regulation, which depended on a common sense approach to regulation on the part of the authorities and the reliability and integrity of those in charge of the companies, could no longer be counted upon to be effective."

The Banking Policy Community

Jordan and Richardson (1987: 91-2) trace the roots of the concept of policy community to US studies of interest group activity conducted in the 1960s. Terms such as "iron triangles", "sub-governments", and "issue networks" all refer to the idea of relatively segmented and specialized subsystems of private actors and government agencies that have established regularized patterns of interchange for managing policy development and policy implementation. The concepts of a "policy community" and of "sub-governments" played a key role in Pross's (1986) survey of interest group politics in Canada and the idea of a "policy network" occupies a central place in recent work on Canadian industrial policy (Atkinson and Coleman 1989a, 1989b).

Similarly, drawing from the work of Rhodes (1987), the concepts of policy community and policy network have assumed a prominent place in comparative government-industry relations research in Britain (Wilks and Wright, 1987; Grant, Paterson and Whitson, 1988; Wright, 1988).

Following the lead suggested by Wilks and Wright (1987: 296-309), I will distinguish between the concepts of policy community and policy network and utilize both in my analysis. Wilks and Wright define a policy community as a group of actors or potential actors drawn from a policy universe whose community membership is defined by a policy focus (Wilks and Wright, 1987: 299). The policy universe refers to all actors or potential actors with a direct or indirect interest in a policy area. A policy focus includes any activity that may be the object of policy-making. Policy communities then tend to be sets of private and public actors that are differentiated readily from other sets, that have their own specialized organizations, and that are relatively interdependent (Grant et al., 1988: 55). Policy communities will vary in their degree of internal integration, in their stability over time, and in the extent to which they share specific professional norms.

A particular policy community will concern itself over time with a number of different issues and programmes. The process for dealing with these various issues and programmes may also vary, implying that different members of the policy community may be involved to different degrees and in different roles depending on the issue or programme (Wright, 1988: 596). The concept of a policy network is reserved for the linking process that brings together different members of the community for resolution of a given issue or development of a programme. The structure of these networks will itself vary depending on a host of circumstances and factors. [11] These structural differences are addressed in this chapter using the typology developed jointly with Atkinson and outlined in Chapter One: pressure pluralism, clientele pluralism, parentela pluralism, concertation, corporatism, and state direction.

In light of these criteria, this chapter argues that a distinct banking policy community exists in Canada. This community has as its policy focus the activity of banking, that is, the provision of a means of payment (Canada. Economic Council of Canada, 1987: 81). A "means of payment" refers to any financial instrument that is widely accepted in payment for goods and services and for the discharge of debt. By this definition, any institution that accepts deposits redeemable on demand or transferable by cheque would be considered to be involved in banking. Hence the banking policy community in Canada includes the chartered banks, credit unions, trust and loan companies, government treasury branches and, to a very limited extent, investment dealers and life insurance companies.[12] It also embraces at the federal level the Financial Policy Sector Branch of the Department of Finance, the OSFI, the Bank of Canada, and the CDIC. At the provincial level, it draws in the relevant regulatory authorities for loan and trust companies and their home departments. Finally, the community includes a number of interest associations and credit union centrals that act as intermediary organizations.

Figure 1
Banking Policy Communities, 1945 and 1987

1945

Bank of Canada		Inspector General
Dept. of Finance		
		PUBLIC
		PRIVATE
Banks		
	CBA	

1987

					Attentive
		Finance Committee			*Public*
Bk. of Canada	OSFI	CDIC	Provinces		*Sub-Gov't*
		Dept. of Finance			PUBLIC
				CPA	
					PRIVATE
		CBA			
A Banks	TCAC		CCCS		*Sub-Govt.*
	Provincial Credit Union Centrals				
B Banks	Trust Cos.	CLHIA	IDAC		*Attentive Public*
	Consumers' Assoc.		TMAC		

CBA:	Canadian Bankers Association		IDAC:	Investment Dealers Association of Canada
CCCS:	Canadian Cooperative Credit Society		OSFI:	Office of the Superintendant of Financial Institutions
CDIC:	Canada Deposit Insurance Corporation		TCAC:	Trust Companies Association of Canada
CLHIA:	Canadian Life and Health Insurance Association		TMAC:	Treasury Management Association of Canada
CPA:	Canadian Payments Association			

Figure 1 summarizes the structure of the policy community and indicates how it has expanded over time. Those organizations closer to the centre of the diagram are judged to be more important members of the community than those further away from the centre. Many members have joined the community since 1945 and several of these new members now enjoy central positions in the community. The sub-government (Pross, 1986) of the community, those members directly involved in policy formulation and implementation, has expanded considerably since the Second World War. In addition, the community now has an "attentive public" that did not exist forty years ago. Looking at the original members of the community, the diagram suggests that the Canadian Bankers' Association (CBA) has moved to a more central position in the community, displacing a little individual representation by the larger chartered banks. Despite these changes, the community is readily identified and remains relatively closed. Agencies dedicated both to supervision of banking and to policy development exist within the state apparatus. The firms in the community have their own interest associations, who have dedicated considerable organizational resources to developing banking policy. Together, these form the sub-government. Financial service consumers represented by the Consumers Association of Canada and the Treasury Management Association of Canada belong to the attentive public.

Several financial sector associations offer educational programmes that help define and maintain a distinctive set of behavioural norms for managers in banking firms. All of the members of the policy community share, albeit to varying degrees, a commitment to prudent management of depositors funds. Most members enunciate a belief that market forces must not be allowed to overwhelm this tradition of prudence. In both of these respects, they differentiate banking activity from other activities in the policy universe: insurance, estates and trust management, securities underwriting. All members believe in the need for a measure of state regulation to protect the overall viability of the financial system. All members also agree that changes in the character of this regulation should take place only after extensive internal consultation.

Organizational Development of Interest Associations

As is evident from Figure 1, interests in the financial sector remain organized around the traditional four pillars—banking, trust and estate management, insurance, securities dealing—with credit unions maintaining a separate identity. One association, the Canadian Payments Association (CPA), acts solely as a private interest government with responsibility for overseeing the payments system. The newest member of the community, the Treasury Management Association of

Canada (TMAC), acts as a lobby on CPA. Detailed analysis of the latter two groups will be reserved for the following section of the chapter on policy. This section will concentrate on the four remaining interest associations that belong to the community's sub-government: the CBA, Trust Companies Association of Canada (TCAC), Canadian Co-operative Credit Society (CCCS), and the Confédération des Caisses Populaires et d'Economie Desjardins. These organizations differ significantly from one another. The CBA has developed a large infrastructure that enables it to perform effectively in both policy participation and policy advocacy roles. In contrast, the TCAC has a structure better suited to policy advocacy. The CCCS and the Desjardins group are not ordinary associations at all; their members are drawn from the financial cooperative movement for which they provide central coordinating functions. But they also assume responsibility for interest representation and have sufficient resources to be described as policy capable organizations.

Although it would be incorrect to say that the CBA dominates interest representation in the banking policy community, it is accurate to note that the association plays hard and well in every policy game that takes place. The association's strength derives from the close integration that has developed between its internal organization and the executive structure of the banks.[13] This integration has emerged since 1980 in particular, when the association appointed its first permanent president.[14] The organizational development of the association has been assisted by a key advantage: by law, all chartered banks must belong to the association and each Schedule A bank must be represented on the association's executive council by its chief executive officer. [15]

Beneath the Executive Council are four major committees: financial legislation and regulation, domestic banking, interbank operations, and financial affairs. Each of these committees has a bank representative at the executive vice-president or senior vice-president level and each is coordinated by a permanent CBA vice-president. The bank representative matches the function of the committee. For example, the members of the Financial Affairs committee are the banks' chief financial officers. Each of these senior committees, in turn, has a number of sub-committees, again with members drawn from the vice-president level in the banks. Although it may appear rather bureaucratic, this structure enables the association to pool the policy expertise of members and staff and to assemble an effective, knowledgeable team of advocates on virtually any issue related to banking.

Not surprisingly, by Canadian standards, the CBA has a large staff of close to 100 persons. It also operates an educational affiliate, the Institute of Canadian Bankers and is responsible for collecting and aggregating some of the statistical information that banks must provide by law to the Bank of Canada. These resources, in conjunction with the close working relationship it has with its members, permit the association in most circumstances to assume the lead role in the policy arena rather than the individual banks. Previously, the association played a role subordinate to the individual banks in the policy process *(see Figure 1)*.

Despite the increased importance of the association, the large A banks also play a direct role in the policy process. Each bank possesses a research department, normally staffed by economists, that provides expertise on policy matters. With the exception of the Toronto Dominion, each bank also has a government relations or legislative affairs officer, usually with a senior rank. The banks remain constant players in the policy community's sub-government for three different reasons. First, they act to complement and reinforce positions taken by the CBA. Second, some policy matters are sufficiently technical and bank-specific that it is difficult to develop an "industry position." Since the largest six banks so dominate the sector in Canada, consultation on a one-to-one basis becomes feasible in these instances. Finally, the banks disagree sufficiently on some policy matters that the CBA cannot develop a common position. When this occurs, the banks follow their own devices.

The Trust Companies Association of Canada provides a sharp contrast to the CBA. Where the two permanent presidents of the CBA have been drawn from the ranks of senior bank executives, John Evans, the President of the TCAC is a former member of parliament. Where the CBA works through an elaborate structure of standing committees, the TCAC has virtually no committees, preferring to create task forces to deal with specific issues. Where the CBA employs a large number of persons, the TCAC has a staff of eight. Where all banks belong to the CBA by law, only 35 of the 75 eligible companies belong to the TCAC. Missing from the roster, in particular, is Canada Trust, the largest trust company in Canada. Such a structure suggests that the TCAC gives primacy to policy advocacy; it concentrates more on using political pressure to achieve its objectives than on seeking a participant role in the policy process. It also means that the larger trust companies sometimes feel themselves to be at a disadvantage when it comes to competing politically with the banks.

The Canadian Co-operative Credit Society received a federal charter in 1953 to provide liquidity for the credit union system in Canada. Its primary members are eight provincial credit union centrals from English-speaking Canada. In 1977, CCCS merged with the National Association of Canadian Credit Unions and has assumed since that time the usual association responsibilities for government relations and communications.[16] This twinning of the functions of liquidity facility and interest intermediation provides CCCS with in-house technical expertise not available to the TCAC. It also encourages a technical orientation to policy that makes CCCS suitable for both policy participation and policy advocacy roles. Financial co-operatives in Québec work through an analogous organization, the Desjardins group. It acts like CCCS in the dual role of liquidity facility and trade association and possesses as a consequence a similar policy style. It differs from CCCS in that it orients its activities primarily to the Québec government rather than the federal government.

The existence of separate organizations representing banks, trust companies, and credit unions is more than an historical legacy. Policy differences exist between the banks and trust companies on the issue of widely versus closely held ownership, commercial firms owning financial institutions, and the regulation of related parties transactions. With a few exceptions, banks also tend to be more active internationally than are trust companies. The credit unions, in turn, espouse a philosophy and possess a structure that distinguish them clearly from banks and trust companies. Banks continue to be regulated largely by the federal government, trust companies may be regulated federally or provincially, and credit unions are supervised by provincial governments.

Capacity and Autonomy of State Agencies

The several state agencies active in the policy community at the federal level, as a group, possess the capacity to define policy in their own right with the Department of Finance playing a lead role. They do not usually formulate policy, however, without extensive prior consultation with the financial sector itself. They thus have the capacity to act autonomously, but are reluctant to proceed without the community's support. On many policy issues, firms in the sector remain somewhat divided and these divisions create additional policy-making space for the federal agencies. Provincial agencies tend to be less well-resourced than their federal cousins but retain a degree of autonomy based on relatively detailed legislation. They operate virtually independently of their federal counterparts (with the exception of the CDIC). Consequently, no formal mechanism for the coordination of policy between the federal and provincial levels exists. Important policy differences also occur in legislative fields occupied by both levels such as the regulation of trust and life insurance companies.

Policy-making at the federal level is coordinated by a body called the "Senior Advisory Committee" that is chaired by the Deputy Minister of Finance and that includes the Governor of the Bank of Canada, the Chairman of CDIC, and the Superintendent of Financial Institutions. This committee is supported by a working policy group chaired by the Assistant Deputy Minister who heads the Financial Sector

Policy Branch in the Department of Finance with corresponding colleagues from OSFI, CDIC, and the central bank and by technical sub-groups staffed at still lower levels. The Department of Finance definitely plays a lead role at the lower working levels of this structure. These coordinating arrangements appear to internalize most differences over policy that might exist among these several agencies. They also facilitate a pooling of technical expertise; each agency has its own policy branch and there is a considerable interchange of position papers and technical information.

The relative autonomy of each of these agencies from the financial sector is difficult to assess. All of them maintain close contacts both with the associations and with individual financial firms. The following statement by one official summarizes a kind of common view.

> Let me start by saying that I am a fan of consultation. I think you have to do it. I think it is essential. It doesn't mean you always do everything that everybody wants but my own view of the policy development process, including the implementation process, is that I am not doing my job, neither is this [agency] doing its job in advising ministers and trying to make decisions if we don't have a sense of what the impacts are and where people are coming from.

This closeness is reinforced by certain common professional ties. Policy development officers in the Department of Finance and the Bank of Canada are virtually always professional economists. The Financial Institutions and Regulations committee of the CBA, which assumes the most responsibility for policy development related to banking, normally has the chief economists of the banks as its members. The head of the TCAC is an economist. This kind of professional background facilitates a certain meeting of minds when policy is being formulated. A different kind of commonality exists between OSFI and the banking community. The superintendent is a former auditor from the corporate sector who is highly respected "on the street." His chief policy person formerly worked for a big A bank and many of the regulatory staff of the Office share common professional (auditor) ties with their client institutions. These ties are reinforced by the pattern of self-regulation based on external auditors that dominates in the sector.

These shared perspectives based on professional norms tend to facilitate negotiations with the financial sector, but do not mean state agencies lack autonomy. Each of the federal agencies has its own independent research capability. Finance houses a "Financial Institutions and Markets Division," the Bank of Canada's Department of Financial and Monetary Analysis has a working group on policy for banking institutions, OSFI a "Legislation and Planning" section and so on. In addition, the legislation governing the activities of firms in the sector tends to be explicit and detailed; the discretion left to the sector's regulators tends to be circumscribed by the willingness of Parliament to define its objectives relatively clearly in law.

To some extent, the need for formal policy coordination at the federal level is a new phenomenon. Previously, the Department of Finance could act alone. CDIC did not become a full partner in the policy process until after the 1984-85 bank failures. Created in 1987, OSFI has a stronger impact than the cumulative contributions of both of its predecessor organizations, the Office of the Inspector General of Banks and the Department of Insurance. Adding to the pluralism of state structure is another rejuvenated player on the scene, the House of Commons Standing Committee on Finance, Trade and Economic Affairs. Chaired for several years by the somewhat unpredictable Donald Blenkarn, the Committee has served as an independent critic of some of the government's policy proposals and has provided an additional forum both for the airing of intra-sector differences and of points of view from those outside the financial sector.

No formal institutional mechanisms link federal government agencies to provincial counterparts.[17] Informal consultation appears to be ad hoc and infrequent. Provincial governments supervise provincially chartered trust and loan companies and credit unions, with the relative importance of these institutions varying from province to province. Trust and loan companies are a much larger component of the financial sector in Ontario than are credit unions; the reverse tends to be true in Québec and Western Canada.[18] Provincial agencies also tend to maintain a degree of autonomy from the sector, but perhaps to a lesser extent than their federal counterparts. They rely on self-regulation to provide them with information on the health of the firms and they do not have the depth of policy expertise possessed at the federal level. But the revisions to legislation that have taken place in the 1980s have strengthened the hands of provincial regulators.

The provinces have begun to develop a structure to facilitate the harmonization (without rendering uniform) of their regulation of financial institutions. Based on an earlier understanding reached by the Western provinces, they have set up a permanent forum of ministers responsible for financial institutions and struck appropriate working groups of officials. There remain, however, important differences in emphasis among the provinces. Ontario tends to give primacy to solvency issues while Québec and British Columbia emphasize economic development and the importance of the financial sector as a provider of jobs. To a certain extent, these differences reflect the differences at the federal level between the Department of Finance (and economists) that emphasize economic growth and markets and OSFI (and inspectors/auditors) that stress prudent firm behaviour.

These kinds of value differences are far from trivial because they slow down policy development and translate into rather distinct kinds of laws and regulations.

To conclude this section on the banking policy community, all of the members of the sub-government of the policy community possess, albeit in varying degrees, a capacity to participate in the making of policy. Societal actors in the sub-government are limited to the financial sector itself; state agencies have considerable autonomy from other parts of the state. Coordination among state agencies at the federal level exists and a useful pooling of policy expertise has resulted, but little interchange exists between the federal and provincial levels. Over the past decade, each of the major associations has improved its policy capacity, particularly the CBA. Larger individual financial institutions possess in-house expertise on policy and government relations matters. With capable and autonomous state actors and organizationally developed societal intermediaries, and given the overriding emphasis on consultation that dominates the policy community, the stage is set for the development of concertation and even corporatist policy networks. Two examples follow.

Policy Networks: Two Case Studies

Standards of Capital Adequacy
In July 1988, the Governor of the Bank of Canada joined other central bank governors in accepting a set of proposals that defined new minimum capital requirements for banks operating internationally. These proposals were developed by an international coordinating committee that had been set up in 1974 by the central bank governors of the Group of Ten (G-10) countries[19] in support of their regular meetings at the Bank for International Settlements (BIS), a kind of central bank for national central banks. The formulation of these proposals and their eventual implementation involved extensive discussions between relevant state actors and the financial sector in each of the countries involved. In Canada, the issue was handled in a concertation policy network that included the CBA and the chartered banks on the one side and the Bank of Canada and the OSFI on the other.

The issue of capital requirements for banks represents only one of a host of questions that have come to the fore with the internationalization of the banking sector. Over the past two decades, there has been rapid innovation in financial products, the expansion of international or (Euro-) currency and securities markets, and the instantaneous linking of national and international markets through advances in communications technology. These globalization trends have increased financial risk whether because of the enormous increases in capital flows, the frequency of transactions, the complexity of new financial instruments, the instability of foreign exchange markets, or the intensification of competition (Mackenzie, 1987). Central bankers in company with banking supervisors have watched and sought to analyze these developments since the mid 1970s, working through a sub-committee of the G10 bank governors set up at the BIS in Basle. Known informally as the Cooke Committee, the Committee on Banking Regulations and Supervisory Practices has promoted increased harmonization of banking supervision practices and more sharing of information among banking supervisors. Canada has been represented on this committee jointly by an Adviser to the Bank of Canada and the Superintendent of Financial Institutions.

Capital adequacy refers basically to the ratio between a bank's total assets and its equity capital plus its disclosed reserves. Increases in interest rate risk, country risk and exchange rate risk in the early 1980s raised the question of whether the capital maintained by banks as a hedge to that risk was adequate and whether different national definitions of this capital were forcing the system to the lowest common denominator definition of capital. Current regulations were failing to capture risks that banks were booking *off* their balance sheets and to reflect the actual asset mix held by a bank (Kapstein, 1989: 338). Britain had reacted earliest to this problem by beginning to move toward a risk-based standard for measuring capital already in 1980. In 1986, the Federal Reserve Board in the US began talks with the UK on a common standard leading to a bilateral agreement between the two countries in January 1987. This agreement provided the impetus for a wider international accord leading to a proposal for common measurement of capital and capital standards published by the BIS in December 1987 (BIS 1987). The paper proposed a two-tier system for capital composed of core capital and supplementary capital. Components of capital were to be weighted by their degree of risk, particularly credit risk. The paper then served as a beginning point for discussion and consultation within each member country because the implications of the proposals varied considerably depending on the country. Final agreement was reached in July 1988, with some discretion being left to national authorities. Members have said that they will abide by the new standards by 1992.

In Canada, discussion of this issue took place in a concertation policy network. OSFI, lead agency on the government side, consulted systematically with the "Capital Adequacy Committee" of the CBA, which was composed of the treasurers of the chartered banks. Some consultation took place between OSFI and individual banks as well, because the Cooke Committee proposals had differential implications depending on the asset structures of a bank. Negotiations with the CBA were particularly intense following publication of the BIS consultative document and then later in 1988 as the discussions turned to how the agreement would be implemented in Canada. For example, one critical issue was whether reserves set aside against Less Developed Country (LDC) loans could be treated as part of a bank's capital. Given that some Canadian banks were more exposed to LDC debt than were others, this issue was a difficult one. Ultimately, the Superintendent decided not to include these reserves as part of capital, a decision that differed from that taken in the United States.

The policy network conforms to the concertation model because one interest group only, the CBA, participated in negotiating the terms of policy with a relatively strong agency, OSFI, backed by the Bank of Canada. No other part of the financial community was included in the discussions although the agreement was bound to affect other financial institutions in the medium-term. Although the chartered banks are more involved in international markets than other firms, some of the trust companies such as Royal Trustco have extensive international operations. Revised provincial legislation and promised federal legislation will reduce significantly the differences in asset structures between chartered banks and other banking firms. It is likely that a risk-based standard will become increasingly common in the Canadian financial system because the need for fair competition dictates that capital requirements imposed on chartered banks be extended to their competitors. None the less, only the chartered banks played a meaningful part in the policy network that developed on this issue.

Managing the Payments System

Concertation networks involving the chartered banks only are becoming increasingly rare in the banking policy community. Pressure pluralism and even corporatism, as the example of the payments system shows, are becoming more common. The payments system refers to the institutions and procedures for distributing and handling coin and bank notes, for transferring deposits through cheques and inter-bank clearing and settlement, and for defining standards for payment innovations such as automated teller machines, credit cards, and point-of-sale systems. The payments system developed originally in Canada under the auspices of the CBA. Its act of incorporation delegated to the association responsibility for setting up and running clearing houses in Canada. At the time, such a step made a certain amount of sense because the banks were virtually the only financial institutions prepared to accept orders for the transfer of deposits. But, as we have seen, in the postwar period, more and more financial institutions have engaged in deposit-taking and hence needed to arrange for cheque clearing and settlement. Accordingly, they set up an arrangement with a chartered bank such that the bank would act as its clearer in the payments system. The position enjoyed by the banks and the CBA corresponded with the dominant position they held historically in the banking policy community (see Figure 1).

As the so-called near banks (trust companies and credit unions) expanded their activities in the postwar period, the inequities between them and the chartered banks became more and more apparent (Canada. Dept. of Finance, 1976: 17). Despite their rising importance in the payments system, not only did they remain dependent on the chartered banks for clearing and settlement, but also they had no voice in the operations and in planning the future development of the system. Furthermore, lacking the status of direct clearers in the system, the near-banks did not have access to the lending facilities of the Bank of Canada and were ineligible to share in the business of receiving deposits from the Government of Canada. Finally, by the mid 1970s, the payments system was about to undergo a fundamental change from one based almost exclusively on paper transactions to an electronic system where paper instruments would play a diminished role. Should such a change take place without the active involvement of all significant participants in deposit-taking activities?

In its White Paper published in 1976, the Department of Finance answered this question in the negative. Following the lead suggested by the Porter Commission 12 years earlier, it recommended the creation of a new organization, the Canadian Payments Association (CPA), that would then take over the running of the payments system from the CBA. Not unexpectedly, the chartered banks resisted this proposal, fearing that the integrity and efficiency of the payments system would be undermined by the admission of trust companies and credit union central liquidity facilities to the club. The banks lost this battle; the Canadian Payments Association Act came into effect on December 1, 1980 and the transfer of the system from the CBA to the CPA took place.

The establishment of the CPA marked a change in the policy network centred on payments issues from clientele pluralism anchored on the CBA to an arrangement that approximates corporatism. Justifying this argument requires a rather careful analysis of the structure of the CPA.[20] The organization meets very well the definition of what Streeck and Schmitter (1985) call a private interest government. It is a (mainly) private association that has received a delegation of public authority from Parliament to run the payments system. By law, all chartered banks must belong to the association; trust companies, credit union centrals, loan companies and other deposit-taking institutions "may" belong.[21] In practice, member institutions account for over 96 per cent of the clearings in the Canadian financial system. It thus resembles a corporatist network because it establishes a forum for competing sets of institutions—banks, trust companies, credit unions to participate with state actors in the design and implementation of policy.

The association is not completely private—the Alberta Government Treasury Branches belong. Even more important, the Bank of Canada is a member, a development that represents a significant change from the previous CBA system. The central bank's role extends beyond simple membership; an Adviser from the Bank chairs the association and possesses one of the 11 seats on the Board of Directors, representing the "public interest." The Deputy Chairman of the association also comes from the Bank and the current general manager (ad interim) is on secondment from the Bank. The other ten positions on the board are divided evenly between the chartered banks and the near banks. This parity rule extends to all the committees of the association, indicating again a corporatist-like attempt to incorporate these competing interests into the system with the Bank of Canada poised to play an arbiter role if necessary.

Evidence to date indicates that the CPA is on its way to realizing the objectives set out in the 1976 White Paper. The clearing and settlement system has become more open to competition. The CPA has defined a set of conditions under which a member firm might become a "direct clearer" in the system.[22] To date, 15 institutions have applied for and received direct clearer status: the big Six A banks, Lloyds Bank Canada, Hong Kong Bank of Canada, the Laurentian Bank, CCCS, the Desjardins group, Canada Trust, Royal Trust, the Province of Alberta Treasury Branches, and, of course, the Bank of Canada. Hence the group has expanded well beyond the chartered banks that dominated the old system.

In addition, the CPA has established a National Planning Committee that has been given the responsibility for planning the steps to a more fully electronic payments system. This committee obviously has as members both banks and near banks and has begun to consult more widely with user communities. It sponsors annual conferences on the payments system and is currently examining EFT/POS (Electronic funds transfer at the point of sale) systems and EDI (Electronic Data Interchange) systems. The CPA has been criticized by some of the users communities for being slow to adapt to the new elecronic world and for being too protective of the interests of deposit-taking firms. In particular, TMAC, which represents treasurers and cash managers in both the private and public sectors, has placed increased pressure on CPA and wondered privately why corporate users could not be given formal representation on the National Planning Committee.

In short, a clientele pluralist network where a private interest group (CBA) assumed virtually complete responsibility for running the payments system has given way to a corporatist network that brings together a highly capable state agency, the Bank of Canada, with a broader range of deposit-taking institutions. Banks and near banks are given equal roles in running an organization that defies easy classification. It is a private association that has been delegated a public responsibility and that is chaired by a publicly-owned corporation, the Bank of Canada. The attempt to accommodate competing sets of firms under this semi-public, semi-private umbrella appears to resemble a corporatist policy network. Yet, like many corporatist networks, it sets up distinct barriers between those private interests that participate in making policy (deposit-taking institutions) and those others (corporate cash managers, retailers, consumers) that wish to influence policy.

Conclusion

Two different kinds of conclusions emerge from this chapter, one related to policy outcomes and the other to theoretical development. Turning first to policy outcomes, what is striking about the changes in the banking policy community is that they have accommodated emergent institutions in the financial sector but not other interested parties. The concertation and corporatist networks that were outlined differed from those previously operating by the addition of an enhanced state presence. Sector strength was matched better by state strength. The increased capacity and autonomy of the state agencies certainly increased the probability of broader public interests being considered. None the less, it is evident that if these interests were to enter the policy process, it would be through state actors and not through societal groups representing financial consumers or workers in financial institutions.

Nor does the expansion of the policy community necessarily mean that the policy process itself is more effective in responding to problems. Provincial governments have become players of considerable force. They have taken advantage of their jurisdiction over credit unions, trust companies, and securities to promote objectives that not only differ from one another, but also from those of the federal government. There appeared to be less in common at the start of the 1990s among provincial and federal laws than there was a decade ago. These differences increase the cost of doing business for financial institutions operating in more than one province and inhibit the possible expansion of some provincially-based institutions. It is arguable whether financial consumers, both individual and corporate, end up being better served and protected against inappropriate business conduct in such circumstances.

Theoretically, this study of organized interests in the banking sector raises several issues of more general significance for public policy studies. First, if the concepts of policy community and policy network are to be used in the study of power and influence, they are best treated in a dynamic, historical context. This chapter joins others in this book in illustrating that the comparison of the membership and structure of a policy community over time often reveals information about changing patterns of power and influence. These changes can then be related to shifts in the economic structure of the sector, changes in government and political priorities, and the evolution of interest group organization. This chapter has illustrated a case where the policy community has expanded by drawing new members from civil society and the state. Yet this expansion was itself limited; the sub-government of the community was restricted to those carrying out banking functions. Groups representing banking consumers, individuals, large corporations, or government bodies doing extensive banking, were not integrated into the core of the community. How the policy community is defined by both state agencies and interest groups will critically affect the values and objectives at the heart of policies being made.

Second, depending on the issue, different policy networks may form within the same policy community. This chapter described the creation of a concertation network on one issue and the transition from clientele pluralism to corporatism on another. Yet these two case studies only hint at the scope of changes in policy networks that have taken place in the policy community. Figure 1 illustrates how the banking policy community is much more pluralistic in the 1980s than it was in the 1940s. In fact, many of the key policy issues that confronted the community in the late 1980s—links between financial and commercial corporations, rules for self-dealing, modalities for networking financial firms—have been dealt with in pressure pluralist networks. In this respect, investigations by several independent commissions and task forces, the forum provided by the House of Commons Finance Committee, and the strong input from provincial governments, particularly Québec, have aided the less organizationally developed groups to enjoin the well-organized bankers in debates over policy. As empirical work on policy networks develops, perhaps it will become possible to develop some theoretical generalizations about the dynamics of changes in networks.[23] This chapter joins others in this book in providing the beginning of an empirical base for this task.

Finally, the example of the payments system, the former role of the CBA in that system, and the structure of the CPA remind us of the need to treat the degree of separation of public and private as a variable in policy analysis. The blurring of public and private responsibilities and of public and private organizations is not a phenomenon easily assimilated by the British-style model of parliamentary government. Tracing the line of accountability for the soundness of the payments system back to Parliament is far from an easy task. Perhaps the need for responsibility is low in this case, perhaps the responsiveness of the payments system to consumer complaints should not be a political matter. None the less, publicly-owned corporations have been criticized because of their lack of accountability. What are we to say about private interest governments whose status is even more unclear and that are even more removed from the institutions of parliamentary democracy?

References

Atkinson, M.M. and W.D. Coleman (1989). "Strong States and Weak States: Sectoral Policy Networks in Advanced Capitalist Economies." *British Journal of Political Science,* 19: 47-67.

_____ (1989b). *The State, Business and Industrial Change in Canada.* Toronto: University of Toronto Press.

Bank for International Settlements, Committee on Banking Regulations and Supervisory Practices (1987). *Consultative Paper: Proposals for international convergence of capital measurement and capital standards.* Basle: BIS.

Canada. Bank of Canada (1988). "The Structure of the Co-operative Credit System of Canada—I." *Bank of Canada Review,* December: 3-20.

_____ (1989). "The Structure of the Co-operative Credit System of Canada - II." *Bank of Canada Review,* February: 3-19.

Canada. Department of Finance (1976). *Canadian Banking Legislation.* Ottawa: Supply and Services Canada.

Canada. Department of Finance (1985). *The Regulation of Canadian Financial Institutions: Proposals for Discussion.* Ottawa: Supply and Services Canada.

Canada. Economic Council of Canada (1987). *A Framework for Financial Regulation.* Ottawa: Supply and Services Canada.

Canada. Inquiry into the Collapse of the CCB and Northland Bank (Estey Report) (1986). *Report.* Ottawa: Department of Supply and Services.

Canada. Royal Commission on Banking and Finance (Porter Report) (1964). *Report.* Ottawa: Queen's Printer.

Canada. Working Committee on the Canada Deposit Insurance Corporation (1985). *Final Report.* Ottawa: Department of Supply and Services.

Coleman, W.D. (1988). *Business and Politics: A Study of Collective Action.* Montreal: McGill-Queen's University Press.

Grant, Wyn P., William Paterson and Colin Whitson (1988). *Government and the Chemical Industry: A Comparative Study of Britain and West Germany.* Oxford: The Clarendon Press.

Kapstein, Ethan, B. (1989). "Resolving the Regulator's Dilemma: International Coordination of Banking Regulations." *International Organization,* 43: 323–47.

Neufeld, E.P. (1972). *The Financial System of Canada: Its Growth and Development.* New York: St. Martin's Press.

Jordan, A.G. and J.J. Richardson (1987). *Government and Pressure Groups in Britain.* Oxford: The Clarendon Press.

Mackenzie, Michael (1987). "Remarks on Financial Risk, Speech of 2 September 1987." *The Financial Observer,* 45: 440-1.

Ontario. Ministry of Consumer and Commercial Relations (1983). *Proposals for Revision of the Loan and Trust Corporation Legislation and Administration in Ontario.* Toronto: MCCR.

Ontario. Task Force on Financial Institutions (1985). *Final Report.* Toronto: MCCR.
OECD (1985). *Trends in Banking in OECD Countries.* Paris: OECD.
Pauly, Louis (1988). *Opening Financial Markets: Banking Politics on the Pacific Rim.* Ithaca: Cornell University Press.
Pecchioli, R.M. (1987). *Prudential Supervision in Banking.* Paris: OECD.
_____ **(1983).** *The Internationalisation of Banking: The Policy Issues.* Paris: OECD.
Pross, A. P. (1986). *Group Politics and Public Policy.* Toronto : Oxford University Press.
Rhodes, R.A.W. (1987). *The National World of Local Government.* London: Macmillan.
Securities Industry Capital Markets Committee (SICMC) (1985). "Submission to the Standing Committee on Finance, Trade and Economic Affairs." Toronto : SICMC.
Streeck, Wolfgang and P.C. Schmitter (1985). "Community, Market, State— and Associations? The Prospective Contribution of Interest Governance to Social Order." In Streeck and Schmitter, eds. *Private Interest Government: Beyond Market and State.* London: Sage: 1-29.
Wilks, Stephen and Maurice Wright (1987). "Conclusion: Comparing Government-Industry Relations: States, Sectors, and Networks." In Wilks and Wright, eds. *Comparative Government-Industry Relations.* Oxford: The Clarendon Press: 275-313.
Wright, Maurice (1988). "Policy Community, Policy Network and Comparative Industrial Policies." *Political Studies,* XXXVI: 593-612.
Young, Brigitte (1990). "Does the American Dairy Industry Fit a Meso-Corporatism Model." *Political Studies,* forthcoming.

Endnotes

1. For a useful overview of these changes, see OECD (1985).

2. For a discussion, see Pecchioli (1987).

3. This change has been noted in Coleman (1988: Chap. 9).

4. This fact was revealed to me in three separate interviews with chartered bank executives conducted in early 1989.

5. The Royal Bank purchased Dominion Securities Pitfield; the Canadian Imperial Bank of Commerce–Wood Gundy; the Bank of Nova Scotia-McLeod, Young, Weir; the Bank of Montreal—Nesbitt Thompson; and the National Bank—Lévesque Beaubien and Géoffrion Leclerc. The Toronto Dominion elected to build its own securities firm.

6. For a more extensive discussion of this topic, see Pauly (1988).

7. Representative offices served only as points of contact for providing marketing information and for establishing business connections (Pecchioli, 1983: 55).

8. For a detailed discussion of the role played by auditors, see the Estey Report (1986: 40ff).

9. The Bank of British Columbia was purchased by the Hong Kong Bank, the Continental Bank of Canada by Lloyds Bank, and the Mercantile Bank by the National Bank of Canada.

10. The review was conducted by the Working Committee on the Canada Deposit Insurance Corporation (1985), chaired by W. Robert Ryman of Pemberton, Houston, Willoughby Inc.

11. Michael Atkinson and I discuss some of these factors in our analysis of industrial policy in Canada (Atkinson and Coleman, 1989b).

12. Investment dealers maintain "cash management accounts" for their customers that resemble deposits; life insurance companies offer short-term, deferred annuities that might also be considered as deposits (Canada, ECC, 1987: 81).

13. The following picture of the CBA organization is based on documents provided by the association, an interview with two association vice-presidents, and interviews with the six largest Schedule A banks and three Schedule B banks. The interviews were conducted between December 1988 and May 1989.

14. Prior to this date, the president had been elected; an executive director was responsible for the administration of the association.

15. Membership is compulsory through an Act of Parliament passed in 1900, nine years after the association's founding. Schedule A banks are "widely held" with no one interest allowed to own more than 10 per cent. At the time of writing, there were seven of these: the familiar big five (Royal, Canadian Imperial, Montreal, Nova Scotia, Toronto Dominion), the National Bank of Canada, and the Canadian Western Bank. Schedule B banks are foreign banks or Canadian banks that are closely held. (Presently there is only one Canadian bank in this category, the Laurentian Bank of Canada). The Bank Act placed restrictions on the size and branching of B banks. B banks have two representatives on the Executive Council of the association and a separate committee in the association representing their interests.

16. The representation of the general interests of cooperatives is assumed by the Canadian Cooperative Association that was formed in 1987 following the merger of the Cooperative Union of Canada and the Cooperative College of Canada.

17. The one exception to this statement is the CDIC. Early in 1989, it established regular monthly meetings with the Superintendent of Deposit-Taking Institutions and the staff of the Trust and Loans Branch of the Ontario government. A similar arrangement, with somewhat less frequent meetings, is planned with the Québec government.

18. For some analysis of these regional differences, see Bank of Canada (1988, 1989).

19. The Group of 10 (G-10) actually includes eleven countries: the Group of Seven (G-7)—the United States, Japan, West Germany, Britain, France, Canada, Italy—plus Sweden, the Netherlands, Belgium, and Switzerland.

20. The analysis that follows is based on documents supplied to the author by the CPA and on interviews with CPA officials and others conducted between December 1988 and May 1989.

21. The difference between chartered banks and other institutions results from a fear of the federal government about treading on provincial government "turf." The Department of Finance White Paper (1976: 18) had proposed that membership be compulsory for all deposit-taking institutions.

22. It must be respnsible for one-half of one per cent of the total volume of cheques, money orders and other payment items in the system; it must be insured by CDIC or CCCS; it must establish operational relations with the Bank of Canada, and it must agree to report to the relevant supervisor any indirect clearer making sizable and repeated borrowings for the purposes of settlement.

23. For one attempt along these lines, see Young (1990).

CHAPTER FIVE

FORESTRY AND FOREST PRODUCTS

Wyn P. Grant

T he forest and forest products industry is of fundamental importance to the Canadian economy. Canada is often termed a "forestry super power," and there is a case for regarding forestry and forest products as the country's single most significant industry. Forestry is particularly important in British Columbia where it accounts for over 40 per cent of the manufacturing Gross Domestic Product (GDP). Canada's forest industries accounted in 1987 for 15 per cent of the total Canadian manufacturing GDP, 13 per cent of manufacturing employment, 21 per cent of manufactured exports, and 17 per cent of total exports. The forest industries make the most important positive contribution of any sector to the balance of trade ($18.3 billion in 1987). There are estimated to be 810,000 direct and indirect jobs in the industry, with 300 remote communities being largely dependent on the industry (Industry, Science and Technology, 1988).

This chapter will consider both the forestry industry, and the manufacture of forest products. To leave the analysis at the point when the felled logs are stacked at the side of the forest road would create an artificial distinction. Even so, some limitations must be placed on the definition of the sector because there are a wide variety of industries that use wood as a major input, for example, construction. For the purposes of this analysis, the industry includes the primary product sector, forestry and logging, sections 121 and 122 of the International Standard Industrial Classification (ISIC), and the principal processing industries, sawmills and wood mills (3311) and the manufacture of pulp and paper (3411).

The industry is regionally diversified since the pulp and paper industries are located in the Atlantic provinces, Québec and Ontario, while wood products predominate in British Columbia and Alberta. The regional division of the industry reflects the availability of fast growing, high quality timber in BC, whereas the industry in Eastern Canada has been shaped by the market for newsprint in the nearby, densely populated parts of the US. In the 1950s eastern interests began pulp and paper production in Western Canada. Moreover, as sawmilling in BC became larger and more advanced, it produced a lot of chips as a by-product which could be used in pulp and paper production. Even with this attempt at creating a significant pulp and paper industry in BC, lumber remains the principal export product from BC.

One cannot, however, simply analyze the industry in economic terms. The forest is the predominant feature of the Canadian landscape, covering nearly half of the total land mass. The forest is important not only as a source of timber, but also as a recreational asset in an urbanized society. It is part of the wilderness, and forms the habitat for much of Canada's wildlife. Political tensions arise between the priorities of producers and those of recreationists and environmentalists, and the claims of native peoples may also become a political issue. The "traditional" forest policy community is under some stress as it copes with these conflicting pressures, an issue which will be returned to later in the analysis.

In this chapter, it will be argued that the state has well developed capabilities for relating to the forest industry at federal and provincial levels. Although there are some intra-bureaucratic tensions at the federal level, mechanisms for promoting federal-provincial discussion and consensus building are quite extensive compared with many other sectors. Industry associations display a high level of organizational development. Linkages within the policy community are institutionalized, and the boundaries of the policy community are well defined.

Apart from the substantive problems that the industry faces— diminution of reserves of high quality, readily available timber;

inadequate research and development; problems in trade relations with the US; increasing overseas competition—the industry's main political problem arises in relation to the growing environmental movement. This point is confirmed in Chapter Six by Wilson's analysis of British Columbia in which he notes that the most extensive challenge to traditional arrangements between the state and capital has been mounted by the environmental movement. The attentive public has changed in composition, has become larger, and has articulated a new set of priorities which are often difficult to reconcile with those of the industry. After a faltering start, the industry has developed strategies of cooption to deal with these new problems. However, if there is a general shift in western societies from the "politics of production" to the "politics of collective consumption," such strategies may not be an adequate response (although the fact that Canadian society is less likely to resort to the courts for resolving policy disputes than that of the US reduces the significance of one means of leverage that is available to US environmental groups).

It is difficult to fit the forestry sector into one of the six different patterns of group-state relations identified by Atkinson and Coleman (1989). First, the structure of the pulp and paper industry differs with that of the extraction of lumber. Even allowing for the trend towards vertical integration, the production of lumber is more fragmented and diverse than the concentrated, capital intensive production of pulp and paper. The character of the pulp and paper industry has also fostered government-industry collaboration (Coleman, 1988: 213-4). Second, the combination in the forestry industry of a high level of organizational development in business interest associations, with relatively fragmented state authority, is not accommodated well by the typology. Admittedly, the provincial governments are the most important actors, and, as Wilson points out in his chapter, forestry policy in British Columbia is developed by a closed policy community centred on the Ministry of Forests. Indeed, the most appropriate paradigm is that of a "company state" (Willis and Grant, 1987; Grant, 1988) in which the government provides a favourable environment for the operations of large companies, with smaller companies complicating the picture somewhat.

The two categories in Atkinson and Coleman's schema that come closest to summarizing the way issues are dealt with are those of corporatism and concertation. As Atkinson and Coleman admit (1989: 58), the two types of networks are "closely-related." However, whereas the incorporation of labour is a key characteristic of corporatism, labour is involved only marginally in concertation networks. Rather, "in a concertation network, it is business, and usually just a single element or fraction of business, that shares policy-making responsibility with the state" (Atkinson and Coleman, 1989: 58). This structure fits well with the analysis later in this chapter of the policy community in forestry and forest products which emphasizes the key role of large firms. The condition of an *autonomous* state agency is less well met in the case of forestry and forest products, but, as Atkinson and Coleman show (1989: 62), the government was able to develop a comprehensive policy for the pulp and paper aspect of the industry through its Pulp and Paper Modernization Program.

Although the structures and processes for the development of forestry policy in Canada are relatively well integrated and effective, concern has been expressed about the policies that emerge from the policy community. Gillis and Roach (1986: 263) go so far as to argue that "what we have witnessed in Canada in regard to the management of forests is a colossal failure of public policy." It is suggested that this apparent paradox can be explained in terms of the policy community's ability to cope with routine policy problems which can be solved incrementally. It faces far greater difficulties in developing comprehensive strategies to cope with major upheavals in the policy environment. This theme is explored more fully later in this chapter with reference to the national forest sector strategy and the softwood lumber dispute with the United States.

The Structure of the Policy Community

Federal-Provincial Relations

This analysis of the state organization in relation to the industry begins with a review of federal-provincial relations. Canada is a highly decentralized, bilingual federal state. Within the grouping of federal states, "Federalism appears to have far greater significance in Canada than it does in other federal countries such as the United States, Australia or West Germany" (Leslie, 1987: ix). Canadian federalism has a number of consequences which are of particular relevance to a consideration of the forest and forest products sector.

The division of responsibility between the federal and provincial governments in forest and forest products is complex, even though forest land is predominantly owned by provincial governments. Constitutionally, forestry is the responsibility of the provincial governments. Provincial legislatures have the power under Section 92A (1.b) of the *Constitution Act,* 1982 to make laws in relation to the "development, conservation and management of non-renewable natural resources and forestry resources in the province, including laws in relation to primary production therefrom". The Sixth Schedule of the Act defines production from a forestry resource as primary production "if it consists of sawlogs, poles, lumber, wood chips, sawdust or any other primary wood product, or wood pulp, and is not a product manufactured from wood." This excludes the wood-using industries from primary provincial jurisdiction.

The federal government, while not constitutionally responsible for forestry, is responsible for international trade, and for providing funds to certain areas of the industry. Federal funding is particularly important in the area of research and development, but, more generally, forest management costs are shared between the federal and provincial governments through Federal/Provincial Resource Development Agreements which were operating in every province by 1987. For example, the Canada—BC agreement signed in May 1985 covers the period 1985-90 with the Federal government agreeing to spend $300 million for re-planting non-satisfactorily restocked forest lands in the province, and for intensive forest management and related research activities. The Pulp and Paper Modernization Grants Program, which was in effect from 1979 to 1985, also operated through a sharing of costs between federal and provincial governments with 54 per cent of the total expenditure of $542 million being provided by the federal government (although the cost sharing ratio varied considerably from province to province) (de Silva, 1988).

One metaphor for federal-provincial forestry relations in Canada is that of "entanglement"; this metaphor has a particular resonance if one visualizes a poorly managed forest. The price of "entanglement" include a lack of clarity concerning responsibility, unnecessary increases in costs, a general lack of accountability, and a failure to meet policy objectives (See Leslie, 1987: 49). Depending on one's perspective, "a rather messy decision-making process" may be called "entanglement or shared responsibility" (Leslie, 1987: 63).

An attempt has been made to improve federal-provincial relations in the forestry industry through the Canadian Council of Forest Ministers (CCFM). One federal civil servant described the CCFM as "the best example of federal-provincial cooperation that has existed for some time. It is an extremely useful body if at the minimum only to promote good collegial relations, but it's much more than that in terms of what it has achieved." An industry association official described the CCFM as "almost unique in terms of the level of federal-provincial co-operation." These comments were echoed by other respondents.

The CCFM held its inaugural meeting in Victoria in September 1985. It generally operates on a basis of one formal meeting of ministers a year, usually in the fall, with a meeting of deputy ministers in the spring, although additional meetings of ministers may be held on particular occasions. The CCFM started work in 1985-86 by sponsoring four forestry forums on labour market issues, multiple use forestry and environmental issues, forest management issues, and trade and investment issues. Each forum was attended by 30 to 35 representatives of various parts of the industry. The objectives of these consultative meetings were to raise the profile of forestry, to increase awareness of forest sector issues, and to develop a consensus on possible solutions to policy problems. In other words, these forums could be seen as an effort to develop linkages within the policy community, and to improve its problem-solving capacity. These meetings led to the development of a national forest sector strategy in 1987, which is discussed more fully later in the chapter.

Federal Government Organization

Canadian federal government organization, particularly in the general area of industrial policy, displays considerable instability, with tasks frequently being shunted from one location to another. As one federal civil servant commented in an interview, "Forestry has been the poor child of a number of different ministries over the course of the past twenty-five years." Even so, "federal forestry grew during the late 1950s and early 1960s into an important national programme" (Gillis and Roach, 1986: 251). In 1960, the Diefenbaker Government created a Department of Forestry. Later in the 1960s, growing environmental concerns, and the submersion of aid to the industry into general regional development programmes, was reflected in a merger of the Department of Forestry with the Department of Rural Development. In 1968 the forestry function was taken into the Department of Fisheries. Subsequently, it was shifted into the Department of the Environment, a location which reflected priorities at the time. Mulroney made aid to forestry one of his campaign planks, and on his initial return to office created a Ministry of State for Forestry under a well-respected minister, Gerald Merrithew. A campaign pledge to create a fully fledged department was not redeemed and forestry remained under the wing of the Department of Agriculture (apparently partly because of bureaucratic rivalries and resistance to the idea from Québec). In September 1988, the Mulroney Government decided to redeem its pledge, and a separate federal department of forestry was created.

A complication in the federal arrangements is that both the Department of Regional Industrial Expansion (DRIE), and its successor, the Department of Industry, Science and Technology (DIST), have had a Forest Products Directorate. This bureau included a Manager, Wood Products and a Manager, Pulp and Paper. Identically described posts (and other examples of parallelism) are to be found in the Industry and Trade Branch of the Canadian Forestry Service (CFS). The CFS had to develop a capability to support its minister across the whole spectrum of enquiries that he might face, leading it to reinforce its traditional strengths in forestry science with a series of industry oriented posts (in some cases, staff were recruited for this purpose from DRIE). Equally, one can understand why the principal industry department in a country such as Canada may wish to have a capability to deal with industrial and regional policy issues that affect the forestry industry. The degree of duplication may, however, point to a tendency in Canada to "fudge" the awkward machinery of government issues. Certainly, within the forestry policy community, the transfer of the Forest Products Directorate from DRIE (now DIST) to the CFS is seen as an essential precondition of a viable federal Department of Forestry (See editorial in *Forestry Chronicle*, June 1984).

Provincial Government Organization

As Wilson emphasizes in his chapter, forestry is an important portfolio at the provincial level, particularly in provinces such as BC, although it is generally combined with some other responsibility. For example, in Prince Edward Island, it is combined with energy, an arrangement that reflects the province's ambitions to build a wood fired power station. An important role performed by provincial forest ministries is as "broker in the bargaining process that balances the demands of logging companies, fishery and wildlife agencies and public groups that have an interest in the details of cutting permits" (Johnson, 1984: 12). Various conflicts of interest arise that have to be mediated within the government machine, or in bargaining with outside groups.

What in effect often happens is a negotiation between the representatives of two policy communities within the government machine. For example, soil erosion resulting from the felling of trees on a steep slope can silt up a salmon stream. Thus, in BC, the provincial Forests Ministry discusses the problems that arise with the industry, and engages in bargaining on possible solutions with the provincial Fish and Wildlife Branch, and the Federal Department of Fisheries and Oceans (DFO). Wilson notes in his chapter that the provincial forests ministry in BC often finds itself in conflict with the DFO and the provincial environment ministry.

Business Associations in the Industry

In his analysis of the associational system in the Canadian forest industry, Coleman (1988: 148-9) subdivides forestry industry associations into general and functionally specialized associations. The second category, which includes safety, professional and research bodies, is considered in the next main section of the chapter when an analysis of the policy community as a whole is provided. At this point, the discussion will be confined to associations representing business interests in the industry.

Coleman stresses a number of features of the associational system in the forestry industry. "Reflecting the divided constitutional jurisdiction in this industry are the strong and plentiful associations at the provincial level. Forest industry associations representing at a minimum the primary extraction components of the sector are found in all provinces except Newfoundland and Prince Edward Island" (Coleman, 1988: 147). Another feature of the associational system that distinguishes it from that of other resource sectors is "its high degree of vertical integration across sector and territory" (Coleman, 1988: 150).

This analysis concentrates on what are argued to be the three most important industry associations: the Canadian Pulp and Paper Association (CPPA), the Council of the Forest Industries of British Columbia (COFI), and the Canadian Forest Industries Council (CFIC). The first two associations, one based in Montreal, the other in Vancouver, are the most important associations in the industry in terms of resources (COFI has a total staff of 110 and CPPA 84) and ability to exert influence. In fact, with the exception of the Canadian Bankers' Association discussed in Chapter Four and the Union des producteurs agricoles noted in Chapter Three, CPPA and COFI are the best-resourced associations analyzed in this volume. They both display a high level of organizational development. CFIC, on the other hand, represents an attempt to develop a body speaking for the industry as a whole at the federal level. This effort has not been as successful as some members of the policy community hoped, and an exploration of the reasons should help to cast some light on the distinctive features of the forestry policy community in Canada.

CPPA is generally regarded as a highly effective organization whose general approach was explained by one of its senior officials in an interview:

> The people here that work with the civil service are very professional people, they deal with civil servants who are as technically expert as they are, so discussions are very peer-oriented. This is done on purpose. We have always sought a professional, high calibre type of person. We realize that the best way to influence policy is when it is being developed. You can only do that if you've got the skills that are required ... Careful management for a long time is paying off dividends now in terms of CPPA's reputation in the departments that we deal with.

CPPA has to represent companies producing a wide range of products as well as single product companies. Since many of the more specialized producers rely on tariff protection to maintain their largely domestic markets, while the more internationally-oriented companies have favoured freer trade with the United States, trade issues have had to be handled with some sensitivity. More generally, the CPPA has a carefully constructed internal structure designed both to filter the views of its members, and to create the widest possible basis of support for its policies. There are special product sections for woodlands, newsprint and wood pulp. Within the Woodlands Section, there is a

Council of Accredited Representatives, made up of the vice-presidents (woodlands) of the 45 member companies with woodlands operations. Chief foresters of member companies are organized in a Forest Management Group. Services are provided to logging equipment manufacturers through the Sustaining Members Group. Individual woodlands personnel can join the Woodlands Section (1,800 have done so), whilst the Technical Section, concerned with mill operating technology, has 5,000 members worldwide. There is also a Human Resources Section with some 600 individual members.

Historically, CPPA has relied on direct contacts with ministers. A federal civil servant commented in an interview that "Up to the 1960s when CPPA wanted something, it was extremely well connected at a very high level. It did not deal with government officials." In the more bureaucratized, post-Trudeau era, the CPPA relies considerably on detailed negotiations with officials where it draws on the stock of goodwill resulting from its ability to offer expert advice on the industry. In particular, CPPA has developed a strong reputation for its industry statistics. A CPPA official argued in an interview that these were CPPA's greatest strength after its people, with about a quarter of its organizational effort going into data collection and dissemination. However the more political side of representation is not neglected. CPPA maintains a "Pulp and Paper MPs' directory" and, where appropriate, the chief executive officers of member companies are mobilized to lobby MPs and senators. In some respects, however, the firms in the industry have been relatively conservative in their outlook, despite having a politically sophisticated industry association. CPPA has encouraged its member firms to hire their own government relations specialists.

COFI fills the gap in CPPA's Woodlands Section, which has branches for various areas in Eastern Canada, but none for Western Canada (Coleman, 1988: 150). Although confined to BC, COFI sometimes functions as the equivalent of a national lumbermen's association, even though it has members in the pulp and paper sector. COFI has particular strengths in overseas offices dealing with issues such as tariffs and standards. Two-thirds of COFI's staff are in its Wood Products Division, which runs the overseas offices and has as one of its most important tasks the promotion of wood products and the development of new markets. The division is closely involved in the Cooperative Overseas Market Development Program, a joint initiative between COFI and the federal and provincial governments aimed at diversifying the markets for BC wood products away from their reliance on the US market. Government relations divisions appear to be more common in firms on the wood products side of the industry than in pulp and paper, and there seems to be a greater emphasis on professional forestry or engineering qualifactions within COFI than in CPPA.

Both the CPPA and COFI would appear to satisfy the key tests of organizational development outlined in Coleman (1987) and summarized in Chapter One. They are both capable of coordinating a range of complex information and activity, and arriving at speedy decisions on sophisticated policy questions. They also have sufficient autonomy from members to be able to take a long-term perspective on policy formation without sacrificing member compliance. These properties are less apparent in the case of CFIC.

CFIC was created in 1983 as an umbrella association that would enable the industry to deal more effectively with trade and resource issues, and to establish a national forest industry data base. It is supported by 17 associations, including CPPA and COFI, and ranging from the Alberta Forest Products Association to the Québec Lumber Manufacturers' Association. Still, not all Canadian lumber producers or manufacturers belong to a member association of CFIC. It was preceded by the Canadian Softwood Lumber Committee which was formed in response to an investigation by the US International Trade Commission into US imports of Canadian softwood. The CFIC was formed because of a perceived need for a federal presence for the industry as a whole, in particular to continue the dialogue with the federal government on trade issues.

CFIC operates in Ottawa from the offices of the Canadian Wood Council (CWC), which is itself an association of associations in the industry. CWC was formed in 1959 to promote the industry's products in the United States, where it participates financially in three US associations. CWC developed as a technical and engineering association with strengths in fire research, and an ability to act for the industry in such areas as building codes, fire regulations and product standards.

CFIC has been something of a disappointment to its supporters both inside and outside the government. It has not provided the input that it was intended to provide, and appears to have difficulty dealing with substantive issues given that the association heads are not in a position to speak for their members. Although CFIC is likely to survive, it is questionable whether it can emerge as an authoritative voice for the industry. CPPA and COFI have been very effective associations, and they will not want to cede too much authority to CFIC.

Perhaps ironically, COFI was directly involved in setting up CFIC because it was bearing the brunt of fighting the softwood lumber case in the US. A BC perception is that the eastern Canadians are not as keen on federal action through CFIC as the westerners are, and so COFI thought that there was a need to create an umbrella organization that would better represent the country. Even so, a COFI source admitted that going to Ottawa to participate in CFIC was time consuming and it was a question of "whether we devote enough time to what everyone agrees is a good idea." From an eastern perspective, the absence of a national lumbermen's association is more of an obstacle (the Canadian Lumbermen's Association is principally a grading organization), although the view expressed was that such a body was unlikely to emerge until that side of the industry was restructured into fewer, integrated operations. There is already a trend in the industry towards greater vertical integration, with the increasing utilization of wood residues in pulp and paper manufacture. "This integration of logging, sawmilling, and pulp and paper manufacturing has tended in some respects to blur the distinction between these industries" (de Silva, 1988: 5). This trend, however, has not yet had any impact on the political organization of the industry.

With two highly effective organizations already serving the sector, and the leading role of provincial governments, it is not surprising that there has been only a limited development of an umbrella organization for the industry at the federal level. The trade policy issue provided sufficient momentum to bring the industry together, but other issues are more divisive. For example, the approach of different parts of the industry to the issue of tax reform is affected by the fact that the pulp and paper side is more capital intensive. One may conclude that, in the absence of an umbrella group to integrate the industry, the political potential of the industry has clearly not been fulfilled.

The Contours of the Policy Community.

This section provides an analysis of the main contours of the policy community in forestry and forest products. As noted earlier, in a concertation policy network, one would expect the main actors to be the state and business. Some empirical data are provided here in support of that contention.

The analysis draws on Pross's subdivision of the policy community into two segments: the sub-government and the attentive public. Pross's use of the notion of "technostructure" is also particularly relevant to the study of forestry. He (1986: 49) defines the technostructure as "a sophisticated communications network of technically proficient specialists that cuts across the lines dividing government and business and in which technical knowledge is the currency of power." Pross argues that government becomes involved in the economy through the need for demand and supply management, and, particularly relevant to forestry, the need to conserve depleting natural resources. This evolution of government's role is related to the development of modern business organization:

> As corporations in the twentieth century sought to integrate geographically distant resources, complex technologies, and sophisticated human skills, they became

increasingly dependent on government to organize and manage the supply of resources to enterprises, and even to take a hand in the regulation of demand ... the forest industries provide a good illustration of these needs. (Pross, 1986: 47)

Table 1

Membership of policy community segments on selected forest industry advisory bodies in Canada (ranked by total number of memberships)

	FSAC	NFSS	FRACC	FIMTF	FFGL	Total
Companies in industry	10	—	5	8	2	25
Provincial governments	—	5	5	5	3	18
Universities	2	1	1	—	6	10
Industry associations	—	3	1	—	3	7
Federal government	—	2	1	1	2	6
Equipment manufacturers	—	—	—	5	—	5
Trade unions	4	1	—	—	—	5
Canadian Inst. of Forestry	1	1	—	—	2	4
Canadian Forestry Association	—	1	—	—	1	2
Others	—	—	—	—	2	2
Environment-alists	—	1	—	—	—	1

FFGL: Forest Forum Group Leaders (moderators and group leaders at national forestry forums)

FIMTF: Forest Industry Machinery Task Force

FRACC: Forest Research Advisory Council of Canada

FSAC: Forest Sector Advisory Council

NFSS: National Forest Sector Strategy Task Force

Table 2

Institutional affiliations of persons attending National Forestry Forum on Research and Development, Edmonton 1988

Provincial governments	34
Federal government	19
R&D institutes	14
Companies in industry	12
Universities	12
Industry associations	7
Others	4
Trade unions	3
Canadian Inst. of Forestry	2
Canadian Forestry Assn.	1
Environmental organizations	1
Equipment manufacturers	1

Pross shows how the development of pulp and paper operations, involving huge capital investments, rendered inappropriate "cut and run" techniques of forestry. Companies had to be assured of a long run supply of timber and reliable supplies of large amounts of electricity. They also needed skilled workers; this was met through specialized university level programmes (Pross, 1986: 47-8).

In an effort to provide a crude map of the extent of the sub-government portion of the policy community, a count was made of the segments of the policy community represented on various advisory bodies operating in the forestry industry at the federal level (Table 1) and of the affiliations of the persons attending the CCFM forum on innovation and technology in the forestry sector held in Edmonton, Alberta, in February 1988 (Table 2). Obviously, there are severe limits to the usefulness of this kind of head counting exercise. One would not expect to find the federal government strongly represented, or even represented at all, on committees set up to advise it. The particular topic of the Edmonton forestry forum meant that there was an over representation of persons from bodies concerned with research and development.

Even so, some useful statements can be made on the basis of this exercise. First, it is possible to list the participants in the policy community: federal government (CFS and DIST); provincial governments; individual companies; business associations; universities; trade unions; research and development institutes; forest equipment manufacturers; the Canadian Institute of Forestry (CIF); the

Canadian Forestry Association (CFA); and (very marginally and a point to be returned to later), environmentalists.

Some other points on the forestry policy community:

- The provincial governments are clearly key actors; numerically, they were more strongly represented than any other group (although they may not act as a group). Moreover, British Columbia is present on all the advisory bodies in which provincial governments are represented, and was present in strength at Edmonton.

- Forest companies are important actors, with MacMillan Bloedel in particular appearing on a number of committees and being strongly represented at the CCFM Forum in Edmonton. An interview with a senior business association executive revealed that MacMillan Bloedel was selected spontaneously for the sophistication of its government relations operation.

- The universities are very important actors, a fact that reflects both their effective monopoly in the training of experts, and a perception that they have an objectivity that allows them to moderate conflicts of interests (a role, for example, which forestry academics were asked to perform in the various forestry forums). A particularly important role is played by the Association of University Forestry Schools and its chairman, Dr. Gordon Baskerville (the dean of the forestry faculty at the University of New Brunswick, Fredericton). He sits, for example, on the Forest Sector Advisory Council (FSAC), and was on the National Forest Sector Strategy Task Force (NFSS). One respondent described Dr. Baskerville as "technically absolutely sound, and articulate—he puts complex things in understandable terms."

Indeed, the membership of the NFSS task force probably gives a good indication of the balance of influence within the forestry policy community. Four of the members were drawn from the provincial governments (including BC, and providing a regional balance so that, for example, PEI represented Newfoundland, New Brunswick and Nova Scotia); two from the federal government; three from industry associations (one each from COFI, CPPA, and a Québec association); and one each from the CIF, the CFA, the unions, the universities, and an environmental organization.

The roles of the CFA and CIF require further examination. As noted earlier, membership of the CFA is open to anyone interested in forests, and its general orientation is conservationist. Coleman (1988: 149) notes, "This conservation wing is tied to other parts of the system through the large forestry companies, which not only are members, but also contribute the largest block of funds." The CFA acted as sponsor of the important 1986 National Forest Congress which led to the NFSS task force. One provincial forester stressed in an interview the symbolic importance of CFA sponsorship, noting that the 1980 congress had been sponsored by the CPPA, with labour only an outside body. He commented, "Government, labour and industry could not in any up front way be seen to be representing the various users of the forest."

As a professional organization, the CIF is particularly involved in the transfer of technical expertise (for example, updating members' knowledge of silvicultural practices and techniques). A chief forester commented in interview that it was difficult to say how much influence the CIF actually had on policy development. In relation to the national forest sector strategy, he felt that the CIF had "missed a golden opportunity as a professional association; people thought it was another government policy that wouldn't go anywhere. We have seen so many proposals come and go."

What emerges is a picture of a relatively tightly-knit policy community in which interpersonal relations are well developed. These close ties did not, of course, mean that there are not lines of tension (for example, between the federal and provincial governments, or the bureaucratic turf fight between DRIE/DIST and CFS within the federal government). There are also personal animosities. In general, however, the boundaries of the policy community seem well defined, and there are a number of established mechanisms for discussing policy issues.

The Attentive Public
When one moves from the sub-government to the attentive public, the picture changes. At one time, the attentive public was largely made up of the forestry policy community: those persons earning their living from forestry and forest products, or related service activities. Over time, however, there has been a growing public interest in forestry issues. This interest is not, of course, entirely new in the United States; the idea of the conservation of parts of the national forest dates back to Teddy Roosevelt's presidency. US data show, however, that there has been a very sharp rise in visits to national parks (mainly in the 1960s); in recreation vehicle sales (in the 1970s, with a downward movement at the height of the energy crisis); in membership of the Wilderness Society (up fourfold between 1960 and 1978); and in membership of the National Audubon Society (1960 onwards) (Hewett and Peterson, 1982). It is clear, as Wilson's chapter shows, that public interest in the fate of the forest has been growing. This increase may reflect a more general growth in "green" politics which reflects a shift from a politics of production (labour-management conflicts, disputes about the distribution of national income) to a politics of collective consumption (consumer concerns, including concerns about the utilization and conservation of natural resources).

The expansion in the attentive public to include environmentalists has forced industry to recognize that it has a serious problem in relation to environmental concerns. Even this recognition has been difficult in some lumber companies where a rugged management style centred on the rapid and cost effective extraction of timber has prevailed. Thus one forest industry company in the US commented to Sonnenfeld (1981: 214), "We have used herbicides and pesticides without causing personal or property damage for decades. It's only now that we are spraying in woods where hippies have planted marijuana that we are having trouble." Sonnenfeld (1981:109) also notes a history of reckless pollution by pulp and paper companies in the US that was only abated by legislative enforcement.

From the late 1960s, Canada has developed environmental regulations in relation to the pulp and paper industry. Firms have appointed environmental vice-presidents. The CPPA organizes them in a special section where they exchange information on technology and measurement problems. COFI has a Paper and Pulp Environmental Committee concerned with pollution control equipment.

A senior COFI official commented on his organization's reaction to increased public interest in environmental issues:

> When the environmental movement hit us in the early 1970s we weren't prepared. We had a tradition of working with the forests without very much interference. As urban centres grew, leisure interests grew. A worldwide movement, it has since become our way of doing things. The knee jerk reaction at the time was, "Who the hell do they think they are?" Then we said, shouldn't we sit down with them? We formed a committee. The committee has met quarterly for 15 years.

COFI's Forest Land Use Liaison Committee discusses issues such as herbicides, pollution in rivers in terms of the effect on fish, and rights of access for recreational purposes (for example, the problem of shutting roads because of fire hazards). As the COFI official interviewed described the committee's work, "We work together and our modus operandi is to form a consensus document that they will all subscribe to."

Provincial initiatives have also been taken. Ontario has attempted to bring wildlife concerns into the management of timber, sponsoring a provincial meeting on forestry and wildlife in December 1988. A senior provincial government offcial commented in an interview on the positive "change in attitude within the last two to three years" including the new understanding by the industry that "you cannot ignore the intervention of other issues on public land, especially if you've got responsibility for management."

Despite the growth of the environmental movement, one should not, as Wilson emphasizes, overlook the industry's structural advantages. A further problem for environmentalists may be that of sustaining the interest of the attentive public in forestry issues. Concessions to environmentalists, such as the designation of the South Moresby national park, may serve to reduce the concerns of the public, if not those of environmental activists. As Wilson shows, it is difficult to focus attention on broader forestry policy issues, as distinct from campaigns to save particular areas of wilderness. A further factor highlighted by Wilson is the emergence of anti-preservation groups made up of industry employees. The industry has had to address the issues posed by environmentalists, but it would be difficult to claim that there have been fundamental changes in decision-making processes to respond to environmental concerns, a point considered further in the following analysis of the national forest sector strategy.

The Policy Community in Action

The National Forest Sector Strategy
The NFSS represented an attempt to build a consensus on the major challenges facing the forest industry. Part of the background to this development was a growing mutual realization in the late 1970s and early 1980s that the sector faced serious problems: inflation, recession, an adequate wood supply.

The forestry forums of 1985-86 sponsored by the CCFM led to a National Forestry Congress in 1986 opened by the Prime Minister. A task force was set up following the 1986 Congress to draft a national forest sector strategy to be considered at a forum in Saint John, New Brunswick in 1987. As noted earlier, this task force was dominated by business and government representatives. A gap developed between government and industry, on the one side, and environmental groups on the other. The latter had a problem in getting consensus among themselves, as a tug of war took place between the Canadian Wildlife Federation (CWF) and Nature Canada. The CWF was seen as being more accommodating than groups further to the left who were displeased with the strategy.

The final draft of the national forest sector strategy emphasized that "the strategy is not a detailed blueprint for the development of the forest sector." (CCFM, 1987: v). After reviewing issue areas—trade and investment, the forest and its management, employment, research, development and innovation, and public awareness—the report concluded with 34 recommendations ranging from the establishment of a full federal department of forestry, through fairly specific recommendations for cooperation between foresters and wildlife managers, to a number of steps to be taken to increase public awareness of the forest sector. A member of the task force noted that the NFSS represented the first time in Canada that groups involved in forestry issues has come together and produced such a document.

The consensus-building process established by the CCFM was effective in securing agreement on the problems facing the industry, and on possible steps to tackle them. What the CCFM cannot do is ensure that provincial governments and the industry themselves do what is needed. A federal civil servant commented that "there is no way that CCFM can dictate to individuals; they can suggest, promote, do all of those nice things. In their own jurisdictions (the provincial ministers) have the clout to leverage companies, but as a body they can't do it." Provincial respondents share the perspective that the strategy is weakest at the implementation phase, which is only now being discussed.

The CPPA's organizational sophistication and effectiveness is reflected in its systematic effort to implement some of the national forest sector strategy recommendations. The CPPA asked its Forest Policy Committee to rank the 34 recommendations in order of priority. The top ten were submitted to the Executive Board (made up of the Chief Executive Officers (CEOs) of member companies) which made some changes to the order. In 1988, the CPPA was concentrating on the first two recommendations which related to the continuation of federal funding of forest management and of federal-provincial agreements, and to the enhancement of the public's understanding of forestry. The first objective has been described as "somewhere between orchestrating and working equally with others in a lobbying and communications effort." In relation to the second objective, CPPA hopes to be able to triple its communications budget. Having worked on these two objectives, the CPPA will move down the list—the third objective relates to the use of pesticides, and includes such tasks as encouraging the development and use of effective alternative means of pest control and accelerating research into the environmental effects of pesticides.

The NFSS, although undoubtedly an interesting exercise in federal provincial cooperation, confirms the traditional strengths and weaknesses of policy-making in the sector. Business-government relations are relatively good, facilitating cooperation in such areas as research and development. Highly integrated, well-resourced business associations are able to contribute effectively to the development of policy, and to participate in policy implementation. However, there are severe limits on what can be achieved through concertation policy networks, a point also developed by Wilson. Environmental concerns were incorporated into the forest sector strategy, but in a rather marginal and industry-orientated fashion as, for example, in the recommendation favouring "converting wildlife information into useable forest technology" (CCFM, 1987: 6). Such crucial questions as the balanced, long-term management of wood supply rely to a great extent on the decisions taken by individual companies, rather than by the policy community as a whole. Although the NFSS represents a comprehensive consideration of the challenge facing the industry, caution is justified in any estimate of whether the necessary changes are likely to be made by the relevant decision market.

The Softwood Lumber Dispute

A discussion of the softwood lumber dispute between the US and Canada permits an exploration of the ability of the forest and forest products policy community to respond effectively to crisis conditions. How well do state agencies and business interest associations perform when they face a fundamental challenge to the basic rules of the economic game, particularly a challenge coming from outside Canada? One member of the industry has suggested that "the forest industry still lobbies very effectively when the changes are marginal. When you get major changes in trends and circumstances (such as the ones affecting trade and attitudes towards forestry) it gets much harder" (*Globe and Mail*, December 15, 1987).

The issue underlying the softwood lumber dispute involved the increasing Canadian penetration of the US market; by 1987 Canada supplied a third of the US market, while 60 per cent of all Canadian softwood lumber exports went to the US. Against a background of growing protectionist sentiment in the US, it was argued that Canada's advantage stemmed from the low stumpage charges levied by provincial governments on forest companies felling trees. The Canadian industry countered that the system of auctioning woodlots in the US forced up prices to unrealistic levels and that much of the Canadian advantage was related to the value of the Canadian dollar relative to that of the US dollar. Indeed, a careful analysis of the problem concluded "that market forces played the major role in increasing Canadian softwood lumber exports to the United States" (Percy and Yoder, 1987: 133).

The relative economic strength of the cases advanced by both sides mattered relatively little in the final outcome. The US case was advanced by the Coalition for Fair Lumber Imports, representing the major forest products corporations in the US. Forest products are a key industry in Oregon and Washington, and these and other states with forest industry interests are strongly represented on key Congressional committees. In particular the "Senate Finance Committee, the congressional body most responsible for international trade policy, is dominated by senators from areas concerned with natural resources"

(Leyton-Brown, 1986-7: 74). In Canada, the Progressive Conservative government did not want a row over lumber to stand in the way of its hopes for a bilateral trade agreement with the US.

The agreement arrived at between the US and Canada at the end of December 1986 provided for the US industry to withdraw its complaint in return for Canada imposing a tax of 15 per cent on softwood lumber exports to the US. The federal government administers the program and collects the tax, returning it to the provinces according to the volume of lumber that each exports. Another route to satisfying the US requirement is to increase stumpage fees to replace the tax. And, in fact, an agreement implemented in December 1987 withdrew the export tax for exports from BC in response to higher stumpage fees introduced by that province. New Brunswick, Nova Scotia and Newfoundland were excluded from the tax at the same time because their timberlands are almost entirely privately owned, and are thus unaffected by provincial stumpage regimes.

Although the immediate impact of the tax on the Canadian industry was not as great as feared because of high demand for lumber in the US, its imposition was clearly a defeat for the industry. It is also apparent that the industry did not handle the situation well politically. Perhaps bolstered by the favourable outcome of an earlier dispute in 1983, the industry initially thought that it could win on the economic merits of its case. However, as Percy and Yoder (1987: 115) point out, "When one reviews the political and economic clout of the various participants acting on behalf of the US softwood lumber industry, it becomes clear Canada could not have won the case on its economic merits."

The CFIC's political strategy was to keep the issue out of the public eye, and to seek to influence key Canadian decision makers, notably then international trade minister, Pat Carney. No effort was made to influence Canadian public opinion, while the US lobby was able to convince "a large portion of the Canadian public that Canada's forest companies were getting a free ride" (*Globe and Mail,* December 15, 1987). Not only did the CFIC fail to perform well at its first major test, but the policy community as a whole failed to work together effectively to defend Canadian interests. "The lack of cohesion displayed by the provinces, federal government, and industry in the negotiations after August 1986 cannot but have hurt Canada's chances before the ITA [International Trade Administration] subsidy determination" (Percy and Yoder, 1987: 130).

Two broader issues also arise from the softwood lumber dispute: the vulnerability of the Canadian state in the international arena, and the extent of decision-making autonomy enjoyed by the provincial governments. Canada is in a weak bargaining position when faced with a determined position taken by a major economic power, notably by the United States to which the Canadian economy is so closely tied. Anderson and Cairns argue (1988: 193) that "agreeing to change *stumpage* policy at the request of the US government *did* affect Canadian sovereignty, in particular, provincial government sovereignty."

One must be careful not to push this point too far. Other Canadian industries, notably the steel industry, seem to have handled their relations with the US government with greater skill and effectiveness (Grant, 1989a: 227-8). It is also evident that the provincial governments have preserved considerable freedom to manoeuvre for themselves. For example, BC refused a request from Ottawa to delay its stumpage fee increases until after a deadline in the free trade talks. BC and Québec were involved in direct presentations of their plans for fee increases to the US Department of Commerce.

Indeed, the individual provinces, notably BC, appear to have come close to behaving as if they were independent states in relation to international forestry trade questions. One BC respondent commented in interview that there was "a suspicion that they [BC Government] might go it alone in Washington. This is when the politics of Canada becomes tricky at times." A federal civil servant referred to the actions of the BC Government as sending "shivers up peoples' spines" and commented that it was "no secret that BC did in fact attempt to negotiate with the US directly during the softwood dispute." This picture was confirmed by a Washington respondent who commented that, seen from a US perspective, "BC always seemed to be like its own government."

The federal government's responsibility for international trade questions is, in practice, qualified by the considerable involvement of the provincial governments in forestry matters. This involvement makes the decision-making process a highly complex one. The effectiveness of the Canadian response on such questions has not been assisted by the inability of the industry to create anything more than a weak umbrella organization representing the sector as a whole.

Conclusion

The policy community in the Canadian forest and forest products industry has responded reasonably well to routine policy problems which can be dealt with in an incremental fashion. It has performed much less effectively in response to major policy shocks, notably the softwood lumber dispute with the US. The national forest sector strategy shows that well established policy linkages in the sector are able to create mechanisms for defining, analyzing and proposing (rather vague and generalized) solutions to the various challenges facing the industry. The key test of this potentially comprehensive strategy rests in whether it can be consistently implemented. For all the organizational assets of the state and the business associations, the key decision makers are ultimately the large forest companies (some of them owned by conglomerates or by non-Canadian forestry companies such as Fletcher Challenge of New Zealand). As Wilson reminds us in the next chapter, their structural power should never be ignored.

The greatest long run challenge to the industry arises from public concern about its impact on the environment, a theme emphasized in Wilson's chapter. A poll of 2,500 Canadians commissioned by Forestry Canada from the Environics Research Group Limited, and carried out in January and February 1989, represents the first comprehensive national survey of public opinion on forestry matters. Of those polled, 75 per cent said that Canada's forests are primarily a national treasure that should be held in trust, and 72 per cent said that the environment is threatened by the forest industry. Sixty-three per cent said the most important thing to consider when deciding how to use forest land is the potential impact on the environment, compared with 19 per cent who cited potential economic value or job creation. (Globe and Mail, May 19, 1989). The attentive public is clearly concerned about the forests, although how sustained that attention will be remains to be seen.

Concern about the environmental impact of forestry has also been expressed in other countries such as the US and Britain, where the industry has also had difficulty creating a sector-wide national organization to respond to the new political challenges it faces (Grant: 1989b). However, the centrality of the forest products industry in the Canadian economy makes the quality of its response to changes in the political agenda an issue of much more central concern. Setting up consultative committees, or giving environmentalists a seat at the edge of the policy table, is unlikely to be sufficient to allay public anxiety about the industry's stewardship of the national forest resource. Objectives, decision-making procedures, and the management culture of the industry may have to undergo fundamental change.

References

Anderson, F. J. and R. D. Cairns (1988). "The Softwood Lumber Agreement and Resource Politics." *Canadian Public Policy*, XIV: 186-96.

Atkinson, M. M. and W. D. Coleman (1989). "Strong States and Weak States: Sectoral Policy Networks in Advanced Capitalist Economies." *British Journal of Political Science*, 19: 47-65.

Canadian Council of Forest Ministers (1987). *A National Forest Sector Strategy for Canada*. Ottawa: Ministry of Supply and Services.

Coleman, W. D. (1987). "Agricultural Policy and the Associations of the Food Processing Industry." In W. Grant, ed. *Business Interests, Organizational Development and Private Interest Government.* Berlin: de Gruyter: 151-65.

_____ **(1988).** *Business and Politics: A Study of Collective Action.* Montreal: McGill-Queen's University Press.

Gillis, R. P. and T. R. Roach (1986). *Lost Initiatives: Canada's Forest Industries, Forest Policy and Forest Conservation.* New York: Greenwood.

Grant, W. (1988). "The Organization of Capitalists in Britain's Company State: A Comparative Perspective." Paper presented to the annual meeting of the American Political Science Association (APSA), Washington D.C.

_____ **(1989a).** *Government and Industry: A Comparative Analysis of the US, Canada and the UK.* Aldershot: Edward Elgar.

_____ **Grant, W. (1989b).** "The Politics of Collective Consumption and Business Interest Organization in the Forest and Forest Products Industry in the US, Canada and the UK." Paper presented to the American Political Science Association (APSA) annual meeting, Atlanta.

Hewett, C. E. and E. Peterson (1982). "The Forest Resource: Emerging Conflicts and the Need for Action." In C.E. Hewett and T.E. Hamilton, eds. *Forests in Demand: Conflicts and Solutions.* Boston: Auburn House: 13-20.

Industry, Science and Technology (1988). "Synergy: A Bonus from Cooperation." Report of the Forest Industry Machinery Task Force, Ottawa.

Johnson, C. M. (1984). "Legislative Mechanisms to Balance Public and Private Interests in Forest Management." Paper prepared for presentation at the International Forest Congress, 1984.

Leslie, P. (1987). *Federal State, National Economy.* Toronto: University of Toronto Press.

Leyton-Brown, D. (1986-7). "Hewers of Woods: the Forest Products Sector." *International Journal,* XLII: 59-77.

Percy, M. B. and C. Yoder (1987). *The Softwood Lumber Dispute and Canada-US Trade in Natural Resources.* Halifax: Institute for Research on Public Policy.

Pross, A. P. (1986). *Group Politics and Public Policy.* Toronto: Oxford University Press.

de Silva, K. E. (1988). "Pulp and Paper Modernization Grants Program an Assessment." Discussion Paper No.350, Economic Council of Canada.

Sonnenfeld, J. A. (1981). *Corporate Views of the Public Interest: Perceptions of the Forest Products Industry.* Boston: Auburn House.

Willis, D. and Grant, W. (1987). "The United Kingdom: Still a Company State?" In M.P. van Schendelen and R. Jackson, eds. *The Politicisation of Business in Western Europe.* Beckenham: Croom Helm: 153-83.

CHAPTER SIX

WILDERNESS POLITICS IN BC:
THE BUSINESS DOMINATED
STATE AND THE CONTAINMENT
OF ENVIRONMENTALISM

Jeremy Wilson

L ike its counterparts across the western world, the Canadian
state was faced after 1965 with the challenge of responding to
a host of new, and newly-assertive, interest groups. The appearance of forceful groups representing previously quiescent components of society such as women and native Indians, along with the
arrival of groups articulating a variety of public interest positions,
transformed the political landscape. Confronted with resistance from
an assortment of groups representing what Offe (Schmitter, 1982: 271)
refers to as "policy takers," the state was forced to consider new
strategies for legitimating its relations with capital. The construction
of these strategies entailed difficult decisions about the extent to which
the new groups should be accommodated or excluded.

In BC, the most extensive challenge to traditional arrangements
between the state and capital was mounted by the environmental
movement. The growth of the movement after 1965 fundamentally
altered the province's "politics of exploitation," adding new layers of

debate concerning environmental externalities to longstanding conflicts over the terms under which rights to Crown resources are granted to companies. Additional dimensions of scarcity impinged on the political system as more and more people, attaching more and more value to goods like wilderness and clean water, organized to challenge industrial users of BC's resources.

Two of these users—BC Hydro and the forest industry—occupied most of the movement's attention in the 1970s and 1980s. The assortment of groups which assembled under the environmentalist banner dealt with issues ranging from urban water pollution and offshore oil exploration to uranium mining and predator control policies. The lion's share of attention, however, was devoted to controlling the forest industry's efforts to liquidate the province's old growth forests, and to derailing BC Hydro's plans to flood several more valleys. BC Hydro issues remained prominent in the 1970s, declining in salience only after a downward turn in the utility's demand forecasts stalled its pursuit of projects such as the Peace Site C dam (Wilson, 1983). Forest land use issues have been a central concern of the movement since the 1960s.

Focussing on the 1975-89 period, this chapter explores the BC government's response to what we will refer to as the forest environment movement. This movement advances two related arguments: first, more of BC's remaining forest wilderness should be preserved; and second, the logging that is done should be carried out in a more environmentally sensitive fashion. Wilderness preservation has been the main thrust. Groups have mounted campaigns to preserve dozens of wilderness areas such as South Moresby, Meares Island and the Stein valley, using a mixture of philosophical, scientific and utilitarian arguments to make the case. Typically, the contention is that wilderness is vital in and of itself for spiritual and cultural reasons; we have an obligation to preserve options for future generations; by saving wilderness we help preserve genetic and species diversity along with ecological benchmarks; and as well as providing recreational opportunities for BC residents, wilderness pays economic dividends by attracting tourists.

The efforts of forest environment groups helped increase the share of BC's land base in protected categories (provincial parks, recreation areas,[1] and ecological reserves along with national parks) from about 5.4 per cent in 1975 to about 6.8 per cent in 1988. Estimates of the amount of land involved in the remaining items on the preservation agenda vary, but roughly speaking, accomplishment of the full agenda would increase the protected land base by between 50 and 100 per cent.[2] The movement points out that less than 30 per cent of land currently protected could be categorized as good forest land, and that the percentage of such land in the areas it seeks is no higher (Fuller, 1985: 28; Sierra Club of Western Canada, 1988; Roemer, Pojar and Joy, 1988).

Since the amount of forest land targeted by environmentalists represents a small fraction of the uncontested industry-controlled land base, the hostility of the industry to the movement may seem surprising. But from its inception, the forest environment movement has been treated as a very threatening phenomenon. Several explanations for the industry's vehement reaction can be offered. Perhaps most importantly, it reflects the industry's conviction that any systematic threat to the sanctity of the tenure system undermines its leverage in financial markets. Although most timber is Crown-owned, virtually all of it is committed to companies under easily renewable, long-term licences. For companies, these licences represent a valuable commodity, an asset whose value is perceived to be jeopardized by any threat to the tenure contract. According to R.V. Smith (1986: 6), the head of BCs largest forest company, MacMillan Bloedel:

> Forest tenures and timber supply and the commitments by which those tenures are held are the fundamental asset by which potential investors or lenders judge the viability of a company. In most cases these tenures are included in present and prospective trust deeds as security for loans. Ask any investment banker how they measure the continuing value of a forest company to the investor. At the top of the list will be security of timber. I can't stress strongly enough my conviction that investor—and lender—confidence is directly related to the frequency and size of timber re-allocations.

Other perspectives on the nature of the environmental challenge help illuminate the industry's hostility. Although this aspect of the challenge is seldom articulated, environmentalism imperils the unwritten code of speculative rights at the heart of the BC capitalist ethos, threatening a system that has long legitimized a profitable traffic in rights to Crown resources. And the movement's plea against commodification of the forests represents a threat to the programme of old growth liquidation inherent in the so-called sustained yield policy adopted in 1947.[3] Once again, it is easy to see why the industry regards the challenge as fundamental. Forty years of investment decisions—and, quite literally, the postwar construction of the province's corporate sector—have been based on the assumption that this programme of liquidation would be pursued to its culmination. For these general reasons, and a host of ancillary ones related to the particular circumstances facing individual companies, industry officials have aggressively campaigned against the environmental movement.

Many adopt domino metaphors, rationalizing a hardline attitude with the argument that any sign of retreat will only encourage further demands for what are referred to as "single use" withdrawals.

It can be appreciated then that the rise of forest environmentalism inaugurated an era of raw, redistributive politics in BC, forcing the provincial state to reconsider the policies it had crafted in response to the legitimation and accumulation pressures of the early postwar decades. On a substantive level, the state was faced with calls for reallocation of a pie already committed to capital. On a process level, it had to contend with attempts by the new groups to elbow their way into a meaningful place in the forest land use policy community, a closed community centring on the lead agency, the Ministry of Forests (MOF); the cabinet committee with ultimate responsibility for resolving land use disputes, the Environment and Land Use Committee (ELUC); and the ten or 12 major forest companies that hold tenure rights to over 60 per cent of BC's forest land (Wagner, 1987: 129; Pearse, 1976: B7).

The literature on environmental groups provides little guidance concerning the sort of dances such groups are likely to engage in with state agencies. But in his book on US public interest liberal groups, Michael McCann (1986: Chap. 5) refers to the proposition that reform-oriented groups will be drawn towards greater dependence on state agencies, a process that takes the edge off their inclination to protest and alienate the publics they purport to represent. Joel Handler (1978, cited in McCann, 1986: 215-17), for example, argues that an inability to surmount the free-rider dilemma may force reform groups to choose between chronic ineffectiveness and some sort of corporatist bargain. Those wanting to have some impact on policy may agree to moderate their demands in exchange for financial help and stable access.

Whatever force it might have had in other situations, the corporatizing logic identified in arguments like these had little impact on the patterns of interest intermediation that evolved in response to the appearance of the BC forest environment movement. Neither the movement nor the state has been favourably disposed to corporatist arrangements. Environment groups, by and large, remain proud outsiders. Mainly because of the high level of issue commitment prevailing among environmentalists, these groups have been able to slough off problems which affect the abilities of other types of groups to attract and retain members, and have thus avoided the slippery slope towards dependence on state resources (for a contrast, see *Chapters 7, 8, and 9*). For a variety of reasons, there has been little movement toward the kind of hierarchical, overarching inter-group structures prerequisite to establishment of stable and binding deal-making arrangements with state and industry. Some groups have entered into close relationships with agencies on the periphery of the forest policy-making process (such as the parks agency), using this access to influence policy on secondary issues (such as the development of use plans for existing parks). But because of concern about the possibility of cooptation, most groups remain suspicious of such linkages.

For its part, the state has shown little inclination to invite environmental groups to play a meaningful role in deliberations on key allocative decisions. This is not to say that its response has been entirely exclusionist. For the Social Credit governments that managed the state's response during the period considered, such a tack would have been too risky. This environmental challenge, after all, comes not from some marginal corner of society, but from groups that draw support from across the class spectrum and, more to the point, are capable of influencing reliable Social Credit voters. So some overtures in the direction of environmental interests were necessary. At the same time, the forest industry's power limited the extent to which those interests could be accommodated. Not surprisingly, the industry prevailed, leading key state actors to treat the forest environment movement as a phenomenon that had to be contained. The movement was offered a mixture of symbolic and substantive concessions, but these were implemented against a backdrop of measures designed to limit the damage to capital.

In short, what is described here is a policy making system in transition. The rise of the forest environment movement transformed a situation bearing the hallmark features of what Coleman and Skogstad label concertation into one that could be described as "contested concertation." MOF-industry attempts to equate their interests regarding forest land use with the public interest no longer go unchallenged. Although it has certainly not achieved a "paradigm shift" in values, the environment movement has influenced many British Columbians' descriptive and prescriptive beliefs regarding the province's traditional resource extraction economy. Further normative shifts may eventually translate into significant changes in policy networks and outcomes. To date, however, the MOF-industry allies have parried threats to the core assumptions underlying their power. They continue to dominate forest land-use policy-making, exerting strong influence over how the wilderness politics issue is defined.

The Forest Land Use Policy Community

The policy outcomes considered here were dropped, one by one, along a path marked by continual institutional change. Key state agencies came and went, a number of those that endured were shifted from ministry to ministry, and the entire bureaucracy was subjected to "downsizing" and privatization initiatives. Despite this flux, the central features of the state forest land-use policy-making system remained fairly constant (Dorcey, 1987; Wilson, 1987: 6-8).

Figure 1

The BC Forest Land Use Policy Community

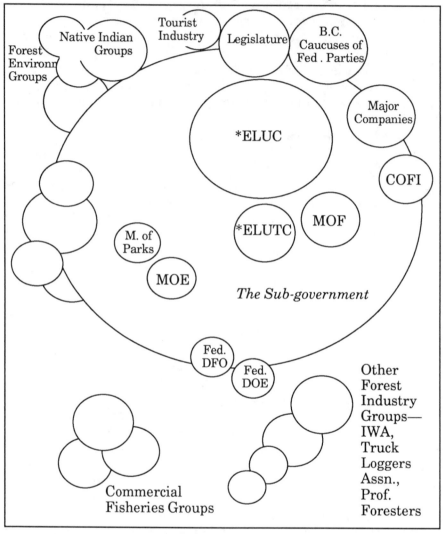

*The ELUTC is composed of the deputy ministers and the ELUC, the ministers of the ministries of environment; agriculture and fisheries; energy, mines and petroleum resources; forests; crown lands; parks; municipal affairs, recreation and culture; tourism and provincial secretary

COFI:	Council of Forest Industries of British Columbia	Fed. DOE:	Federal Department of Environment
ELUC:	Environment and Land Use Committee	IWA:	International Woodworkers of America
ELUTC:	Environment and Land Use Technical Committee	M. of Parks:	Ministry of Parks
		MOE:	Ministry of the Environment
Fed. DFO:	Federal Department of Fisheries and Oceans	MOF:	Ministry of Forests

The system is dominated by the Ministry of Forests (MOF). By dint of its jurisdiction over land in "Provincial Forests", it is responsible for over 85 per cent of the province's 94 million hectare land base (and about 93 per cent of Crown land). The MOF delegates extensive management responsibilities to companies holding Tree Farm Licences (TFLs) and Forest Licences, but it retains power to enforce the levels of management it deems appropriate. As we will see, a late 1970s shift in the MOF's mandate made it responsible for integrating a range of nontimber values into its management and planning. Two agencies with environmental mandates—the provincial Ministry of Environment (MOE) and the federal Department of Fisheries and Oceans (DFO)—often find themselves in adversarial relationships with the MOF. The MOE's Wildlife Branch (formerly the Fish and Wildlife Branch) is particularly inclined to advance views on forest land management that conflict with those of the MOF. Both the MOE and the DFO must try to achieve their goals through bargaining. Over the years, inter-agency bargaining processes have become increasingly institutionalized, but this has not changed the fact that results generally reflect the bureaucratic pecking order. Neither the MOE nor the DFO has the political resources needed to fare consistently well in bargaining with the MOF. The same can be said of the two agencies most disposed to push for preservation of wilderness, the tiny bureaucracy responsible for the Ecological Reserves Programme and the Parks Branch (since 1988, the Ministry of Parks).

Inter-agency differences that cannot be resolved through negotiation among lower ranking officials are passed up the ladder to a committee of deputy ministers from ministries with jurisdiction in the resources area, the Environment and Land Use Technical Committee (ELUTC). Those which cannot be resolved at this level go to the corresponding cabinet committee, ELUC. This committee has been at the centre of the province's natural resource management structure since 1969. The various state actors are represented (at more or less central positions) in the core, "sub-government" zone, of the policy community diagram presented in Figure 1. In accordance with Pross's (1986: 98) conceptualization, this zone is reserved for agencies and interest groups most centrally involved in policy-making in the sector.

Five other features of the forest land use policy sector bear noting. First, the provincial legislature plays virtually no role in the process. Second, the process is a closed one. The province has no freedom of information legislation, and the legislative mandates of the MOF and other agencies were framed so as to limit severely statutory obligations regarding the release of information or the openness of decision processes. Third, the mandating legislation leaves extensive pools of discretionary power in the hands of cabinet ministers and their officials. Fourth, forest policy is made against a backdrop of deep technical uncertainty. For example, 60 or 70 years after attempts began to develop an inventory of the forest resource, there remains considerable debate over how much wood fibre is available in the province's forests. And likewise, there is no consensus on what sort of future forest (and future forest economy) is likely to be produced by the regeneration programmes so far undertaken or planned. Fifth, the decision-making freedom of forest policy-makers is constrained by policies adopted by previous governments, which did much to determine the silvicultural condition of the province's forest land, and long ago conveyed rights to virtually all of the province's timber to companies under long-term tenure contracts. These characteristics of state structure and the policy sector have different consequences for the political resources of the environment movement and the forest industry.

The forest environment movement consists of four components: first, fish and wildlife clubs and their umbrella organization, the BC Wildlife Federation (BCWF); second, naturalist groups and their provincial organization, the Federation of BC Naturalists (FBCN); third, nonconsumptive outdoor recreation clubs and their federations, the Outdoor Recreation Council (ORC), and the Federation of Mountain Clubs of BC (FMCBC); and fourth, groups concerned exclusively (or mainly) with environmental advocacy, including some with province-wide, multi-issue perspectives (such as the Sierra Club) and others with a local or regional focus (such as the Friends of Clayoquot Sound). The distinction between the last category and the first three highlights the fact that the naturalist and recreational groups engage in a range of activities besides advocacy. These include, for example, organizing bird counts (FBCN), providing courses on such things as mountaineering (FMCBC), and carrying out salmon enhancement and wildlife re-location projects (BCWF). These categories are not mutually exclusive; many individuals belong to two or more types of groups.

The fish and wildlife, naturalist, and outdoor recreation movements all have deep historical roots in the group life of the province. The first fish and game clubs appeared in the 1880s, and the province-wide federation which was to become the BCWF took shape in 1947-48. This step quickened the movement's evolution from one preoccupied with regulatory issues (such as the size of bag limits and the length of hunting seasons) to one concerned with a broad array of environmental and natural resource issues (Terpenning, 1982). Naturalist and alpine clubs appeared prior to the First World War. Although groups such as the BC Mountaineering Club and the Natural History Society of BC did campaign for creation of early provincial parks like Garibaldi, such groups were slower than their fish and game counterparts to gear up for concerted political action. The first steps in this direction were taken in the 1960s with the establishment of province-wide coalitions. Various alpine clubs set up the Mountain Access Committee in 1963 and then formed the FMCBC in 1971. Naturalists followed a similar path, establishing the BC Nature Council and then the FBCN. In both instances, greater emphasis on environmental advocacy followed federation.

Groups devoted exclusively to advocacy began to appear after 1965. By 1975, the list of organizations actively involved in forest environment issues included the Sierra Club and several groups established to pursue specific wilderness proposals, including the Okanagan Similkameen Parks Society (OSPS), the Valhalla Wilderness Committee (later, Society), and the Islands Protection Committee (later, Society). Advocacy groups continued to proliferate after 1975. Groups like the Friends of Clayoquot Sound sprang up to battle against logging in particular areas, while the ranks of multi-issue groups were joined by the Western Canada Wilderness Committee (WCWC), the Friends of Ecological Reserves (FER), and the Valhalla Wilderness Society, which began to pursue a range of issues after winning its battle to preserve the Valhalla in 1983.

Groups vary considerably in size, ranging from single issue groups with fewer than 100 members to large umbrella federations like the BCWF (38,000 members in 176 clubs) and the ORC (100,000 members in 47 associations). They share many of the organizational characteristics of reform-oriented US groups, including low overhead operations, heavy reliance on deeply committed volunteers, and a tendency to reject complex, formal structures. Decision-making approaches vary, but most can safely be characterized as benign, open oligarchies (McCann, 1986: Chap. 4; Berry, 1977: Chap. 3).

The socio-economic complexion of these groups varies but, generally speaking, like environmental groups elsewhere, they draw most of their members from the upper two-thirds of the class ladder.[4] Selective and solidary incentives play some part in decisions to join and remain; that is, some members are influenced by the opportunity to receive benefits unrelated to the group's policy goals (such as magazines or access to courses and field trips) or by a desire to make or maintain contacts and friendships (Berry, 1977: 36-44). Purposive incentives, however, provide the main motivation for participation in advocacy groups (and in the advocacy efforts of the recreation and naturalist groups). Clark and Wilson's conclusion is applicable: "the intrinsic worth or dignity of the ends themselves are regarded by members as justifying effort" (1961: 146; cited in Berry, 1977: 42).

The intensity with which large numbers of wilderness proponents pursue the movement's ends represents its greatest political resource. Although this high level of issue commitment is rooted in a web of factors, it derives most directly from a recognition that there are no second chances to win wilderness battles—once an area is logged it is lost as wilderness.

The movement's diversity represents another important political asset. Available evidence indicates that a significant minority of British Columbians actively support environment groups, and that a much larger portion of the population is sympathetic to key parts of the movement's platform.[5] The movement's diversity also manifests itself in a wide repertoire of political approaches. Drawing as it does on a broad cross-section of society, it is not surprising that the movement encompasses a variegated assortment of political talents and dispositions; expert analysts operate alongside skilled symbol mongers, merry pranksters who are ready to consider a range of radical tactics alongside cautious birders who are convinced that progress requires diligent research and patient lobbying. Though it does create some potential for strain, this diversity of approaches represents an obvious political asset. It means that the movement as a whole is able to cover a range of tactical bases, and that some segment of the movement can usually be counted on to gravitate quickly to the approach deemed most appropriate in a particular circumstance. The movement's opponents have found it to be something of a hydra. The value of diversity has also been revealed in the movement's alliance-building activities. For example, the groups that spearheaded the early stages of the Meares, Stein and South Moresby campaigns were able to establish productive alliances with the native Indian groups which became increasingly involved as those campaigns progressed.

The movement's diversity is also apparent in the way it performs its most central tactical approach of building public support and galvanizing sympathizers to express their views to decision makers. Both the emotional and intellectual sides of arguments for wilderness and better forest practice have been well articulated. The WCWC and its allies have led the way on the first front, using calendars, posters and videos to juxtapose the horrors of clearcut logging against the special features of areas proposed for preservation. Between 1980 and 1988, it distributed over 2 million copies of tabloid-style handouts on areas such as Meares Island and the Stein Valley. Meares, South Moresby and the Stein were all glorified in special books full of striking photographs (Friends of Clayoquot Sound, 1985; Islands Protection Society, 1984; M'Gonigle and Wickwire, 1988).

Efforts along these lines are generally backed by strong, research based arguments about the benefits of wilderness preservation. Groups like the WCWC, FER, and the Islands Protection Society have tried to combine the two approaches, while other groups have rejected emotional appeals, choosing instead to concentrate on trying to win converts with arguments based on thorough homework. The OSPS and one of the groups active in the struggle to preserve the Stein, the Save the Stein Coalition, are good examples of this approach. Both have developed complex technical arguments concerning the diseconomies of logging (Jones, 1983). Most groups are able to cite considerable evidence in support of arguments about the tourism benefits of wilderness preservation.

Attempts to mobilize public support are, of course, combined with behind-the-scenes lobbying of politicians and bureaucrats. The movement brings some significant resources to bear on its lobbying campaigns. Its leaders are generally well prepared, persistent and personable. And movement members enjoy good access to parts of the bureaucracy. Many environmentalists are linked to bureaucrats by friendship or acquaintance ties based on shared educational backgrounds or common recreational interests. For example, BCWF leaders are on very friendly terms with staff in the fish and wildlife bureaucracies, while members of advocacy, recreational, and naturalist groups often have close links to officials in the environment and parks ministries. The movement has also usually contained at least a few people enjoying friendship ties or old school ties to key cabinet level bureaucrats.

Turning to the movement's principal political weaknesses, its access to MOF officials is not nearly as good as to peripheral parts of the forest land use decision-making structure. For all of its diversity, the movement has included very few people capable of relating easily to recent forest ministers. And few environmentalists manage to bridge consistently and effectively the cultural chasm separating the movement from the professional foresters who populate the MOF bureaucracy.

Second, the movement is not, to say the least, awash in money. Although various fund-raising devices are used, most of the movement's campaigns must be funded out of members' dues and donations. The latter limits the range of tactical approaches available. None of the groups considered here has sufficient funds to support media advertising campaigns, or to maintain a full time lobbyist in Victoria. The volunteers and staff members who do carry out public relations and lobbying activities usually subsidize expenses out of their own pockets. Were it not for the intense commitment of its activist members, the movement would not be able to maintain anything close to its present level of activity.

The extent to which the movement's effectiveness is impaired by intergroup divisions is debatable. Geographical and issue cleavages create a certain amount of strain and the willingness of groups to countenance multiple use solutions has always varied. In terms of their views about the scope of institutional changes needed and their visions of what the future forest economy should look like, groups range from moderately reformist to fairly radical (Wilson, 1987: 25-30). The issue of native land claims has caused some divisions. Many members of naturalist, recreation, and advocacy groups are not at all sympathetic to the hunters who make up a significant portion of the BCWF membership, and BCWF leaders have hit back at those they consider aggressively anti-hunter. The BCWF and other groups which perceive themselves to be moderate, "homework and lobbying" organizations sometimes express resentment at the approaches employed by groups such as the WCWC.

Yet the movement has managed to avoid the kind of strife that has broken apart other progressive organizations; its leaders have not had to devote a lot of energy to counteracting inter-group discord. Although differences like those noted have certainly discouraged any thoughts about groups merging into an umbrella organization, they have not prevented the formation of a number of productive issue-specific alliances. Here as elsewhere, problems that might have been expected to bedevil the movement seem to have been neutralized by high levels of issue commitment.

The outsider status of forest environment groups is depicted in Figure 1. These groups sit on the periphery of the sub-government zone, closely enough connected to allow them to monitor and influence policy decisions but excluded from regular policy participation. In dynamic terms we can think of these groups as having edged steadily towards the centre, exerting more and more pressure on the concertation pattern of policy-making represented by the inclusion of the major forest industry actors within the sub-government portion of the diagram.

The latter placement is based on an assessment of the structural advantages enjoyed by the forest industry. First, the state is impelled to protect the interests of the industry because, by dint of their control over key decisions on investment, employment and the like, major companies shape the general level of economic prosperity which government actors regard as a crucial determinant of their re-election chances.[6] The longstanding belief that the forest industry is responsible for 50 cents of every dollar's worth of economic activity in the province is far from accurate; in fact, in most years its direct contribution to the province's gross domestic product is in the 10-15 per cent range (BC. Ministry of Economic Development, 1985). But together, the wood and pulp-paper industries do account for about 50 per cent of all manufacturing shipments (COFI, 1988; Price Waterhouse). In recent years, the industry has directly employed between 75,000 and 85,000 workers, and the percentage of workers who are directly or indirectly dependent on the industry for their jobs is usually estimated to be in the 15-20 per cent range.

Second, BCs major forest companies have the technical resources and opportunity to influence governments; most importantly, they possess the financial resources needed to mount extensive lobbying efforts and public relations campaigns, and they have good access to the state elites at the core of the forest land use policy community. The political influence of these companies is channelled through a peak association known as the Council of Forest Industries of British Columbia (COFI) as well as through the lobbying-public relations operations of individual companies and regional associations. Small lumber producers and logging contractors are represented by the Truck Loggers Association. COFI members account for over 90 per cent of all forest products output in the province.

Operating with a yearly budget of about $10 million, COFI provides its members with services in a variety of areas including trade promotion, product research, statistics gathering, and government relations. Its Government and Public Affairs division includes lobbyists responsible for both the Ottawa and Victoria scenes. It shares a Victoria office suite with MacMillan Bloedel, whose Victoria lobby operation was estimated in 1987 to cost about $150,000 per year (Sopow, 1987: 10). Officials from other major companies make regular calls in Victoria.

The industry enjoys good access to all levels of the MOF power structure. Perhaps the most telling way of making this point is to focus on the career moves of the man who heads COFI, Mike Apsey. Over the past decade he has engaged in a classic bit of elite hopping. After a stint on the government-appointed advisory committee that translated the recommendations of the Pearse Royal Commission into the new Forest Act of 1978, Apsey left his position as a COFI vice-president to become Deputy Minister of Forests in mid-1978. After six years in that position, he returned to COFI, assuming the presidency in mid-1984. There is also considerable lower level personnel interchange between companies and the MOF. And close ties between government and industry foresters are fostered by common values and educational experiences, along with membership in the foresters' organization, the Association of BC Professional Foresters (ABCPF).

Over the past decade, the ABCPF has become quite vociferous in its support for the industry, releasing position papers which (with some qualifications) endorse industry positions on issues such as clearcutting, wilderness, and the need to resist reductions to the forest land base. The industry's major players receive less consistent support from the Truck Loggers Association, and from the organization representing most industry workers, the International Woodworkers of America (IWA). The Truck Loggers carry on a long tradition of hostility to large companies and the policies they see as benefitting them, taking some positions on forest management and the tenure system which parallel those taken by environmentalists. But they are certainly not sympathetic to the main demands of environmentalists. Likewise, while it is a harsh critic of many aspects of government-company forest administration, the IWA supports the industry position that the government should emphasize management of forest land for multiple uses (including harvesting and recreation) rather than seeking to preserve additional amounts of land in parks.

It should also be noted that some forest industry workers, along with their spouses and supporters, have begun to establish anti-preservation groups with names such as "Share the Stein." Taking strategic guidance from a US organization known as the "Center for the Defence of Free Enterprise," these "share groups" use the media, public meetings, and WCWC-style tabloids to push the idea that multiple use approaches will allow for the preservation of industry jobs as well as recreational opportunities. There has been considerable debate over the extent to which these groups are instigated and bankrolled by companies. Some claim to be free of such connections, but others have admitted receiving company support. The Share the Stein group, for example, received $200,000 in 1988 from COFI, BC Forest Products (which became Fletcher Challenge Canada), and others.[7]

In recent years, COFI has also been responsible for a major public relations initiative. Centred on the "Forest Forever" theme, the apparent aim of this campaign is to implant or reinforce the notion that the industry is doing a good job of managing the province's forests. Now in its third year, the campaign's annual cost is estimated to be in the $1.5–$2.0 million range, with a significant portion of this amount spent on TV ads.[8] MacMillan Bloedel has maintained a parallel campaign.

The State Response

Given the above assessment of the relative resources of the protagonists there is nothing surprising about the way the post-1976 Social Credit regime responded to the forest environment movement. Guided by the MOF's dispositions and concerned not to upset the forest industry, it resisted measures that would have fundamentally altered the traditional, concertation pattern of policy-making. The forest environment movement could not be totally ignored; its growing influence on public opinion necessitated some concessions. These, however, were offered in the context of a strategy aimed at containing the movement. One would hesitate to describe this containment strategy as "carefully crafted." As always in describing policy processes we must be careful not to overestimate the coherence or consistency of the government response.

Social Credit's response was patterned around certain recognizable elements which can be grouped into three families. First, conceding that forest management practice needed improving, the government embarked on some well-publicized initiatives to polish the image of the province's three-decade-old sustained yield policy and to bolster the impression that logging was being done in accordance with strict environmental standards and sound multiple use precepts. In a closely related step, it extended the opportunities for public involvement in the forest land use policy process. The symbolism of the sustained yield, multiple use and public involvement initiatives was of course every bit as important as the substance. These served as the legitimating cornerstones underlying other facets of the government's response to environmentalism, particularly its concerted campaign against "single use" alienations of forest land for purposes such as parks. Second, the government took steps to strengthen MOF-industry control over the land base, allowing the MOF to incorporate large additional amounts of land into "provincial forests," and adopting tenure system changes which enabled the industry to tighten its grip. Third, by denying requests for a comprehensive assessment of the wilderness issue, and insisting instead on a piecemeal process for resolving wilderness conflicts, the government maintained maximum room for political manoeuvre and ensured that the wilderness debate would be "about" a limited list of wilderness area candidates nominated by environmentalists rather than about all of the province's remaining wilderness. This way of defining the agenda put environmentalists at a disadvantage.

Terms like multiple use, integrated resource management, reforestation, and public involvement were never far from the lips of MOF officials after 1976. Some substantive improvements were apparent behind this wall of symbols. The commitment to multiple use was clearly enunciated in the new forest legislation adopted in 1978. The Ministry of Forests Act [s.4(c)] states that the forest and range resources of the Crown are to be developed in a coordinated way, with recognition of the importance of fisheries, wildlife, water, outdoor recreation and other natural resource values. In a similar vein, a sibling piece of legislation, the Forest Act, includes a clause [s.7(3)(a)(v)] stipulating that in calculating the allowable annual cut, the Chief Forester must consider "the constraints on the amount of timber produced from the area that reasonably can be expected by use of the area for purposes other than timber production." Building on this statutory base, the MOF expanded its own planning capacity while extending arrangements which allowed other agencies to have input in its planning processes. By 1988, the ministry was able to point to a number of signs of progress, including establishment of a new Integrated Resources Branch, participation with officials from other agencies in studies of logging impacts on wildlife and fish habitat, development of interagency protocols governing roles and responsibilities, and numerous successful applications of the Coordinated

Resource Management Planning process to resolve or avoid local-level conflicts among competing interests.

The MOF's high profile initiatives on the sustained yield front formed another important cornerstone of its campaign. Alarm about the state of the province's forest resource began to grow after 1970 with the release of several studies questioning whether levels of timber commitment could be maintained, and suggesting for the first time that the transition from first growth logging to second growth forestry would likely be accompanied by a "falldown" in timber supply (Wilson, 1987: 23-26). By 1976, the sustained yield security blanket that had reassured British Columbians throughout the 1950s and 1960s was beginning to seem a bit threadbare.

Although its decision to do so required it to chant a few preliminary rounds of mea culpa, the MOF joined in the chorus of concern about worrisome timber supply prospects. The ministry was willing to take a lead role in sowing alarm because it knew that it could employ the new atmosphere to advantage, using it to support both its claims for increased funding and its arguments about the need to secure the ministry's control over the forest land base. After convincing the cabinet that action was necessary, the MOF announced ambitious five year plans for forest renewal in 1980 and 1981. These called for sharp increases in the amounts spent on both basic replanting and intensive silviculture. The restraint programme of the mid-1980s knocked the latter dimension of this programme off target, but with the federal government's help the MOF did increase the area of Crown land planted each year from about 50,000 hectares in 1978-79 to over 90,000 hectares in 1986-87. The MOF's efforts in the area of public involvement were also stepped up after 1976. By the early 1980s, members of the public were participating in an advisory capacity on a variety of bodies, including public advisory committees set up to deal with a range of issues arising in government-managed Timber Supply Areas (TSAs), special inter-agency teams struck to develop integrated management plans for logging of environmentally sensitive areas, and other inter-agency teams brought together to advise cabinet on how specific logging versus preservation conflicts might be resolved. In 1981, the MOF adopted a formal policy on public involvement, directing its officials to provide the public with opportunities to see and discuss plans ranging from those for large management units (TSAs and TFLs) down to those for small subunit areas like watersheds (BC. Ministry of Forests, 1981).

In the end, none of the cornerstone initiatives had the kind of impact the government hoped for, largely because of the half-hearted or flawed implementation of these measures. To take some examples, the MOF's attempts to refurbish the image of sustained yield were

undercut in the early 1980s by recession-related moves to reduce
planned spending on intensive silviculture, and by revelations that the
Deputy Minister (Apsey) had directed staff to "sympathetically
administer" logging regulations in order to help companies experienc-
ing cash flow problems.[9] Doubts about the quality of forest management were later reinforced by sharp cutbacks in MOF staff levels and
by ongoing moves to "privatize" management responsibilities. Government restraint measures had a parallel impact on the MOF's attempts
to gain acceptance for its approach to integrated resource management. In the eyes of environmentalists, this approach was suspect
because it denied other agencies the statutory bases and resources
needed to bargain effectively with the MOF. In addition, attempts to
sell the approach were undermined at an early stage by an embarrass-
ing episode known as the Riley Creek affair (Bryant, 1983: 59-73;
Overstall, 1979-80). Thus, environmentalists were handed the ammunition needed to update continually their critique of forest management. Their assessment of the government's public involvement
measures was no more positive. By 1985, it was clear that most agreed
with the assessment offered by one of the province's most respected
environmentalists, Ken Farquharson (1984):

> Overall, the results of public participation in governmen-
> tal planning have been very limited, if you are an optimist or
> virtually zero if you are a pessimist. It is my opinion that
> public participation only really works where the conflicts
> being considered can be resolved by minor adjustments to
> logging or development plans and do not compromise the
> overall intent. Where a public group wishes to change a land
> use designation, such as to prohibit logging, I see the public
> participation process as a trap designed to exhaust the par-
> ticipants and to shield politicians and civil servants from
> discomforting confrontations.

As weak as the government's cornerstone initiatives were in the
eyes of environmental activists, they can be assumed to have had at
least some of the intended impact on other sectors of the public, helping
to win or hold support for the counter-offensive elements of the containment strategy. This part of the strategy combined a well-
publicized campaign against "single use withdrawals" with quieter
moves to secure MOF and industry control of the forest land base.

The MOF's glowing characterizations of the multiple use alternative were usually linked to dark predictions about the impact of single
use withdrawals. For example, in a 1983 speech to professional
foresters, Deputy Minister Apsey (1983) argued that the land base had
to be protected from unwise alienations:

The potential impact of land alienations on our forest land base is staggering. At present, province-wide, the ministry is faced with more than 200 resource use conflicts, each of which could have an adverse effect on the rate of harvest. If we fail to live up to our responsibilities in this area, if we permit the Balkanization of the forest land base into single-use fragments we will have failed in our most basic duty.

Using the multiple use concept as a rationalizing symbol, the MOF mounted a concerted campaign to bring as much land as possible under its jurisdiction. Following passage of the 1978 legislation it began a push to have Crown lands "... on which the optimum use is long term integrated management of renewable natural resources" incorporated into "Provincial Forests." This programme, it said, was "urgently needed" because "there are increasing demands for alienation and single uses" and because "the security afforded by provincial forest status will protect existing investments and provide the necessary climate for further investments in intensive management and utilization of our renewable resources" (BC. MOF, Planning Division, 1979).

The MOF's drive to incorporate land under the provincial forest designation coincided with tenure system changes that tightened the industry's grip on the resource. During the NDP's term (1972-75) the forest industry had begun to worry about the renewal of its existing tenures, particularly the TFLs due to expire in 1979. These concerns pretty well evaporated with the defeat of the NDP. Any residual doubts were removed with passage of the new Forest Act in 1978. This legislation is often regarded as having implemented the recommendations of the Pearse Royal Commission Report of 1976. But in drafting the new legislation, the minister ignored Pearse's calls for moderate increases in competitive bidding, opting instead to enhance the degree of security enjoyed by existing companies. The legislation extended the length of TFLs to 25 years and established a replacement procedure which allowed the TFL holder to obtain a new 25 year licence every ten years (Schwindt, 1979). Forest Licences, the new instrument for granting rights to Crown timber in the government-controlled Timber Supply Areas, would be for 15 years (rather than ten as suggested by Pearse), and those wanting to renew such licences would not have to face the sort of competition recommended by Pearse. The government clearly wanted to assure the major forest companies (the ten largest of which controlled nearly 60 per cent of all harvesting rights by 1975) that their hold was secure (Pearse: B7).

The government's determination to provide assurances regarding the sanctity of the tenure contract was also evident in a section of the new Forest Act which clarified tenure holders' rights where land or timber is withdrawn for purposes such as parks. Previously, rules regarding the compensation owed licence holders in such instances had been set out in individual tenure contracts but not in legislation (Pearse, 1976: 94-95). The new Act removed any doubts, providing that the licence holding company had to be compensated by the Crown if a withdrawal reduced its annual allowable cut by more than 5 per cent (BC. MOF, 1985: 21-2). According to the MOF, "this provision was required in order to ensure the security needed for investments in the logging industry" (BC. MOF, Planning Division: 9).

The 1978 legislation sent two clear signals to the environment movement. First, in no sense should it think of timber land as being "up for grabs" at renewal time. The state's commitments to tenure holders were, for all intents and purposes, in perpetuity; the government was under no obligation to re-examine land use options before granting a replacement licence.[10] Rather than using the tenure system review process as an opportunity to attain some additional flexibility for future governments, Social Credit further limited the options. Second, the new legislation made it explicit that withdrawals entailed a direct cost in the form of compensation. If the movement wanted to make a case for withdrawing forest land, then it had better be prepared to convince society that the benefits of preservation would outweigh the costs of compensating the company(ies) involved. The negotiations that have followed the declaration of the South Moresby national park reserve have made clear the potential magnitude of these costs. The federal and provincial governments have offered compensation of $31 million to Western Forest Products, the company holding TFL rights over part of the area. Western is apparently demanding at least $100 million.

We turn finally to those elements of the government's containment strategy apparent in its direct response to demands for wilderness preservation. Despite the government's campaign against forest land alienations, demands for wilderness preservation continued to grow after 1975. When Social Credit regained power the list of major proposals being pushed by preservation groups included South Moresby, the Tsitika-Schoen, the Stein, the Valhalla wilderness, and the Cascade wilderness. Over the next decade, areas such as the Khutzeymateen, the South Chilcotin wilderness, the Tahsish-Kwois, Meares, and the Carmanah were added to the agenda. The government resolved a number of these issues between 1975 and 1989, handing the environment movement a mixture of wins and losses. The Valhalla and South Moresby areas were preserved, the former by creation of a provincial park in 1983, the latter through the 1987 federal-provincial agreement to create a national park reserve. The Tsitika, the Tahsish-Kwois, and a large part of the original Cascade wilderness proposal area were opened for logging. A number of other issues, including the Khutzeymateen, Meares Island and the Stein, resisted resolution, the last two in spite of what appeared to be final pro-logging decisions.

The supporters of these and other proposals spent the years after 1975 engaged in "long marches through the institutions." [11]In every case, the campaign for preservation became an expanding multi-chapter story featuring innumerable battles over procedural and substantive issues. The Valhalla story is indicative. For the Valhalla Wilderness Society the creation of the park culminated a nine year effort marked by repeated campaigns for renewal of the logging moratorium placed on the area in 1974, a long struggle to persuade the parks branch of the area's worth, running battles over the claims and performance of the area's dominant logging company, and a major campaign to influence a provincial government-regional district planning process set up to address the Valhalla and other regional development issues. As well as dealing with the practical difficulties involved in lobbying officials in a provincial capital over 700 kilometers away, the Society's leaders faced numerous problems stemming from the closed nature of the decision-making system.

Public involvement mechanisms were tried out on most of the major wilderness conflicts (Wilson, 1987: 9-17). Usually this involved grafting an element of public participation onto the normal inter-agency advisory instruments; committees of officials were transformed into "planning teams," "task forces," and the like with the addition of representatives from companies, unions, and other interests, including in several instances, environmental groups and native bands. In a couple of high profile cases (Meares and the Tsitika) environmentalists won representation only after launching strong protests.

Adoption of the planning team approach involved a minimal concession to environmentalists. While some of the committees were given mandates broad enough to allow consideration of the preservation option, others were constrained by terms of reference that allowed only consideration of an integrated resource management plan, or that is, a plan premised on a prior decision to log and aimed at identifying ways to mitigate logging impacts. And the committees were strictly advisory. The government was careful to avoid any prior commitment to action (or to a timetable for action) in response to committee reports. In the face of these limitations, most environmental participants were left asking themselves whether the educational side benefits outweighed the costs in terms of time, out-of-pocket expenses, and frustration. Most, as we said, ended up adopting some variant of the cooptation thesis (Farquharson, 1984; George, 1981).

The mix of wilderness area decisions handed the environment movement was, of course, determined by a complex web of factors. (Indeed, the same could be said of any particular decision.) In general, the government recognized the political costs of denying all of the proposals. It knew that considerable political mileage could be extracted from decisions like those on the Valhalla and South Moresby. Although concessions like these did little to reduce the pressure exerted by proponents of other areas, they did allow the government to portray itself as having crafted a balanced outcome, one which cut a middle course between the demands of environmentalists and those of the industry.

The government's success in selling this interpretation has been abetted by its refusal to replace its piecemeal approach to dealing with wilderness proposals with a more comprehensive one. In a comprehensive approach, decisions about what to preserve would be derived from a process that combined, first, full assessment of the amount and distribution of different types of wilderness remaining, and second, an examination of the future benefits of (demand for) the wilderness resource. Calls for adoption of such an approach were commonplace by the mid-1980s. The argument was made, for example, by a number of those who appeared before the Wilderness Advisory Committee (WAC), the advisory body asked by the Minister of Environment in late 1985 to review 16 areas being considered for protected status and to examine boundary adjustments to 8 existing parks. The committee heard both strong criticism of the existing system (Fuller 1985:20, for example, noted that it allowed "continuing incremental destruction of wilderness ... before it is properly evaluated as a resource") and well-conceived blueprints for a comprehensive approach. Murray Rankin (1986: 10-22), Professor of Law at the University of Victoria, for example, suggested that a semi-permanent advisory committee be established with a mandate to evaluate a comprehensive inventory of possible wilderness areas to be drawn up by the Ministry of Environment.

The government has remained wary of such an approach. The decision to set up the WAC represented a small step in the direction of comprehensiveness, but the committee was asked to consider only a partial list of wilderness candidates. And following release of its report, the government reverted to piecemeal consideration while ignoring WAC's proposal for a permanent advisory body.[12]

There are no doubt a number of reasons why BC governments have been reluctant to adopt a comprehensive approach to wilderness decision-making. Most importantly, such a tack would run against the "incrementalist grain." Governments generally prefer to move in small steps, trying to minimize risks while retaining maximum room for political manoeuvre. Another reason is that a switch to a truly comprehensive approach would have markedly changed the way the wilderness issue was defined, making it difficult for the government to depict the mix of wilderness decisions it made as a balanced outcome. This point needs elaboration.

Wilderness politics has been "about" a list of preservation candidates nominated by the environmental movement, rather than about all of the province's remaining wilderness. This definition of the issue places environmentalists at a disadvantage. It obscures the fact that they are asking for preservation of only a small fraction of the remaining wilderness and it renders them vulnerable to attacks depicting them as greedy and unreasonable, to attacks which, for example, say: "We gave them South Moresby, now they want the Stein and the Carmanah—they want it all."

In order to understand the importance of the politics of agenda definition here we need only consider the very different political dynamics that would have operated had the game been about all of the province's remaining wilderness. It would have then been more apparent that in asking for preservation of the areas highlighted in its campaigns of the last decades, the movement was really just asking for a quarter-loaf (or indeed, for a crust). The movement would have been able to make more effectively the point that while it has been fighting to save a watershed here and an island there, the industry has continued to liquidate old growth wilderness, actually increasing the area clearcut each year from about 130,000 hectares (325,000 acres) per year in the early 1970s, to over 200,000 hectares (500,000 acres) per year by the mid-1980s (Pearse: 275; BC. Ministry of Forests and Lands, 1986-87: 52).

The environmental movement itself must bear some responsibility for the way the agenda has been defined. This agenda has reflected the movement's pluralism and geographical fragmentation—different groups throughout the province have simply nominated areas of special concern. It is probably also true that the logic of political mobilization confronting the movement has led it to concentrate on specific areas with strong emotional appeal rather than on wilderness preservation generally. However, the main force shaping the definition of the wilderness issue has been the government's approach, and its implications were not a totally unintended consequence.

Conclusion

The rise of forest environmentalism transformed the group structures surrounding BC's forest land use policy agencies. Forest industry monopolization of societal power became merely forest industry domination. Concertation became contested concertation. Prior to 1970, the forest industry had little difficulty identifying its interests regarding forest land use with the public interest; after 1970, its attempts to generalize this part of its ideology began to be challenged. Realizing that environmentalism threatened Social Credit's electoral support (or, if one would prefer, that new legitimation initiatives were required to maintain the conditions needed for capital accumulation), state managers responded with a rough-hewn containment strategy.

Accommodation played some part in this strategy. A desire to appease environmentalism contributed to a 25 per cent increase in the share of the land base in protected categories between 1975 and 1988, figuring particularly large in decisions to preserve South Moresby and the Valhalla wilderness. Pressure from environmentalists also helped to change the norms governing forest management, bringing a greater emphasis on the need for reforestation along with increased sensitivity to the impacts of logging on other resources. Fish and wildlife values received particular emphasis in the government's attempts to develop an integrated resource management (or multiple use) response to environmentalism.

Concessions to environmentalism were offered against a backdrop of moves designed to establish the MOF's place atop the bureaucratic pecking order and to consolidate the industry's hold on the land base. After 1976, the government adopted a MOF-centred concept of integrated resource planning, allowing the MOF to incorporate most Crown land into the provincial forest category, and rejecting alternative models of land use planning that would have given agencies with environmental protection mandates the resources needed to bargain on a "between equals" basis with MOF officials. Concurrent changes to the tenure system enabled the industry to tighten its grip on the province's forests. Despite increasing concern about the sustainability of the resource, the industry expanded operations, increasing by over 60 per cent the amount of land clearcut annually in the decade after 1976. Meanwhile, the state dealt with those wilderness preservation issues which the environmental movement managed to push onto the front burner, handing the movement some significant defeats as well as the victories just noted. The state continued to deal with such issues on a piecemeal basis, rejecting calls for a comprehensive approach to wilderness preservation, an approach which would have had some advantages for environmentalists.

This mix of outcomes is, in the final analysis, as much as forest environment groups could expect to accomplish given the resources the forest industry is able to invest in protecting the concertation pattern of policy-making. Indeed, much less would have been achieved had it not been for some special characteristics of the movement. Most importantly, the high level of issue commitment prevailing among group members helped to counteract shortages of other types of resources, enabling the movement to maintain lobbying and public relations efforts far stronger than would have otherwise been possible. It has also been argued that the diversity of groups making up the movement represented a significant strategic asset.

In contributing to a problematic definition of the wilderness issue, diversity also proved to be something of a liability for the forest environment movement. It cannot, however, be accepted that the movement consigned itself to a limited advocacy role by failing to develop a unified (or coordinated) front. It is true, as Coleman and Skogstad note in Chapter One, that a cohesive inter-group structure must be in place before groups can move beyond advocacy to policy participation. But this is only one of the preconditions necessary for such a transition in roles; key state actors would also have to be willing to grant the newcomers a meaningful policy participation role. In this case they were not. Forest environment groups have remained outsiders, able to achieve a modicum of success only because of their resourcefulness. These groups have translated gains made in terms of public consciousness into a fair bit of influence.

One future possibility is that environment groups will continue to make advances in changing public values, eventually bringing about a paradigm shift that would necessitate fundamental restructuring of forest land use policy-making patterns. Another possibility is that such a restructuring will be brought about as a result of other forces or events. An NDP victory, for example, might precipitate major change in the positions of various actors in the policy community. No new government, however, could ignore the measures the industry would use to protect its position, including threats of capital withdrawal. In addition, the NDP's strong links to the IWA would limit its willingness to engage in fundamental restructuring. A third and most likely possibility is a continuation of contested concertation; the MOF-inustry nexus will continue to protect its position through a combination of defensive manoeuvres and tactical retreats, with the latter element of the containment strategy likely to be more pronounced under an NDP government. The forest environment movement will continue to win some battles, but large-scale liquidation of old growth forests will proceed unabated.

Can the results of this case study be generalized to other corners of the environmental policy field? Caution is advised. This case had at least three elements which may not be replicated elsewhere.

First, the state's response to environmentalism was dictated here by a pro-business government which, in the middle of the period analyzed, embraced a "hypercapitalist" ideology of the sort which led other of its adherents to emphasize exclusion over accommodation as a response to reform groups (Amott and Krieger, 1982, cited in McCann, 1986: 235). And this case featured what we earlier termed raw, redistributive politics. Despite the presence of compensation clauses that appear to socialize costs (risks), the forest industry perceives itself to be involved in a high stakes battle against attempts to reallocate a pie already committed to it. If we take away any or all of these elements, we might expect different patterns of interest intermediation and policy-making. For example, without leaving BC or the groups considered, we would find something quite different were we to look at interactions between the Parks Branch and outdoor recreation groups on park use issues, or at interactions between the Wildlife Branch and the BCWF on wildlife management policy.

Second, what happened in this case was coloured by the fact that the environmental groups involved are numerous and geographically and programmatically diverse. In other matters of environmental politics, there is probably a greater likelihood of one group monopolizing representation or at least of there evolving a highly integrated coalition of the sort needed to strike and enforce binding agreements with state actors and competing interests. Given a willingness on the part of other actors, different policy-making arrangements could be expected.

Third, the developments observed here reflect the intensity of our groups' supporters, an aspect of the "logic of membership" which derives ultimately from the "once it's gone, it's gone" reality facing the wilderness movement. Although environmentalists are generally highly committed, we would not expect those engaged in normal budgetary or regulatory politics (such as campaigns for increased renewable energy funding or tougher pollution control enforcement) to be as zealous as wilderness campaigners. Differences on this dimension might have a number of implications. Perhaps most importantly, groups with less committed members might be vulnerable were state agencies to use promises of funding and access in order to induce groups to accept weak, "compromised" positions in corporatist arrangements.

Even this brief bit of speculation reminds us that in the environmental policy sector there may be almost as many patterns of interest intermediation and policy-making as there are environmental groups and issues. Indeed, it makes little sense to talk of an environmental policy sector. Over the past few decades environmental groups have pushed their way into dozens of sectors, forcing alteration of pre-existing state-industry relations. While most environmental groups appear to have accomplished versions of the "win some battles, but not the war" outcome chronicled here, differences in group characteristics and state-industry reactions obviously translate into a wide variety of outcomes. The latest wave of public concern over the environment may allow environmental groups to advance to new planes of achievement, but it is unlikely to iron out this variation.

References

Amott, Teresa and Joel Krieger (1982). "Thatcher and Reagan: State, Theory and the 'Hyper-Capitalist' Regime." *New Political Science,* 8: 13-26.

Apsey, T.M. (1983). Speech to the Association of BC Professional Foresters Annual Meeting, Kamloops, BC, 17 February 1983.

BC. Caucus of the Canadian Assembly on National Parks and Protected Areas (1985). Peter J. Dooling, Coordinator. *Parks and Protected Areas in British Columbia in the Second Century.* Vancouver.

BC. Ministry of Economic Development. Central Statistics Branch (1985). *British Columbia Economic Accounts, 1971-84.* Victoria.

BC. Ministry of Environment, Wildlife Branch (1986). *Report on the British Columbia Survey of Non-hunting and other Wildlife Activities for 1983.*

BC. Ministry of Forests (1980 and 1981). *Five Year Forest and Range Resource Program. Victoria.*

____ **(1981).** *Public Involvement Handbook.* Victoria.

____ **(1985).** "Brief to the Wilderness Advisory Committee."

____ **(1985a).** "Natural Areas, and Wilderness-Type Recreation Policy." A draft discussion paper released to the Wilderness Advisory Committee. (WAC 1058).

BC. Ministry of Forests and Lands (1986-87). *Annual Report.* Victoria.

BC. Ministry of Forests, Planning Division (1979). *Provincial Forests: A Discussion Paper.*

BC. Ombudsman of BC (1985). *The Nishga Tribal Council and Tree Farm Licence No. 1.* (Public Report No. 4). Victoria.

BC. Wilderness Advisory Committee (1986). *The Wilderness Mosaic.* Vancouver.

Berry, Jeffrey M. (1977). *Lobbying for the People: The Political Behavior of Public Interest Groups.* Princeton: Princeton University Press.

Bryant, Raymond L. (1983). "Federal-Provincial Relations in the Management of British Columbia's Fishery and Forestry Resources: Conflict and Cooperation in a Context of Growing Scarcity." Unpublished Honours B.A. Essay, University of Victoria.

Clark, Peter B. and James Q. Wilson (1961). "Incentive systems: A Theory of Organizations." *Administrative Science Quarterly,* 6.

COFI (Council of Forest Industries of British Columbia) (1988). *British Columbia Forest Industry Fact Book 1988.* Vancouver.

Dorcey, Anthony H.J. (1987). "The Management of Super, Natural British Columbia." *BC Studies,* 73: 14-42.

Drushka, Ken (1985). *Stumped: The Forest Industry in Transition.* Vancouver: Douglas and McIntyre.

Evans, Garth (1980). "Islands Protection Society et al. v. Minister of Forests et al.: Supernatural Goes to Court." *All Alone Stone,* IV: 623.

Farquharson, Ken (1984). "Public Participation: Lessons from the Failure." *The Sierra Report,* 3(3).

Fuller, Stephan (1985). "Wilderness: A Heritage Resource." Presented to the Wilderness Advisory Committee (WAC 383). With addendum (WAC 1106).

George, Paul (1981). "How to muzzle environmental critics." *Times Colonist,* 29 December.

Gitlin, Todd (1987). *The Sixties: Years of Hope, Days of Rage.* New York: Bantam.

Friends of Clayoquot Sound and Western Canada Wilderness Committee (1985). *Meares Island: Protecting a Natural Paradise.* Vancouver.

Handler, Joel F. (1978). *Social Movements and the Legal System: A Theory of Law Reform and Social Change.* New York: Academic Press.

Hays, Samuel E. (1987). *Beauty, Health, and Permanence: Environmental Politics in the United States, 1955-85.* Cambridge: Cambridge University Press.

Islands Protection Society (1984). *Islands at the Edge: Preserving the Queen Charlotte Islands Wilderness.* Vancouver: Douglas and McIntyre.

Jones, Trevor (1983). *Wilderness or Logging: Case Studies of Two Conflicts in BC.* Vancouver: FMCBC.

Lindblom, C.E. (1977). *Politics and Markets.* New York: Basic Books.

_____ **(1980).** *The Policy-Making Process* (2nd ed.) Englewood Cliffs: Prentice Hall.

McCann, Michael (1986). *Taking Reform Seriously: Perspectives on Public Interest Liberalism.* Ithaca, New York: Cornell University Press.

M'Gonigle, Michael and Wendy Wickwire (1988). *Stein: The Way of the River.* Vancouver: Talonbooks.

Milbrath, Lester (1984). *Environmentalists, Vanguard for a New Society.* Albany, N.Y.: State University of New York Press.

Overstall, Richard (1979-80). Essays on the Riley Creek affair. *Telkwa Foundation Newsletter*, 2(5), 2(6), 2(7), 3(1).

Pearse, Peter H. (1976). *Timber Rights and Forest Policy in British Columbia.* Report of the Royal Commission on Forest Resources (2 vols). Victoria: Queen's Printer.

Price Waterhouse. *The Forest Industry in British Columbia, 1986 and 1987.* Vancouver.

Pross, A. Paul (1986). *Group Politics and Public Policy.* Toronto: Oxford University Press.

Rankin, Murray (1986). "Submission to the Wilderness Advisory Committee." (WAC 779).

Roemer, Hans L., Jim Pojar and Kerry R. Joy (1988). "Protected Old Growth Forests in Coastal British Columbia." *Natural Areas Journal*, 8(3): 146-59.

Schmitter, Philippe C. (1982). "Reflections on Where the Theory of Neo-Corporatism has gone and where the Praxis of Neo-Corporatism may be going." In Gerhard Lehmbruch and Philippe C. Schmitter, eds. *Patterns of Corporatist Policy-Making.* Beverly Hills: Sage.

Schwindt, Richard (1979). "The Pearse Commission and the Industrial Organization of the British Columbia Forest Industry." *BC Studies*, 41: 3-35.

Sierra Club of Western Canada (1988). "Fact Sheet—BC Forests." Victoria.

Silva Ecosystem Consultants (1985). *Forest Management Practices in the Nass Valley: Summary of Technical Evaluation.* Nishga Tribal Council.

Smith, R.V. (1986). "Forest Land Use Planning and Management in British Columbia." Presented to the Wilderness Advisory Committee (WAC 855).

Sopow, Eli (1985). *Seeing the Forest: A Survey of Recent Research on Forest management in British Columbia.* Victoria: Institute for Research on Public Policy.

_____ **(1987).** "How to Lobby the Government." *BC Business*, July: 104-119.

Taylor, Serge (1984). *Making Bureaucracies Think: The Environmental Impact Statement Strategy of Administrative Reform.* Stanford: Stanford University Press.

Terpenning, John Gordon (1982). "The BC Wildlife Federation and Government: A Comparative Study of Pressure Group and Government Interaction for Two Periods, 1947-1957, and 1958 to 1975." Unpublished M.A. Thesis, University of Victoria.

Valhalla Wilderness Society (1988). *British Columbia's Endangered Wilderness: A Proposal for an Adequate System of Totally Protected Lands.* New Denver, BC: The Valhalla Society.

Van Liere, Kent D. and Riley E. Dunlap (1980). "The Social Bases of Environmental Concern: A Review of Hypotheses, Explanations and Empirical Evidence." *Public Opinion Quarterly*, 44: 181-97.

Wagner, William Leroy (1987). "Privateering in the Public Forest? A Study of the Expanding Role of the Forest Industry in the Managementof Public Forest Land in British Columbia." Unpublished M.A. Thesis, University of Victoria.

Wilson, Jeremy (1983). "Environmentalism and BC Natural Resources Policy: 1972-83." Presented to the Annual Meeting of the Canadian Political Science Association (CPSA). Vancouver.

_____ **(1987).** "Resolution of Wilderness vs. Logging Conflicts in British Columbia: a Comparison of Piecemeal and Comprehensive Approaches." Presented to the CPSA Annual Meeting, Hamilton.

_____ **(1987-88).** "Forest Conservation in British Columbia, 1935–85: Reflections on a Barren Political Debate." *BC Studies*, 76: 3-32.

Endnotes

1. It should be noted that most environmentalists regard the recreation area category as offering a second or third class form of protection against resource development.

2. For example, a comprehensive list of proposals developed by the Valhalla Wilderness Society (1988) called for the area protected to increase to 13 per cent. A list of 187 proposals compiled by the BC Caucus of the Canadian Assembly on National Parks and Protected Areas (1985) was estimated to involve an additional 3 per cent of the land base. See also Fuller (1985).

3. A concept which has always been the subject of debate, sustained yield is premised on the notion that it makes good economic sense to liquidate old growth forests (an asset whose value is static or wasting since the trees are no longer growing and possibly subject to disease and rot) so that land can be used to grow new crops. Land currently producing nothing thus begins to produce yearly increments of wood fibre. Considerable debate has focussed on how quickly the old growth should be liquidated. The general notion guiding BC's policy has been that old growth should be rationed to the industry so as to ensure that the last of the old growth is not harvested until second growth forests sufficient to support the industry are available. See Drushka, 1985: ch. 3; and Wilson, 1987-88.

4. There is a large literature (most of it focussing on American groups) on the class composition of the environmental movement. See for example, Milbrath, 1984: 76-78; Van Liere and Dunlap, 1980; and papers in the "Whither Environmentalism" symposium, Natural Resources Journal, 20 (1980).

5. For example a Decima survey of 1,000 British Columbians done in 1986 found that 19 per cent of those interviewed belonged to or financially supported an environmental group and that 12 per cent claimed membership in an outdoor group. (See "Study on Forestry Issues for the Canadian Forestry Service."). Estimates of the level of public sympathy can be deduced from evidence on outdoor and wildlife-related activities. For example, surveys conducted by the

BC MOE and the Canadian Wildlife Service in the early 1980s estimated that 70-75 per cent of British Columbians participated in some wildlife related activity in the previous year, with 23.5 per cent reporting at least one trip to observe wildlife. (See BC. Ministry of Environment, Wildlife Branch, 1986.) About 60 per cent of those polled in the Decima survey reported using forests for recreation very or fairly often, while BC park surveys indicate that about two-thirds of residents make at least one visit to a provincial park each year.

6. Here and in the next paragraph we parallel Lindblom's (1980:71) general arguments concerning "the privileged position of business" in liberal democratic systems.

7. Vancouver Sun, 19 May 1988; Forest Planning Canada 5(1) (January/February 1989), 5-8; and Alberta Report, 6 June 1988.

8. After receiving complaints, the CBC stopped running these ads in late 1988, ruling that they violated rules forbidding ads that attempt to influence public opinion on a contentious issue.

9. See Sopow, 1985: 67-68 and Forest Planning Canada, 1(4), 18. Some of the manifestations of this policy were illustrated in two reports on the management of TFL No. 1, both released in 1985. See Silva Ecosystem Consultants, 1985 and BC. Ombudsman of BC, 1985.

10. The absence of any such obligation was confirmed by the courts when the Islands Protection Society tried to challenge replacement of the TFL which covered much of the South Moresby Wilderness area. See Islands Protection Society: 134-36 and Evans, 1980.

11. Gitlin (1987) attributes the coinage to Rudi Dutschke.

12. See BC. Wilderness Advisory Committee, 1986: 26-27. Although WAC recommended a permanent Natural Areas Advisory Council, it stopped short of endorsing the critical part of Rankin's recommendation, that is, the suggestion that the advisory body should consider a comprehensive list of all possible wilderness areas.

CHAPTER SEVEN

OFFICIAL LANGUAGE MINORITIES AND THE STATE: DUAL DYNAMICS IN A SINGLE POLICY NETWORK

Leslie A. Pal

R ecent work on interest groups and public policy has focussed on policy communities consisting of state agencies and economic associations. Such an approach stresses the meso or sectoral level, urges a more disaggregated view of the modern state, emphasizes variables such as state autonomy and capacity, and poses several interesting models of organizational development of associations within sectors. In the first chapter of this volume, Coleman and Skogstad raise the question of how applicable these models are to non-economic associations and policy sectors. "Non-economic" in this context refers to associations whose members' interests are not *primarily* defined in terms of production or economic exchange, though, of course, their demands often have economic consequences.

This chapter argues that these models are generally applicable, but that caution must be exercised when they are used to analyze policy sectors defined primarily by concerns over citizenship and the mobilization of identity, such as language policy, multiculturalism, and gender equality. Models designed to deal with economic associations and their relationship to the state have at least four limitations when applied to the analysis, for example, of official language minorities in Canada. First, the ontological categories of "minority", "majority", and "official" are firmly rooted in concepts of citizenship and the nature of the political community. This characteristic of these categories inevitably enhances the impact of factors such as state capacity, autonomy, and tradition, since these are preeminently political or state categories. Second, associations that manoeuvre on the terrain of community and citizenship have, in the Canadian context (though I expect this applies in other countries as well), developed a rights-based discourse. Thus, the language of politics in this and similar sectors is significantly different from that in economic sectors, and the resolution of conflict will tend to occur in judicial as opposed to administrative institutions. Third, official language minority groups (OLMGs), like their counterparts in other social movements, are burdened by the collective action problems outlined by Olson (1965). One strategy of survival is to accept public funding, but this raises the question of cooptation and the degree to which these groups become mere instruments of government policy. Fourth, while OLMGs provide services, they are primarily designed to act as policy advocacy organizations, and often must be critical of the very agencies that provide them with financial support.

This chapter illustrates these points through an analysis of the evolution of Canadian policy towards OLMGs. It shows how the launching of the policy was directly linked to an intra-state crisis and a resultant statist strategy of national unity, and how the policy's subsequent trajectory was at best an example of severely compromised autonomy due to the factors outlined above. An additional factor, one that has only emerged clearly in recent years, is the extent to which federal policy towards linguistic minorities pertains largely to matters of provincial jurisdiction, such as education, and health and social services. By the late 1980s, a coherent policy network had emerged to deal with linguistic issues, but that single network had a dual dynamic. In Atkinson and Coleman's (1989) terms, one dynamic was "state-directed" while the other resembled "pressure pluralism". This dualism arises because official languages policy in Canada has always had the character of a revolution from above, with strong federal priorities about the development of linguistic communities and the provision of provincial services to help these communities survive. In this dynamic, Ottawa has deliberately aided advocacy organizations that support federal policy concerns in the provincial jurisdiction. But these advocacy organizations, although fiscally dependent on Ottawa, are not mere ciphers or clients. They, in turn, also pressure Ottawa for policy commitments that will further their interests as players in the network and as representatives of language minority communities.

Organization of the State

Responsibility for Canada's official policy of bilingualism rests with the Secretary of State of Canada (SSC), a department with an annual budget in excess of $3 billion. Most SSC spending is statutory, and the department's prime discretionary and policy activities lie in citizenship development (which includes disabled persons, natives, voluntary organizations, women and youth), multiculturalism, and official languages. The latter is in turn divided among (1) educational support programmes to the provinces and territories to facilitate the teaching of minority official languages at all levels, (2) translation services for the federal government, and (3) promotion of official languages. It is the final category that is the focus of this chapter, since it is the one that provides grants and support to OLMGs. Although there are several service delivery programmes within this broad category of promotion, the philosophical foundation of "promotion" lies in trying to shape the social landscape. Although Canada never officially adopted a policy of biculturalism to complement its policy of bilingualism, it was clear from the beginning (as we shall see below) that language could not be completely divorced from culture or from living communities. In this regard, a linguistic policy inevitably had to be a social policy in support of communities and identities, assisting their struggle against assimilation. But in addressing this objective, Ottawa would face another inevitability: it would have to help the advocacy organizations whose role it was to protect the political interests of their communities. Its main form of assistance to these organizations is grants.

Despite the contemporary importance of governmental support for advocacy groups, the antecedents to the 1969 *Official Languages Act* did not emphasize such support for interest groups. The Royal Commission on Bilingualism and Biculturalism (RCBB), for example, whose report laid the basis for the Official Languages Act, was virtually silent on the question of OLMGs, though it did touch obliquely on the question of community representation and the voluntary sector. With few exceptions, whenever the Royal Commission discussed linguistic minorities, it only looked at various communities comprising those minorities, and not at the organizations that might represent and lobby on behalf of those communities. Nowhere in its five volume report did the Commission recommend support for the groups that represented and sustained the linguistic minorities. In part, this approach may simply have been a reflection of the way in which the linguistic communities had represented themselves to the

Commission. For example, out of 404 individuals, associations and organizations that presented briefs to the Commission over its five year span, only 71 could be counted as francophone. More importantly, most of those were private companies (e.g., radio stations), educational institutions, and chambers of commerce (RCBB, 1965: Appendix III).

However, the Commission did not completely ignore the question of voluntary associations. Although it did not closely study businesses, trade unions or political parties, it did undertake some analyses of groups in the recreational and community fields. Its assumption was that Canadians participate in a wide variety of such organizations, and true equality between the linguistic groups would demand equitable opportunities to participate, openness of groups to minority needs, and some effort to foster cross-cultural and linguistic exchange. The Commission also assumed, however, that voluntary associations are by definition free, or largely free, of government constraint. It clearly did not want to treat the voluntary sector as just another transmission belt of government policy. "Voluntary associations are, by definition, private organizations catering to an enormous variety of interests of their members. In a free society they must be allowed to function with a very high degree of freedom" (RCBB, 1970: 128).

Canada's first Official Languages Act was passed in 1969, and closely followed most of the Royal Commission's recommendations. At its May 29, 1969 meeting the federal Cabinet approved new spending proposals for the Social Action Branch of the SSC, and by July 31, the Treasury Board had authorized an allocation of $1.3 million under this programme chargeable to the Official Languages Programme. The Social Action Branch was to spend this money in support of associations and organizations representing the interests of linguistic minorities, but as the programme title suggested, these expenditures were intended less for the traditional type of community based linguistic or cultural group than for the new ideal of "social animation." This policy was the genesis of the core funding programme described at the outset of this chapter. But how did it arise when the Royal Commission itself had made no reference to it, and indeed had appeared to cling to the classical liberal idea that voluntary associations were almost purely private, even though their activities had public effects? The answer to this question involves the nature of the SSC at the end of the 1960s, particularly its Citizenship Branch, the national unity crisis to which the Royal Commission on Bilingualism and Biculturalism was a response, and the decade's atmosphere of "social animation" and participatory democracy.

The Citizenship Branch of SSC had been created in 1945 out of the old Nationalities Branch of the Department of National War Services (Dreisziger, 1988; Pal, 1989). The role of the Nationalities Branch had been to encourage and facilitate domestic support for Canada's war effort among ethnic communities. Never well funded, the Branch was nearly disbanded at the war's end. Instead it was transformed into the Citizenship Branch in the hope that it might play a broader role in the integration of new immigrants into Canadian society. Without much money or staff, and buried in first the SSC (1945-1950), and then the Department of Citizenship and Immigration (1950-1966), the Branch did its work largely through liaison and education. In practice this task involved establishing and maintaining broad contacts with dozens of community service organizations, recre-ational groups, church affiliations, youth groups, and adult education agencies.

It is therefore not surprising that the Citizenship Branch played an active role in helping those same organizations, especially linguistic minority groups, prepare their presentations to the Royal Commission on Bilingualism and Biculturalism. As the Citizenship and Immigration Annual Report for 1963-64 noted:

> Bilingualism and biculturalism concern many volunteer organizations in Canada. In October 1963, the Branch (including many field officers), met the staff of the Royal Commission on Bilingualism and Biculturalism to discuss ways in which it could be of assistance to the Commission. As a result of these meetings, Liaison Officers worked with organizations studying topics related to the activities of the Commission, with groups planning to present briefs to the Commission, and with the staff of the Commission in organizing public meetings at the community level (Department of Citizenship and Immigration, 1964: 10).

Over the years the Branch's activities became so broad and amorphous that one official criticized it for becoming a "sort of generalized adult education and community service organization."[1] The Branch was almost disbanded at one point, but was saved by Québec nationalism and ultimately separatism, which forced both the Pearson and Trudeau governments to address directly the question of national unity. One of Pearson's responses was the Royal Commission on Bilingualism and Biculturalism; one of Trudeau's was a concerted federal strategy to encourage allegiance to national institutions, national symbols, and ultimately to the national political community. SSC, under Trudeau's friend, Gérard Pelletier, was to be the lead agency in this offensive. The Citizenship Branch, once it was transferred to the SSC, became ensnared in this agenda, and was perceived as possibly having a role to play in fostering national unity through the development of citizenship. As early as 1965, the Senior Liaison Officers in the Branch collectively agreed that Canadian unity was to be the "central concern of the Branch from which all our other work should be derived."[2]

In October 1969, Robert Stanbury was appointed Minister without Portfolio responsible for Citizenship and Information Canada, and he launched a comprehensive review of citizenship policy. In May 1970, the Cabinet approved five new broad objectives as the mandate of the Citizenship Branch within the SSC: the Branch would, first, "reinforce Canadian identity and unity"; second, "encourage cultural diversity within a bilingual framework"; third, "preserve human rights and fundamental freedoms"; fourth, "increase and improve citizenship participation"; and, fifth, "develop meaningful symbols of Canadian Sovereignty."[3] Bernard Ostry was appointed Under-Secretary of State for Citizenship in January 1970 and was encouraged by the Prime Minister himself to "shake up" the Branch and expand its role in promoting national unity (Jaworsky, 1979: 61).

A simple focus on national unity would not in itself have been enough to shift the Branch into a more activist stance, particularly in the area of group funding. For this to happen, there had to be a re-definition of the meaning of citizenship and a new articulation of the proper role and relationship of government to voluntary organizations. This re-definition had been gradually occurring since the early 1960s, but was given a tremendous boost with the idea of citizen participation. Indeed, Pierre Trudeau was able to capitalize on this change with his famous 1968 campaign phrase that the role of government was to foster a "Just Society."

The SSC of course was the logical place within which to house this new effort, at least insofar as it involved government funding of voluntary organizations that would in turn try to animate society. The Citizenship Branch in the SSC represented a "state capacity", in Skocpol and Finegold's terms (1982), for this sort of activity. In the 1950s, funding had been undertaken gingerly and reluctantly, even by politicians who might have been expected to see some political gain in it. However, year by year, the grant requests grew, as did the number and amount of grants. The Branch's view always was that it preferred to give project rather than core funding, and for the most part it held to this commitment. By 1966, for example, the Branch was dispensing $250,000 in grants to organizations and groups. One quarter of that amount went to native friendship centres. Only two organizations received sustaining grants. (The Canadian Citizenship Council and the Indian Eskimo Association each got $15,000.) These sustaining grants had been authorized by the Treasury Board on October 31, 1963. The remainder was distributed through supporting grants among 27 organizations (exclusive of groups involved in native issues) active in citizenship promotion and human relations.[4]

Grants under this category had been approved by Treasury Board in August 1962. The Branch, in short, was active in the granting area, but had expanded its efforts cautiously, in part because of the constant pressure it received from Treasury Board about spending monies that were not strictly authorized by statute.

Gérard Pelletier, appointed Secretary of State by Pierre Trudeau, wanted to apply the doctrines of the "Just Society" and "participatory democracy" to the cultural scene. Bernard Ostry describes how "the money flowed in and out. I was appointed Assistant Under Secretary of State for Citizenship shortly after Charles Lussier left for the Public Service Commission in January 1970. The Branch was supposed to develop and strengthen a sense of Canadian citizenship, chiefly through programs that would aid participation and assuage feelings of social injustice" (Ostry, 1978: 117).

Funding of OLMGs cannot be understood apart from this context, since virtually up to the threshold at which they began (mid-1969), they had been anathema to the very Branch of the SSC that was given the responsibility for administering them. But the new priority for national unity, the momentum created by the Official Languages Act, the atmosphere for support for community development and participatory democracy, and the new personnel with new ideas together provided the impetus for public funding of OLMGs. Clear evidence of the importance of this context is that the OLMG financing was not originally part of the bilingualism programme in the SSC at all. It was a component of a larger Social Action branch that paralleled the Citizenship Branch's activities in providing project grants to voluntary organizations. The difference was that the Social Action branch also deliberately provided core funding for provincial associations.

In 1969, the SSC received responsibility for the official languages programme, creating four new branches that reported to the Assistant Under Secretary of State: bilingualism programmes branch, social action branch, language administration branch, and research and planning branch. The objectives of the Social Action Branch were, "to ensure that official language minorities continue to flourish and to encourage their participation in Canadian society without the risk of losing their identity; and to promote a better understanding between the two official language communities" (SSC, 1964: 4). The Branch came into operation in August, 1969, and immediately launched programmes in several provinces. The 1970 Annual Report noted that "an attempt is being made to meet the needs of associations and agencies whose objectives correspond to those of the government as defined above. Organizations and groups receiving grants must play a part in carrying out their own projects" (SSC, 1979: 4). In addition to sustaining funds, the Branch was prepared to make funds available for the following activities and projects:

- cultural exchanges organized for the purpose of bringing cultural events to isolated communities;

- social animation programmes designed to encourage communities to play a greater role in their own social and cultural development;
- seminars and conferences enabling cultural and regional groups to exchange views on such subjects as bilingualism and national unity;
- youth activities which meet the special needs of young people;
- cultural centres whose activities enrich the cultural heritage of isolated groups;
- international participation enabling heads of organizations to participate in international conferences and events;
- special or national projects designed to assist national and ethnic organizations and special or experimental programmes which do not fall under the previous categories (SSC, 1970: 4).

During 1969-70, 109 grants were approved for a total of $1,015,680 (though this included Citizenship Branch grants before the Social Action branch was established). Under the sustaining grants component, provincial associations received $115,600 in direct aid. The social animation component gave eight provincial associations grants amounting to $312,621 (SSC, 1970: 5). The 1970 Report on the Social Action Branch described the latter as "a programme which, by utilizing the services of professionally trained community development officers, attempted an in-depth attack on mass apathy and, concentrated, during the past months, on sensitizing and preparing confirmed or potential leaders through group dynamic sessions and leadership training courses" (Social Action Branch, 1970: 5). The report claimed to have involved over 20,000 people at the community level in such sessions.

The 1969-70 policy design remained in place for the next twenty years, though under the new Official Languages Act passed in 1988, the support of official language communities was given a higher status and increased funding. The government's 1988 Funding Manual makes it very clear that the Official Language Communities (OLC) programme is intended to be proactive, to help change institutions and attitudes, and not simply deliver services. It is also clear that the instruments for this goal are to be, in part, advocacy organizations that happen to agree with the government's policy vision.

The Funding Manual poses the following as the overriding objective of the OLC programme: "To make Canadians aware of the country's linguistic duality and to help non-federal public administrations and the private sector set up and deliver adequate services to minority official language communities" (SSC, 1988: v.1.1.). Along with assistance for the "creation, development and maintenance" of institutions, the Manual envisages assistance "to organizations for lobbying activities." Eligible applicants are non-profit organizations, non-governmental institutions (established, non-profit, and not under the control of any government), provincial/territorial/municipal governments, and individual persons. The section on lobby groups shows that the programme is prepared to encourage a broad range of activities.[5]

An interesting feature of the activities is that virtually all pertain to items in provincial jurisdiction. One of the less appreciated aspects of Canada's *federal* policy of bilingualism is how much of it must be directed at *provincial* services like education. This property arises, in part, because of the dual nature of the policy: the provision of bilingual services by the federal government throughout the country and the nurturing of linguistic communities. The former can be done with institutional changes and the development of services by federal agencies; the latter depends to a great degree on creating a supportive economic, social and linguistic environment at the local level. The conflicts between francophone minorities and western provincial governments as well as the battles over the linguistic rights of anglophones in Québec illustrate the problem. In all these cases, the linguistic minorities, with the aid of Ottawa, were targeting provincial language policies that they claimed made it difficult if not impossible for them to thrive as communities.

The Associational System

The associations in this policy area exist to serve their respective communities, and so can only be understood in terms of the history and current distribution of those communities. Because these individual histories would take us too far afield, we note simply that each province has a long standing linguistic minority. The English in Québec can trace the existence of an organized community of British origins back to 1763, and Acadians in the Maritimes and French-speaking minorities in Ontario and the West have roots in the earliest French settlements and explorations connected to the fur trade. According to the 1986 Census, out of a total of 25 million Canadians, 15 million list English as their mother tongue and 6 million list French. Of those 6 million French speakers, however, only about 838,000 or 14 per cent live outside Québec. The largest numbers of Francophones outside of Québec live in Ontario (422,770 or 4.6 per cent of the provincial population) and New Brunswick (223,675 or 31.8 per cent of the provincial population). In the other provinces they range from a low of 0.3 per cent of the population in Newfoundland to a high of 4.2 per cent in Manitoba. Anglophones in Québec account for 8.9 per cent of the provincial population, but three-quarters of them live in Montreal, where they make up almost 20 per cent of the city's population. These statistics are based on the province's mother tongue, but the 1986 Census also provided information on language spoken at home. If this measure is used to gauge the size of the official language minority groups outside Québec, they are even smaller, dropping in some cases (Saskatchewan and Alberta) by more than half (Statistics Canada, 1989: Table 1).

The associational system built around these communities may be divided into three tiers (SSC, 1983: 47-48). The first includes nation-wide umbrella groups, consisting principally of la Fédération des francophones hors Québec (FFHQ), la Fédération des jeunes canadiens-français, la Fédération nationale des femmes canadiennes-françaises, la Fédération culturelle des canadiens-français, and l'Association de la presse francophone hors Québec. The second tier consists of province-wide organizations that represent the minority language communities. These ten organizations are: la Fédération des francophones de la Terre-Neuve et du Labrador, la Société St-Thomas d'Aquin, la Fédération des Acadiens de la Nouvelle-Ecosse, la Société des Acadiens du Nouveau-Brunswick, l'Alliance Québec, l'Association canadienne-française de l'Ontario, la Société franco-manitobaine, l'Association culturelle canadienne-française de la Saskatchewan, l'Association canadienne-française de l'Alberta, la Fédération des Franco-Colombiens. The third tier is virtually uncountable, and con-sists of hundreds of community based organizations such as day care centres, festivals, youth clubs, home and school associations, and so on. These exist primarily as service organizations, and are actors in the policy network.

Many of the organizations in the first and second tiers have long histories, though the character of the political activity has changed in the last twenty years. L'Association canadienne-française de l'Ontario, for example, can trace a continuous organizational history back to 1910, when its forerunner was established to fight for francophone educational rights. Education was also the original core concern of la Société franco-manitobaine (established 1916) and l'Association canadienne-française de l'Alberta (established 1926). Other organiza-tions are of more recent vintage. L'Alliance Québec was created only in 1982, with the amalgamation of several Anglophone organizations. The FFHQ was formed in the mid-1970s to provide national repre-sentation for the provincial francophone minorities.

These provincial organizations share several broad characteristics that distinguish them from analogous associations in the economic sphere. First, although most of them were originally established to fight for educational rights, since the 1960s they have increasingly tried to represent the broad political, social and cultural interests of their communities. Second, as their names suggest, the linguistic minorities have increasingly developed a regional identity as, for the francophone communities, the pan-Canadian bonds of religion and connections to a Québec "homeland" have diminished. Third, among the francophone groups, the linguistic communities that they represent are so small and the tasks they set for themselves so broad that they have had little choice but to depend on government financial assistance. As the previous section showed, this assistance became a formal part of federal policy after 1970, and programmes have been developed to fund groups in all three tiers.

In 1987-88 there were two broad categories of grants that appeared to support hundreds of organizations and projects. The first programme category, Promotion of Official Languages (POL, component 2210), gave up to about $20,000 with an average of around $3000 for translation services. The Alzheimer Society of Canada, Canadian Meat Council and the Fraternity of Canadian Astrologers, for example, each got small grants for translation of conference proceedings. By contrast, Canadian Parents for French received over $132,000 in this grant category. The second category, Official Language Communities (OLC, component 2220), provided the operational funding for key organizations. In 1987-88, the POL (National Projects) funded 360 separate projects, for a total approved amount of $7,389,636. Most of these projects were for translation services for conferences and exhibitions, and bilingualism development plans. The only group to receive operational funding, as opposed to project funding for the implementation of a bilingualism programme or the translation of a conference, was Canadian Parents for French. It received $132,525 in operational funding for 1987-88, plus $39,525 in supplementary grants, for a total of $172,050. Canadian Parents for French also received federal funding in every province except Québec. In five regions—Newfoundland, Nova Scotia, Saskatchewan, Alberta, and British Columbia/Yukon—the organization is a key player on a short list of recipients. Once the total grants are adjusted to exclude transfers to governments for translation services, Canadian Parents for French is the recipient of between one-half and all grants to non-governmental organizations. In some cases—Nova Scotia, Saskatchewan, and British Columbia/Yukon—it is the only recipient in this category. This finding suggests that the Promotion of Official Languages Programme of the Secretary of State is largely the funding vehicle of one organization: Canadian Parents for French. Under the OLC programme, the five national groups listed earlier managed to capture 60 per cent of all grants and contributions for national groups.

The FFHQ received one-fifth of the total. At the regional level, the ten organizations (out of almost 300 applicants) listed earlier captured just under 40 per cent of available funding.

These data show that the core of the POL and the OLC programmes consists of support for organizations representing the interests of OLMGs, through Canadian Parents for French lobbies for French language instruction and immersion programmes for non-francophones. While at first glance the number of grants and groups seems high, in fact there is substantial concentration of funding for the main francophone and main anglophone organizations in and outside of Québec.

The contours and nature of organized interests and the state in the language policy field thus show some curious features. First, although there are over 300 groups that receive state support through the POL and OLC, the main actors (in terms of representatives of the linguistic communities themselves) in fact consist of six national associations (the five listed earlier and Canadian Parents for French) and ten regional ones. Second, these organizations are explicitly oriented towards policy advocacy, and not merely service provision. Third, these organizations receive millions of dollars of operational and project funding from Ottawa, and this support constitutes a major source of revenue for the groups. For example, the 1987-88 annual reports of leading francophone organizations show that the proportion of revenues accounted for by federal grants is quite high: FFHQ (83%); la Fédération nationale des femmes canadiennes-françaises (91%); l'-Association canadienne-française de l'Ontario (49%, with another 40% from the Ontario provincial government); la Société franco-manitobaine (84%).

Since much of the advocacy of these federally supported groups is aimed at provincial governments, it would appear to point to a state-directed paradigm wherein Ottawa controls, or at least heavily influences, a range of groups that press for changes in policies within jurisdictions from which Ottawa is constitutionally barred. However, the history of the OLMG programme, and the complaints from the organizations themselves, as well as information from such respected sources as the Commissioner of Official Languages, suggest a more complex and compromised picture.

The Evolution of the Policy Network, 1970-88

In the early 1970s, it clearly appeared as though Ottawa, through the Social Action Branch, was taking a strong lead in shaping the associational system, reaching out to stimulate interest and assist groups to form and lobby. The programme's guiding principles did indeed reflect an activist orientation of statism, but they also were hedged by incantations of traditional liberal ideas of the autonomy of social actors in the voluntary sector. In this sense the programme was assumed to be both pro-active and reactive.

The kind of social action undertaken by the Social Action Branch is non-directive in nature, i.e., it seeks to respond to the needs of the groups with which it works and to strengthen, support and improve the quality of the work undertaken by associations or organizations which have similar objectives and which make a contribution to the Programme objectives. Where organizations or programmes do not exist that can respond to specific social and cultural needs the Social Action Branch may initiate action on its own (Social Action Branch, 1970: 2).

This statement reflected the ambivalence at the heart not just of the OLMG programme but the other citizenship development programmes that were operating at the time or would emerge shortly to support youth, women, ethnic minorities, and community groups. The prevailing Canadian tradition of state/civil society relations in respect of the associational system had, until the late 1960s, been grounded in classic liberal principles about the autonomy of the voluntary sector. Faced with a regime crisis and new ideas about the stimulative role of the state vis-à-vis social change, programmes were developed that involved a much more direct state presence, and for the first time, an established practice of sustaining grants for advocacy organizations. But the new mode could not completely replace the old tradition, and so the two coexisted uncomfortably within the SSC. By 1974 the regime crisis seemed to have passed, the issue of fiscal constraint was rising on the public agenda, and many of the key defenders of social action programmes (for example, Pelletier and Ostry) had left the SSC. The OLMG programme was sufficiently entrenched that it was in no danger of dissolution, but these changing circumstances did pose the threat of tepid support and inconsistent policy development. That is precisely what happened over the next 15 years.

The SSC was reorganized into three major sectors in 1974: Cultural Affairs, Citizenship and Corporate Management. The responsibility for the OLMG programme (which until the previous year had been designated simply as the Social Action Programme) was transferred from Cultural Affairs to Citizenship. The OLMG programme still had the same components: aid to provincial associations (purely operational grants); social animation (develop group pride in heritage and so on); French-English relations; cultural centres; cultural exchanges; youth activities; special and national projects; and international participation. In 1975 an OLMG Directorate was established within the Citizenship Sector of the SSC. Its expenditures amounted to $2.9 million. The original 1969 allocation to the programme had been $1.3 million (of which only $1 million was spent), and so over six years the budget had barely tripled. In 1975, the Multiculturalism Directorate spent $2.2 million, and SSC allocated $3.6 million to the Student Community Service Program (SSC, 1975: 24, 31).

This apparent low priority for OLMGs was reversed to some extent in the next five years. There were two key stimulants. The election of a separatist government in Québec raised the question of national unity once again, and Ottawa realized the advantages of a statist strategy of fostering linguistic minority communities. The other stimulant came from the client groups themselves. It would have been surprising, even with the small resources devoted to social animation, if sustaining grants to provincial OLMGs and leadership training had not had some mobilizing effect. The Official Languages Act and the federal policy of bilingualism had created a policy commitment that could be criticized, and had helped to institutionalize the critics by supporting groups whose main purpose lay in seeing expansions in the programme. As Keith Spicer, the Official Languages Commissioner noted in his 1976 Annual Report:

> Federal policy and funding have also enabled the provincial associations to emerge as more useful pressure groups. In Ontario, New Brunswick and Manitoba, to cite only the strongest, these groups now command attention from press and government, even if their views must always be fought for. In 1976, on advice from the report *C'est le temps ou jamais* (It's Now or Never) commissioned by the Secretary of State, the Government encouraged creation of a national common-front body called the Fédération des francophones hors Québec (FFHQ). This body, with extremely limited means, is already doing its job well by shaking up quite a few people in Ottawa (Official Languages Commissioner, 1976: 9).

The following year, the new Commissioner, Max Yalden, was even more critical of the SSC, calling it "Characters in Search of an Author": "After eight years of dealing with the official languages and official language minority groups, it appears that the Secretary of State's Department is still wondering where it is going and how it will get there" (Official Languages Commissioner, 1977: 22). The Commissioner noted acerbically that "present misunderstandings result in considerable measure from a virtual breakdown of reasonable human intercourse between a government agency and a group it is designed to serve"(Official Languages Commissioner, 1977: 24).

The government responded in a variety of ways to the new situation and the new criticisms. First, in its 1977 Throne Speech it promised to develop a new "comprehensive policy for official-language minorities." Second, in October the Secretary of State (John Roberts) announced that resources for linguistic minorities would increase from $30 million to $75 million over the next five years. Third, at the end of the year, the SSC established a consultative mechanism to communicate with OLMGs. An interdepartmental committee, chaired by the Assistant Under Secretary of State, would report biannually to the Secretary of State. Regional officers were designated to act as channels of communication for the OLMGs (Official Languages Commissioner, 1977: 22). Over the next three years, the OLMG programme was shifted around various sectors and branches of SSC, to settle finally as Citizenship and Official Languages in 1981.[6] In 1979 the programme helped in the formation of the Council of Québec Minorities, which in 1982 came together with other groups to form Alliance Québec (Malvern, 1985: 205). In 1980, the FFHQ received pilot money to establish, through training sessions, new francophone associations, and the next year it enjoyed the right of regular meetings with the SSC (SSC, 1980-81: 15-16). Despite these efforts, a 1980 Departmental Task Force noted that "some Sector staff question its *raison d'être*, its underlying philosophy" (Secretary of State of Canada, 1980: 4). In his 1980 Annual Report, the Official Languages Commissioner characterized the SSC's activities in the OLMG areas as a "mixed bag of piecemeal reactions to community pressures interspersed with heavy insinuations that father knows best" (Official Languages Commissioner, 1980: 19).

In part, the problem was linked to the success of the OLMG programme itself, as illustrated in the fortunes of the FFHQ. The passage of the Official Languages Act and the establishment of the Social Action Program in 1969 had refocussed OLMG energies and directed them to the national level. The FFHQ itself noted that with Ottawa's involvement, the provincial associations gained both the confidence and resources to tackle a whole range of problems concerning the economy, education, community development, communications, and social policy. It was possible, in short, to begin to elaborate "une stratégie globale" (FFHQ, 1981: 1). Provincial OLMG lobbying led the SSC to establish a Working Group on linguistic minorities that in 1975 released the report entitled *C'est le temps ou jamais*. The recommendations urged better consultative structures between the OLMGs and the SSC, and in November the FFHQ, as an umbrella association for the nine provincial associations, was established. The FFHQ took it upon itself to follow through on the other recommendations of the Working Group's report, but it was clearly intended to change the contours of the policy field in two ways.

First, as already indicated, the FFHQ would concentrate on "global" strategies for the language issue. This decision meant designing an approach that would integrate all elements of community life around language and culture, rather than isolating them as discrete components that might be addressed by other means. In practical terms, such an approach implies control over education and the adoption of French as an official language in each of the provinces. The FFHQ's goals have led the organization to the forefront of defining the linguistic issue in terms of fundamental rights rather than as simply a technical matter of services. For the FFHQ, any government service, whether it be education or community development, must be grounded in the "fundamental guarantees" of individual and collective rights inscribed in the Constitution (FFHQ, 1981: 6-7). Second, the FFHQ was designed to loosen the paternalism of the SSC and develop direct consultative mechanisms wherein the provincial associations and the FFHQ would become partners in policy development. In practical terms, this decision has meant demands for regular meetings at senior levels, and ultimately for some form of tripartite policy group comprised of politicians, senior administrators and representatives of the FFHQ.

The FFHQ has had some notable successes in its short history. In November 1977, the organization persuaded the Québec government, through the Ministère des affaires intergouvernementales, to provide it with financial and technical support.[7] It issued several well publicized reports on the status of French minority communities in Canada, and in late 1979 reached a tentative agreement with the federal Conservative government to establish a joint commission of government and OLMGs to oversee language policy development. However, after the February 1980 election, the new Liberal government declined to follow through with the idea. Nevertheless, over the next several years an informal system of quarterly meetings between the government and the FFHQ emerged. This organization was involved in consultations over the new Official Languages Act (Bill C-72) proclaimed on September 15, 1988. The FFHQ has been a persistent critic of federal bilingualism policy and provincial educational policies, and has acted to forge contacts with other groups in the linguistic policy field such as Canadian Parents for French and Alliance Québec. Perhaps its greatest recent success was the new Official Languages Act which contained a new and stronger commitment to OLMGs and government support for them. In testimony before the Standing Joint Committee of the Senate and of the House of Commons in September 1988, however, Secretary of State, Lucien Bouchard illustrated the ambiguities and difficulties that even this modest victory entailed.

In his introductory remarks, Minister Bouchard acknowledged that most of the priorities of the official language communities (for example, social, cultural, and communications services) came under provincial jurisdiction (Standing Joint Committee, 1988: 16). In the course of Committee questioning, Bouchard noted how the government had recently committed itself to spending an additional $4 million on OLMGs, though the exact funding formula had not been decided. The anglophone minority group in Québec has roughly the same population as all francophone minority groups outside of Québec, and yet gets only 1/8 of the available funding. This turned out to be a somewhat contentious item in the Minister's presentation, but his defence was that these were historical funding patterns and that the needs of francophone minorities were greater because of their dispersion and size. The Minister preferred to focus on the new money that would be available, suggesting that it would probably be distributed as an across-the-board increase of 10 per cent for all groups, with some getting slightly more depending on circumstances. In addition, there would be "a development fund which will allow us to finance ad hoc projects on their merit, not according to geographical, ideological, linguistic or ethnic considerations, but on merit" (Standing Joint Committee, 1988: 23). While this strategy of mixed funding went back to the earliest days of the programme, it had another rationale: "We are, of course, interested in adjusting the core funding, but we would not like to create a bureaucracy inside each organization. We would not like to have many Ottawa governments everywhere in Canada" (Standing Joint Committee, 1988: 28). There could be only one Ottawa government, which while it might consult with the OLMGs (as it did in the Alberta and Saskatchewan cases dealing with provincial accommodations to linguistic minorities), would have to be alone at the negotiating table with its provincial counterparts.

Conclusion

The associational system for official language minorities in Canada has evolved into a paradoxical and curious creature. The FFHQ has received government funding from both federalists and separatists. The federal government has provided core funding for organizations that it then persistently has been reluctant to integrate into its policy making machinery. These same groups, most of them sorely dependent on federal largesse for operations and projects, have become the most articulate critics of a policy that seems suspended between the simple provision of services and the social support of living human communities. What began as "social action" ended in a Minister worrying about creating two many little Ottawas around the country. In terms of Atkinson and Coleman's schema of policy networks (Atkinson and Coleman, 1989), this pattern does not fall clearly into any of the three variants of pluralism (pressure, clientele, or parentela). The state is sufficiently well-organized at the federal level to be more than reactive, and it clearly seized the initiative in the late 1960s. This would seem to place the linguistic associational system into the state-directed category. State decision-making capacity is "concentrated and well-coordinated." But the history of the development of policy and the associational system encrusted around it suggests that there has been a progressive attenuation in the state's directive and dominating role. In short, while the categories are useful, they do not capture the *dynamics* of policy development within a field, wherein the policy network may evolve from one form to another, or indeed show evidence of different dynamics operating simultaneously.

These differing dynamics arise in part from the tension between factors that tend to encourage state autonomy and those that tend to constrain it. The former would include the "regime crises" of the late 1960s and in 1976, when federal politicians perceived real threats to national unity, indeed national existence, in Québec. The existence of the Citizenship Branch and its practices of community development provided a capacity (though a somewhat anemic one) that could then be used by state actors to shape the social landscape. A sense of crisis engendered by a threat that struck at the very existence of the state itself was twinned with a pro-active philosophy of "social animation." That phrase itself conjures an image of the body politic lying inert and cramped on a cold slab, ready to have its stiff limbs exercised back into life through bureaucratic interventions. The whole enterprise was made easier by the fact that the pre-existing associational system was so weak. Francophone minorities outside of Québec had few resources to devote to community development, and their representative institutions faced all of the classic problems of collective action because they were trying to fight for almost pure public goods.

If the contemporary policy field began with a network that might be best described as statist, it was not uninhibitedly so. Constraints were operating then and in some respects even increased as the years passed. The Citizenship Branch, for example, had wrestled with the question several times during its early history, and had evolved a practice that reflected fairly classical notions of the separation of the state and civil society. At the macro level, even today, this is the prevailing structure that sets the boundaries for policy interventions that involve a degree of statism. Canadians have to justify departures from this framework at the meso-level, and they have become quite imaginative defenders of state action. But by 1975, the OLMG programme was stalled, no one spoke seriously anymore of "social animation," and new organizations like the FFHQ were coming on to the scene to demand more "global" policies. The context had changed. The national unity crisis that seemed so pressing in 1969 had abated, and the participatory discourse had been overwhelmed by fiscal restraint and some doubts about administrative hubris. But while the state's warmth towards the organizations it helped support had dissipated, the organizations themselves, as a result of state funding, were now able to organize and lobby. Increasingly, since the terrain of policy had shifted so clearly to the federal level, they oriented themselves to the federal government, leading to the formation of the FFHQ. The OLMG programme received a slight boost again in 1976 with the PQ provincial election victory, but Ottawa knew that the battlefield, for several years at least, would be in and not outside, Québec. With the referendum defeat and the constitutional negotiations in 1980-82, the sense of crisis abated again, and the OLMG programme remained mired at the margins of Ottawa's bilingualism policy. Even the recent increase in core funding is modest, and hedged with project grants to give Ottawa flexibility.

Therefore, the contemporary OLMG policy network began in a highly statist mode and, while it retains statist characteristics, also shows increasing evidence of pressure pluralism. Although the OLMGs are fragmented, confined to policy advocacy, and fiscally dependent on Ottawa, with Ottawa's help they have grown in prominence and become more developed organizations in the last twenty years. Moreover they speak with the legitimacy of representatives of whole communities striving to maintain distinct identities. This political project makes it virtually impossible for Ottawa to direct significantly the policy network. It was able to do this for conjunctural reasons in the early 1970s, but its own policy helped create a political terrain upon which unrestricted movement was no longer possible, despite the apparent weakness of the OLMGs and their client status. There is now more of a balance between state and civil society. The OLMGs are advocacy organizations, and, moreover, see themselves as fighting for the very survival of their communities. Ottawa's official policy is sufficiently ambiguous to give the groups ample opportunity to criticize the government. The logic of the relation of sponsor and client in this case leads to antagonism. Ottawa finds the OLMGs useful at the provincial level in pressuring governments for policy changes consistent with federal aims, but most of these aims involve provincial services. This logic leads groups to demand that they be at the negotiating table, and Ottawa to resist fragmentation of its authority.

Ottawa's paradoxical weakness in the policy area is clear; discontinuation of support to the OLMGs is all but inconceivable. The groups are useful not only in a practical political sense, but also because an official languages policy that does not help official language communities becomes nonsensical. Moreover, the policy field has developed around the concept of linguistic rights, articulated in the early 1970 and now enshrined in the Charter. A rights-based discourse has given the OLMGs opportunities to pursue their interests in the courts, though not always successfully. The point is not how successful they are, but rather that one of the key "sites" of policy development is no longer clearly under the government's control. The linguistic policy network therefore promises to become even more complex over the next decade, and the liaison between Ottawa and the OLMGs more uncomfortable.

References

Atkinson, M. M. and W. D. Coleman (1989). "Strong States and Weak States: Sectoral Policy Networks in Advanced Capitalist Economies." *British Journal of Political Science,* 19: 47-65.

Department of Citizenship and Immigration (1964). *Annual Report.* Ottawa.

Dreisziger, N. F. (1988). "The Rise of a Bureaucracy for Multiculturalism: The Origins of the Nationalities Branch, 1939-1941." In Norman Hillmer, Bohdan Kordan, and Lubomyr Luciuk, eds. *On Guard for Thee: War, Ethnicity, and the Canadian State, 1939-1945.* Ottawa: Canadian Committee for the History of the Second World War, Directorate of History, Department of National Defence: 1-29.

FFHQ (1981). *La fédération des francophones hors Québec: son origine, son orientation, ses membres, ses objectifs, ses programmes.* Ottawa: FFHQ.

Jaworsky, John (1979). A Case Study of the Canadian Federal Government's Multiculturalism Policy. Unpublished M.A. Thesis, Carleton University.

Malvern, Paul (1985). *Persuaders: Influence Peddling, Lobbying and Political Corruption in Canada.* Toronto: Methuen.

Official Languages Commissioner (1976). *Annual Report.* Ottawa: Ministry of Supply and Services.

Official Languages Commissioner (1977). *Annual Report.* Ottawa.

_____ **(1980).** *Annual Report.* Ottawa: Ministry of Supply and Services.

Olson, Mancur (1965). *The Logic of Collective Action.* Cambridge, Mass.: Harvard University Press.

Ostry, Bernard (1978). *The Cultural Connection: An Essay on Culture and Government Policy in Canada.* Toronto: McClelland and Stewart.

Pal, Leslie A. (1989). "Identity, Citizenship and Mobilization: The Nationalities Branch and World War II." *Canadian Public Administration,* 32: 407-26.

Royal Commission on Bilingualism and Biculturalism (1965). *Preliminary Report,* Appendix III. Ottawa: Queen's Printer.

_____ **(1967).** *Report,* Volume 1, Book 1. Ottawa: Queen's Printer.

Secretary of State of Canada (1964). *Annual Report.* Ottawa.

_____ **(1970).** *Report,* Volume 5, Book 1. Ottawa: Queen's Printer.

_____ **(1970).** *Annual Report.* Ottawa.

_____ **(1975).** *Annual Report.* Ottawa.

_____ **(1979).** *Annual Report.* Ottawa.

_____ **(1980).** *Report of the Task Force on Improving Certain Aspects of the Administration of the Official Languages and Citizenship Programs.* Ottawa.

_____ **(1980-81).** *Annual Report.* Ottawa.

_____ **(1983).** Program Evaluation Directorate, *Evaluation Report of the Official Language Minority Groups Program (OLMG), 1970-82.* Ottawa.

Secretary of State of Canada (1988). *Grants and Contributions Manual, 1988.* Ottawa.

Skocpol, Theda and Kenneth Finegold (1982). "State Capacity and Economic Intervention in the Early New Deal." *Political Science Quarterly,* 97: 255-278.

Social Action Branch (1970). *Annual Report.* Ottawa.

Standing Joint Committee of the Senate and of the House of Commons on Official Languages (1988). *Minutes of Proceedings and Evidence.* September 28.

Statistics Canada (1989). *Dimensions: Language Retention and Transfer.* Ottawa: Minister of Supply and Services.

Endnotes

* I would like to thank Sylvia Bashevkin, Stephen Brooks, William Coleman, and Grace Skogstad for their comments on an earlier draft. Research for this chapter was supported by an Association for Canadian Studies Writing Award and the Social Sciences and Humanities Research Council, grant no. 880360.

1. National Archives of Canada, RG 26, Department of Citizenship and Immigration Files, volume 65, file 2—2-4, C.M. Isbister (Deputy Minister, Department of Citizenship and Immigration) to George F. Davidson (Secretary, Treasury Board), October 8, 1964.

2. National Archives of Canada, RG 6, Department of Secretary of State, volume 661, file 2-4-8, volume 1, "Report of SLO's Staff Conference May 18-20, 1965," p. 1.

3. National Archives of Canada, RG 6, Department of Secretary of State, ACC. 86-87/320, volume 1, file 10-1, part 1, "Some Thoughts on the Application of the 'New Concept of Ministry Organization' to the Portfolio of the Secretary of State and the Responsibilities of the Minister 'without Portfolio' for Citizenship and Information Canada," Appendix B, March 3, 1971, p. 1.

4. National Archives of Canada, RG 6, Department of Secretary of State, volume 661, file 2-4-8, volume 1, memorandum from Hean H. Lagass (Director of Citizenship Branch) to C.A. Lussier (Assistant Deputy Minister—Citizenship), March 23, 1966.

5. Financial assistance will be provided to lobby groups for activities whose aims include:

   a) access to or improvements in minority language education from pre-school to post-secondary institutions and minority community control over primary and secondary education services;

   b) the passing and implementation of legislation recognizing the equal status of the two official languages;

   c) access to improvements in social, judicial, economic and cultural as well as health, sports and recreation services in the minority language;

   d) access to or improvements in telecommunications services, including the print media, radio and television and data information systems such as Telidon (SSC, 1988: v.1.4).

6. In 1984 Official Languages, split into Promotion and Official Language Communities, was established as a separate concern, and OLMGs were redesignated Official Language Communities.

7. In 1988–89 the Québec government allocated $2 million for the support of francophone communities outside Québec.

CHAPTER EIGHT

ORGANIZED WOMEN'S GROUPS AND THE STATE

Sandra Burt

S ince the late 1800s, women's groups in Canada have sought
policy changes from governments. Their activity has been continuous, although varying significantly over time in both intensity and focus. The first clustering of political action occurred in the
early 1900s when social feminists, who wanted to transfer the values
prevalent in the private world of the family to the public world of
politics and labour, worked to obtain franchise rights for women.
Beginning in the 1960s, liberal, radical and socialist feminists (Code,
1988: 43-46) have sought changes ranging from equality rights to a
reshaping of the values informing all facets of social, economic and
political life. And more recently anti-feminists have lobbied for a
return to traditional family forms and life styles.

The literature on these groups and their interactions with the
Canadian state has grown dramatically in the past ten years (Black,
1988; Burt, 1986, 1988a, 1988b; Findlay, 1987). Yet although the
amount of information on women's groups has increased, an

understanding of the relationships that have developed between these groups and policy-makers has not developed at the same rate. Analyses of the overall policy patterns have concentrated on feminist theory in the general context of policy-making frameworks, and conclusions have focussed on the end result of feminist lobbying rather than on the processes that lead to these results.

It is now clear that, over time, Canadian policy-makers have become increasingly sympathetic to the feminist claim that women should have equal access with men to the competitive spheres of politics and work. But they have consistently resisted demands for a fundamental restructuring of relations among both women and men to reflect the feminist values of participation, nurturing, caring, and peace. To a somewhat lesser degree, they have resisted as well attempts by feminists to redefine gender roles within the family. This pattern is similar to that found in other Western, industrialized countries, and in the case of Canada at least reflects the growing emphasis on individual rights developing since the end of the Second World War, and accelerated by the adoption in 1982 of a Charter of Rights and Freedoms. The most dramatic manifestation of the federal government's commitment to the equal rights claim of feminists came in 1981 when the Ad Hoc Committee on the Constitution convinced both levels of government to give notwithstanding status to section 28 in the Charter of Rights and Freedoms (Burt, 1988a).

But within the boundaries of this equal rights thinking, the process of interest accommodation is not well understood. Paul Pross (1986) discusses the qualities needed by groups that seek a consultative role in the policy-making process, and some studies (Adamson et al., 1988) have examined the level of institutionalization of women's groups. On the basis of these studies it can be concluded that the strongest groups, such as the National Action Committee on the Status of Women (NAC), the Business and Professional Women, (B&PW) or the Canadian Congress on Learning Opportunities for Women (CCLOW) have, on most issues, undergone organizational development that equips them to move from policy advocacy to policy participation. The nature of their policy participation, the pattern of women's group-government interaction *within* the general boundaries of the prevailing policy climate, is best furthered by a sectoral level of analysis.

With sectoral-level analysis "much greater attention must be paid to specific bureaucratic arrangements and to the relationships that the officials involved maintain with key societal actors" (Atkinson and Coleman, 1989: 50). The relationships among groups as well as between groups and governments within a policy sector are important. Women's groups have rapidly proliferated and diversified since 1970. And although these groups have moved away from the state direction exercised in the 1960s, they are still fragmented, diverse in their goals and organizationally weak, partly as a consequence of their continued reliance on government funding. At the same time, the federal government has put in place a set of agencies and status of women officers to accommodate the claims of women's groups. These government agencies are fragmented as well. The argument advanced here is that the network linking women's groups with the state has evolved from state direction in the 1960s to pressure pluralism in the 1980s. This transition (see Figure 1) is explored in the context of two issue areas: maternity leave in the 1960s and child care in the 1980s.

Figure 1

The Changing Community on Status of Women Issues at the Federal Level

1965

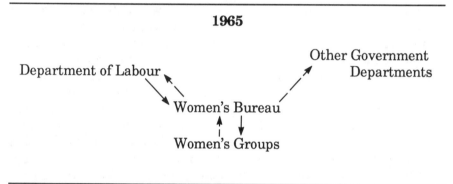

1989

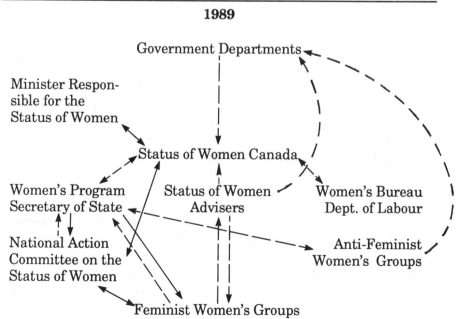

Women's Groups and their Policy Community

Prior to 1970, only a small number of groups were concerned with women's roles and status in Canada. Some, like the National Council of Women, which was formed in 1893, were still committed to social feminist principles (Black, 1981). Other groups, such as the B & PW, formed in the 1900s in the context of women's growing labour force participation, sought equal opportunities for women in the work world. Links between the early groups and public officials were weak, and often limited to yearly formal presentations to Cabinet. Although the groups lobbied successfully for changes in women's status—notably improved family property and labour laws—they lacked organizational skills, were only weakly coordinated, and were few in number.

In the 1970s, the number and range of women's groups increased dramatically.There are now thousands of women's groups across Canada which focus on a wide variety of issues affecting both women's and men's roles, such as abortion, maternity leave, employment equity, and equal opportunity. The largest increase in numbers occurred after 1970, for a variety of reasons. First, throughout the 1900s, but most dramatically in the past two decades, women's labour force participation has increased. The wages paid to women have been lower than those paid to men, leading to demands for equal treatment and equal opportunity in the work place. A second catalyst to mobilization was the United States example of action, with Betty Friedan leading women into the liberation movement. Third, in 1970, the federal government published the report of the Royal Commission on the Status of Women. This report directed the government's and the public's attention to the status of women in Canada, and recommended federal government support for women's groups working to improve women's status. In 1973, in the context of preparations for International Women's Year, the federal government acted on this recommendation and created the Women's Program in the Secretary of State to provide both core and project funding for women's groups.

The goals of women's groups today are much more diverse than those of the groups in existence before 1970. From a survey conducted in 1984,[1] it is possible to identify three major categories of feminist groups. The largest category consists of service providers—groups that make counselling, referral, educational, or shelter services available to women. Equal rights groups are almost as numerous. They seek to break down the barriers to equal opportunities in employment and politics. Finally, there are still some groups committed to social feminist goals. Since the 1984 study, a fourth category of groups, those seeking to maintain the traditional division of responsibilities between women and men, has gained significance as well.

About one-half of these groups are small in size (with less than 50 members) and operate with annual budgets of less than $50,000. A national umbrella group, NAC, has attempted to serve as a coordinator of women's claims since its origins in 1972. With a membership of over 500 groups, NAC tries to accommodate most of its members by serving as a lobbyist on issues with policy relevance to women. Issue priorities are set each year at the annual general meeting, and positions on these priority issues are then presented to the federal cabinet at an annual lobby session. In addition, informal links with public officials, especially those in Status of Women Canada, together with the publication of position/research papers, help to publicize their positions (Morris, 1983).

NAC has had some difficulty exercising its leadership. Since it brings together a wide variety of women's groups, some of which hold conflicting positions, NAC's strength as a national lobby group is sometimes weakened by internal dissension. In 1980, for example, NAC lost its position as the leading lobby group in the struggle for women's equality rights in the Charter of Rights and Freedoms. Today, some member groups oppose NAC's pro-choice position on the abortion issue. In addition to problems arising within NAC, the group has recently faced a loss of legitimacy with the federal government as the major representative of women's views in Canada. For the first time, in 1989, the Minister responsible for the status of women refused to meet with NAC in a closed session to receive its annual cabinet submission.[2]

Overall, since 1970, women's groups have improved their organizational skills, and developed lines of communication with both levels of government. Although the groups are fragmented, many of those committed to feminist goals work with NAC on issues upon which there are common positions, and their commitment to the principle of cooperation also leads to some collaboration. For example, in the 1984 survey 17 per cent of the groups interviewed reported spending at least one-quarter of their time networking with other women's groups. But the links among feminist groups are still weak, and the emergence of new anti-feminist positions suggests that the women's organizational community is becoming increasingly pluralist.

In the 1970s, a further factor contributing to pluralism in the policy community is that a separate set of policy advisers was established by the federal government. These Status of Women advisers sometimes have been important in affecting the impact of the women's lobby on policy formation. There is even evidence that they have performed an advocacy function within government when interest groups have been silent on an issue. And there have been variations over time in their autonomy or ability to insulate themselves from societal influence while drawing on their own internal resources and expertise in defining policy objectives. There have been variations as well in their ability to operate independently of their host agency or other parts of the federal bureaucracy.

The federal government made its first administrative arrangements for the development of policy for women in the 1950s. At that time, its main interest was the employment status of Canadian women. In the booming postwar economy, the focus was on increasing the labour force, and governments started to look to women for help. By 1951, already 24 per cent of women were working for pay outside the home, an increase from only 16 per cent at the turn of the century. Gradually women were being accepted as long-term and low-wage labour, and the proposals of the 1945 reconstruction committee following the Second World War included the recommendation that a women's bureau be established in the Department of Labour. The Minister of Labour, Milton Gregg, a Liberal member from New Brunswick who throughout his career was concerned with the removal of discriminatory practices from the employment field, announced in 1953 in the House of Commons the creation of a women's bureau. It was charged with the following functions:

- providing research on women workers;
- through speeches, etc., making information on women workers available to the public;
- developing channels between the Department of Labour and other public and private agencies;
- advising the Department of Labour on its programmes affecting women workers.[3]

The Bureau was formed in 1954, and from the outset it served as a vehicle for bringing the positions taken by groups to the attention of policy-makers. But the Bureau was not autonomous within the Department of Labour, with its weak administrative position being demonstrated in many ways. Marion Royce, the first Director, complained in 1955 that, although she was a member of an interdepartmental committee to examine the problems of older workers, she was not invited regularly to meetings.[4] In 1965, she was overruled in her effort to have the Women's Bureau housed in the Research and Development Section of the Department of Labour, rather than the less supportive Labour Standards Section. The Bureau was moved to Standards, where it remained until 1985. It is a tribute to Royce's skills that the Bureau survived the transition.[5] Royce was forced to work with a small staff (never more than five people) and a starting budget of $24,000. She concentrated on the publication of information about women's changing labour status, together with liaison work with women's groups. Under her directorship, the Bureau began a listing of national women's organizations. When Royce retired in 1966, she was replaced by Jessica Findlay, a woman with no involvement in women's groups or awareness of status of women concerns. During her brief directorship, the staff of the Bureau shrank to three full-time people, including the director, and a budget of $45,000. Findlay resigned after one year, and her resignation sparked a debate in the House of Commons which focussed on the Director's lack of authority and funds to carry out her functions. Findlay was replaced by Sylva Gelber, and under her directorship the Bureau became a much stronger working unit within the Department of Labour. The functions shifted from information-gathering to coordination of policies affecting women in the federal government. To this end, an interdepartmental committee was established "consisting of representatives of the main government departments concerned with women's affairs in general and with working women in particular."[6]

However, the Bureau's greatest successes remained within the realm of information gathering and dissemination. Under Gelber's leadership, the Bureau upgraded the yearly publication begun by Royce of facts and figures about women in the labour force, and undertook studies of the needs of these women. But her efforts to promote interdepartmental cooperation failed. This setback is obvious from her letter to the assistant deputy minister of Labour on the subject of the wording in the 1969 publication, Labour Highlights: "The inclusion of the Interdepartmental Committee on Women's Affairs as a highlight of the work of the Bureau is not only a source of annoyance but a source of real embarrassment. You will recall that we discussed the failure of the Interdepartmental Committee as long ago as last spring."[7] Gelber was most successful in pointing out the pattern of women's labour force participation, using this knowledge as her ammunition in the fight to gain equality rights. Under her leadership the Bureau developed a reputation within the Department of Labour for conscientious research and expertise.

But the Bureau's new-found autonomy was short-lived. In 1970, the Royal Commission on the Status of Women submitted its report. The Commission recommended that the federal government improve the process for implementing policy changes to enhance the status of women. The government struck an Interdepartmental Committee to consider implementation of the report. The committee, chaired by Freda Paltiel, a senior bureaucrat from Health and Welfare with an interest in status of women issues, proposed that many of the Bureau's functions be redistributed to new agencies. When these new agencies were created, the Bureau suffered a loss of power and personnel. It now focusses on the publication of information related to women in the labour force; activities associated with the International Labour

Organization; and the administration of a small grants programme (started in 1985 with a budget of $25,000) designed to assist individuals or groups with projects to improve the situation of women in the workplace. In 1985, the Bureau was moved from Labour Standards to Policy within the Department of Labour. The staff was increased to 13 person years in 1987, and the budget reached $1,002,000 (Neilsen Task Force, 1987: 128).

Between 1970 and 1975 the federal government decided to accept the recommendations of the interdepartmental committee studying the Royal Commission's report, and put in place a collection of status of women agencies. This decision reflected cabinet's commitment to the principle of equal opportunity. In later recollections about the process, Florence Bird, the Commission Chair, reflected that the creation of multiple agencies was a mistake. The Commission had pressed for several, hoping to get one. Of these new agencies, the most powerful was Status of Women Canada, a central agency that was situated first within the Privy Council Office, and was designed to assist the Minister Responsible for the Status of Women. In addition, Status of Women was involved in "monitoring the activities of government departments, and coordinating new initiatives to improve the status of women."[8] This responsibility included the former Bureau function of serving as a link between women's groups and the government.

From the outset Status of Women encountered difficulties. Unlike the Women's Bureau, which by the 1970s had developed a strong working relationship with its host department, Status of Women Canada was an independent agency, without close links with any departments. Officials charged with the task of considering status of women concerns who were placed within some departments (for example, Health and Welfare, the Public Service Commission, and the Justice Department) had only nominal power to recommend policies, and real power only to promote research and offer advice.

The relationship between the Women's Bureau in Labour and women's groups was further weakened by the development of a granting programme within the Women's Program of the Secretary of State. The Women's Program provides both core and project funding for groups which serve to "promote increased understanding of, and action on, women's issues among women and the general public in the form of advocacy and information exchange" (Canada. Secretary of State, 1982: 1). The first budget of the Women's Program was only $223,000, but by 1987 over 650 groups received funding from a total budget of $12.4 million. Of this amount, 61 per cent was targeted for special projects, and 39 per cent for operational grants. National groups received 37 per cent, and regional, provincial, or local groups the rest (Canada, Secretary of State, 1987: 10). According to the funding guidelines, operational funding, the most sought-after commodity, is available to groups that promote action and provide information to the public on women's issues. The granting guidelines have been interpreted by some groups as an attempt by the federal government to exert control over programmes which lie within the boundaries of provincial responsibility. Social service groups in particular (rape crisis centres, transition homes, and educational counselling groups) have been granted both types of funding. The government controls the groups' agenda by setting a priority list for funding. For example, in 1983-84, funding priorities were violence against women, communication, and women in the economy. In addition, the government directs money to be spent in specific activity areas, requires its approval for budget transfers, and, according to some groups, discourages service providers from taking public stands on issues related to women (Saskatchewan Action Committee, 1983).

The Women's Program acts as "the main federal programme of financial assistance, advice and information to women's and other voluntary organizations" (Secretary of State, 1987: 2). Until 1989, directors of the programme understood these guidelines to mean that only those groups which work to improve the status of women in Canada (that is, improve the potential for equal opportunity) are eligible for funding. They have worked within what they have interpreted as the federal government's commitment to equality. However, that interpretation may be changing. In 1989 a group seeking a return to pre-feminist definitions of women's roles, Realistic Equal Active for Life (REAL women), received funding, in accordance with the recommendations in the 1987 report of the Standing Committee on the Secretary of State, "Fairness in Funding."

Throughout their existence, the status of women agencies within the federal government have struggled to develop autonomy. Some of them have been assisted by central policy directives. The cabinet has been particularly anxious to improve the position of Status of Women Canada. In 1975, in the context of International Women's Year, the minister responsible for the status of women (Marc Lalonde) undertook a review of the government's record in advancing women's claims to work as equal partners with men in the economy. His report led cabinet to declare in 1976 that "each department or agency should establish or designate a mechanism to ensure the integration of status of women concerns into all phases of department activity." It recommended as well that each departmental mechanism maintain continuing contacts with the Office of the Coordinator, Status of Women.[9] At the same time, Status of Women Canada was granted independent status as a central agency, reporting directly to the minister responsible for the status of women. Somewhat later in 1987, the Neilsen Task Force studying government organization recommended that the

Minister Responsible for the Status of Women be a member of the Priorities and Planning Committee in cabinet, and that each Minister mandate an existing assistant deputy minister to ensure that all departmental proposals contain a thorough study of their impact on women.

The record of Status of Women has been mixed. Successive coordinators have worked to establish good working relationships with women's groups, and the agency houses the past publications and policy recommendations made by these groups. Status of Women grew to 43 person years by 1986, with a budget of $2,804,000. But the agency has not been able to coordinate the activity of other departments on status of women questions. Status of Women advisers meet only occasionally, and rarely to discuss policy concerns of mutual interest. The Neilsen Task Force concluded that the main success of Status of Women Canada lay in pulling "the provinces together for national awareness of issues relating to women and for consensus building." It further concluded that the agency's coordination function was hampered by the fact that, with the exception of Labour Canada, no federal department systematically reviews its policies to determine their impact on women (Neilsen Task Force, 1987: 109, 111).

In summary, the agencies within the government for dealing with status of women issues have never enjoyed positions of autonomy within the bureaucracy. But some organizations, especially the Women's Bureau in the Department of Labour in the late 1960s and Status of Women Canada after 1975, have been more capable of generating their own "professional ethos" (Atkinson and Coleman, 1989: 52) than those embedded in existing department bureaucracies. And the overlap of mechanisms across bureaucratic divisions, without effective coordination among them, creates the potential for conflicting interpretations of status of women needs. The policy networks linking women's groups to these status of women agencies have undergone significant changes as both the groups and governments have become more fragmented. In the 1960s, the pattern was one of state direction, with the Women's Bureau performing the leadership function. But whereas Coleman and Skogstad, in Chapter One, suggest that a true state-directed network is characterized by "highly autonomous, coordinated state agencies," (see page 29) the Bureau always held a weak administrative position within the Department of Labour and within the federal bureaucracy generally. Responsibility for developing policy on status of women issues rested within the various departments concerned with the multiple items on the agenda of both the Bureau and women's groups. Progressively since the 1970s, with the proliferation in the number and goals of women's groups and the shift from one government bureau to several status of women mechanisms, the network has evolved to one of pressure pluralism. But again, the public officials who focus on status of women concerns are embedded in a subordinate position within the state.

Two Case Studies: Maternity Leave and Child Care

The two issues of maternity leave and child care illustrate this transition in the policy network over time. The first, maternity leave legislation, took effect in 1970, and federal child care policy was developed in the 1980s.

Maternity Leave
The maternity leave issue was introduced to the federal agenda as early as 1943, when the Marsh Report recommended the awarding of benefits for pregnant women in the labour force (Guest, 1985: 113). But until the 1960s maternity leave was not an important issue among women's groups, partly because of the relatively small number of women involved. In 1951, for example, only 11 per cent of married women were in the labour force, compared to 58 per cent of single women. The Women's Bureau, under Marion Royce, took a leading role in introducing the issue to policy-makers. Royce was convinced of the need to focus on the personal and family problems of married women employees, and she tried to sensitize her department on this issue. At the time, the Department of Labour was still caught up in the philosophy that "in the long run the big contribution to the nation's work is made by women who, like the men, are permanently committed to the labour force as few mothers are."[10] In the Department's view, this excluded married women with family responsibilities.

Royce began with an investigation of existing arrangements in private companies and in the federal public service, and found a precedent for action in 1941-42 maternity leave regulations. These guaranteed a woman's right to return to work at her discretion after the pregnancy, but entailed no payments during leave. When the restriction on the employment of married women in the federal public service was lifted in 1955, the problem of maternity leave became more important for female public servants. While the early research efforts of the Bureau did not result in policy changes, they did focus some attention on the problem within Labour. At about the same time, in 1949, the Unemployment Insurance Commission (UIC), which was still located within Labour, received requests from pregnant women within the public service for unemployment insurance. Without firm guidelines on the question, the UIC granted the unemployment benefits. And so the administrative practice of dealing with maternity leave within the unemployment framework was established.

Again in 1965, the Bureau tackled the question of maternity leave in a study on the employment of women with family responsibilities, and organized a conference on the same theme. But maternity leave clearly was not a high priority among other governments or other federal departments. British Columbia, New Brunswick, and Newfoundland refused to send representatives. And at the federal level, the National Employment Service responded to the invitation to attend the conference with an angry memo, complaining that "it is most difficult for us to devote the time of so many officers to this sort of meeting."[11]

A 1967 report of the Bureau surveyed the maternity leave provisions for women in the private labour force, and noted the growing momentum for legislation in other countries as well. The Bureau's position was that many women of childbearing age work, "not only because they want to or must work, but because there is a demand for them." As a principle, a high standard of working conditions (which would include maternity leave protection) should be part of the labour code. The Bureau proposed legislation to grant women 14 weeks of unpaid leave, with guaranteed job protection at the same level. Cash benefits were viewed as desirable but impracticable at the time, and were to be considered in the next stage of negotiations. The Bureau recommended that this maternity leave protection be introduced as part of the Canada Labour (Standards) Code.[12]

The Bureau did not act alone on this issue. The national B & PW had included maternity leave protection among its recommendations. But the group was organizationally underdeveloped, and limited its lobbying strategy to annual presentations to cabinet. At that time, women's groups had not yet developed links with policy-effective public officials. There was support as well from Grace MacInnis, a New Democratic member of the House of Commons. From the time of MacInnis' first election to the House, she had championed the cause of women in the labour force, urged government to reformulate its policy on gender roles, and drawn media attention to the issue. But the most consistent and best-informed pressure came from the Women's Bureau, lobbying the federal government from within.

By 1967 the deputy minister of Labour, George Haythorne, was convinced by Royce's arguments of the merits of maternity protection, but wanted to see it introduced under the Canada Labour (Safety) Code. [13] However, Haythorne was not anxious to proceed with maternity legislation in any form before considering the recommendations of the newly appointed Royal Commission on the Status of Women. So the project was placed on hold. Then in 1968, Jessica Findlay, as the new Director, quickly concluded that maternity leave legislation would be premature in 1968, and removed Bureau pressure for action.[14]

When Sylva Gelber resumed the call for maternity leave legislation in 1968, her recommendations included the provision for paid leave. This was supported by the 1970 Royal Commission report. The federal government decided to adopt the policy of promoting equal opportunities for women and in his reflections on this period Bryce Mackasey, Minister of Labour at the time, noted the significance of Prime Minister Trudeau's commitment to the Just Society. Thus, in spite of resistance from officials within the Unemployment Insurance Commission, in 1971 the Canada Labour (Standards) Code was amended to guarantee women employed in jobs under federal jurisdiction a total of 17 weeks of leave without dismissal. At the same time, maternity leave benefits were included within the unemployment insurance programme. After a waiting period of two weeks, women who had completed 20 weeks of work within the 52 preceding their claim were awarded 15 weeks of unemployment insurance benefits. According to Gelber, the decision to implement the legislation through the unemployment insurance programme was the direct result of the federal government's decision to use the insurance instrument to enter an area of provincial jurisdiction. "Later there were provinces ready, but at that time no province was ready. So we started to take a good look at our constitution, and I said, well marvellous, we'll get maternity leave under unemployment insurance, and that's the story. It became federal."[15] The decision to include maternity leave benefits within the unemployment insurance system later angered women's groups who argued that pregnancy is not equivalent to unemployment, and were concerned about a possible overlap between unemployed and pregnant status.

In summary, the policy network was dominated by the Women's Bureau which slowly achieved recognition within government as the authority on "women's issues", although it never achieved autonomy within the Department of Labour. There was little challenge or support from women's groups which had not yet been drawn into the network of government funding and policy participation. Until the 1970s, the government had no clear policy on status of women issues, and the Bureau provided the expertise and the pressure to create the conditions for change. The policy proposals generated by the Bureau were ultimately accepted by the federal government for a variety of reasons: the rights claims of women were increasingly popular with a government committed, after 1968, to the Just Society; the necessary contribution of women to the developing economy was acknowledged and nurtured; and the opportunity to influence provincial programmes through federal status of women programmes was welcomed.

Day Care

The day care issue provides evidence of a different pattern of interaction between women's groups and the federal government in the 1980s, one where initiatives for policy action have come from a plurality of women's groups and day care associations, rather than from government agencies. Concern for day care had been on the agenda of the Women's Bureau in the Department of Labour since the 1950s, but it had not received priority treatment. The issue was significantly less visible than either maternity leave or equal pay throughout the 1950s and 1960s. The Bureau assumed an advisory role on the issue in the 1960s, but was not in the forefront of activity. In 1965 it was the National Employment Committee that proposed sponsoring the Canadian Welfare Council to undertake a study of day care needs in the country. The Bureau was asked for advice, and recommended that the Department of Health and Welfare play an important role in the provision of day care services. This advice was accepted.[16]

The issue remained dormant until 1970 when the Royal Commission on the Status of Women included day care in its report as one of the issues requiring federal and provincial attention. But on this issue, it was primarily women's groups which promoted policy action. Like maternity leave, this issue properly belonged to the provinces. Indeed, most of the early child care legislation was provincial in nature—primarily in the form of licensing regulations. (See, for example, the Ontario Day Nurseries Act, first passed in 1946.) And the earliest lobby group on this issue, the Day Nursery and Day Care Parents Association, was an Ontario group that concentrated its energies on lobbying Queen's Park and Toronto city council (Prentice, 1988: 108).

Then in the midst of the second wave of feminist activity in the 1970s, women's groups made day care a major issue in their lobbying campaigns. NAC included day care on its initial action list, and has since continued to work for a policy of universal non-profit centres. It was soon joined by the Canadian Labour Congress and the Canadian Congress on Learning Opportunities for Women, who wanted non-profit, accessible, affordable, quality centres set up across the country. Again, most of the energy of women's groups on this issue was concentrated at the provincial level, since responsibility for most centres came under provincial jurisdiction. Provincially-based day care advocacy groups began to form across the country. In Ontario, the Ontario Coalition for Better Child Care formed in 1981, following a series of public meetings on the subject organized by the Ontario Federation of Labour. This advocacy group-labour coalition was a common pattern. In Québec, the Fédération des Femmes du Québec took the lead on the day care issue, and was soon joined by locally based groups pressing for non-profit centres. In British Columbia and Alberta the pattern was somewhat different, with some of the advocacy groups pressing for either public or private centres.

But the federal government was involved through funding. Federal assistance for day care was administered by the Department of Health and Welfare under the Canada Assistance Plan. In the 1970s, each dollar of provincial day care funding was matched by a federal dollar, and the programme was open-ended. This ad hoc arrangement had been worked out by the two levels of government in federal-provincial conferences, and represented the indirect impact of lobby groups' success at the provincial level.

By the early 1980s, this system was clearly inadequate. Not only were there too few day care spaces, but also rising costs made likely a ceiling on federal government day care expenditures. A second National Day Care Conference, funded by Health and Welfare Canada, was held in Winnipeg in 1982 (the first had taken place in 1971). Both labour and women's groups such as NAC sent representatives, and the emerging day care advocacy groups have maintained alliances with these groups since that time. At that second conference there was a split between delegates on the issue of profit versus non-profit centres, and the participants (about one-third) who supported profit centres broke away to form their own group. The remaining participants discussed the need for a national lobbying group, and subsequently formed the Canadian Day Care Advocacy Association (CDCAA). The federal Department of Health and Welfare supported financially the first meeting of CDCAA, but the group had a very limited budget, and the organizing work was done by volunteers. Health and Welfare discontinued its financial support after that first meeting, ostensibly on the grounds that CDCAA did not have charitable status, and the group was forced to look elsewhere for financial help. After about one year it was awarded operational funding ($220,000 in 1989) by the Women's Program in the Secretary of State, and was able to establish a formal office in Ottawa with a paid staff which grew from two to three person-years by 1989. However, since 1987, when the Women's Program began to define a women's group as one that is run exclusively by women, CDCAA's funding has been in jeopardy. The group was singled out for criticism by anti-feminist groups during the 1987 hearings on the funding programme within Secretary of State.

At the outset, CDCAA focussed on the provision of spaces, and was prepared to press for non-franchised private as well as public centres. But within a few years, it adopted the principle of exclusively non-profit day care services, and this is now the bottom-line position of the group. Over the years CDCAA has developed skills in analyzing policy and preparing press releases. The Association has undertaken as well intensive lobbying of politicians. It relies heavily on NAC for lobby support, and many day care activists are involved in NAC work. Most of its bureaucratic contacts are with the lead ministry, Health and Welfare Canada, "but when that isn't working, Barbara McDougall (Minister responsible for the Status of Women) has been an ally in Cabinet." And Status of Women Canada has provided beneficial information about the government's intentions and publicized the group's position within the bureaucracy. But help has not been available from the Status of Women's Adviser in Health and Welfare.

In the 1970s, the community of policy actors expanded to include the for-profit day care operators, who, at the outset, focussed their energies at the provincial level. One of the strongest provincial groups was the Association of Day Care Operators of Ontario (ADCO) which has 250 members and an annual budget of $15,000. In 1988, the founder of ADCO, Herb Goldsmith, created a direct membership national group, the Canadian Childcare Management Association (CCMA) to pressure the federal government to permit government subsidies of for-profit centres. Unlike the advocacy groups, these associations of private day care operators do not receive government funding. They rely exclusively on membership fees that are assessed on the basis of the number of children supervised within the member day care units. Fees range from $100 to several hundred dollars.

The Childcare Management Association does not maintain an office in Ottawa, and relies on its members to develop contacts with relevant bureaucrats and ministers. The Association is hampered by the absence of effective organizations like ADCO in some provinces which can bring the private operators together to make their views known to government and the public. The Association believes that society needs a variety of day care options to fulfil the growing need for spaces, and that the key is effective licensing rather than ownership. "Parents must have the freedom to choose the type of care they believe is appropriate and best for their children." (ADCO, 1988: 3).

A third group, active at the federal level, is the Canadian Child Day Care Federation formed by child caregivers following a federal government funded conference of early childhood educators in 1983. The Federation focusses on the provision of services and support, and publishes a review, *Interaction*, that is sent to members. Throughout the Federation's early years, it was encouraged to continue by Health and Welfare Canada, which has provided operating funds since 1986 (the award was $100,000 in 1986 and $400,000 in 1989). In addition, extra money is made available by Health and Welfare for specific projects such as national conferences. There has been some speculation, particularly among the non-profit advocacy groups, that the federation was "set up" by government to help resolve the public versus private day care issue. But the present executive director feels that, though this may be true, in any case "there needs to be a mechanism for bringing very disparate groups together." Mediation is one of the federation's central concerns. It sees its role as an information broker rather than an advocacy group and refuses to take a stand on the public-private issue, focussing on quality rather than auspices. The Director noted the presence of representatives from ADCO at the Federation's conference in 1989, and proposed that this could be the beginning of dialogue between the non-profit and for-profit factions within the lobby.

The Federation has individual rather than group links with the women's movement and the non-profit day care advocacy groups. Several members of the current board have feminist group connections, but strong national feminist organizations such as the NAC on the Status of Women remain outside the Federation's formal ranks. The labour movement also has remained aloof. At the same time, private operators have been wary of the group's intentions. ADCO sent representatives from its Board to the 1989 conference organized by the Federation, and there is some evidence that these board members were impressed with the Federation's work. But the links are still tenuous. So the constituency of the Federation is, in most respects, very different from that of the two groups noted above.

Throughout the early 1980s, all three groups became involved in discussions with the federal government. Primarily as a consequence of rising costs in the area of day care, the federal government decided to develop a policy on the issue when the Liberals were still in power, before 1984. To do so, the Trudeau government commissioned an external study, reflecting both the fact that day care was a controversial issue on which relatively little good research material had been produced up to that point, and the lack of leadership by Status of Women Canada on the issue. In the National Plan of Action, developed jointly by Status of Women Canada and Health and Welfare Canada in 1979, the priorities selected were violence against women, gender-role stereotyping, and the financial problems of older women. They did not include day care. At the time the coordinator of Status of Women explained this omission as a consequence of the federal-provincial character of day care funding.

The Liberal government's plans to act on the issue ended with its defeat in the 1984 federal election. The new Conservative government established its own day care study group, the Special Committee on Child Care, and looked for a solution within its own terms of reference. In the context of its philosophical commitment to privatization, and in the absence of overwhelming evidence to support the proposition that non-profit centres provided better quality care, [17] the federal government was prepared both to listen to the arguments made by the private day care operators as well as to advance funds to the Canadian Child Day Care Federation, which seemed to offer a compromise position.

The Conservative strategy was made easier by conflicting messages from its own bureaucrats. While Status of Women Canada had strong ties with the non-profit advocacy groups, Health and Welfare was firmly committed to supporting the child care educators who were at least ambivalent on the question of ownership. In that context, it was easy for the Conservative government to listen to the ideologically welcome argument advanced by the rather poorly organized for-profit CCMA. When the government announced its federal day care strategy in 1987, it provided clear evidence of its decision to follow ideological rather than lobbying dictates. The short-lived 1987 strategy acknowledged a role for private day care operators in Canada. It called for a new Child Care Act which would allocate $6.4 billion to child care over seven years. Included in the plan was the development of 200,000 new spaces, through cost-sharing with the provinces; a $100 million child care initiatives fund to support innovative approaches to providing child care services; and a phased-in $200 supplement to the Child Tax Credit for children six and under as well as an increased deduction from $2000 to $4000. The plan placed no restrictions on the ownership of childcare facilities, and fell short of providing for the estimated 750,000 needed spaces. The Strategy failed to pass Senate reading before the 1988 federal election, and the 1989 federal proposals, while similar, allocate an even smaller amount to day care funding.

This issue illustrates the policy deadlock that developed as the number of status of women advisers grew, and the range of group positions expanded. Since the early 1970s, women's policy has been dispersed among several, sometimes competing agencies within government. Status of Women Canada has not been able to develop either a strong coordinating or advisory role on this issue. At the same time a plurality of groups, most of them well-organized, have presented government with sometimes conflicting demands.

Conclusion

These two issues demonstrate the complex and changing nature of relations between women's groups and the federal government over time. As the groups have become more diverse, partly as a consequence of government funding, the government mechanisms set up to deal with status of women concerns have become more numerous. There has been a transition within the status of women sector from a largely state-directed policy network in the 1960s to a pressure pluralist network in the 1980s.

There were indications in the 1970s that the emerging network might become one of clientele pluralism. When Status of Women Canada was accorded increased legitimacy as the state agency most authoritative on status of women questions, it developed closed links with feminist groups, especially NAC and the National Association of Women and the Law. But the proliferation in the 1980s of groups seeking policies on status of women issues, combined with a change in government in 1984, led to a breakdown in the clientele relationship. The child care issue illustrates the new pluralism that has emerged.

There are several reasons to suppose that, in future, the government may be reluctant to act on status of women issues, or may move away from feminist positions in its policy directions. Combined with the plurality of interests represented within women's groups is the new climate of privatization within the federal government. It has become as important as the equal rights mentality in setting policy limits. Partly as a consequence, women's groups that have relied on government funding in the past are finding it difficult to obtain operating grants. And they have not yet worked out strategies for obtaining funds from other sources. Government funding provided women's groups with financial stability, and improved their claim to legitimacy. Without these funds, the groups will gain greater freedom to develop their own set of policy directions, but they may lose their foothold within the bureaucracy. At the same time, problems with organization and member mobilization which have always plagued women's groups—in particular, the multi-function status of women's organization—will remain. In the context, it will become increasingly easy for governments to refuse to act, on the grounds that the "women's lobby" is divided. Alternatively, governments may select policies that correspond with their own pre-set goals, comfortable in the knowledge that, within the new plurality of interests represented among the groups, they can find support for their actions.

References

Adamson, N., Linda Briskin and Margaret McPhail (1988). *Feminist Organizing for Change: The Contemporary Women's Movement in Canada.* Toronto: Oxford University Press.

Association of Day Care Operators of Ontario (1988). "More and Better Childcare!" November. Toronto.

Atkinson, M.M. and W.D. Coleman (1989). "Strong States and Weak States: Sectoral Policy Networks in Advanced Capitalist Economies." *British Journal of Political Science*, 19: 47-67.

Black, Naomi (1981). "Introduction." In Elsie Gregory MacGill, *My Mother the Judge*. Toronto: Peter Martin Associates: xi-xxiv.

_____ (1988). "The Canadian Women's Movement: the Second Wave." In Sandra Burt, Lorraine Code, and Lindsey Dorney, eds., *Changing Patterns: Women in Canada*. Toronto: McClelland and Stewart.

Burt, S. (1986). "Women's Issues and the Women's Movement in Canada." In Alan Cairns and Cynthia Williams. *The Politics of Gender, Ethnicity and Language in Canada*. Toronto: University of Toronto Press.

_____ (1988a). "The Charter of Rights and the Ad Hoc Lobby: The Limits of Success." *Atlantis*, 14:74-81.

_____ (1988b). "Legislators, Women, and Public Policy." In Sandra Burt et al., eds. *Changing Patterns*. Toronto: McClelland and Stewart.

Canada. House of Commons, Task Force on Program Review (Neilsen Task Force) (1987). *Report*. Ottawa. Ministry of Supply and Services.

Canada. Secretary of State (1982). *Funding Guidelines*. May.

_____ (1987). "Notes for the presentation of the Undersecretary of State Before the Standing Committee on the Secretary of State." February 3.

Code, Lorraine (1988). "Feminist Theory." In Sandra Burt et al., eds. *Changing Patterns*. Toronto: McClelland and Stewart.

Findlay, S. (1987). "Facing the State: The Politics of the Women's Movement Reconsidered." In H.J. Maroney and M. Luxton, eds. *Feminism and Political Economy*. Toronto: Methuen.

Griffin, Sandra Jean (1985). "Canadian Child Day Care: Translating Research into Policy." Unpublished M.A. Thesis, School of Child Care, University of Victoria, Victoria, B.C.

Guest, D. (1985). *The Emergence of Social Security in Canada*. Vancouver: University of British Columbia Press.

Morris, C. (1983). "Pressuring the Canadian State for Women's Rights: the Role of the National Action Committee on the Status of Women." *Alternate Routes*, 6:87-108.

Prentice, S. (1988). "Kids are Not for Profit: The Politics of Childcare." In F. Cunningham et al., eds. *Social Movements / Social Change: The Politics and Practice of Organizing*. Toronto: Between the Lines.

Pross, A. Paul (1986). *Group Politics and Public Policy*. Toronto: Oxford University Press.

The Royal Commission on the Status of Women (1970). *Report*. Ottawa: Information Canada.

Saskatchewan Action Committee, Saskatchewan Status of Women (1983). "The Pink Papers: Government Funding and Government Control in the Women's Movement." Unpublished document available from Canadian Women's Movement Archives. Toronto.

Endnotes

*Much of the information reported in this paper was obtained from interviews conducted with activists within women's groups, status of women officials in the federal government, and elected officials responsible for the policies discussed. These interviews were conducted between 1984 and 1989, and were supported by Grant 410-86-0170 from the Social Sciences and Humanities Research Council of Canada.

1. This study was conducted by the author in 1984. The 686 women's groups listed in the 1982 publication of the Women's Program, Secretary of State, were sent questionnaires. The response rate was 24 per cent.

2. See Paul Koring, "Antibudget Campaign by Women's Group Off to Confused Start," Toronto Globe and Mail, May 16, 1989, A13.

3. National Archives of Canada, RG 27, vol. 1903, file 38-2-2, part 1, "Seminar on the Work of the Women's Bureau, Department of Labour," May 5, 1960.

4. Canada, Department of Labour, Women's Bureau Library, memorandum from M. Royce, Director, Women's Bureau to H.L. Douse, January 18, 1955.

5. National Archives of Canada, RG 27, vol. 3209, file 1-4-12, "Interim Report of the Task Force on Manpower," December 30, 1965.

6. National Archives of Canada, RG 27, vol. 4160, file 722-4-3, memo to J.P. Despres from S.M. Gelber, October 23, 1968.

7. National Archives of Canada, RG 27, vol. 38-6-2-8, letter to J.P. Despres from S. Gelber, Dec. 29, 1969.

8. National Archives of Canada. RG 106, vol. 29, "Report of the Ad Hoc Committee on Mechanisms to Integrate the Status of Women." Appendix A, p. 2.

9. National Archives, RG 106, vol. 29, "Briefing for Deputy Ministers on Status of Women Policy," p. 3.

10. Canada, Department of Labour, Women's Bureau Library, "Paper to be delivered by W.R. Dymond, Seminar on Women's Bureau," May 5, 1960.

11. Canada, Dept. of Labour, Women's Bureau Library, memo from W.T. Thomson, Director, National Employment Service, to G.V. Haythorne, Deputy Minister of Labour, Jan. 25, 1965.

12. National Archives of Canada, RG 27, vol. 1904, file 38-11-6-3, "Notes on Maternity Protection," Women's Bureau, Dept. of Labour, August 9, 1967.

13. National Archives of Canada, RG 27, vol. 1904, 38-11-6-3, memorandum from George Haythorne, Deputy Minister of Labour to M. Royce, Director, Women's Bureau, January 1967.

14. Canada, Dept. of Labour, library, memo to G.V. Haythorne from J.-P. Despres, 1968.

15. Information obtained in an interview with Sylva Gelber, Ottawa, March 1987.

16. National Archives of Canada, RG 27, vol. 1903, 38-11-6-41, "Memorandum from M. Royce to G.V. Haythorne re resolution on child-care facilities."

17. See, for example, Griffin (1985:30) who notes that there is a weak research base in this area. She argues that studies of the effects of day care are few in number and on less than 300 Canadian children over the past 15 years.

CHAPTER NINE

THE POVERTY POLICY COMMUNITY IN CANADA'S LIBERAL WELFARE STATE

Rodney Haddow

T
he last quarter-century has witnessed three major turning points in national income security and social service measures for the poor in Canada: a reform of traditional social assistance measures in 1966; a comprehensive review of poverty measures which started in 1973 and ended in failure five years later; and a debate which began in 1984 and shows no signs of abating about improving social security for the needy, possibly by abandoning universal elements in Canada's welfare state. This chapter will examine these developments, identifying for each the constellation of organized interests speaking for or on behalf of the poor, the state institutions with responsibilities in the area, and the major policy concerns.[1]

In doing this, the chapter will also assess the merits of sectoral analysis as a tool for analyzing the poverty policy. Coleman and Skogstad, in Chapter One of this collection, point out the value of policy studies that avoid an exclusive focus on such macro-level factors as parliamentary politics, class relations and state structures and that seek to remain sensitive to the impact of sectoral level variables on policy-making in a given field. Sectoral studies pay particular attention to the impact of organized interests and state institutions with a specific interest in a policy field on developments in the field. Sectoral analysis does have an application in the poverty field. Throughout the postwar years poverty policy has been an identifiable "sector." Poverty constitutes a discrete "focus" of policy-making: income security and social service measures directed at needy Canadians, rather than at the broad mass of citizens. An identifiable "associational system" of organized interests outside the state, and a discrete set of bureaucratic institutions within the state, have constituted the "policy community" for the sector. This core has remained even though the community has broadened significantly in the postwar period. Because of this growth, the sectoral policy "network" evolved from being "state directed" in the 1960s to a condition best described as "pressure pluralism" in the 1970s. The contemporary policy network still includes significant elements of pressure pluralism, but cannot be fully described in sectoral terms.

To adequately understand Canada's poverty policy network during the postwar years, the sectoral approach must be complemented by macro-level analysis (as Coleman and Skogstad note in *Chapter One*). Fundamental aspects of the poverty sector have been determined by characteristics of Canada's state system and social relations. First, the role of state institutions in the policy community, for each period, has been shaped by prevailing structures of the federal cabinet system and by federal-provincial relations. These macro-level qualities of the state have influenced the kind of policy network that has emerged at the sectoral level.

Second, the importance of poverty as a policy "focus" in Canada—the extent to which Canada's social security system has been constructed around measures directed at disadvantaged people—reflects what will be called the "liberal" character of Canada's welfare state. This property, in turn, is related to the historical pattern of class politics in Canada.

Ameliorating the lives of poor people is far more prominent as an objective of social policy in Canada and in other Anglo-Saxon countries than in most European welfare states, where social security has developed in a more universalist direction (Jones, 1985: 202-203; Lawson and Walker, 1984: 303-304; Kahn and Kamerman: 1983). Poverty "sectors" therefore vary considerably in extent, implying the existence of different welfare state "models" and policy instruments in capitalist democracies. Korpi (1980) and Esping-Andersen (1985) have elaborated a typology of three models that can account for international differences in the importance of poverty policy. Most

Western European welfare states, such as Scandinavia, West Germany, or Austria, conform either to a "conservative" or a "social democratic" model. Both rely on comprehensive social insurance and universal benefits—in either case, social programmes that provide benefits to the broad mass of citizens and are not intended exclusively, or primarily, for use by poor people. In these welfare states, programmes targeted at the poor are very secondary. The preferred approach is one of meeting the needs of disadvantaged people through universal and social insurance programmes. A "liberal" welfare state prevails in a number of societies, especially Anglo-Saxon ones, including Canada. Here, in contrast to the first two models, "means-tested assistance, modest universal transfers, or modest social insurance plans predominate" (Esping-Andersen, 1989: 25). Liberal welfare states include some limited universal and social insurance programmes, but these are inadequate to meet the needs of the disadvantaged.

Esping-Andersen and Korpi contend further that different welfare state models emerged from distinctive patterns of class power at the historical origin of the welfare state. Political parties played a central role in mediating the impact of class. Once in place, welfare states shape electoral preferences, thereby conditioning the alternatives for reform available to politicians (Esping-Andersen, 1989: 30). Social democratic welfare states emerged under the dominance of democratic socialist parties; conservative welfare states were founded by anti-bourgeois conservative political forces. In either case, the resulting welfare state emphasized broad coverage and, consequently, attracted the loyalty of the many non-poor voters who benefitted from it. Such is not the case in liberal welfare states, established by pro-business parties and subject to limited subsequent modification by socialist ones. Here, modest social insurance and universal measures emerged, and voters are therefore less committed to social security.[2]

Canada's welfare state emerged, historically, along liberal lines. It has some noteworthy income security programmes of a universal type, such as family allowances and old age security, non-actuarial elements in its social insurance programmes, especially Unemployment Insurance, and an important universal programme for the provision of health insurance. But these developments are modest by international standards. Canada's welfare state also developed in a context of weak working class parties and the dominance of national politics by pro-business parties; there has never been a social democratic government nationally, and the influence of the Co-operative Commonwealth Federation/New Democratic Party (CCF/NDP), usually on minority governments, has been sporadic (Wolfe, 1989: 113-114).

Canada's liberal model has shaped poverty policy developments in two ways. First, in each postwar poverty reform period, policy-makers have reached for measures directed at the poor in recognition of the inadequacy of Canada's universal and insurance-based programmes. Second, these programmes have engendered only modest support for the welfare state among Canadians, permitting conservative politicians to advocate a residual, "poverty" orientation in social policy. This development has definite consequences for the contemporary political debate over poverty in Canada.

The next three sections will trace developments in the poverty sector in the postwar years. For each reform period, the chapter "maps" the policy community, identifying state and societal interests in the sector, and the relationship among them. The main interests are summarized in Figures 1, 2 and 3. These facilitate the identification of the kind of policy network that existed in each period, using the typology of Atkinson and Coleman (1989: 54-59) noted in Chapter One. Each section also assesses the impact of macro-level factors on developments within the sector.

From the first to the second reform period the poverty policy network evolved from state-direction to pressure pluralism. The associational system has been consistently weak, despite expanding considerably over the years. Its members have shown only a limited capacity for independent policy advocacy, inter-group relations have been fragmented, and the system has had modest success in mobilizing the consumers of poverty programmes to fight for improvements. There have been tensions between middle class organizations and "consumer" groups which can lay some claim to representing poor people.[3] By contrast, during the 1960s, state actors possessed autonomy and considerable policy capacity with the state's involvement in the sector being concentrated in parallel federal and provincial departments. The state continued to have considerable autonomy during second phase, the Social Security Review, but capacity declined because of a substantial diffusion of decision-making authority within the state.

In the third and current phase, state authority remains fragmented, and autonomy is now also compromised. For the first time, poverty reform is driven by the preferences of a governing party. The contemporary interest of politicians in poverty cannot, we suggest, be understood to mean the autonomy of sectoral state actors. First, this political interest is not a sectoral phenomenon; it is linked to an agenda for reform of the welfare state as a whole. Second, it reflects broad ideological objectives of the governing party, and its successful implementation will require the consent of voters. And, as was suggested above, electoral preferences reflect the social forces underlying the genesis of distinctive welfare states. Consequently, we conclude by suggesting that Atkinson and Coleman's sectoral network typology does not fully accommodate the contemporary network.

Origins of the Canada Assistance Plan, 1958-1966:
A State-Directed Policy Network

In the early 1950s the federal government passed three "categorical" assistance acts, permitting it to share the costs of assistance payments to the blind, the elderly between the ages of 65 and 70, and the disabled. A much more significant step was passage of the Unemployment Assistance Act in 1956, which shared the costs of assistance payments to the unemployed. During the 1950s, then, the federal government accepted increasing responsibilities in the assistance area, but its involvement consisted of four uncoordinated programmes which excluded many aspects of provincial welfare programmes, especially mothers' allowances and the costs of social services and administration. The Canada Assistance Plan of 1966 (CAP) consolidated and expanded the federal government's involvement in the assistance field. It eliminated the categorical programmes by integrating all existing legislation in one comprehensive act, and covered those parts of provincial assistance programmes that were previously excluded from federal cost-sharing.

The Associational System
Almost all of the assistance reforms of the 1960s were first proposed, in general terms, by the Canadian Welfare Council (CWC), a middle class, non-governmental organization concerned with social policy. The CWC dominated the non-governmental poverty sector in the 1950s and early 1960s (*see Figure 1*). But in the assistance field, the CWC was less a disinterested organization outside the state able to engage in effective policy advocacy, than a structure "captured" by state actors who permitted them to establish a policy consensus and propagandize on its behalf (Haddow, 1988: 5).

The CWC was a highly decentralized body. Its main policy-making functions were concentrated in a number of divisions which had jurisdiction over specific "fields" of social policy. Social assistance policy was the responsibility of the Public Welfare Division (PWD), and its major decision-making body consisted largely of public welfare officials. In 1961, for instance, 62 of its 77 members were welfare officials from one of the three levels of government, including a substantial representation of very senior welfare officials—consisting of almost all deputy ministers—from the federal and provincial governments. The Council's main policy statement was co-authored by the Deputy Minister for Welfare for Nova Scotia, and by another specialist in welfare policy, who had professional experience in social welfare, and who subsequently obtained employment in the federal Health and Welfare

Figure 1

Poverty Policy Community, 1960s

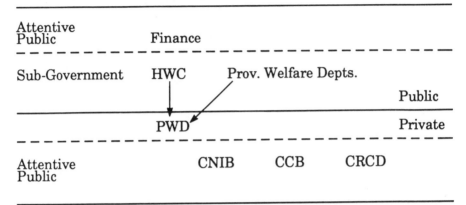

CCB: Canadian Council of the Blind
CNIB: Canadian National Institute for the
       Blind
CRCD: Canadian Rehabilitation Council for
       the Disabled

HWC: Health and Welfare Canada
PWD: Public Welfare Division (Canadian
       Welfare Council)

Department as CAP was being developed. The policy statement was also the subject of considerable consultation among welfare officials from across the country, most of whom belonged to the Division.

Real policy-making power resided in the divisions, but the CWC's formal power structure was capped by its Board of Governors. The Board included an impressive cross-section of Canada's business, academic and governmental elites. CWC policies were drawn up within the PWD and then endorsed by the Board before release. The Board actually had very little to do with preparing them, and did nothing to alter their content before publication. Endorsement by the Board attached considerable prestige to the documents, which the CWC would claim represented the considered opinion of a number of prominent Canadian citizens. Although nominally reflecting the views of disinterested opinion-leaders outside the state, the CWC's public assistance policy was the product of deliberations among welfare officials from different levels of government who used the Council's policy-making procedures to camouflage their activities.[4]

The CWC largely monopolized the associational system at this time, but there were a number of "consumer" organizations with an interest in assistance issues. These groups represented exclusively recipients of the various categorical assistance programmes and they resisted efforts to eliminate the measures which privileged them in comparison with other, less "deserving", categories of the needy. Consequently, to the extent that the needy themselves had a voice in policy-making, this voice spoke for them very selectively, and it encouraged the maintenance of the status quo.

Organizations representing the blind were, by far, the most vocal, although groups speaking for the disabled also made their views heard.[5] Because they had limited resources to deploy in lobbying (being mainly devoted to providing services to their members), little knowledge of policy options under discussion within government, and objectives that were antithetical to those preferred by officials, these recipient organizations had little access to officials. When they did manage to meet a minister, federal welfare officials convinced the minister to ignore their advice.[6]

The State

The contours of the poverty policy community in the 1960s were shaped by macro-level qualities of the federal state and federal-provincial relations. The federal state was organized along "departmentalized" lines in these years: individual programme departments had considerable independence from central agencies, and were able to negotiate policy agreements with provincial officials without obstruction, as long as discussions did not move beyond traditional departmental policy prerogatives. Provincial participants in negotiations would usually represent programme departments that parallelled those of federal officials, and would therefore share a common agency philosophy. Consequently, federal-provincial relations were frequently harmonious (Dupré, 1985: 5-6).

During the 1950s and 1960s, policy-making in the poverty sector reflected these structures that were almost entirely confined to federal and provincial welfare departments (Dyck, 1976). Officials who worked in the sector usually shared a common professional background in social work and, when they did not, quickly became assimilated to the reformist norms that predominated in welfare departments. Shared values meant that there was little intradepartmental conflict about policy objectives and that federal-provincial discussions were conducted by officials with similar outlooks. CAP emerged from this cooperative group of welfare officials. They reached a general consensus on reform in the PWD in the late 1950s, and elaborated this in direct federal-provincial negotiations from 1960 to 1964. Thereafter, the major impediments to reform were political. Although most politicians were indifferent to assistance issues, some remained committed to the categorical measures and the benefits that they gave to the supposedly "deserving" poor. The major tool used by federal welfare officials to overcome this resistance was to demonstrate the consensus achieved with provincial welfare officials (who successfully lobbied their own ministers on the reform). In 1965, Joe Willard, the federal Deputy Minister of Welfare, used this provincial consensus to convince Tom Kent, Prime Minister Pearson's most prominent political advisor, of the merits of a comprehensive assistance act. With Kent on side, passage of CAP was assured. The Department of Finance resisted and delayed the legislation on fiscal grounds, but Mr. Kent's endorsement was enough to allow the reformers to get most of what they wanted.

The welfare bureaucrats who instigated CAP were explicitly motivated to support reform of measures targeted at the poor by a perception that Canada's meagre universal and social insurance programmes could not meet the needs of the disadvantaged. The main CWC policy statement emphasized this point; federal welfare officials made the same point in 1963 while convincing their minister of the need for assistance reform. Finally, the inadequacy of any potential changes in universal measures was cited by Prime Minister Pearson in defending CAP after it was tabled in the House of Commons in 1966.[7]

During the 1960s, the policy network in the poverty sector was, in Atkinson and Coleman's terms, state-directed. Public welfare officials experienced considerable autonomy from non-state interests, and this autonomy was not threatened by politicians who had little interest in the sector. The main sectoral organization, the CWC, far from challenging this autonomy, served as an important basis for it. Organizations that could claim, in a very limited way, to speak for client groups did not share bureaucratic objectives, but lacked the resources to challenge them. Welfare officials also had substantial policy-making capacity, because decision-making was effectively centralized within federal and provincial welfare departments.

CAP also reflected the impact of macro-level factors. First, the concentration of policy-making in the hands of welfare officials was facilitated by the prevailing departmentalized structure of the federal cabinet, and the harmonious federal-provincial relations that typify a departmentalized cabinet. Second, reflecting the imprint of Canada's liberal welfare state, the reform consensus presupposed that universal and social insurance programmes would not meet the needs of the disadvantaged. Actors in the policy community assumed that measures targeted explicitly at the poor had to be improved in order to assist needy Canadians.

The Social Security Review, 1973-1978: From State-Direction to Pressure Pluralism

CAP came under attack after a "rediscovery of poverty" occurred in Canada during the late 1960s. Alternatives that received attention included a guaranteed annual income and social services made available on a more inclusive basis than was possible in a needs-tested programme. These ideas, which together constituted a new agenda for reform in the poverty sector, implied a much broader conception of the problem of need—one that extended to the working poor for example—than had existed previously. In 1973, a Social Security Review was launched by the federal government based on this new reform agenda. It ended five years later without realizing any of its objectives.

The Associational System

The associational system in the poverty sector changed in two fundamental ways in the late 1960s and early 1970s. First, the CWC, the major middle class organization, became the Canadian Council on Social Development (CCSD), a body less subject to "capture" by state actors. Second, organizations that involved poor people in decision-making roles much more explicitly grew dramatically. "Poverty" emerged as an identity capable of mobilizing needy citizens, and demands increased for client participation in the operation of welfare programmes. Narrower groups representing the old "categorical" recipient groups for a time receded into the background. These changes in the associational system are illustrated in Figure 2.

The CWC was overhauled because its fragmented structure and its reliance on the professional expertise of actors in public welfare bureaucracies came to be seen as anachronistic at a time when the focus of concern with poverty had transcended traditional assistance measures; appropriate policy responses increasingly demanded the skills of highly trained social scientists, especially economists. The Council therefore abolished its divisions, including the PWD, and developed a broadly focussed research capacity, relying much more than in the past on experts in the social sciences (Haddow, 1988: 10). The Council's changed structure gave it greater autonomy from bureaucratic interests in federal and provincial governments.

However, this autonomy was not complete, and the Council's influence on the state was weak. Its ambitious research objectives required government financing and Council staff were well aware of the need to mute criticism of government policy; on at least one occasion a failure to exercise sufficient self-restraint led to a threat to cut government funding for an important Council project. Relations between Council staff and leading state actors were cool during the 1970s; in 1976 there was a highly publicized quarrel between the CCSD's executive director and the federal welfare minister about who was responsible for the impending demise of the Review. Also, the Council's policy-formulation autonomy was largely irrelevant in a context where, as we demonstrate below, the federal state had expanded its own capacity to act independently on the new reform agenda.

Figure 2

Poverty Policy Community, 1970s

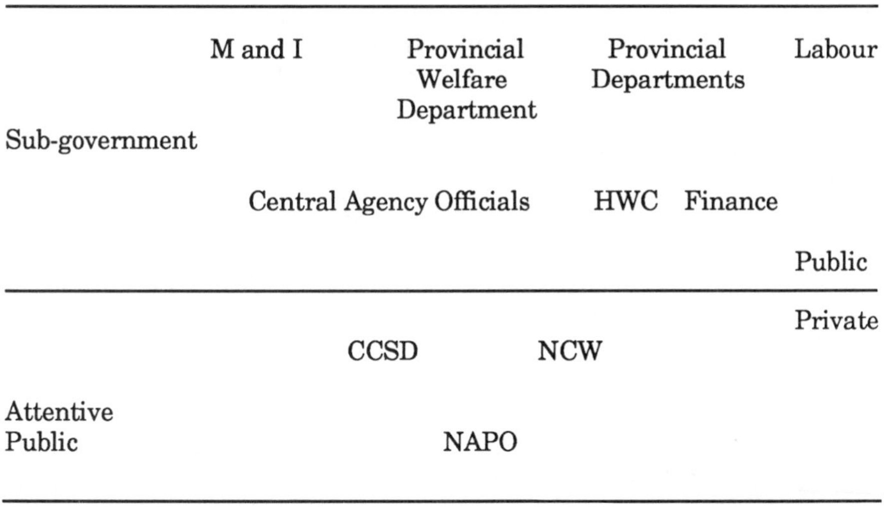

	M and I	Provincial Welfare Department	Provincial Departments	Labour
Sub-government				
		Central Agency Officials	HWC Finance	
				Public
				Private
		CCSD	NCW	
Attentive Public				
			NAPO	

CCSD:	Canadian Council on Social Development	NAPO:	National Anti-Poverty Organization
HWC:	Health and Welfare Canada	NCW:	National Council of Welfare
M and I:	Manpower and Immigration		

The late 1960s witnessed the development of numerous local "welfare rights organizations" across Canada, run at least partly by poor people. These emerging poverty organizations were financed and their behaviour powerfully constrained by the federal government (Felt, 1978; Loney, 1977). When poverty groups at the local level adopted a position or used tactics that were considered too radical, their financing could be cut off, and the group effectively disbanded.[8] In at least one case—Toronto's Praxis Corporation—efforts to mobilize the poor by middle class activists were considered dangerous by some leading officials, and were subjected to more severe sanctions.[9] It was only after 1970 that organizations of the poor began to emerge at the national level; here the imprint of the federal state was especially transparent. The first national organization to acquire at least the partial mandate of representing the poor was the National Council of Welfare (NCW), created in 1970 by the federal government as an advisory committee to the minister of National Health and Welfare. The NCW acquired offices in the Department's main building; it was (and is) wholly financed by the government.

In establishing the NCW, federal politicians stressed particularly the organization's potential as an effective spokesman for the poor. In its early years about one half of the NCW's membership consisted of poor people, and appointments were largely free of patronage. But it nevertheless had little success either in influencing effectively government policy-making or in representing the poor. Major actors within the Council at the time do not feel that they had a significant impact on the government's policy deliberations during the Social Security Review, and key actors within the state agree with this assessment. The organization's status as an advisory body sponsored by government meant that it could not directly lobby on behalf of policy proposals that it publicized. Moreover, there was no real effort to have poor members act as "representatives" of specific poverty organizations across the country. Finally, the Council's staff, and the one half of its members who represented service "producers", were middle class. The NCW was not, and was not intended to be, exclusively representative of the poor (Wharf and Halladay, 1984).

The National Anti-Poverty Organization (NAPO) came into existence in 1971 as Canada's first (and only) national non-governmental organization of the poor. In its early years, however, it was singularly incapable of fulfilling its mandate. Although an almost complete reliance on federal government financing was one reason for this, the main limitation was self-inflicted. NAPO was, in the eyes of other major actors within the associational system, beset by substantial mismanagement that destroyed its credibility as a voice for the poor. Its resources were never effectively employed. Only a major reorganization in 1981 saved NAPO from dissolution.

Neither the NCW nor NAPO, then, were able to influence the federal government by mobilizing Canada's poor. The CCSD, despite its admittedly middle class composition, made some efforts during the 1970s to act as an umbrella organization for the poor, but it largely failed in this endeavour. In 1974 poor people associated with NAPO disrupted proceedings at the CCSD biennial conference and questioned the credibility of the middle class activists from the CCSD. At the 1976 conference there were sharp exchanges between poverty groups and Council staff about the contribution of each to the Review (*Toronto Star*, 17 June 1976).

Before the Social Security Review began, each of these non-governmental organizations took positions on the Guaranteed Annual Income (GAI) and social services, and continued to do so as the Review proceeded. While usually asking for more ambitious reforms than those eventually contemplated by the federal and provincial governments, they broadly agreed with the objectives of a GAI and more comprehensive social services (NCW, 1973; Hartling, n.d; CCSD, 1973). But they had little to do with the inception of the Review, were largely ignored as it proceeded, and were regarded with skepticism by officials when they diverged from bureaucratic objectives on important details. Indeed, senior federal actors consciously avoided involving non-governmental organizations to any significant extent in the Review, feeling that they would only complicate the already difficult task of reaching agreement among the federal and provincial governments.[10]

During the 1970s, the poverty associational system developed important qualities that were lacking a decade earlier. There were now significant organizations attempting to speak for all poor people. The major middle class organization developed a policy-making autonomy that had not existed before. But the system remained fundamentally weak because of its minimal resources, financial dependence on the state, internal fragmentation and very limited capacity to mobilize the poor. Consequently, the impact of the associational system on the Social Security Review was minimal.

The State

During the Social Security Review the state maintained its autonomy from sectoral organizations. The Review owed its origins to state actors: the new poverty reform agenda was largely popularized in Canada by agencies of the federal and provincial governments. Second, the Review was launched in response to imperatives that emerged within the Canadian state system and its subsequent development was also shaped by state institutions.

But the policy-making capacity of the state diminished considerably, as public authority in the poverty sector was diffused among a number of federal and provincial departments and agencies (Haddow, 1988: 10-17). This diffusion of authority, reflected in Figure 2, undermined the Review. Before 1966, poverty reform had been almost exclusively the preserve of federal and provincial public welfare departments, staffed by line officials. But the range of relevant institutions broadened over the next few years, and included a major role for central agencies; consequently, the policy-making capacity of the federal-provincial state system was reduced substantially.

Diffusion of authority in the poverty sector reflected macro-level changes in the Canadian state system. The departmentalized cabinet system was supplanted in the late 1960s by a more "institutionalized" one, that put much greater emphasis on central agencies and, to a lesser extent, public research bodies, as government-wide policy coordinators. The new system was more capable of producing broad policy initiatives involving the jurisdiction of a number of programme departments. Consequently, policy-making, both at the federal and provincial levels, was far more likely to involve an array of heterogeneous institutional interests and, therefore, to produce conflict (Dupré, 1985:7).

Poverty came to the top of the policy agenda in Canada because it was the focus of a number of studies by federal royal commissions, senate committees and research councils; the Québec government also contributed a massive commission of inquiry study in 1971. These bodies each had an ample grounding in the social scientific expertise that permitted study of the new poverty themes. Although many of these themes–including the GAI concept and many ideas for social services reform–originated in the United States, they were largely introduced to Canada by these state-based research bodies.

When the Social Security Review was launched in April 1973, it was neither non-governmental actors nor public welfare officials, but bureaucrats in Ottawa's central agencies, who were the key instigators. In 1970, Québec, at the behest of leading officials and policy analysts, one of whom (Claude Castonguay) became an important provincial minister, made the reform of poverty policy, based on a GAI, a major demand in its relationship with the federal government. Officials in federal central agencies also developed an interest in poverty reform. In contrast, federal politicians of all parties showed little real interest in or understanding of the GAI or other current reform ideas. Québec's persistent demands, and the fluid situation created by a minority federal government elected in November 1972, provided interested officials in federal central agencies with an opportunity to launch reform. Once it was under way, these officials transferred to the Health and Welfare Department, displacing line officials from key policy-making roles.

All of these state actors, in recommending poverty reform, explicitly rejected the possibility that Canada's meagre universal and social insurance programmes could meet the needs of the disadvantaged. A common theme in most of the government-sponsored research studies of the period was that these programmes were inadequate to alleviate poverty and must be supplemented with more targeted measures (Adams 1971: 152-167; Québec, 1970: 247). Similarly, in the early 1970s, federal officials who launched the Review resisted extensions of such non-targeted measures as Unemployment Insurance and Old Age security, arguing that these could do little to help the disadvantaged.

The Review involved a variety of highly heterogeneous federal actors: staff officials from central agencies, labour market specialists in the Manpower and Immigration Department, and programme officials at Health and Welfare Canada (HWC). In addition, the provinces contributed the participation of their public welfare and labour officials. Tensions among the conflicting objectives of these groups played an important role in undermining reform. But the actors most responsible for destroying the Review were officials within the federal Department of Finance. In the worsening economic climate of the mid-1970s, they convinced the Liberal government, which had been restored to a majority in 1974, that the country could not afford a GAI. By 1978, their thinking permeated the Prime Minister's Office, and destroyed any chance of significant reforms of social services. Most politicians had never been very concerned with poverty reform, and with increased pressures for restraint emanating from Finance and the business community, they were easily convinced to drop it.

In the 1970s, the poverty policy community formed a pressure pluralist network. The associational system expanded significantly in the late 1960s and early 1970s, but its membership was weak and fragmented. It therefore failed to challenge the autonomy of the state bureaucracy, which was also given a relatively free hand by politicians. But state policy-making capacity was significantly eroded because authority for poverty issues was dispersed among a number of conflicting federal and provincial bureaucratic interests. Poverty reform failed because of intra-bureaucratic rivalries and, in particular, because of a vociferous attack from the Finance Department.

The dispersion of federal and provincial state authority in the poverty sector reflected macro-level changes in the Canadian state system. An institutional cabinet created conditions favourable to much broader policy initiatives involving many bureaucratic interests, and to a resulting pattern of conflict. The Review also reflected Canada's liberal welfare state. Actors who initiated the reforms advocated measures targeted at the poor because other social security programmes had failed to alleviate poverty.

Poverty and the Contemporary Debate on Canada's Welfare State: The Role of Partisan Politics

The most recent debate on poverty arose in the wake of Canada's unsatisfactory economic performance in the 1980s. For the first time, poverty reform was being championed, in an important way, by a governing political party. Unlike the 1960s and 1970s, poverty reform was also now discussed as an alternative to retaining more universal elements of Canada's welfare state. The Progressive Conservative government proposed to finance enriched selective social programmes for the poor from savings in expenditures on universal and non-actuarial social insurance programmes; hard economic times, they argued, made this the only affordable route to poverty reform. And because this proposal for poverty reform implied the curtailment of programmes that affected the majority of voters, it gave rise to a political debate about the future of Canada's welfare state that continued into the 1990s.

Consequently, opposition parties, as well as sectoral interests, played an important role in developing a contrasting vision of poverty reform. Although there is a need to improve selective measures, they said, addressing the needs of the poor would also require that universal elements of the welfare state be preserved and enriched. Universality was depicted as an integral and necessary element of an attack on poverty (Rice, 1987: 211, 218-219).

This larger debate still involved a poverty policy community; a number of sectoral interests and state institutions shared a preoccupation with poverty issues. What changed was that debates within the sector about poverty were linked to debates about the future of Canada's entire welfare state, and were driven to an important extent by partisan politics. The capacity of sectoral actors to realize their goals depended on developments in the political arena. Unlike the second phase, the poverty policy community was far less self-contained as a sectoral phenomenon.

The Associational System
The poverty associational system has continued to develop in the 1980s with some organizations becoming more capable policy advocates. For the first time, there was an effort to develop umbrella organizations to foster cohesion within the sector. The system also became markedly more differentiated: it included more organizations that contributed greater specialization of interest and (sometimes) greater expertise. These changes are illustrated in Figure 3.

The CCSD remained the major non-consumer organization. Professional staff established objectives in conjunction with a largely middle class Board of Directors. The CCSD had, by far, the largest financial and professional resources in the associational system. Its annual budget in 1988 was $3,232,165 (CCSD, 1987-88: S-15). It had nine full-time staff engaged in research and policy analyses; their efforts were supplemented by several contract positions. About one-quarter of staff time was spent on purely poverty-related issues, and other projects often involve poverty concerns. The Council was invited to participate in some programme evaluations for the Health and Welfare Department, and it has sponsored a lengthy series of meetings across the country between local social policy critics and the Department of Finance's Assistant Deputy Minsters. Personal relations between Council and state actors have improved since the 1970s. Nevertheless, the CCSD re-mained financially dependent on government. Almost 90 per cent of the Council's budget came from government in the form of sustaining or project grants. And despite having the largest research staff in the associational system, it was tiny in comparison to government departments. Consequently, it did not possess expertise that state actors had to rely on, and it was not consulted in detail by officials preparing legislation.

Figure 3

Poverty Policy Community, 1980s

Partisan Arena (Macro-level)	Progressive Conservative Party

Sub-government   Prov. Welfare and Labour Depts.
                 HWC   E and I
       Finance   *Public*

Attentive   SPRG   *Private*
Public
      CCSD / NCW | | NAPO
        NAC   NPSCF ⌐CASW   CACSW   Child
                                            welfare
                                            Organizations

CACSW:	Canadian Advisory Committee on the Status of Women	NAPO:	National Anti-Poverty Organization
CASW:	Canadian Association of Social Workers	NCW:	National Council of Welfare Organization
CCSD:	Canadian Council on Social Development	NPSCF:	National Pensioners and Senior Citizens Federation
E and I:	Employment and Immigration	SPRG:	Social Policy Reform Group
HWC:	Health and Welfare Canada		
NAC:	National Action Committee on the Status of Women		

The NCW was now universally seen by actors in the sector as an invaluable body. Its access to government research resources made it a key source of poverty research for other organizations. None the less, the public status of the Council still precluded it from lobbying on its own behalf, and despite its official status as an advisory body to the Minister of Health and Welfare, it had no intimate relation with the minister or with other government actors as a policy advocate. With a research staff of two and an annual budget of $310,000 in 1989 (which, of course, was provided by the federal government), the Council remained a very modest entity; its prestige largely reflected the stature of its director.

NAPO joined the CCSD and the NCW in forming the nucleus of the contemporary associational system. Since the reforms of 1981, NAPO had become a far more effective body, due mainly to the high quality of its last two executive directors. They have improved NAPO's capacity to develop informed positions on policy issues and enhanced its credibility with the media and government. But NAPO was limited as an independent policy advocate. It remained almost entirely dependent on government for financing and had little capacity to generate policy positions based on independent research. In recent years, it decided to devote little of its meagre resources to research, concentrating instead on its representational role. Internal research resources consisted of the Executive Director, and a full-time "advocacy researcher." NAPO had four full-time employees, and its annual revenues in 1988 were a paltry $306,374 (NAPO, 1987-88: 8). For much of its research it depended on other organizations, especially the NCW. Government actors recognized that NAPO's level of expertise was, of necessity, lower than that of CCSD or NCW.

Consumer groups organized around identities other than poverty have become far more prominent in the last decade in addressing poverty policy reflecting the general broadening of the policy community. Women's organizations became particularly important: the National Action Committee on the Status of Women (NAC) and, to a lesser extent, the Canadian Advisory Committee on the Status of Women (CACSW), were now identified by sectoral actors as important participants in poverty debates. The National Pensioners and Senior Citizens Federation (NPSCF), the main national organization tapping emergent "grey power", and national organizations of the disabled, were also considered important players. These groups each contributed a unique area of interest and expertise to the associational system. But poverty was always secondary in their objectives, and they were not considered to be as significant as the CCSD, NAPO and the NCW as actors in the field. A variety of organizations that have concentrated their energies primarily on child poverty also became active in the sector, and retained a similarly secondary position in the associational system.

With so many more members, the associational system has made unprecedented efforts to coordinate its policy advocacy. These efforts were particularly stimulated by alarm at the direction of government policy after the 1984 election. The most noteworthy result was the Social Policy Reform Group (SPRG), created shortly after Finance Minister Michael Wilson's economic statement of November 1984. SPRG initially consisted of CCSD, NCW, NAPO, NAC, the CACSW, and the Canadian Association of Social Workers (CASW). The CACSW later left SPRG and was replaced by the NPSCF.

SPRG concentrated its efforts on lobbying the Department of Finance. Forging a common front on the future of Canada's welfare state forced member organizations to reconcile obvious policy disagreements that had lessened their collective influence on the government.

SPRG has, however, encountered severe limits. In fact, it was only in a very qualified sense that it could be referred to as a "peak organization." Its members retained complete autonomy in formulating policies, and have continued to act independently in consultations with departments other than Finance, and in informal interaction with the latter as well. SPRG lacked such formal structures as a board of directors, budget or its own staff. Participants, who were selected by constituent groups, met in informal settings and only occasionally decided to take a common public position.

In addition, tensions among member groups emerged almost from the beginning. By 1989, some of SPRG's members felt that the Group might have exhausted its usefulness. The CACSW left SPRG because it was less willing than other members to be critical of government policy. The requirement that organizational spokesmen in the Group have "plenipotentiary" authority to agree to common positions was a problem for other members. Some actors involved in SPRG felt that it only achieved a "lowest common denominator" because of deeper conflicts between some member groups.

SPRG's membership was not comprehensive. The child welfare organizations did not belong to SPRG and have developed their own umbrella group, itself a very temporary and precarious body, to respond to Conservative child care policies. Other assemblies have emerged that were considered more satisfactory than SPRG by some participants. The CCSD sponsored a "last Wednesday of the month" club, that permitted social policy groups to meet informally in Ottawa to discuss common projects. NAPO, labour organizations and some church groups also created a "Working Committee on Solidarity" to pursue common objectives.

The failure to develop a *bona fide* organization reflected the diverse perspectives of those within the associational system. The major groups broadly agreed that there should be improved income supplementation and services for the poor and that the principle of universality must be preserved. But there was disagreement on the appropriate mix of universal and selective measures. The CCSD, for instance, was firmly committed to the retention of universal income maintenance programmes such as Family Allowances and Old Age Security, while important actors in NAPO and the NCW were willing to consider diverting these to needy people. The non-poor consumer groups tended to support universality on this question because of their specific concerns: NAC saw family allowances as a women's benefit, and the Seniors group was a champion of the Old Age Security payment. NAPO and the CCSD disagreed on income transfers versus employment as a tool to alleviate poverty. Finally, personal animosities among leading actors in sectoral organizations inhibited cooperation.

Despite the significant expansion of the poverty associational system in the 1980s, it remained weak and fragmented in important ways. Organizations had limited resources and these were provided almost entirely by the state. Differentiation threatened to exacerbate fragmentation in the associational system, and new coordinating bodies were only partially successful.

The associational system also remained largely incapable of mobilizing the poor. In the late 1980s, the NCW had completely lost any capacity to represent poor people. Since the 1984 federal election, only one brief appointment has gone to a poor person; at the time of writing all Council members were middle class. In addition, Council staff no longer had any influence in the selection of members. These were now chosen as patronage appointments by political staffers in the Prime Minister's Office. The NCW has therefore lost its status as a consumer group.

NAPO saw representing the poor as its main priority. In recent years its membership has grown significantly to include, in 1989, about 1000 individuals and 150 organizations. Most individual members were middle class, but NAPO's executive bodies were largely filled by the approximately one-fifth of its members who have had some experience of poverty. Most staff members also had a poverty background. In keeping with its representational objectives, NAPO aggressively recruited local and provincial organizations that consisted mainly of poor people. NAPO was therefore able to represent poor people better in the late 1980s than it had been in the 1970s. Nevertheless, obviously, the vast majority of poor people remained "almost totally unorganized and collectively inarticulate" (Van Loon, 1979: 253).

In another effort to enhance its representative role, NAPO strengthened the accountability of staff to executive bodies, with mixed success. The Executive Director and other staff became answerable to NAPO's executive committee, and its composition had to be ratified by the NAPO membership. But it is not inaccurate to describe the executive, as one actor did, as "self-appointed." A committee of executive members draws up the list of individuals for new positions as they become open and the membership rarely opts for an alternative.

NAPO could not claim to have mobilized more than a small fraction of Canada's poor people. That this was true in the late 1980s was not due to deficiencies in the organization's leadership, but was probably a consequence of the well-documented barriers impeding participation in political life by socially marginal people (Piven and Cloward, 1977: 352-353; Schlozman and Verba, 1979).

The State

In the third phase, the state remained largely autonomous from non-state organized interests. But because poverty debates were now entangled with a partisan dispute about Canada's entire welfare state, sectoral state officials did not have nearly as much autonomy as in the

The State

In the third phase, the state remained largely autonomous from non-state organized interests. But because poverty debates were now entangled with a partisan dispute about Canada's entire welfare state, sectoral state officials did not have nearly as much autonomy as in the past. Figure 3 portrays the contemporary pattern of policy-making authority within the state.

The federal state continued to have an institutionalized cabinet system in the 1980s.[11] In keeping with this macro-level structure, bureaucratic authority in the poverty sector remained dispersed among a number of federal bureaux with differing objectives. The tensions in federal-provincial relations that typify an institutionalized cabinet remained.[12] The major change in the macro-level structure of the federal state was Finance's heightened stature, a change that permitted it to displace HWC as the lead department in the poverty sector. Finance's greater prominence, like other recent developments in the federal state, was "designed to pursue the government's substantive policy priorities and in so doing to alter the configuration of power in the executive-bureaucratic arena." It therefore reflected partisan factors, especially the more restrictive fiscal priorities of recent federal governments (Aucoin, 1989: 335, 338), and the selectivist objectives of the Conservative government in social policy.

In the past, Finance's involvement had consisted of efforts to restrict potentially costly recommendations from elsewhere in the bureaucracy. By the late 1980s, Finance's Social Policy Division had become an active policy-maker in its own right, concentrating on the potential use of the tax system as a mechanism for meeting social policy objectives in a selective manner. The department also developed a Consultation Division to conduct pre-budget discussions with interest groups; as a result, poverty organizations, through SPRG, had far more formal interaction with government officials than in the past and, far more with Finance than with other departments. Nevertheless, the department appeared to share the Conservative government's social policy goals, and SPRG had little impact.

Health and Welfare remained an important actor in the poverty field, but policy-making there became largely incremental. Where the department had been involved in a more significant way, the objectives of its officials were curtailed by the government's, and Finance's, goals. For instance, in the day care area, while Health and Welfare participated in drafting the abortive, federal proposal of 1988, it was Finance who drew up the basic design, which was considered far too restrictive by many Health and Welfare officials. As one of the latter put it, "I'm still healing from this myself." Because of its concern for manpower programmes, the Employment and Immigration Department (the successor to Manpower and Immigration) retained a role in the poverty sector. Changes in federal legislation also still required consultation with provincial labour and welfare officials. Within the federal bureaucracy, Finance's selectivist social policy goals now prevailed over competing bureaucratic objectives because these goals mirrored those of the governing party.

The poverty debate continued to be premised on the inadequacy of Canada's universal and social insurance measures to meet the needs of the disadvantaged. All participants accepted the need for improved measures targeted at the poor. What was new in the contemporary context was the Conservative argument that hard economic times required a reduction in broader elements of the welfare state to meet better the needs of the poor. Throughout its first term, the Conservatives advocated redirecting universal income security and non-actuarial social insurance payments to the needy; they became more determined in pursuing this objective after the 1988 election. A restrictive view of social security was also reflected in the government's treatment of social services (Johnson, 1989: 273-278).

Conservative policy preferences have not been implemented without resistance, and sectoral organizations played an important role in mounting opposition. These "rearguard" actions against policy developments were confined to measures that affected the interests of the non-poor; and, in such cases, public opinion could sometimes be galvanized against them. The partial success of organized interests was therefore explained by the broader focus of the contemporary debate on poverty, and the resulting creation of issues that concerned large numbers of voters. Sectoral interests had to have the public "on their side" to have any success in confronting the Conservative agenda. For instance, various groups, especially the NPSCF, played an important role in thwarting a 1985 attempt to partially de-index the universal old age security benefit, once public interest was attracted to the issue. The government's restrictive child care proposals, also, were attacked by a number of organizations; child care and women's organizations were particularly effective here. The proposals were withdrawn in the April 1989 budget, in part because these groups discredited them with the public (Prince, 1985; Rice, 1987; NAPO, 1987-88: 3).

Sectoral organizations obtained a friendly hearing from officials, at least at Finance, or from Conservative ministers, when they made specific proposals that were compatible with the overall agenda of the government. These were implemented in the context of broader policies with which the organizations disagreed. One sectoral actor aptly referred to this process with the phrase "one step forward and two steps backwards." For instance, the NCW played a role in convincing the federal government to introduce a sales tax credit, and to increase it substantially in the 1989 budget; various groups, especially these changes were in keeping with the government's desire to deliver social benefits more selectively through the tax system, and the overall impact of tax changes since 1984 was far from progressive.

Despite resistance from sectoral organizations, the Conservative government implemented important elements of its agenda. Rice (1987), Johnson (1989) and O'Connor (1989: 141-42) have documented the increasingly selectivist and restrictive guise of Canada's welfare state in recent years. The Conservatives have introduced a number of significant changes: the partial de-indexation of family allowances in 1985; the elimination of the government's financial contribution to the Unemployment Insurance fund, and a "claw back" of family allowance and old age security benefits for the affluent in 1989; numerous tax changes which benefit the rich most, while adding to the tax burden of other Canadians; and attempts to increase the incentive for welfare recipients to join the work force. Just as sectoral organizations require public support to impede the Conservative agenda, success for government would require that Canadians accept reductions in universal and non-actuarial social insurance benefits. Minimal public resistance to a vigorous reassertion of the agenda in the 1989 budget augured well for Conservative objectives in the years ahead.

In the period since 1984, the poverty policy community has retained elements of pressure pluralism. The associational system is still weak, and state actors have retained considerable autonomy from sectoral organizations. In addition, public authority in the poverty community remains diffuse; it includes a number of competing bureaucratic interests. But a sectoral focus no longer affords the explanatory import it once did; macro-level factors now figure more prominently. The poverty debate has become linked to supra-sectoral issues and has been driven primarily by partisan politics and the ability of governing politicians to, at least, obtain public acquiescence to their preferred policies. Sectoral state institutions retained an important role in developing policy, but within a broader macro-political debate.

The macro-level factors that set the parameters for earlier reforms remained relevant. The diffusion of policy-making authority in federal and provincial states continued to occur in the broader context of an institutional cabinet system. Finance's recent ascendancy in the poverty sector also reflected its more general rise in stature within the federal state. Second, Canada's liberal welfare state remained a presupposition of reform debates. All participants in policy debates presumed that improvements were needed in social measures directed at the poor, because of the relative underdevelopment of non-targeted social security measures in Canada.

Canada's debate over poverty policy provides evidence that the liberal welfare state can influence policy developments in another way.

We noted earlier that, for Esping-Andersen, popular allegiance to social security, especially in the middle class, depends on the prevailing model of the welfare state. The underdevelopment of universal and social insurance programmes in a liberal welfare state results in limited support, or shared loyalty, among middle class citizens, to such broad-based programmes (Esping-Andersen, 1985: 242-244; see also, Goodin and LeGrand, 1987). This weak pattern of support is apparent in the contemporary social policy debate in Canada, which is witnessing increasing public acceptance of an erosion of universal social programmes.

Conclusion

There is a distinctive poverty policy community in Canada, and it has experienced certain continuities throughout the postwar period. Despite growing since the 1960s, the associational system has remained weak, consisting of organizations that have a limited capacity to engage in independent policy advocacy, are highly fragmented, and have little ability to mobilize the consumers of poverty programmes to support policy reform. The state has been consistently autonomous from sectoral interests.

Since the 1960s, there has been a considerable dispersion of authority over poverty issues within the federal-provincial state system. This decentralization has caused friction among competing bureaucratic interests, and a reduction of policy-making capacity. Consequently, the policy network evolved from state-direction in the 1960s to pressure pluralism in the 1970s. In the most recent period elements of pressure pluralism remained, but an exclusively sectoral typology of networks no longer described the poverty sector, because developments within it became driven by broader partisan conflicts. As Coleman and Skogstad remind us in Chapter One, the relationship between macro and sectoral level phenomena must be treated as a variable.

Sectoral analysis must be complemented by two macro-level factors that have set the parameters of poverty policy-making throughout the postwar years. First, account must be taken of prevailing structures of the federal state and of federal-provincial relations. The concentration of public authority for poverty in federal and provincial welfare departments during the 1960s reflected the existence of a departmentalized cabinet system at the federal level, and of cooperative relations between the two levels of government. The institutionalized cabinet of the 1970s facilitated a dispersion of state policy-making capacity that destroyed the Social Security Review. In the late 1980s, similarly, divergent bureaucratic interests persisted within the sector, under the overall domination of a Finance Department that was also the dominant department in the federal state.

The second macro-level parameter of the poverty sector is Canada's liberal welfare state paradigm. Throughout the postwar period, policy-makers have taken it as a given, in face of the relative underdevelopment of universal and social insurance programmes, that the extension of measures targeted at the poor must be central in any attempt to alleviate destitution. Because Canada's universal social measures are modest, they have not eliminated a need for measures targeted at the most needy. In 1986, consequently, approximately one-sixth of Canada's social security expenditures were devoted to public assistance and associated services; 1,892,900 Canadians were assistance recipients in that year, representing 7.5 per cent of the national population (NCW, 1987: 8; Canada, Health and Welfare Canada, 1985: 70, 78). Assistance therefore persists as an important element in Canada's welfare state, and measures targeted at the poor remain a focus of policy debates.

In Canada's contemporary debate, the ideological heritage of a liberal welfare state is also having an impact. Although there certainly has been public resistance to reductions in the modest universal and social insurance elements of Canada's welfare state, the Progressive Conservative government appears to be gaining public acceptance for cuts in these measures. Internationally, recent attacks on the welfare state have been most vociferous in other countries, such as the US and Britain, where the liberal model prevails (Mishra, 1984: 25). In liberal welfare sates, formative political class coalitions precluded the development of generous social insurance or universal social measures, and widespread loyalty to the welfare state did not emerge. Thus, the pleasant prospects for the Progressive Conservative reform agenda are related to the historic pattern of social relations embedded in Canada's welfare state.

References

Adams, Ian, et al. (1971). *The Real Poverty Report.* Edmonton: Hurtig.

Atkinson, Michael and William Coleman (1989). "Strong States and Weak States: Sectoral Policy Networks in Advanced Capitalist Economies." *British Journal of Political Science*, 19: 47-67.

Aucoin, Peter (1989). "The Mulroney Government, 1984-1988: Priorities, Positional Policy and Power." In A. Gollner and D. Salée, eds. *Canada Under Mulroney.* Montreal: Véhicule Press: 335-56.

Canada. Health and Welfare Canada (1985). *Social Security Statistics, Canada and the Provinces, 1960-61 to 1984-85.* Ottawa: Supply and Services Canada.

Canadian Council for Social Development (1973). *Social Security in Canada* Ottawa: CCSD.

_____ **(1987-88).** *Annual Report.*

Canadian Welfare Council. Public Welfare Division (1957-58). *Annual Report.*

_____ **(1958).** *Social Security for Canada.* Ottawa: CWC.

Dupré, Stefan (1985). "Reflections on the Workability of Executive Federalism." In R. Simeon, ed. *Intergovernmental Relations.* Toronto: University of Toronto Press, 1-32.

Dyck, Rand (1976). "The Canada Assistance Plan: The Ultimate in Cooperative Federalism." *Canadian Public Administration,* 19: 587-602.

Esping-Andersen, Gosta (1985). "Power and Distributional Regimes." *Politics and Society,* 14: 223-56.

_____ **(1989).** "The Three Political Economies of the Welfare State." *Canadian Review of Sociology and Anthropology,* 26: 10-36.

Felt, Lawrence (1978). "Militant Poor People and the Canadian State." In D. Glenday et al., eds. *Modernization and the Canadian State.* Toronto: MacMillan: 417-41.

Goodin, Robert and Julian LeGrand (1987). *Not Only the Poor.* London: Allen and Unwin.

Haddow, Rodney (1988). "Class Interest, State Structure and Social Marginality; Poverty Policy in Canada, 1963-1978." Paper presented to the 60th Annual Meeting of the Canadian Political Science Association, Windsor, Ontario.

Hartling, Marjorie, Executive Director, National Anti-Poverty Organization (n.d.). "Toward a Guaranteed Annual Income." NAPO: Ottawa.

Johnson, Andrew (1989). "Canadian Social Services Beyond 1984: A Neo-Liberal Agenda." In A. Gollner and D. Salée, eds. *Canada Under Mulroney.* Montreal: Véhicule Press: 265-83.

Jones, Catherine (1985). *Patterns of Social Policy.* London: Tavistock.

Kahn, Alfred and Sheila Kamerman (1983). *Income Transfers for Families with Children.* Philadelphia: Temple University Press.

Korpi, Walter (1980). "Social Policy and Distributional Conflict in Capitalist Democracies. A Preliminary Framework." *Western European Politics,* 3: 296-316.

Lawson, Roger and Robert Walker (1984). "Lessons for the United Kingdom." In Walker et al., eds. *Responses to Poverty.* London: Heinemann.

Loney, Martin (1977). "A Political Economy of Citizen's Participation." In L. Panitch, ed. *The Canadian State: Political Economy and Political Power.* Toronto: University of Toronto Press, 446-72.

Mishra, Ramesh (1984). *The Welfare State in Crisis.* Brighton: Wheatsheaf.

National Anti-Poverty Organization (1987-88). *Annual Report.*

National Council of Welfare (1973). *Incomes and Opportunities.* Ottawa: NCW.

_____ **(1987).** *Welfare in Canada.* Ottawa: NCW.

O'Connor, Julia (1989). "Welfare Expenditures and Policy Orientation in Canada in Comparative Perspective." *Canadian Review of Sociology and Anthropology,* 27: 127-150.

Piven, Frances and Richard Cloward (1977). *Poor People's Movements.* New York: Pantheon.

Prince, Michael (1985). "Startling Facts, Sobering Truths and Sacred Trusts: Pension Policy and the Tories." *How Ottawa Spends: 1985.*Toronto: Methuen: 114-61.

Québec. Commission of Inquiry on Health and Social Welfare (1970). *Report.* Vol 5, tome 1, title 1.

Rice, James (1987). "Restitching the Safety Net: Altering the National Social Security System." *How Ottawa Spends: 1987.* Toronto: Methuen: 211-35.

Schlozman, Kay and Sidney Verba (1979). *Injury to Insult.* Cambridge, Mass.: Harvard University Press.

Van Loon, Richard (1979). "Reforming Welfare in Canada." *Public Policy*, 27: 569-504.

Wharf, Brian and Allan Halladay (1984). *The Role of Advisory Councils in Forming Social Policies.* Hamilton: McMaster University.

Wolfe, David (1989). "The Canadian State in Comparative Perspective." *Canadian Review of Sociology and Anthropology*, 26: 95-126.

Endnotes

1. Much of the evidence for each case is based on confidential interviews with leading actors from sectoral organizations and relevant departments of government. Many points from the first two cases are treated at greater length in Haddow (1988).

2. Thus, Britain's welfare state is mainly liberal because liberal principles were embedded in the welfare state at its origins, and the Labour Party, although it has sometimes held office, was unable subsequently to win middle class support for social measures designed on other than liberal principles. Extensive reliance on benefits targeted at the poor remains a feature of the British welfare state (Esping-Andersen, 1989:29).

3. The large number of poverty organizations at the provincial and local levels in Canada have been excluded from the analysis. National organizations have been the most important poverty actors in federal policy-making.

4. A PWD director at the time spoke frankly about the purpose of this practice (CWC, 1957-58:2).

5. The main organizations were the Canadian National Institute for the Blind, the Canadian Council of the Blind and the Canadian Rehabilitative Council for the Disabled.

6. The attitudes of federal officials are reflected in a departmental memorandum of August 8, 1961; PAC RG 29, vol. 1682, file 20-J-9A.

7. Canadian Welfare Council (1958:9), Willard to LaMarsh, April 29 and May 20 and 23, 1963, RG 29, vol. 2311, file 251-15-1, pt. 7; Bryden (1974: 152-153).

8. This was the fate of a Hamilton Welfare Rights organization in 1971. See Health and Welfare Minister Munro's press statement at the time; PAC RG 29, vol. 1605, file 7.

9. The Praxis Corporation organized a poor people's conference in 1970. The Corporation's files were rifled and its premises burned while it was making arrangements for the conference. The RCMP later acknowledged having the missing files, and returned some of them.

10. Federal policy-makers expressed these misgivings at private conferences with the provinces. The minutes are in PAC RG 29, vols, 1296-12, 99.

11. Coordination and collegial decision-making remain central in the Mulroney cabinet. This is only partly qualified by recent changes in the cabinet system; see Aucoin (1989:345-347).

12. For instance, federal cuts in Established Programme Financing transfers to the provinces, used in part to finance universal health insurance, have caused friction with the provinces.

CHAPTER TEN

INSTITUTIONS AND INTERESTS IN THE OCCUPATIONAL HEALTH ARENA:
THE CASE OF QUÉBEC

Carolyn Tuohy

Those who study Canadian politics in comparative perspective have wrestled in recent years with the possibilities and the implications of establishing tripartite policy-making structures in the Canadian context. In European settings, the establishment of structures drawing together representatives of labour, business and the state has made possible the negotiation of policy packages in which, typically, labour trades off some measure of wage gain for increases in social security benefits and the maintenance of high levels of employment. Where these tripartite structures have developed most fully, they have usually been preceded by the emergence of "encompassing organizations" of labour and business. Furthermore, they are most likely to develop where a comprehensively organized labour movement is both strengthened by the presence of a strong social democratic party ally and made vulnerable by a domestic economy open to international forces (Maier, 1984; Katzenstein, 1985).

The conditions under which labour is able and willing to pursue a strategy of collaboration with business and the state through tripartite structures, then, are fairly limited. And the implications of such a strategy for the advancement of labour interests in capitalist systems is a matter of considerable dispute. Cameron has demonstrated that labour "quiescence" (as indicated by moderate wage demands and low levels of strike activity) was associated, across eighteen OECD nations from 1965-1982, with relatively low levels of unemployment and relatively high levels of social spending. However, "neither quiescence nor militancy over the long term has a great deal of impact on the distribution of income between capital and labour" (Cameron, 1984:170-174). In a solidaristic sense, full employment and "social wages" may be seen as gains for the working class; but the lack of redistribution between capital and labour gives some credence to Panitch's earlier contention that corporatism within liberal democracies is merely another vehicle for reinforcing class dominance (Panitch, 1977:81).

Canada would not appear to be a strong candidate for the emergence of tripartite structures: the organization of both labour and business interests is fragmented at the national level; there is a long history of markedly adversarial labour relations; and organized labour remains highly skeptical of the benefits of tripartism. Furthermore, Canada lacks the strong "state tradition" with which these structures have been associated (Atkinson and Coleman, 1989). Nonetheless, Canada's moderately open economy has placed labour (as well as business) under increasing pressure to adjust to international economic developments. Furthermore, labour has social democratic allies in government. Social democratic parties have held power at the provincial level; and, at the federal level, the New Democratic Party continues to exert electoral and parliamentary pressure from the left. The limited experimentation with tripartism in economic policy arenas has been viewed at best with caution and more typically with skepticism by academic observers (Banting, 1985) and within the labour movement itself.

There is, however, one policy arena in which tripartite structures are somewhat more fully developed—that of occupational health and safety. In this arena, primary responsibility is held at the provincial level; this development has allowed for experimentation with tripartite structures where business and labour are *relatively* cohesively organized and where social democratic parties have been in office. Such experimentation has progressed furthest in Québec. In the Canadian context, this is not, at least initially, surprising. Among Canadian provinces, Québec has the highest level of unionization in Canada; and, with British Columbia, is the only one with an umbrella employers' federation. It has the strongest tradition of "corporatism" among Canadian provinces, and its citizens evince the most "statist" attitudes.[1] The development of the tripartite structures under review here, moreover, occurred under the social democratic Parti Québécois. On a broader international perspective, however, Québec tripartism presents a somewhat anomalous case. Although the level of unionization in Québec, at just over 43 per cent, is high by Canadian standards, it is modest by European standards. Furthermore, the Québec labour movement is organizationally fragmented into rival federations and independent unions. The largest labour federation, the Fédération des Travailleurs et Travailleuses du Québec (FTQ), affiliated with the Canadian Labour Congress, comprises unions representing about half of the organized workers in the province. The next largest federation, the Confédération des syndicats nationaux (CSN), represents about 30 per cent of organized workers; the remainder are represented by a small federation of unions primarily in the textile and clothing sectors, the Centrale des syndicats démocratiques (CSD) and a number of independent unions. Furthermore, there is a significant radical syndicalist tradition in the Québec labour movement, most closely idenified with the CSN, but also espoused to varying degrees by public sector unions such as those affiliated with the Centrale de l'nseignment du Québec (CEQ) and the independent Syndicat des Professionels du Gouvernement du Québec (SPGQ).[2] Those who adhere to this tradition hold that unions should concentrate their efforts where they have the most effective sanctions to back their demands— that is, in the workplace, where they can confront employers with the ultimate threat of a strike. They are highly suspicious of centralized collaborative tripartite models, believing that labour is inevitably out-gunned in forums in which the relevant resources are the information and analysis to which employers and governments have disproportionate access, and in which, moreover, the capitalist state is the employers' natural ally. The syndicalist tradition is not the only, or even the dominant force in organized labour in Québec, but it militates against the smooth development of tripartite structures.

Similarly, Québec business is organizationally cohesive only by North American, and not by European standards. The Conseil du Patronat du Québec—the umbrella employers' organization—has as members both individual firms and other employer associations. The Canadian Manufacturers Association—Québec division, for example, is a member with guaranteed representation on the CPQ board, as are the Montreal Board of Trade and a small-business federation, the Centre des Dirigeants d'Entreprise (CDE). As Coleman (1985:267) notes, however, the CPQ has some difficulty in speaking for small business. The Québec and Montreal Chambers of Commerce, whose memberships are primarily composed of small businesses, are not CPQ members. The ability of the CPQ to maintain formal and informal coalitions with other business organizations has varied over time, especially as different partisan factions are advantaged by changes in the political executive.

Notwithstanding these inhospitable aspects of the climate, the most full-blown model of tripartism in the occupational health arena in North America has developed in Québec.[3] The bureaucracies charged with both regulatory (so-called "prevention and inspection") matters and workers' compensation are overseen by a single board, the Commission de la Santé et de la Sécurité du Travail (CSST), which was established by the PQ under 1979 legislation, and reports to the Minister of Labour. The governing board of the CSST comprises equal numbers of part-time labour and management representatives appointed by government in consultation with the major labour and employer federations in the province, and is chaired by a full-time government official. In addition, there are a number of "sectoral associations" funded by the CSST to perform information and training in occupational health and safety matters in particular industrial sectors. The governing structure of these associations is "bipartite" in that they are comprised of representatives from labour and management, but not from the government. A third significant component of the Québec system is the Institut de recherche en santé et en sécurité du travail du Québec (IRSST), a research institute funded primarily by the CSST. The governing board of the CSST also functions as the governing board of the IRSST, although decision-making is, *de facto*, in the hands of a scientific advisory council composed of labour, management and scientific representatives.

In short, looking at the occupational health arena, Québec presents us with an example in which tripartite institutions have been established in the context of an essentially North American structure of fragmented interests. The structure that has developed in Québec forms part of an intriguing comparative case. The comparative literature on occupational health policy has suggested that there are essentially two models under which labour can advance its interests in the occupational health arena, at least insofar as that advance can be measured by the adoption of protective health standards. On the "US" model, a fragmented labour movement can attempt to deploy its limited resources strategically in a pluralist state—influencing the establishment and staffing of executive agencies, manoeuvering to have cases heard in sympathetic courts, and so on. Coordination is not required, indeed a certain redundancy can perform a "fail-safe" function. This model is close to the model of "pressure pluralism" described by Coleman and Skogstad in the first chapter to this volume. On the "European" model, cohesively organized labour can attempt to function as a "social partner" with business and the state, as a full participant within tripartite regulatory structures. This is Coleman and Skogstad's "corporatist" model. Notably, in the occupational health field, the policy outputs of these two models appear to be roughly similar—the most protective regulatory exposure limits for major hazardous substances have been adopted by European corporatist systems (the Scandinavian countries, West Germany and Austria) and the United States (Tuohy forthcoming).

The European corporatist/American pluralist dichotomy does considerable violence to the variation among European jurisdictions (not to mention the rather procrustean efforts required to fit certain nations, notably Japan, within either category), and in particular implies a neglect of important differences in the power of labour in different "European" jurisdictions. Nonetheless, it is possible to identify at least four major points of difference between these two approaches:[4]

- *Internal vs. external representation of interests*: In the European model, affected interests are incorporated within the structures of executive decision-making; in the American model they are granted rights to challenge executive decisions from the outside at various stages of the process, through "notice and comment" provisions and opportunities for judicial review.

- *Closed vs open processes*: The judicialization of the US process has meant that, in contrast to European processes, it is remarkably open to public view and even to public participation. In contrast, European deliberations are conducted among relatively small groups of labour, business and government representatives, well out of the public eye. These closed processes are an intrinsic part of the European tripartite model: they are necessary to foster the close, small-group dynamics of collaboration upon which this model depends.

- *Accommodative vs punitive enforcement*: European inspectors have been described as adopting an accommodative style, negotiating schedules and levels of compliance and offering advice; whereas American inspectors are said to adopt a punitive style, citing violations and imposing fines. Comparisons are, in fact, difficult because of the differences in the sanctions available. US inspectors are empowered to levy administrative fines; whereas European inspectors must rely upon a prosecutorial framework.

- *Bureaucratic continuity vs political volatility*: European structures for the making and enforcement of occupational health standards, although they have undergone various organizational reforms, generally exhibit a tradition of bureaucratic continuity. Furthermore, the role of labour (and business) within these structures does not change sharply with changes in the government of the day. In the US, on the other hand, the Occupational Health and Safety Administration was established in 1970 as a new "zealot" agency; and its role and orientation changed dramatically with the coming of the Reagan administration in 1981.

On the surface, Québec's tripartite and bipartite structures look remarkably "European". They do not, however, function on the European model; with closer examination, the effects of their lack of fit with the fragmented organization of interests in Québec become apparent. The structures are politically contentious and less stable than their European counterparts. Furthermore, institutional differentiation allows for the use of multiple instruments and strategies—some collaborative, but others markedly adversarial. There is, nonetheless, a *reciprocal* causality between these institutional structures and the structure of organized interests. Some institutional sub-structures, because of the nature of their mandates or because of the structure of interests in particular sectors, may be better able than others to function effectively as tripartite institutions. The "demonstration effect" of these more successful sub-structures may allow the tripartite model to survive even in an inhospitable partisan climate, and even in the face of competing adversarial strategies. Over time, then, organized interests not only shape but also adapt to institutional change. The incentives established by tripartite structures may encourage fragmented interests to develop inter-organizational networks and to adopt collaborative strategies, at first with regard to certain sub-structures and then more generally.

The rest of this chapter examines these distinctive features of the Québec hybrid: contention and instability, the use of multiple instruments and strategies, and the development of inter-organizational networks and strategies. The discussion draws upon CSST documents, previous academic work, and interviews with key participants.[5] Given the scope of this chapter, the emphasis is primarily on the representation of labour interests, although developments in the representation of employer interests will be treated insofar as they affect the context within which organized labour functions.

Political Contention and Instability

Throughout its history, the CSST has been marked by controversy: controversy surrounding its original creation by the Parti Québécois (PQ) government in 1980, the development of its institutional structure, and the changes made by the Liberal government in 1986 and 1987.

The Creation of the Commission de la Santé et de la Sécurité du Travail

The creation of the CSST, like other tripartite experiments under the PQ (Tanguay, 1984; Fournier, 1985), was very much a governmental initiative. For some within the PQ, support for tripartism was ideologically linked to Québec nationalism. As one of the architects of the CSST put it in an interview, "an alliance of the social partners in Québec is essential if Québec is to remain a distinct society". The sense of economic vulnerability which has given impetus to the development of tripartism elsewhere is complemented in Québec, it would seem, by a sense of political and cultural vulnerability. In 1978, the government published a White Paper on *Occupational Health and Safety* (Québec, 1978), which outlined problems with the current structures and policies for the prevention and compensation of industrial injuries and diseases, and proposed comprehensive reforms. The principal problems identified were the fragmentation of authority over occupational health and safety, the "absence of workers" from the decision-making system, and the inadequate attention given to occupational disease as opposed to traumatic injury.

The structural reforms proposed were centred upon the creation of a new body, the CSST, that would replace the former workers' compensation board, the Commission des accidents du travail (CAT), and that would also have authority over "prevention and inspection" activities, including the making and enforcing of occupational health and safety regulations. The Board of Directors of the CSST was to be composed of equal numbers of representatives of management and labour, to be chosen from lists submitted by the "most representative" organizations of employers and employees, plus a government-appointed "director general" as a full-time chair and two non-voting assistant directors. At the sectoral level, the White Paper also proposed the withdrawal of CAT funding from existing "safety associations" of employers in favour of bipartite "sectoral associations". And at the workplace level, it proposed the establishment of joint labour-management health and safety committees.[6]

In developing its reform proposals both before and after the publication of the White Paper, the PQ government drew eclectically from a variety of international models. In September 1978, one month before the publication of the paper, Québec hosted the annual meeting of the International Association of Workers Compensation Boards and Commissions, a major theme of which was the greater participation of the "partners" in prevention and compensation regimes (Pontaut, 1986:120-21). The White Paper itself made little reference to international models, merely drawing attention to the contrasting approaches of the US (characterized as "very interventionist") with the British emphasis on self-regulation at the workplace level under the general authority of the Health and Safety Commission (Québec, 1978:61-62). In the period between the publication of the White Paper and the introduction of legislation, however, the president of the CAT, who was spearheading the reforms, made an information-gathering tour of the Netherlands, Sweden and the UK, which "confirmed the directions taken by the Québec White Paper" (Pontaut, 1986:121).[7]

In June 1979, Bill 17, which gave legislative form to the principles set forth in the White Paper, was introduced into the National Assembly. Reaction to the proposed legislation, as to the White Paper, revealed divisions on both labour and management sides. The CPQ, in its brief to the parliamentary committee considering the legislation, lauded the objectives of the legislation, but objected to the proposed powers of workplace committees, and to the fact that sectoral associations were to be jointly governed but financed only by employers' worker compensation premiums. Several major firms and associations from within and outside the CPQ's membership, including the Québec Chamber of Commerce, echoed and endorsed the CPQ's views. The language of the Canadian Manufacturers Association- Québec division was even more conciliatory. It hoped that the state would "assume its responsibilities toward all concerned partners not only in seeking to innovate but also in seeing to a stricter enforcement of existing legislation" (Pontaut:126). Other management voices were more hostile. The Association des Mines de Métaux du Québec (a CPQ member), for example, opposed the proposed structural reforms as creating "an enormous technocratic structure"; and the Fédération of Catholic School Boards charged that the employer would no longer be "maître chez lui" and decried the fact that the sectoral associations would "extinguish" employer associations (Pontaut, 1986:125-26). Most opposed, however, were groups representing small and medium-sized business, who saw the legislation as leading to increased powers for unions and increased unionization, and, through the sectoral associations, to multi-employer bargaining (Plasse, 1985:132).

As for the unions, the FTQ was generally supportive of the legislation—indeed it was the government's major ally in this instance. The CSD was somewhat less supportive, expressing concerns about excessive centralization and technocracy (Pontaut, 1986:127-28). These concerns may in fact have reflected fears that the proposed regime might actually reduce incentives to unionization (since non-unionized plants could receive from sectoral associations various information and consulting services which unions normally provide to their own members), and fears that the regime might come to be dominated by a small group of union activists (a particular concern for a small federation such as the CSD) (Plasse, 1985:150-51). Nonetheless, the CSD's long-standing support for participatory mechanisms ultimately led it to support the legislation overall.

The CSN, the CEQ and a number of independent unions, however, strongly opposed the legislation as constraining union activity. The CSN central argued that it "erected hindrances to union action," and constituent CSN unions attacked the proposals as a "machiavellian plan attempting to counter union action" and as seeking "the elimination of the union." For the CEQ, only union "force" could counter the logic of profit which drove the capitalist organization of production. And for the SPGQ, the legislation would too tightly constrain the union "fight" for occupational health and safety (Pontaut, 1986:126-28). The language of their criticisms reflected the radical traditions of these unions.

The legislation was also opposed by the opposition Liberal Party. However, with a majority in the National Assembly, the PQ secured passage of the legislation in December 1979. Political action then shifted to different ground: the appointment of the CSST Board, and the establishment of sectoral associations.

Appointments to the Commission de la Santé et de la Sécurité du Travail Board, 1980-82

The first two rounds of appointments to the Board were of key significance in launching the new CSST structure. And two things were crucial to this process: the character of the first President (chair) of the Board, and the alliance between the PQ government and the FTQ. In appointing Robert Sauvé, the former President of the CAT and one of the principal architects of the new design, as the first President of the Board and Director General of the CSST, the government clearly signalled its commitment to the structure and provided it with strong, labour-oriented leadership. Sauvé was, ironically, a former secretary of the CSN and a former deputy minister of labour. In the latter capacity, he had promoted the concept of sector-based negotiations, and implemented it in the construction sector. He had been appointed to the CAT in 1977 to begin the process of reform.

The second crucial factor in the launching of the CSST was, as noted, the existence of an effective alliance in this arena between the PQ government and the FTQ. This alliance required that the CPQ (which was not indisposed to collaborative mechanisms in any event) take seriously the establishment of the CSST. Eventually but not immediately, even unions and union federations opposed to the establishment of the CSST fell in line. Finally, the PQ-FTQ alliance meant that the FTQ would hold the majority (four) of the seven labour seats on the CSST Board.

The way in which the first appointments were made established several important precedents. The legislation required the seven labour and seven management members, who were to be appointed for two year renewable terms, to be chosen from lists provided by the "most representative" union associations and employer associations respectively. This left unspecified the allocation of seats among associations. It soon became clear that this was to be a matter for the government's own discretion, and that the government did not feel bound by the lists presented, but rather considered them subject to negotiation.

On the labour side, the appointment process was complicated by the internal division within the CSN regarding participation in the new structure. This division reflected long-standing tensions in the CSN regarding participation in *any* government structures: the view that such participation constrained unions in their "struggle" was pitted against the belief that it was necessary to participate in decisions which affected the interests of union members (Fournier, 1985:306; Plasse, 1985:156-57). In general, these views split along public sector/private sector lines, with public sector unions opposing participation and private sector unions supporting it. In 1980, the CSN central refused to participate; but two of its affiliated federations in forestry and construction independently agreed to take seats on the CSST Board after being approached directly by the Minister of Labour.

As for the FTQ, its first concern was to secure the majority of labour seats on the Board, basing its case on the fact that it represented a majority of union members. From the government's point of view, however, allocating four seats to the FTQ severely constrained its own ability to offer representation to other federations or unions. Given the FTQ's support of the government, and the opposition of the FTQ's major rival the CSN, the FTQ was able to strike a deal with the government establishing its majority at the outset. However, the need to defend this principle over time has had important implications for FTQ strategy. It has, for example, come to determine the allocation of seats *among* FTQ affiliates: it must fend off challenges from other unions and union centrals by allocating seats to those sectors in which other unions are strong but the FTQ has a majority or plurality of membership—notably construction, the public sector and resource industries.[8] The need to defend against challenges to the FTQ majority has also led to a decision that members of the FTQ executive, and not specialists in health and safety, should occupy the FTQ seats.[9] The reasoning has been that only members of the executive have the stature to make the claim to a seat on the board stick. The quintessential example of such "clout" is that wielded by the FTQ president, Louis

Laberge, who holds one of the FTQ seats and a seat on the Executive Committee of the CSST as well. With four seats allocated to the FTQ, and two to CSN affiliates, the government was left in 1980 with only one seat to allocate to one of a number of contenders. The major contenders were the CEQ and the CSD. In this case, the CSD may have paid an initial price for its general support of the new structures: the Minister of Labour allocated the seat to the CEQ in an attempt to bring these opponents of the new structure "on board". In the subsequent round of appointments in 1982, however, this seat was allocated to the CSD.

On the management side, the appointment process was dominated by the relationship between the government and the CPQ. Five of the seven management seats were allocated to the CPQ. The CPQ's internal allocation of these seats was accepted by the government—with one exception.[10] The final allocation of CPQ seats included one seat to the executive vice-president (later president) of the CPQ, Ghislain Dufour; two to association members of the CPQ (the Canadian Manufacturers Association (CMA)-Québec division and the Association des Mines de Métaux du Québec); and two to individual member firms.

One of the two remaining management seats was allocated by the government to an organization of cooperatives as a signal of support for that form of management. The ambiguous status of this association as a "management" association, however, meant that its claim to a management seat was ultimately untenable, and its representative's term was not renewed in 1982. The final management seat went to the Association des Hôpitaux du Québec, which was not a member of the CPQ.

The Establishment of Sectoral Associations
The 1979 legislation provided for the establishment of sectoral associations, to be administered by boards "composed, in equal numbers, of representatives of the employers associations and representatives of the union associations." Such associations were to be voluntary in every sector except construction, in which specific groups were required to come to an agreement regarding the establishment of a joint association.[11] Only one association per sector was to be recognized and funded by CSST.

As conceived, these sectoral associations mirrored to a limited extent the bipartite accident insurance associations of West Germany and France. Their structures, with bipartite governing boards reporting to bipartite general assemblies, were similar; but the functions and powers of the Québec associations were much narrower than those of the European bodies—they were essentially to provide "training, information, research and counselling services to employers and workers" in their respective sectors.[12] These provisions nonetheless constituted a sweeping repudiation of the employer-governed and CAT-funded "safety associations" that had existed for decades, and no small measure of disgruntlement on the part of employers had to be overcome in the process of putting these new structures in place. And in fact, this process has been lengthy and incremental.

The legislation specified little more than the requirement of "parity" representation on the governing boards of sectoral associations. A subsequent CSST regulation established a few other parameters relating to the holding of an annual general assembly and the appointment of an executive committee. All other matters related to the establishment and functioning of the associations—notably the mechanisms of representation and voting and the very definition of sectors—were to be dealt with in agreements between unions and employer associations, which were to be approved by the CSST. The CSST did, however, publish guidelines as to how the various parties were to proceed with establishing sectoral associations, beginning with a steering committee, and proceeding to a general assembly which was to elect a board of directors.

The ease of establishing these sectoral associations varied widely across sectors. Two agreements were approved in 1981, two in 1982, three in 1983, five in 1985, and one in 1986 (CSST, 1987a). In construction, the only sector in which the establishment of a joint sectoral association was mandated in the legislation, the incorporating agreement was not reached and approved until February 1985. And in some significant sectors, such as forestry and foundries, no sectoral association has been established to date. The willingness of groups to enter into agreements varied across sectors. The disgruntlement of some employer groups has been noted. On the labour side, CSN affiliates in the public sector were generally less willing than CSN-affiliated private sector unions to enter into these agreements, although a CSN affiliate participated in the first sectoral association created. The union and management demography of particular sectors varied as well: some were clearly dominated by one or two associations on each side; others were considerably more pluralistic. In several cases, the definition of the sector was far from straightforward, and the way in which the sector was defined had important implications for the ability of various associations to claim to be "representative" (George, 1986:53).

The FTQ and various of its affiliated unions were very active in the formation of sectoral associations. In most sectors, they replicated the strategy which had proved successful at the CSST Board level. That is, they attempted to establish a claim to a majority of labour seats on the association's governing board, on the basis that their membership constituted a majority of union members in the sector. Of the 13 sectoral associations that had been established by 1987, FTQ unions (or the FTQ central) held all union seats on the governing board of one, an outright majority on another five, and a plurality on another two. Voting mechanisms on the governing boards varied, but in at least five and possibly seven cases, they afforded a potential veto to FTQ unions (CSST, 1987a). The realization of these advantages, of course, depended upon the extent to which the actions of FTQ unions were coordinated and in some cases, the FTQ members of the CSST Board "had words" with affiliates which took different positions in sectoral associations (George, 1986:87).

Notwithstanding the predominance of FTQ unions, the agreements reached also tended to favour the over-representation of small unions (and, on the management side, small employer associations as well) (George, 1986; Plasse, 1985). This resulted primarily from the active encouragement by the government (through the CSST) of broad participation. In at least one case (automobile services), it resulted as well from the recognition even on the part of large unions and employer associations that changing economic circumstances could leave them, over time, less "representative" (George, 1986:86).

To some extent, this over-representation of smaller unions, together with the predominance of FTQ unions, left other medium-sized unions "squeezed" in terms of their representation. Voting mechanisms, however, tended to be designed to require the building of coalitions across unions (and across employer associations)—most associations operate on the basis of "double majority" or "bloc" voting. The building of these coalitions entails complex relations among individual unions, between unions and the central federations, and among the central federations—relationships charged, in the arena of sectoral associations as elsewhere, with the force of ideological differences and economic rivalries.

Appointments to the Commission de la Santé et de la Sécurité du Travail Board, 1984

The most significant change relating to Board appointments in 1984 was the decision of the CSN central to participate. A number of factors entered into this decision: the CSST Board had clearly become an important forum in the health and safety arena; CSN affiliates were participating centrally and at the sectoral level; and the CSN's internal polling suggested that health and safety issues were second only to job security issues for its rank and file members. The CSN executive took pains to portray this decision as a "strategic" choice that did not imply an endorsement of tripartism. In presenting its recommendation to the membership in June 1983, the executive committee affirmed "with force the absolute necessity for our organization to be present wherever the interests of our members are being discussed and are at issue," while emphasizing that the CSN was still engaged in the "syndicalism of struggle, of class, of the masses and of combat." (Reported in Plasse, 1985:156; author's translation) In explaining the decision to participate on the CSST Board ratified at the May 1984 CSN convention, the CSN president declared that "our policy of participation is a strategic, rather than an ideological or political policy ... and it is important not to underestimate our capacity to influence, to promote and to persuade" (Reported in Fournier, 1985:306).

The two CSST Board seats which had been occupied by CSN affiliates were filled with a member of the CSN central executive and a member of the CSN central staff. The staff member was assigned full-time to CSST matters. This decision by the CSN to fill one of its two seats with a full-time health and safety specialist contrasted with the FTQ's strategic decision to appoint only executive members, but it underlines the pragmatism with which the CSN approached its role on the CSST Board.

With two seats, the CSN was somewhat under-represented on the Board: it had about 29 per cent of union membership but 21 per cent of labour seats. The FTQ, in contrast, with 53 per cent of union membership, has 57 per cent of union seats. But the distribution of seven seats is inevitably "lumpy", and to have given one of the FTQ's seats to the CSN would have resulted in an even greater imbalance in the other direction. The FTQ was able to make this point with relatively little difficulty. The CSD continued to occupy the remaining seat on the Board. At least two other groups, the CEQ and the independent public sector union, the Syndicat des Fonctionnaires Provinciaux du Québec (SFPQ), had a stronger claim to representation on the basis of the size of their memberships, but the deteriorating relationship between the PQ government and these public sector unions at the time, together with the fact that another public sector union, the Canadian Union of Public Employees (CUPE), occupied one of the FTQ seats, militated against their appointment.

On the management side, the 1984 appointment process was a rather rocky one. Relationships between the government and business, especially small business, were worsening in this period. In the health and safety arena, these relationships were increasingly dominated by compensation issues, as the government prepared a set of amendments to workers' compensation legislation that tended to liberalize compensation policy. Attempting to build bridges to small and medium-sized business, the government allocated to the Chambre de Commerce de la Province du Québec the seat which had been occupied by the Association des Hôpitaux du Québec. In a very controversial move, however, the government again refused one of the nominees of the CPQ. It responded to a division within the construction sector by choosing a construction representative other than the one nominated by the CPQ on behalf of one of its constituent organizations, the Association des Entrepreneurs en Construction du Québec (AECQ). The representative appointed, however, resigned in January, 1985, as did a CPQ representative in October 1985. These seats were not filled until the first round of appointments under the Liberal government in 1987.

Changes Under the Liberal Government, 1986-87

The election of a majority Liberal government in December, 1985 dramatically altered the balance of power in the occupational health and safety arena. Business interests, particularly those which had felt most disadvantaged under the PQ government and looked to the Liberal government to enhance their position, initially found considerable comfort. Committees of inquiry were appointed to look into the potential for deregulation and privatization—and, within their more general mandates, addressed issues of CSST reform. Pierre Paradis, from the right wing of the party, was appointed Minister of Labour. Robert Sauvé was replaced as President and Director-General by Monique Jerome-Forget, a former federal civil servant with a reputation for managerial expertise and also with Liberal connections (as the spouse of a former Québec Liberal cabinet minister). Indeed, as part of a re-organization intended to model the CSST more closely on business corporations, the title of Director-General was changed to that of Chief Executive Officer. In the course of this re-organization, three of the four vice-presidents (the staff tier immediately below the president) were also replaced. [13] As shown in Table 1, the authorized complement of the CSST declined more sharply in the Liberals first year in office (1986) than had been the case in any previous year, and was frozen in 1987. The declines in actual complement are even more marked. However, in comparison to the complement changes in the US and even in the UK after changes in government, these changes in Québec appear modest. [14]

The triangular relationship between the government, the FTQ, and the CPQ had clearly been broken. On the government side, internal tensions were apparent. Paradis had been a leadership candidate in the contest won by Robert Bourassa; and considerable rivalry and ideological disagreement continued. Jerome-Forget was Bourassa's choice; and Jerome-Forget and Paradis established separate task forces to review the CSST. The alliance of different factions of the Liberal party with different segments of business vastly complicated the task of the CPQ in maintaining a business coalition—essentially, the Liberal party was assuming the role of brokering among business interests. [15] The more extreme business opponents of the CSST, moreover, accused the CPQ of having "collaborated" with the PQ government. [16]

Table 1

Percent Change in Complement, CSST 1981-87

| | Percent Change from Previous Year | |
	Authorized*	**Actual**
1981	+10.8%	NA
1982	- 1.0	+6.9
1983	- 3.0	-0.4
1984	+ 1.3	-0.5
1985	- 1.0	-0.1
1986	- 4.6	-2.4
1987	0.0	-4.1

Source: CSST Rapports Annuels

*Authorized refers to budgetary allocation of person years that may or may not be taken up.

Of the three principal players, the FTQ maintained the greatest degree of cohesiveness, due in large part to the stature of its president, Louis Laberge. This was most apparent in the first round of appointments to the CSST Board under the Liberal government, in the fall of 1987.[17] Paradis offered the FTQ three, not four seats on the Board; Laberge immediately informed Bourassa that the FTQ would boycott the CSST unless it retained its four seats. Bourassa was not prepared to risk the destabilization of labour-management relations that would be precipitated by a boycott of the CSST by a group which had been one of its pillars. As a result, the entire labour side was re-appointed unchanged in 1987.

The management side, however, changed almost entirely. Only one CPQ nominee, the president, Ghislain Dufour, was accepted. Others were selected from various associations, some chosen by Paradis, others by Bourassa. Appointees included representatives of sectors that had previously opposed the CSST[18] or felt excluded from it. Representatives of large firms dominated; only one represented small and medium-sized business.

This section has emphasized the political contention and instability that have characterized the first eight years of the CSST's existence. To leave the discussion at this point, however, would neglect important changes which have been brought about by the intersection of the institutional structures with the structure of labour and management interests. The next two sections address these changes.

Multiple Instruments and Strategies

Introduced as they were into the context of a relatively fragmented structure of interests and an adversarial tradition of labour-management relations, the CSST structures have not functioned smoothly on the collaborative "European" model. But neither have they disintegrated into adversarialism. Rather, collaborative strategies have been used in some settings, adversarial strategies in others.

Some mandates, indeed, may lend themselves better to collaboration than others. This section of the chapter briefly reviews the use of collaborative and adversarial strategies in various sub-arenas.

The Research Institute

Perhaps the best example of collaboration in the Québec system is in the sub-arena of research. As noted above, the CSST has a research arm, the IRSST. Although separately constituted, the IRSST is funded by a CSST grant[19] and the CSST Board of Directors also functions as the IRSST Board. Effective decision-making power in the IRSST is, however, held by its advisory Scientific Council composed of four labour representatives (two from the FTQ and two from the CSN), four management representatives, and five "scientific" representatives from academe and industry. The scientific representatives are appointed after informal consultation with labour and management, and have been drawn from academic centres of industrial relations as well as from occupational hygiene, engineering and health science backgrounds. The IRSST operates an accredited occupational health laboratory and funds research in both university and industrial settings.

Relationships among the members of the Scientific Council are closely collaborative—especially within labour and management "caucuses" but also across caucuses. The development of these networks is encouraged by the fact that the FTQ and the CSN have appointed members of their occupational health and safety staffs to the council, and some management representatives have also had experience in occupational health and safety. A number of IRSST-funded projects and initiatives have drawn praise from both labour and management sides.

The IRSST survived the transition under the Liberal government with relatively little change, despite the view of the new management members on the CSST (and hence the IRSST) Board that researchers needed to be held on a "tighter rein." The CSST grant to the IRSST was slightly reduced, and research teams were held more closely accountable for specific research projects; but the members of the Scientific

Council, and their collaborative working relationships, remained unchanged.

The Sectoral Associations

At the level of the sectoral associations (SAs), a mix of strategies has been apparent. As noted above, the system of sectoral associations is one to which employer associations and unions must agree to "opt in": that is, a SA is established only where unions and employer associations can agree on the definition of the sector and the structures and processes of the SA. The genius of this model has been to allow for a certain variety of structures and processes suited to the nature of union-employer relations in particular sectors. It has meant that the highly adversarial nature of significant but delimited sectors, such as forestry, has not prevented the establishment of SAs in other sectors. It has also allowed successful SAs to have "demonstration effects."

The mechanisms which various SAs have adopted for resolving disputes give a rough indication of their tendency toward, or at least their anticipation of "collaborative" or "adversarial" strategies. Eight of the 13 SAs provide for matters that cannot be settled by their governing boards to go to arbitration—a mechanism clearly patterned on a adversarial collective bargaining model. Four SAs provide for disputes to be settled "without arbitration" or through "conciliation," and one provides for either arbitration or conciliation (CSST, 1987a).

The functioning of the SAs has fostered the development of networks among the staffs of unions, employer associations and the SAs themselves. In most cases, each union or employer association sends one staff member to meetings of staff, regardless of its proportionate representation on the board of the SA—an arrangement which tends to reduce the perception of power differentials and to promote collaborative relationships. Indeed, participation in such staff networks has allowed unions effectively to augment the staff expertise available to them, and has provided incentives to greater participation.

The Review Boards

The most adversarial element of the Québec system is the process of appealing decisions made by officials of the CSST in compensation cases and workplace inspections. These decisions may be appealed to tripartite Review Boards established by the CSST for each of its regional offices. These boards are composed of a CSST official as chair and two members nominated by the CSST Board members representing labour and management respectively. For each region, the labour and management Board members submit a list of individuals, who are drawn in turn to form review board panels. In the case of labour, the Board members agreed that their lists would comprise 60 per cent FTQ nominees, 32 per cent CSN nominees and 8 per cent CSD nominees. Again, the CSN has indicated the seriousness of its pragmatic commitment to these structures by assigning staff fulltime to the review boards; the FTQ and the CSD assign union activists who have other duties as well. Decisions of the Review Boards may be appealed to the Commission d'Appel en Matière de Lesions Professionelles, an administrative tribunal under the Minister of Justice.

The "litigiousness" of the parties in the Québec system is indicated by the heavy workload of the Review Boards and the Commission d'Appel. Inspectors' decisions appealed to the review boards numbered about 375 in 1986 and about 200 in 1987. By contrast, in Ontario, despite a workforce 1.5 times as large and with twice as many annual inspections, about 100 inspectors' decisions per year are appealed through the Ministry of Labour's internal appeal process. Furthermore, the relatively few appeals in Ontario are more likely to be resolved through mediation or other settlement mechanisms (McKenzie and Laskin, 1987: Vol.2:47). Not only does the Commission d'Appel receive more appeals of review board decisions on inspection matters (Commission d'Appel, 1987:10) but several cases, indeed, have been taken beyond the Commission d'Appel to judicial review. The Review Boards, the Commission d'Appel, and their predecessor agencies[20] have substantial case backlogs.

The flow of appeals of inspection decisions in Québec is a mere trickle, however, when compared with appeals of worker compensation matters. Compensation matters accounted for 63 per cent of appeals in 1986 and 70 per cent in 1987. Combining compensation and inspection matters under the same body, indeed, may have allowed the litigiousness and rancour associated with compensation issues to spill over into the inspection arena, and to have increased the likelihood that inspectors' decisions will be appealed. We will return to this point later.

Enforcement and Compliance Mechanisms

CSST inspectors themselves take a relatively "punitive" or "prosecutorial" approach. The CSST prosecution process involves a "prior notification" phase: offenders who fail to comply with inspectors' orders receive a prior notice of violation stating the fine to be paid. Payment of the fine constitutes a guilty plea. Those who fail to respond to the notice within a specified time period are liable to prosecution before the Labour Court. As indicated in Table 2, the CSST appears to take a more punitive approach than does, for example, the Ontario Ministry of Labour. The CSST does not report the size of fines, so it is not possible to compare its approach with those of US and European agencies. If the cases in which the CSST cites violations are equivalent to US "serious violations," however, the CSST would appear to take punitive action at roughly the same rate as do the US Occupational Safety and Health Administration (OSHA) and state agencies.[21]

Table 2

Prosecutions under Occupational Health and Safety Legislation

	Québec		Ontario
	Prior Notice	**Labour Court**	
1983	481	297	398
1984	895	459	333
1985	1534	746	441
1986	1335	911	481
1987	1145	715	NA

Sources: CSST Rapports Annuels; Ontario Ministry of Labour Annual Reports

The compliance strategy of the CSST is premised not only on inspectors' activities but on the encouragement of joint labour-management health and safety committees at the workplace level—an element modelled on systems in place in Europe and in other Canadian jurisdictions.[22] The legislation requires that such committees be established in sectors defined by regulation, in workplaces where twenty or more workers are employed, and where the union (or 10 per cent of the workers where there is no union) so request. The CSST Board put these requirements into effect by a 1983 regulation in ten "priority" sectors, employing about 13 per cent of the workforce covered by the legislation. By 1987, committees had been established under the legislation in just over 30 per cent of establishments with more than 20 employees in these sectors. The committee requirements were to have been extended to another group of "priority" sectors, including public administration, in 1985. The PQ government at the time, however, facing its own difficulties as an employer with public sector unions in an election year, delayed publication of the legislation and the Liberals have not yet acted on it.

The Commission de la Santé et de la Sécurité du Travail Board

At the apex of the structure, the CSST Board has generally managed to avoid the adversarialism and acrimony which characterize some segments of the system. The Board has generally not been plagued by strategic "leaks" and boycotts as have other tripartite structures in this and other arenas in Canada (although as noted the FTQ did threaten a boycott in order to preserve its four seat allocation in 1987). Regular meetings of both labour and management "caucuses" are held, and staff networks link the participants on a ongoing basis. Relationships between the two sides are generally characterized by pragmatic negotiations. Perhaps the best example of this pragmatism is the fact that representatives on the political extremes of the Board—from the CSN and the management of a forestry firm—each report that they can "deal" with each other to find practical solutions to specific problems.

The regulation-making processes of the Board favour face-to-face negotiations in small groups rather than broad and open participation. Initial drafts of regulations, prepared by CSST staff, are discussed and revised, first in task forces appointed by the Board, and then by the Board itself. In some cases, such as the development of standards for aromatic hydrocarbons in the mining industry, the sectoral association has also become involved. After a regulation has been approved by the CSST board, it goes to Cabinet for approval. After Cabinet approval, as in the case of other regulations in Québec, there is a 60 day public comment period before the regulation becomes final. The period between CSST approval of a regulation and its becoming final provides an opportunity, not so much for hitherto unrepresented interests to participate, as for interests who perceive themselves to have lost at the CSST level to lobby at the Cabinet level. In some cases, particularly in the period immediately prior to the 1985 election, these lobbying efforts resulted in the "shelving" of regulations—Cabinet simply did not act to approve regulations sent forward from the CSST.

The regulatory output of the Board has so far been concerned largely with structural and procedural matters—relating, for example, to sectoral associations and workplace joint health and safety committees (discussed above) and to workplace "prevention programs." With regard to the latter, all employers in 15 designated "priority sectors" (accounting for about one quarter of the workforce) are required to adopt a written prevention programme according to CSST criteria and to submit it for comment to the workplace joint health and safety committee were one exists. Employers in establishments with more than 20 employees are to submit the programme and the committee's comments to the CSST. As of 1987, 70 per cent of such employers had complied with these requirements.

The process of revising and updating the overlapping sets of occupational health and safety standards which the CSST inherited from its predecessor agencies, however, has been protracted and fruitless. If we use Permissible Exposure Levels (PELs) for hazardous substances as representative indicators of the "protectiveness" of Québec's regulatory standards, Québec appears to lag behind the leaders in this respect, such as Sweden, West Germany and the United States. Québec adopted universally applicable standards for about 600 hazardous substances by regulation in 1979[23] at the same time as it adopted the Act Respecting Occupational Health and Safety. Previous regulations for industrial establishments and foundries, specifying less protective standards, were continued in force, however, and differences between these regulations have not yet been reconciled. Assuming that the most protective standard takes precedence, Québec's PEL's are in about the same category of protectiveness as Britain, but behind the US and the European corporatist systems (Tuohy, forthcoming). Revisions to these standards have been periodically considered, but no formal action has yet been taken.

In part, this delay may have been due to "stalling" tactics as various parties have waited for more favourable political climates in which to press their advantage. For example, labour respondents allege that employer representatives stalled Board activity in the run-up to the elections of 1981 and 1985, anticipating (in the first case incorrectly, in the second case correctly) a Liberal victory. More importantly, however, the attenuation of the regulatory process is attributable to the increasing preoccupation of the CSST with compensation matters. From 1984 onward, the agenda was dominated by the preparation, passage and implementation of new workers' compensation legislation. The passage of this legislation occasioned even more controversy than had the passage of the Act respecting Occupational Health and Safety in 1979. It occupied 135 hours of committee hearings and debate, which generated over 100 amendments and passed over Liberal opposition.

The financial significance of the compensation function dwarfs that of "prevention" (that is, the setting and enforcement of standards and other regulatory requirements, the provision of health and safety training and the funding of research). In 1986, for example, compensation programmes (not including administrative costs) accounted for over $1.25 billion of the CSST's total expenditure budget of $1.49 billion (CSST, 1986). Compensation issues, because they involve employer financing of worker benefits, are even more likely to be seen as "zero-sum" issues than are prevention measures. The latter, although they entail compliance costs for employers (and in some cases for workers), arguably "pay off" in terms of decreases in the lost time and disruption attributable to occupational injuries. In the case of the CSST, certainly, compensation issues have generated more conflict than any other matters. Of the three occasions on which the chair has had to exercise the casting vote, all have had to do with compensation.

Reciprocal Casuality

The functioning of the institutional structure of the CSST has been shaped by the organization of labour and management interests in Québec, and the relationship of those interests to political parties. But the causality is reciprocal: the organization and the strategies of interest groups themselves are beginning to be shaped by these structures. The most arresting example of this effect is the participation of the "anarchico-syndicalist"[24] CSN in these structures. While the CSN remains somewhat dubious as to whether the gains from participation are worth the substantial commitment of its resources ("We fight and fight", said one respondent, "for a word on a page."), it is becoming increasingly integrated into the labour "caucus" and staff networks.

For the most part, these reciprocal effects have occurred within organized labour. In the face-to-face process of developing common positions vis-à-vis employer representatives, links have been forged among representatives of unions that regularly confront and raid each other in the industrial relations arena. These links have been forged at the sectoral level through sectoral associations, and at the centre through the CSST Board and associated task forces, and the IRSST.

Effects on relationships between labour and management are somewhat less apparent. Some sectoral associations, such as the one for metalworking, have adopted a pragmatic, problem-oriented approach (for example, to the reduction of noise) which has won praise from both employers and unions. And the scientific council of the IRSST has been a forum for labour-management cooperation in the definition of research priorities. Even on the CSST Board, as noted, pragmatism has generally governed relationships. There is, indeed, a considerable irony in the pragmatic relationships between the left (CSN) and the right (forestry) on the Board. Both saw the Board, at least initially, as "fighting ground"[25] and hence allowed their representatives to commit a great deal of time to Board activities. These representatives consequently developed a considerable familiarity with the issues and have become accustomed to dealing with each other—factors that have encouraged a degree of pragmatism.

However, relationships amongst employer groups, at least at the central level, have been little affected by experiences within CSST structures, and much more affected by shifts of power within and between the PQ and the Liberal party. The few "high profile" businessmen appointed to the Board in the 1987 round of appointments by Premier Bourassa, have had little time to devote to Board activities. At the level of some sectoral associations, however, linkages among employer associations may be fostered through participation in joint projects.

Summary

As an example of an attempt to establish "European" tripartite institutions in the context of a North American structure of fragmented interest organizations, it is not surprising that the Québec system contains elements of each of the (American) pluralist and (European) corporatist models discussed in the first section of this paper. Joint decision-making bodies on the European model find parallels in the boards and task forces of the CSST, the IRSST and the sectoral associations; but the "litigiousness" of the American model, the external challenging of decisions, finds an analogy in the heavy use of administrative appeal procedures in Québec. In general, the policy-making process is characterized by face-to-face collaboration and negotiation among a delimited number of interest representatives, rather than by American-style open hearings and debate. The development and passage of statutory legislation is an exception to this rule: the 1979 occupational health and safety legislation and the 1985 workers' compensation legislation involved legislative hearings, numerous submissions and lengthy partisan debate. Enforcement by CSST inspectors has tended toward "punitiveness" on the American model; but a complementary concept of enforcement (so far not widely implemented) is premised on the ability of workplace joint health and safety committees to ensure compliance with standards.

Finally, the effects of the partisan complexion of government on the system have been mixed. On the American model, the institutional framework was created virtually *de novo* by "zealots" within government. In this case, the zealotry had to do as much with the concept of "social partnership" as with occupational health and safety issues *per se*. A change of the party in power led, again on the American model, to substantial changes in organization and personnel in the CSST bureaucracy, including the President, and to a slowing down in the development and implementation of policy. It also led to a change in all but one of the employer representatives on the CSST Board. But the labour caucus on the Board remained intact, as did the Scientific Council of the IRSST. Furthermore, the bipartite sectoral associations, as structurally independent of (though funded by) the CSST, were relatively untouched by the partisan change in government.

What is most distinctive about the Québec system, in short, is the *institutional differentiation* that allows tripartite collaboration to thrive in some contexts, bipartite collaboration in others, and adversarialism in yet others. Furthermore, the Québec case demonstrates a degree of *reciprocal causality* between institutions and interests. Institutional processes have clearly been shaped by the strategic behaviour of fragmented interests. But tripartite and bipartite institutions have provided certain niches in which collaborative relationships have developed—a process that has had a slow and incremental but nonetheless important effect on organized interests, especially labour interests. Ongoing face-to-face discussion and the development of staff networks are forging organizational and strategic bonds among rival labour federations and unions, and are accustoming both labour and employer groups to pragmatic collaboration.

References

Archibald, Clinton (1984). "Corporatist Tendencies in Québec." In Alain G. Gagnon ed. *Québec: State and Society*. Toronto: Methuen: 353-64.

Atkinson, Michael and William Coleman (1989). *The State, Business and Industrial Change in Canada*. Toronto: University of Toronto Press.

Badaracco, Joseph (1985). *Loading the Dice: How Institutional Arrangements Shape Business-Government Relations*. Boston: Harvard Business School.

Banting, Keith, ed. (1985). *The State and Economic Interests*. Toronto: University of Toronto Press.

Brickman, Ronald, Sheila Jasanoff and Thomas Ilgen (1985). *Controlling Chemicals*. Ithaca: Cornell University Press.

Cameron, David R. (1984). "Social Democracy, Corporatism, Labour Quiescence and the Representation of Economic Interests in Advanced Capitalist Society." In John H. Goldthorpe, ed. *Order and Conflict in Contemporary Capitalism*. Oxford: Oxford University Press: 143-78.

Campbell, Stewart (1986). *Labour Inspection in the European Community*. Brussells: Health and Safety Executive.

Coleman, William D. (1985). "Canadian Business and the State." In Banting, 245-90.

Commission d'Appel en Matière de Lesions Professionnelles (1987). *Rapport annuel, 1986-87*. Québec. Ministère de la Justice.

Commission de la Santé et de la Securité du Travail (CSST) (1980-87). *Rapports annuels*. Québec. Ministère du Travail.

_____ **(1981a).** *Loi sur la santé et la securité du travail: sources, buts, commentaires*.

_____ **(1987a).** *Associations sectorielles paritaires: fiches signaletiques*.

Dion, G., ed. (1973). *La politisation des relations du travail*. Québec: Les Presses de l'Université Laval.

Fournier, Pierre (1985). "Consensus Building in Canada: Case Studies and Prospects." In Banting, 291-336.

George, Kenneth (1986). *Entre syndicats, entre patrons: Alliances fragiles*. Montréal: Agence d'Arc.

Goldthorpe, John H., ed. (1984). *Order and Conflict in Contemporary Capitalism*. Oxford: Oxford University Press.

Hudon, Raymond (1984). "Polarization and Depolarization of Québec Political Parties." In Gagnon, 314-30.

Katzenstein, Peter (1985). *Small States in World Markets*. Ithaca: Cornell University Press.

Kelman, Steven (1980). "Occupational Safety and Health Administration." In James Q. Wilson, ed. *The Politics of Regulation*. New York: Basic.

_____ **(1981).** *Regulating America, Regulating Sweden*. Boston: M.I.T. Press.

Lehmbruch, Gerhard (1984). "Concertation and the Structure of Corporatist Networks." In Goldthorpe, 60-80.

Lipsig-Mummé, Carla (1984). "The Web of Dependence: Québec Unions in Politics Before 1976." In Gagnon, 286-313.

Maier, Charles S. (1984). "Preconditions for Corporatism." In Goldthorpe, 39-59.

McCaffrey, D.P. (1982). *OSHA and the Politics of Health Regulation.* New York: Plenum.

McKenzie, G.G. and J.I. Laskin (1987). *Report on the Administration of the Occupational Health and Safety Act.* Toronto: Ministry of Labour, Government of Ontario.

Noble, Charles (1986). *Liberalism at Work.* Philadelphia: Temple University Press.

Office of Technology Assessment (1985). *Preventing Illness and Injury in the Workplace.* Washington, D.C.: U.S. Congress.

Ornstein, Michael D., H. Michael Stevenson and A. Paul Williams (1980). "Region, Class and Political Culture in Canada." *Canadian Journal of Political Science,* XIII: 227-71.

Panitch, Leo (1977). "The Development of Corporatism in Liberal Democracies." *Comparative Political Studies,* 10:61-90.

Plasse, Micheline (1985). *La loi sur la santé et la securité du travail: une analyse de sa mise en oeuvre.* Thèse du doctorat, l'Université du Québec à Montréal.

Pontaut, Alain (1986). *Santé et securité.* Montreal: Boréal.

Presthus, Robert (1973). *Elite Accommodation in Canadian Politics.* Toronto: Macmillan.

Québec (1978). *Santé et securité au travail.* Québec: Editeur Officiel du Québec.

Simeon, Richard and Donald E. Blake (1980). "Regional Preferences: Citizens' Views of Public Policy." In David J. Elkins and Richard Simeon, eds. *Small Worlds: Provinces and Parties in Canadian Political Life.* Toronto: Methuen: 77-105.

Tanguay, A. Brian (1984). "Concerted Action in Québec, 1976-1983: Dialogue of the Deaf." In Gagnon, 365-85.

Tremblay, Louis-Marie (1972). *Le syndicalisme québécois: Idéologies de la CSN et de la FTQ, 1940-1970.* Montreal: Les Presses de l'Université de Montreal.

Tuohy, Carolyn (forthcoming). *Tripartism without Corporatism: Labour, Business and the State in the Occupational Health Arena.*

Endnotes

1. On Québec corporatism, and the historical role of the Roman Catholic church and the state in its development, see Presthus (1973: ch. 2) and Archibald (1984). Simeon and Blake (1980) and Ornstein et al. (1980) have demonstrated a greater "statism" in public attitudes in Québec than in other provinces since the 1960s.

2. For discussions of the syndicalist tradition and its place in Québec labour politics, see Dion (1973), Tremblay (1972) and Lipsig-Mummé (1984).

3. Two other provinces (British Columbia and New Brunswick) entrust both compensation and regulation to semi-independent boards on which labour and management are represented. Alberta, Saskatchewan, Manitoba, Ontario and Prince Edward Island maintain "advisory councils" on occupational health and safety, on which labour, management and other interests are represented. Ontario also provides for labour and management representation within the structures of the Workers' Compensation Board. No other province however, has developed as comprehensive a system of tripartite institutions as exists in Québec.

4. These points are developed more fully in Tuohy (forthcoming). See also Badaracco (1985), Brickman et al. (1985), Campbell (1986), Kelman (1980; 1981), McCaffrey (1982), Noble (1986), Office of Technology Assessment (1985).

5. Interviews were conducted with members of the CSST Board, and staff of the CSST, labour federations and sectoral associations.

6. The White Paper also proposed a massive re-organization of occupational health services which is beyond the scope of the present discussion.

7. In 1981 the CSST published an annotated version of the Québec Act Respecting Occupational Health and Safety which drew attention to provisions in Swedish, Ontario, and Saskatchewan legislation.

8. Since 1982, these seats have been allocated to the International Brotherhood of Electrical Workers, the Canadian Union of Public Employees, and the United Steelworkers of America respectively.

9. In the first round of appointments, the FTQ did allocate one of its seats to the director of its health and safety department, but since 1982 the strategic decision has been to nominate only executive members.

10. The CPQ nominated an industrial physician, but the government, which wished to have a representative of the Association des Hôpitaux du Québec on the Board, believed that to have an industrial physician as well would introduce too strong a medical perspective into what was intended to be a labour/management/government Board, and required the CPQ to produce another nomination.

11. If the parties failed to come to an agreement, the CSST was empowered to prescribe the terms and conditions for the establishment of a sectoral association.

12. *An Act Respecting Occupational Health and Safety*, R.S.Q. 1980, Chapter S-2.1, s.101.

13. Like the President, the vice-presidents are appointed by the government for renewable terms of "not over five years." Other personnel fall under the *Public Service Act*.

14. Reductions in complement in the occupational health field were common across western industrial nations in the early 1980s, after a buildup of staff in this area in the 1970s. In Sweden, this pattern was virtually unaffected by partisan change in the governing party; the nonsocialist coalition did not reverse the pattern of increase upon its election in 1976 nor did the Social Democrats reverse the declining trend upon their return to power in 1982. In the UK, retrenchment may have begun somewhat earlier under Thatcher in 1979-80 than it might otherwise have done; the occupational health and safety complement, after a period of increase in the 1970s, declined by 1.4 per cent in 1979-80 and 5.5 per cent in 1980-81. These reductions pale in comparison to experience in the US, however, where the Occupational Safety and Health Administration suffered a 21.8 per cent reduction in complement in the first fiscal year (1981-82) of the Reagan administration.

15. This incident demonstrates the weakness, in international perspective, of the CPQ as a peak association of business. That it cannot claim a representational monopoly provides a rationale for government allocation of seats. And the inability of the CPQ to manage its own internal coalition in 1986 allowed the Liberal government to assume a brokerage role, and hence for partisan factors to come to the fore.

16. The class-based adversarialism of the relationship between the Liberals and the PQ, which persisted despite what Hudon (1984) has called the "deradicalization" of the PQ during its period in government, has undoubtedly elevated the significance of partisan factors in the destabilization of tripartite institutions. There is a parallel in this sense between Québec and British

experience. The Confederation of British Industry lost legitimacy in the eyes of the Thatcher Conservative government for having collaborated with the previous Labour regime.

17. The legislation provides that members continue to serve until replaced, even if their terms have expired.

18. This opposition may have been in part due to the strong opposition to multi-employer bargaining structures in these sectors, and fears that CSST structures constituted one step in that direction.

19. Between 1981 and 1986, the CSST provided $47 million to the IRSST, and the Québec government provided another $5 million. The government ceased funding the IRSST in 1986. CSST grants to the IRSST were approximately $11 million in each of 1986 and 1987.

20. Prior to 1985, the CSST had separate bureaucratic review offices for matters arising under the Act Respecting Occupational Health and Safety and the Workmen's Compensation Act.

21. The CSST is at the low end of the American range in this respect. The CSST covers about 2.4 million workers and cites about 1200-1300 violations per year; OSHA and state agencies, cover about 94 million workers and cite between 47,000 and 79,000 "serious", "willful" or "repeat" violations per year (Calculated from Office of Technology Assessment, 1985:375). The CSST hence cites violations at the rate of about 500-550 per million workers; the US rate is about 500-840 per million workers. (Note that both employers and workers are cited for violations; using the number of workers as the denominator in these ratios is simply intended to control for the size of the workforce covered by the respective agencies.) These rates are much higher than those for European agencies, again assuming that we are dealing with roughly similar sanctions. The US, with an employed labour force about 4.5 times the size of those of Britain, France and Germany, takes "punitive" action at about 30-50 times the rate of Britain, 200-400 times the rate of Germany, and 7-13 times the rate of France (Tuohy forthcoming).

22. In its 1981 commentary on the Act Respecting Occupational Health and Safety, for example, the CSST cited provisions of the legislation of Sweden, Ontario, and Saskatchewan related to the establishment of worker representatives and workplace committees (CSST, 1981a:112-28).

23. With few exceptions, Québec adopted the standards recommended in the 1979 list of the American Conference of Governmental Industrial Hygienists (ACGIH), an American professional organization which establishes and annually reviews and revises a list of Threshold Limit Values (TLVs) for some 600 toxic substances. A number of jurisdictions adopt the ACGIH list, either formally or informally, as PELs; and in other cases, the ACGIH list is given heavy weight in regulatory decision-making.

24. This characterization was offered by a CSN staff member.

25. The phrase is from a CSN respondent.

CHAPTER ELEVEN

LABOUR AND LOBBYING:
A POLITICAL ECONOMY
APPROACH

Charlotte Yates

W ork on the Canadian labour movement's involvement in the lobbying process has been restricted to that undertaken by elite pluralists (Kwavnick, 1972). Canadian political economists, while cognizant of lobbying as the primary means by which organized labour has attempted to influence policy, have ignored this aspect of labour-state relations. Instead political economists have focussed their studies of labour-state relations on either the brief moment when corporatism was on the political agenda (Panitch, 1979; McAllistair, 1984; Giles, 1982) or times of intense class struggle when workers are argued to have forced either the provincial or federal governments to take political action to stave off the growing challenge to the state (Finkel, 1977; Cuneo, 1979, 1980). The absence of a systematic study of trade-union lobbying and its effects on organized labour has led to a remarkable gap in political economists' understanding of how labour-state relations were stabilized in the postwar period. Moreover, it has led many political economists to accept some of the basic assumptions made by elite pluralists concerning lobbying. This chapter aims at filling this gap.

There are two key assumptions that can be found in existing Canadian studies on labour and lobbying. First, organized labour is assumed to be one organized interest among many that participate in the politics of a pluralist society. Labour has no particular pre-eminence as an interest group and the basis for its influence in lobbying is assumed to be similar to that of other groups (expertise, financial resources and legitimacy). Second, lobbying is assumed to be the "natural" form of interest intermediation in a pluralist society. Elite pluralists appear to overlook the history of labour's involvement in lobbying. They also do not perceive other forms of interest inter-mediation which if developed would signify a *fundamental* change in labour-state relations.

The following chapter calls both these assumptions into question. It argues that the regularized lobbying relationship which emerged between trade unions and governments in Canada was part of the Fordist mode of regulation (see below), a mode originally intended to stabilize social relations and ultimately the postwar economy. Moreover, this particular form of labour's interest intermediation was put into place after failed struggles by the Canadian labour movement to institute tripartite forms of decision-making and due to the peculiar-ly private nature of Canadian Fordism. Once established, single inter-est group lobbying by trade unions prevented the Canadian labour movement from politically mobilizing itself as a class, and instead encouraged labour's acceptance of a pluralist discourse which defined its position in society as one interest of many. The political discourse and practice of lobbying tended to demobilize unions, therefore under-mining their basis of power which lay in their organization of large numbers of workers involved in the production process. The chapter concludes with an examination of how the crisis of Canadian Fordism in the 1970s and 1980s led to attempts at rearticulating labour-state relations such that lobbying would no longer constitute the dominant mode of interest intermediation for organized labour.

This chapter focusses on one union—the Canadian branch of the United Auto Workers (UAW)—and pays particular attention to the auto industry. The reasons for this are several. First, individual trade unions, not central labour federations, are the centre of power in the Canadian labour movement. Second, the characteristics of a pressure pluralist policy network encourage a focus on a particular union (or set of unions) in a specific economic sector. As the Canadian UAW holds a virtual monopoly of representation of workers in the auto industry, it is appropriate to limit discussion to this union. Third, the centrality of the auto industry to both the Canadian and Ontario economies makes the case of the Canadian UAW especially important for understanding

Fordist regulation and labour-state relations. At its peak employment year of 1979, the auto industry directly employed 124,000 workers, most of those in Ontario. This figure does not include the spin-off employment in sectors such as steel, electrical equipment and rubber. Moreover, the auto industry in 1982 contributed $30 billion in trade to the Canadian economy (Lavelle and White, 1983: 21-5). For these reasons the auto industry is considered the lynchpin of the industrial economy, making it an especially important case study. The final reason is empirical: the long period of history under discussion and the variability of labour-state relations in different economic sectors make it impossible to analyze more than one union.

The Régulation Approach: A Summary

Regulation theorists characterized the post Second World War period as one when the Fordist regime of accumulation was put into place. The concept "regime of accumulation" "describes the fairly long-term stabilization of the allocation of social production between consumption and accumulation" (Lipietz, 1987:14). Fordism, as one particular regime of accumulation, denotes two historically distinct but interrelated processes. First, it encompasses a particular mode of capitalist accumulation that is based upon a labour process organized around the semi-automatic assembly line. Such changes in the organization of the labour process are accompanied by a rise in productivity and output, that is, mass production. Capital accumulation in this process requires a corresponding increase in society's consumption. Therefore, the second process denoted by the term Fordism consists of the continual adjustment of mass consumption to match the growing productive capacity. More specifically, this means ensuring the existence of a mass market for the goods produced, something that ultimately can only be achieved by increasing and stabilizing relative wages of workers.

These two processes are not naturally linked and therefore do not develop simultaneously out of the logic of the market. Rather, the Régulation Approach holds that production is prone to crises because production and consumption do not naturally develop in tandem. Such crises may emerge when productivity outstrips consumption, as occurred in the 1930s, or as a result of conflict between capital and labour. The solution to these crises becomes a mode of regulation, defined as a set of rules (both explicit and implicit), social norms and institutional arrangements which encourage types of behaviour consistent with the regime of accumulation (Lipietz, 1987:15). If and when a mode of regulation becomes entrenched it has the effect of constructing a balance between consumption and production and peace between labour and capital.

In general, the mode of regulation which emerged in the post-1945 period in western capitalist countries consisted of two interrelated processes. First, the state intervened in the economy with a series of macro—and micro—economic policies aimed at demand management, that is, Keynesian economic policies. Second, wage labour-capital relations were institutionalized. This development had the effect of allowing simultaneous increases in production and consumption and preventing disruption of this cycle by trade-union conflict with corporations. This component of regulation centred on the stabilization of collective bargaining between unions and employers, with varying national degrees of state intervention. This institutionalization consisted of linking wages to productivity and inflation and engaging trade unions in an exchange of higher wages and benefits for decreased disruption of production. According to Aglietta (1976: 189-92), regulation of union-employer relations also entailed the articulation of politico-legal and social relations between workers and management and backed up by the state, which were consistent with the new economic relations.

Both the regime of accumulation and the mode of regulation are, according to Lipietz (1987:15), *"chance discoveries* made in the course of human struggles." Thus, the specific form of accumulation or regulation which comes to dominate in different capitalist countries will vary (Boyer, 1989). Moreover, capitalism is full of failed experiments to construct such modes of regulation. Therefore, postwar political arrangements in capitalist countries, that can now be characterized by their regularities and apparent systematic incorporation of the working class into capitalism, are not seen as part of a design by the state or capital. Rather they are seen as the product of political struggle which put into place a system of behaviour and institutions that had as its result, the stabilization of relations in capitalist society.

Forms of political interest intermediation constitute part of the mode of regulation as they contribute to the stabilization of social relations. Due to the centrality of labour in the Fordist regime, the mode of representation of labour's interests is of particular significance as it contributes to the successful regulation of the economy and society. The dominant form of interest intermediation is in no way given, however, by the regime of accumulation. Rather structures of representation are the product of struggle. Once established, these structures of representation will tend to reinforce a particular political discourse which defines the limits of group action and behaviour vis-á-vis the state and legitimates a certain language of communication between groups in society and the state. This has profound ideological effects on the group in question (Jenson, 1989b).

Corporatism, and its various forms, have been the most often studied mode of representation of labour's interests. Corporatism emerged out of struggles by certain Western European labour movements that had consolidated their position in the national economy and in party politics (Martin, 1986). According to Jenson (1989a), this mode of representation encourages a productivist discourse based on class-based collective identities. Although participation by organized labour in corporatist structures will tend to encourage the redefinition of trade-union demands around capitalist growth criteria (Panitch, 1986), labour movements that participate in these structures still retain an ideological and organizational basis for class action.

In contrast to the experience of many Western European countries, Canada and the US did not see the emergence of corporatist structures as the dominant Fordist mode of representation of labour's interests. Rather, organized labour became part of pressure pluralist policy networks wherein trade unions advocated policy but remained outside the decision-making process. This structure of political interest intermediation is based on the relations between the state and leaders representing various group memberships. Pressure pluralism involves a process of dialogue between a number of competing interests and the state, with the assumption that the state, acting as umpire in the negotiations, will construct a consensus based on a compromise of interested parties. Groups allowed entry into such deliberations are expected to behave responsibly and accept the "win and lose" process of constructing such a compromise, without resorting to confrontational methods of input. A pressure pluralist network organizes politics around the political discourse of pluralism. Such politics are structured by concepts of compromise and competition between various groups which are defined according to their "interests" and which compete for a share of limited resources.

Ongoing participation in this policy network necessitated that certain preconditions be met by the group seeking access to and input at the governmental level. For the labour movement, these preconditions were twofold. First, unions had to consolidate their position as organizations that represented the "interests" of workers. The failure of the Canadian labour movement to consolidate its position in party politics or in the national economy required that this process of consolidation be achieved by individual trade unions in their own workplaces. Ideally this entailed organizing the monopoly of workers in a particular industry or sector, constructing a stable and enduring relationship with employers, and developing enough leadership control over union members that collective agreements would be honoured by union members and spontaneous disruptions of production curtailed.

The second precondition consisted of proving the union a responsible actor willing to accept the limits of pluralist politics. Although this stance was partially achieved through organizational consolidation in the workplace, it also entailed the elimination of radical, and in particular Communist, elements within the labour movement and the replacement of militant political strategies, such as politically motivated strikes, with less confrontational methods, such as the presentation of briefs. As these preconditions took some time to achieve for industrial unions, the development of a stabilized relationship between these unions and government was delayed.

Once established, involvement in a pressure pluralist network has two adverse effects on organized labour. First, trade-union participation in lobbying tends to reinforce divisions within the working class along the dimensions of the varying and competing interests of different types of workers represented by different unions. In Canada, this fragmentation has been buttressed by the federal system of government and labour laws that encourage the certification of "skill-based" unions. This process encourages a plurality of interchanges and relationships between different unions and governments and their agencies, without one labour federation or union having the exclusive role of articulating the policy interests of organized labour. Consequently, labour-state relations are highly variable and heavily dependent upon the power of individual unions.

Participation in pluralist politics therefore erects structural barriers to the definition of class-based interests by workers. The structure and practice of lobbying (otherwise referred to as policy advocacy) mediates and redefines class-based interests in terms consistent with pluralist discourse, thereby reinforcing unions' likelihood of understanding their place in society and the economy as one interest of many. Thus, although Fordism tends to make trade unions central to the regulation and stability of this regime, the particular form of political interest intermediation that becomes dominant may preclude labour from seeing itself in such central terms, and from organizing itself in politics to take advantage of its structurally pre-eminent position in the Fordist regime of accumulation (Berger, 1981:13).

Furthermore, by encouraging the dissolution of class-based interests and cross-union alliances, a pressure pluralist policy network establishes the basis for sectoral union-corporate cooperation. Because the "interests" of a union and corporation may be similarly based on the health of a particular industry or economic sector, when necessary or expedient, these two groups could construct a compromise as a basis for joint lobbies of government. Moreover, the identification of union interests with those of a particular industry or sector will tend to encourage the development of sectoral, rather than functional, relationships between unions and government agencies. Thus, rather than assuming that the Department of Labour becomes the primary site for union-government interaction, the site for union-government interaction will vary.

Involvement in a pressure pluralist policy network also tends to have the effect of demobilizing unions, therefore undermining the very basis of their power and influence. For most unions their key resource, and hence the basis of their power, lies in the large numbers of workers they represent. Yet having this resource does not in itself guarantee a union influence. Rather, a union must have the capacity to mobilize its resources effectively, and in particular its membership, behind a common course of collective action. In the absence of successful mobilization behind a political party of labour, the final sanctioning act in this mobilization becomes a strike or threat thereof. It was the threat or experience of massive strike activity in North America that tended to prompt governments and companies to seek stabilized relations with unions in the postwar period. In short, unions not only gain influence via strikes but also they must have the capacity to threaten such collective action if their political influence is to be sustained.

Yet this mobilizational capacity will tend to be undermined by the structures of regulation put into place. Once collective bargaining is institutionalized and unions accept and enter into policy advocacy, forms of direct membership action, such as strikes, are rationalized and increasingly controlled by the leadership. Such centralization of decision-making tends to reduce the capacity of the membership for collective action because it structures union politics around the "politics of representation." According to Przeworski (1980: 29), the very nature of representative politics tends to have a demobilizing impact on unions as it erodes the possibility for direct action by workers. This demobilization is sustained by the pluralist discourse and practice of lobbying.

In accepting the limitations of lobbying and trying to sell this to their memberships, union leaders may become incapable of representing those membership interests that either conflict with accepted compromises or that challenge the existing ideological parameters of pressure politics. This failing may have one of two results. On the one hand, union members may mobilize against their leaders in a bid to regain control over their union and force their issues onto the political agenda. In so doing, the union's legitimacy as representative of workers is undermined, ironically reducing the union's influence in the very lobbying process which led to this membership backlash. On the other hand, in finding their union incapable of or unwilling to represent their interests, workers may seek redress to their problems through alternative organizations (Davis, 1980). Although this route does not constitute a direct challenge to the union leadership, it will tend to restrict future possibilities for the union to mobilize its membership when necessary. Finally, by accepting the limits of a pressure pluralist policy network and institutionalized collective bargaining, unions will tend to limit the strategic options they see as available for political action. In other words, trade union leaders may be incapable of providing an alternative interpretative framework for politics that would legitimate forms of mass-based collective action as a means of forcing labour's demands on the political agenda.

Policy advocacy in a pressure pluralist network remained the dominant form of Canadian labour's political interaction with the state until the late 1960s when economic troubles led governments to seek a reformulation of labour-state relations along tripartite lines. From this point onwards, as the Fordist regime came under increasing strain, trade unions, governments and corporations have struggled to rearticulate their relations. These struggles and the prevailing uncertainty over the economy have opened up the space for trade unions, such as the UAW, to once again try and push for a reformulation of labour-state-capital relations more favourable to workers. While these struggles continue and the shape of any new mode of regulation remains unclear, the labour movement's capacity for structuring a more pre-eminent position for itself in Canadian society appears restricted due to Canadian Fordism's legacy of working-class fragmentation.

Lobbying and Labour: Consolidating Fordist Regulation in Postwar Canada

The institutionalization of labour-management relations and the Fordist wage relation in Canada was primarily constituted in the sphere of private production (Yates, 1988). Both the stabilization and increase of domestic demand and the negotiation of labour-management peace were largely the product of conflicts between employers and unions and were codified in collective agreements. Canadian governments' commitment to Keynesian demand management, to regulation of the economy, and in particular to structuring the labour market was half-hearted, leading to relatively low spending on the welfare state and crisis-oriented management of the economy. Canadian governments demonstrated an interest in, if not a preference for, privately organized structures that would both regulate the economy and structure the labour market. This approach had profound effects on the politics of Canadian trade unions in the postwar period.

Canadian trade unions' demands for tripartite forms of decision-making for planning the Second World War economy and the transition from war to peacetime failed. Business was opposed to tripartite arrangements and the federal government was lukewarm. Organized labour was too weak to force tripartism onto the government's agenda. Despite its massive mobilization during the war, the Canadian labour movement was ideologically and organizationally fragmented

(Panitch, 1979). Trade unions were therefore forced to abandon their demands for tripartism.

Demands for tripartite decision-making were linked with pressure by labour on the federal government for greater government regulation of the economy. The Canadian UAW, in a policy brief called the "Win the Peace Plan" submitted to the federal government in 1945, demanded government intervention in the economy to ensure full employment, adequate wages and a better quality of life for all workers. This intervention would, according to the union, ensure increased demand, expanded production and ultimately stability in the industrial arena.[1] Despite the Liberal government's pronouncement in its White Paper on Employment and Income Security in April 1945, the federal government proved less committed to regulating the economy and ensuring adequate wages for workers than its policy pronouncements suggested. Rather than acting on trade union demands for paid vacations, a government sponsored health plan and a guaranteed annual wage for all workers, both the federal and Ontario governments appeared more interested in leaving the running of the economy to the private sector.

These governments' major contribution to this process lay in establishing the ground rules for collective bargaining between trade unions and employers through peacetime labour legislation passed in 1948. Despite the labour movement's attempts to have input into this legislation, both the Ontario and federal governments denied organized labour access or input to government deliberations.[2] Thus it seemed by the late 1940s, that not only had tripartism failed but any labour input into government legislation was to be denied. The combination of a weak commitment to government regulation of the economy and the exclusion of unions from political decision-making left trade unions with little option but to make gains through collective bargaining. In the absence of a powerful Canadian labour federation, this process had to be undertaken by individual trade unions.

For the Canadian UAW, as with other unions, this approach meant negotiating and striking for measures intended to stabilize unions' position in the workplace, ensure regular and increasing wages for members, and provide a safety net for workers who suffered from illness, lay-offs or retirement. This was no easy task as employers appeared more determined than ever in the immediate postwar years, to take back what few gains unions had made during the war and once again establish union-free workplaces. Thus, Fordist regulation of wage labour-capital relations was put into place piecemeal and varied sector by sector, depending upon the strength of the union or unions in each industry. After many long and bitter strikes, the Canadian UAW had succeeded by the end of the 1950s in gaining the automatic check-off of dues, substantial and stable wage and benefit increases, and a system of bargaining that prevented whipsawing by corporations and rationalized costly strikes. In their turn, corporations gained predictable, non-competitive wage costs tied to industry productivity and reduced disruption of production caused by spontaneous rank-and-file action.[3]

Perhaps the most interesting development in the 1950s was the private negotiation of a social security net for workers that in most other Western capitalist countries was provided for by the state. The UAW demanded pensions, paid vacations, health care insurance, and other social benefits. In many cases, corporations joined the union in lobbying governments to assume the responsibility for such social security provisions. Governments resisted these efforts, apparently preferring privately negotiated arrangements. Hence, it was in collective agreements that these social security provisions were first established. One example can illustrate this argument. In Canada, 1951 and 1954 were recessionary years, marked by high levels of unemployment. Although the Canadian UAW pressured the federal government for solutions to the unemployment problem, the government refused to act. The union therefore once again resorted to collective bargaining to provide some protection for its membership. In 1954-55, after a number of strikes, the UAW won a Supplementary Unemployment Benefit programme (originally known as the Guaranteed Annual Wage) under which laid-off workers would be paid, from a fund financed by forfeited workers' wages, most of the difference between their unemployed insurance earnings and usual wage.

By the late 1950s, Fordist regulation of labour-management relations had been secured through private negotiations. The UAW had consolidated its position in the workplace. This process had been wrought with conflict, however, between union leaders and a radical union caucus determined to maintain rank-and-file control over the union and to pursue a more wide-sweeping programme of political and social change. Purges of communists and militants alike by union leaders gradually weakened this caucus and the ideological basis for alternative visions of the union's role in the economy and society. The end result of these purges and the emergent structures of collective bargaining established many of the preconditions for a structured relationship between the UAW, employers and ultimately, governments. With the purging of radicals, the UAW proved itself a responsible actor and severely restricted the possibility for class-based discourse. Moreover, collective bargaining developments had secured leadership support from and control over its membership such that deals struck with either employers or governments could be enforced.

Nonetheless, governments had played a minimal role in securing regulation of labour-management relations. Moreover, despite some attempts, the UAW had failed to become part of a policy community at either the federal or Ontario level of government.

The 1958-61 recession changed all this. In 1957, Canada suffered from declining rates of investment that triggered a falling rate of growth. Between 1957 and 1961 unemployment doubled. The auto industry was particularly hard hit as consumers sought cheaper means of transportation that led to a jump in imported vehicles as a percentage of new car sales in Canada from 12.9 per cent in 1957 to 28.1 per cent in 1960. Canadian motor vehicle production therefore plummeted and was accompanied by increased automation both of which resulted in very high levels of unemployment in the auto industry (Wolfe, 1984:51; Beigie, 1970:13).

The crisis that faced Canadian Autoworkers as a result of this economic downturn was compounded by corporate responses to the recession. To meet small car competition, North American automakers replaced domestic Canadian production with imports, from either the US or those European plants where corporations such as General Motors (GM) produced their own small cars. Many smaller companies shut down their Canadian operations or relocated their plants to avoid the union.

Collective bargaining solutions to the economic recession were of limited value in tackling the more fundamental problems facing the Canadian auto industry, of which the most important was the importation of small cars for sale in Canada. Consequently, the Canadian UAW vigorously pursued a legislative programme, putting pressure on the federal government both to respond to short-term problems of unemployment and to develop an industrial policy to revitalize the auto industry. To accomplish the latter, the UAW proposed a Royal Commission to study the Canadian auto industry.[4]

In complete contrast to earlier union experience, the federal government demonstrated a willingness to act and, more importantly, to involve the Canadian UAW in at least the periphery of decision-making. Part of this willingness stemmed from the centrality of the auto industry to Canada's industrial complex. When the auto industry declined so too did other sectors such as the steel and rubber sectors. Thus the federal government appointed the head of the Canadian UAW, George Burt, to a number of government committees, increased the value added taxes on auto parts imported into Canada from the US, and in 1960 appointed a Royal Commission (known as the Bladen Commission) to study the auto industry.

The UAW took these moves as signs of success of its policy advocacy. To keep up the pressure on the federal government, the UAW prepared to submit a brief to the Bladen Commission. The union's position was weakened, however, by internal union splits over recommended solutions to the auto industry crisis. Union officials and their supporters favoured greater integration between the American and Canadian auto industries. Radicals in the union opposed these suggestions and instead put forth a proposal to the union membership that would lead to greater national control and ownership of the auto industry and the production of an all-Canadian car. Although the union officially endorsed the leadership's integration option, four UAW briefs were submitted to the Royal Commission, therefore placing in question which proposal constituted the "legitimate" representation of autoworkers' interests.

In spite of these splits, the Bladen Commission Report released in 1961, added credence to the union's official policy position. The report recommended a series of measures intended to lower the price of Canadian-produced vehicles sold in Canada and proposed a comprehensive policy of freer trade for Canadian produced parts and vehicles (Bladen, 1961). The UAW favoured this recommendation. To take advantage of the opening doors of government, however, and to increase the pressure for government action based on the Royal Commission Report, the UAW had to consolidate its own position as the sole representative of the autoworkers. This necessitated elimination of organized opposition to the union leadership, something finally achieved by 1961.

Concerned for Canada's industrial economy, the federal government moved quickly to restore the fortunes of the Canadian auto industry. In 1962-63, the government of Canada instituted a tariff incentive plan that made lowered tariffs on imported vehicles and auto parts dependent upon investment in Canada. When this plan was opposed by the corporations, the federal government, and in particular the Minister of Industry and Trade, solicited the UAW as an ally. As the UAW supported the tariff programme, it willingly demonstrated support for this government action that, in turn, provided them with increased access to government.

These unilateral tariff changes by the federal government strained Canadian-American relations. The threat of retaliatory measures by the US government led to a series of hasty and secret negotiations between Prime Minister Pearson and President L.B. Johnson that produced the Autopact, a managed trade agreement that allowed freer trade in auto parts and vehicles in exchange for Canadian content (Beigie, 1970). The trade agreement was approved by both the major auto corporations and the UAW. To manage effectively the economic transition that would accompany the Autopact, the government sought continued support of both the corporations and the union.

The Canadian UAW's commitment to pressure pluralist politics and desire for continued involvement in the auto policy network were quickly tested. Although the Autopact increased overall employment in the auto industry, it led to extended layoffs of many union members who worked in plants that were undergoing restructuring. The Canadian UAW demanded a government-sponsored transitional assistance benefit programme to protect these workers, but the federal government was hesitant to act. When it did finally introduce a Transitional Assistance Benefit Programme (TAB), government monies were limited to autoworkers not covered by the previously privately-negotiated Supplementary Unemployment Benefit Programme that had been funded by forfeited workers' wages. In other words, many autoworkers were to pay for their own adjustment to the Autopact.

As rank-and-file autoworkers demanded withdrawal of their union's support for the Autopact and mobilization against the government, the UAW found itself caught in the contradictions of pressure pluralist politics. The union had been pressing for closer consultation with the federal government throughout the 1950s and the Autopact had provided it. Since early government moves to correct auto industry problems, the UAW had developed a regular, ongoing communications network with certain government ministries. Outright opposition to the Autopact might once again shut government doors to the union. Second, policy advocacy by the union appeared to have had some effect. Integration of the Canadian auto industry had been achieved and although the assistance programme put into place by the government fell short of UAW recommendations, its very implementation suggested that the government would listen to the union if it behaved responsibly and accepted the rules of pressure politics. The UAW began walking a fine line, tokenly withdrawing its full support for the Autopact to quell growing internal discontent, while continuing to consult with both companies and the government.

In the short-term, the union's strategy of staying within the limits of pressure-pluralist politics appeared to pay off. After undertaking a concerted lobby, the UAW pushed the government into modifying the TAB programme to conform with some union demands. In the long-term, however, this strategy was less clearly successful in retaining the influence of the UAW in government. As the Autopact proved economically successful and administrative problems were overcome, the UAW, despite its abandonment of militancy and enforcement of membership compliance with the terms of responsible union behaviour, found itself gradually pushed to the fringes of decision-making. Top level meetings to evaluate the Autopact, to which the UAW had been promised involvement, excluded the union. Finally, meetings with the Department of Industry, Trade and Commerce became less frequent and the UAW's point of access to government was gradually restricted to the less powerful Department of Labour.

Nonetheless, the UAW had become both ideologically and strategically committed to policy advocacy in a pressure pluralist network. This commitment, in turn, restricted the UAW's ability to envision an alternative structure of union-government relations. Rather than mobilizing its members and hence utilizing its key resource, the UAW leadership continued to discipline "irresponsible" members and engage in leadership-dominated pluralist politics. Although the 1960s secured the political regulation of UAW-federal government relations, the structure of pressure politics tended both to demobilize the union and to reinforce a non-class political discourse and practice.

Hints of Tripartism[5]: Holding the Fordist Regime Together, 1969-79

Ironically, almost at the very moment that political regulation was secured, this arrangement came under strain. The late 1960s saw a marked increase in union rank-and-file discontent, evidenced in the growing number of illegal and wildcat strikes. At the same time, the Canadian economy showed signs of declining productivity and increasing inflation. These trends were evidence of the limits of Fordism as the ability of unions to control their memberships was called into question and the economic growth of the postwar regime faltered.

While individual unions sought, often unsuccessfully, to regain control over their memberships, both the federal and Ontario governments attempted to restabilize the Fordist regime. For the federal government, inflation was the number one problem. Both in 1969 and 1974-75, workers' wages, and in particular those of public sector workers, were targeted as the primary cause of inflation (Maslove and Swimmer, 1980:3-11). The government's preferred solution to this problem was voluntary wage restraint. It was hoped that wage restraint could be achieved through tripartite arrangements in which unions would be responsible for controlling their membership's wage demands. In both 1969 and 1974-5, organized labour, through the Canadian Labour Congress (CLC), entered into preliminary talks with both government and business with an interest in establishing tripartism. Two factors ultimately forced the CLC to withdraw from these discussions. The first centred on the federal government's unwillingness to control profits and the cost of services such as lawyers fees, in exchange for wage restraint. The second, which became more pronounced in 1975, was the inability of the CLC and its affiliated unions to gain membership support for tripartism that was tied to wage restraint. The failure of the Canadian labour movement to secure support for tripartism, combined with the weakness of the CLC, rendered concerted action by unions impossible. Once again it was left up to individual unions to fight their own battles against government restraint measures.

In both 1969 and 1975, when voluntary and mandatory wage controls were respectively introduced, the UAW sidestepped the wage guidelines through collective bargaining and strikes. These strikes threatened to devastate the auto industry at a time when auto corporations were enjoying prosperity. Consequently, the corporations, rather than risk a return to open confrontation with the union, increasingly cooperated with the UAW in its bid to resist the wage restraint programme (Yates, 1988:400-418). This corporate desire to protect private regulatory structures of collective bargaining rather than return to open conflict and workplace disruption, combined with the threat of mobilization by Canadian autoworkers, meant the UAW successfully resisted the worst effects of mandatory wage controls.

The mobilization of the Canadian UAW and the growing militancy of autoworkers strained political relations between the union and the federal government. Not only was the Canadian UAW able to defy the wage control programme, it was also instrumental in encouraging the shift of CLC political strategy away from responsible pluralistic politics towards mass mobilization. The change in strategy resulted in a number of mass demonstrations by trade unions culminating in the one day general strike in October 1976 and the 1979 concerted labour campaign on behalf of the NDP. Ironically, the federal government's attempts to gain organized labour's cooperation in restraining its membership produced, instead, a return by many unions to a more militant form of politics. Although this union strategy did not influence government policy away from wage restraint, it changed the perceived limits of union strategy and made ever more fragile the existing mode of political regulation.

In contrast to the experience of the federal government, the Ontario government succeeded in restructuring government-union relations along tripartite lines. Consequently, the UAW's relationship with the Ontario government, which had hitherto been sporadic and of lesser importance to the union, became at once more highly structured and crucial in the union's quest for political change.

The Ontario government's corporatist initiatives in the 1970s were the result of a number of factors. The primary factor lay in the Ontario government's analysis of the underlying cause of the economic malaise. Since the late 1960s, Ontario industrial productivity had declined precipitously. Two of the identified causes of this were low quality work resulting from workers dissatisfied with the quality of their life on the assembly line and increased numbers of lengthy and bitter strikes in the 1970s. These problems led the government to investigate new ways of bringing organized labour "on side" in the fight to restore economic

prosperity. Second, existing structures of labour's political representation appeared to have reached their limits as more and more unions
turned to confrontational methods of making demands on government.
Thus, if the government wished to secure a labour-management accord, some new structures of labour representation had to be put into
place. Finally, as tripartism had already been placed on the political
agenda by the federal government, and given many unions' expressed
interest in this arrangement, such structures seemed a feasible means
of restructuring labour-state relations.

The Ontario government reformulated postwar regulation on two
dimensions. First it restructured labour-management-government
relations along tripartite lines. Second, it addressed some of workers'
shop floor concerns with the objective of formulating a new human
relations strategy for motivating workers. Specifically, this approach
meant addressing health and safety and broad "quality of working life"
issues. The Ontario government's linkage of solutions to productivity
with this two-dimensional reformulation of postwar arrangements
was clearly summarized by Ontario Premier Davis as follows: "productivity is a key factor in relation to objectives we all share, including
improved standards of living, security of employment and quality of
working life. It is my belief that joint action by labour, business and
government in this area could reap many benefits."[6]

The first preparatory step towards encouraging trade union support for the Ontario government's agenda was the appointment of Tim
Armstrong, first to the Ontario Labour Relations Board, and not long
after, as Deputy Minister of Labour. Armstrong was a liberal social
democrat who had acted as the UAW's legal counsel for years. His
appointment was met with strong approval by unions, and by the UAW
in particular. Armstrong played a crucial role in orchestrating compromises between the provincial government and the UAW, and,
therefore, in constructing the basis for closer relations between this
and other unions and the government. Shortly thereafter, the Ontario
government appointed the Ham Commission to investigate health and
safety measures in the province.

It was only after the federal government's 1975 introduction of
wage and price controls and internal union debates over tripartism,
however, that the Ontario government pushed for restructuring of
labour-management-government relations. Although the Ontario
government opted for the federal government's anti-inflation
programme, the provincial government was shielded from responsibility for wage controls and hence growing conflict with the labour
movement. The introduction of this legislation under the Peace, Order
and Good Government Clause of the BNA Act and the federal
government's exclusive role in enforcing the controls programme

meant that the Ontario government's tripartite initiatives were not tied to or tarnished by wage restraint.

The first effort by the Ontario government to draw labour into closer policy discussions came in 1975 when an advisory committee on health and safety was established (Yates, 1988:419-26; Fournier, 1986). More important than this development, however, was Premier Davis' call for a meeting between key labour, business and provincial government representatives "to discuss the subject of productivity improvement," including in its purview the issue of quality of working life. Dennis McDermott, then leader of the Canadian UAW, was one of the few labour representatives invited to attend.

This initiative and other similar informal dinner meetings served as a basis for the establishment of a more permanent top-level tripartite body. Early in 1977, the Ontario government established a Centre for Quality of Working Life (QWL) with a mandate to coordinate QWL programmes. More significant than the actual programmes was the creation of a tripartite Committee on the QWL, later renamed the Labour-Management Committee. This body, consisting of top business, union and government representatives (including the Canadian Director of the UAW) met regularly over dinner to discuss broad economic issues of concern to the Ontario economy. Although the committee was not vested with formal decision-making powers, it served as an important forum of communication and, for the Ontario government, was used to sound out reactions to politically controversial issues.

This restructuring of labour's role in political decision-making combined with the Ontario government's apparently determined bid to bring organized labour "on side" to restore economic prosperity resulted in a flurry of legislation favourable to unions. Besides the very important Health and Safety legislation introduced in 1979, the UAW used its participation on the new tripartite bodies and the Ontario government's desire for labour's cooperation to press the Ontario government into legislating the automatic check-off of dues, an issue around which a number of bitter strikes were fought in the late 1970s. The economic malaise of the 1970s was indicative of the limits of Fordism and, in particular, of existing regulatory structures governing the wage labour-capital relationship. In response, both the federal and Ontario governments sought to reformulate this relationship by drawing labour into the decision-making and planning process. Yet, when tied to wage restraint as in the federal case, these initiatives faltered. At the provincial level, however, there was established an informal network of tripartite consultation. This restructuring of political interest intermediation gave the UAW increased leverage with and access to senior Ontario government officials, something which the UAW would seek to use to its advantage in the upcoming economic crisis of the 1980s.

New Directions for Canadian Autoworkers: The Crisis of Fordism in the 1980s

Between 1979 and 1983, the Canadian economy went into serious economic decline along with the rest of the world economies; the Fordist regime had reached its limits. The 1970s "latent crisis of Fordism," characterized by declining US productivity and a profit squeeze, became full blown in the 1980s as the increased competitiveness of Japan and West Germany in the world economy threatened US economic hegemony. Higher North American wage costs and the rigid structures of collective bargaining, that is, the particular mode of Fordist regulation in postwar Canada, were targetted as the root of this declining competitiveness. The Fordist wage relation appeared as a fetter on continued capital accumulation and came under attack. The result was intensified conflict between corporations, unions and governments and uncertainty for trade unions.

The North American auto industry was at the centre of this crisis. Between 1979 and 1983, Japanese vehicle imports into Canada rose dramatically (Lavelle and White, 1983). High interest rates and lowered relative incomes due to the recession made lower-priced vehicles more attractive to the consumer. Existing production techniques and marketing strategies of North American automakers contributed to the competitive edge of imports.

Corporations were uncertain about how to respond effectively to the downturn. Consequently, individual corporate strategies differed in timing as well as in nature, depending upon each company's structure, economic viability and perceived strategic capacity. Whatever the strategy adopted, however, corporate responses to the crisis particularly hurt workers. Plants were closed and extended layoffs initiated. The number of unemployed autoworkers increased to almost 25 per cent of the auto workforce. Corporations also undertook a major assault on existing Fordist structures of collective bargaining and labour relations, upon which the UAW had come to rely for its organizational strength. Automakers demanded wage concessions, changes to workers' pay regimes, the dismantling of master and pattern bargaining, and changes to seniority and job posting practices in order to introduce a more flexible labour process. The UAW found itself besieged.

Government responses to the economic downturn were similarly variable. Federally, after a brief interlude of Conservative rule, the Liberal party returned to power on a nationalist platform which held promise that this government would use its leverage to ensure continued auto production and employment in Canada. As the economy ground to a halt, however, the federal government, like the corporations, targeted workers' wages and unions as well as the costs of the welfare state as key factors in prolonging the economic crisis. Consequently, the federal government's nationalist direction was eclipsed by a move towards fiscal conservatism. The result was high interest rates, increased unemployment, cutbacks in social programmes and the restriction of union rights. Finally, the federal government adopted a wait-and-see attitude about the auto industry and Japanese imports.

Only with the Ontario government did the UAW find some receptiveness to its concerns. Although this government readily curbed the rights of public-sector unions, the importance of the auto industry for the provincial economy and the government's 1970s strategy of increased consultation with unions, led it to support many UAW calls for change to the industry.

UAW political strategies reflected the changing nature of corporate and government responses to the economic decline and recent experience with wage controls. During 1979 and the early months of 1980, UAW strategies reflected an uneasy optimism about the economy. Collective bargaining remained peaceful and the union continued to lobby the government. By mid-1980, however, when the economy plunged into recession and mounting numbers of autoworkers were laid off, the UAW found that "politics as usual" based on compromise and negotiation was no longer enough. Policy advocacy brought few results to problems, such as plant closures, which needed immediate and radical solutions. Moreover, the collective bargaining strategies on which the union had come to rely in the face of an impasse with government were turned upside down by corporate determination to dismantle existing collective bargaining arrangements and to undercut the UAW's position in the workplace.

Compounding these problems for the Canadian UAW was a serious internal weakening of the union which threatened to prevent the union from taking any meaningful political action. On the one hand, the union was weakened by declining memberships, greater job competition between workers and heightened job insecurity brought on by the economic crisis. On the other hand, the union found itself wracked with internal union conflict over the appropriate union response to corporate and government attacks on unions. Concessions and corporate attempts to introduce a more "flexible" labour process found Canadian Autoworkers divided between those willing to accept such changes in the hope of saving their jobs and more militant workers who insisted on fighting back. Furthermore, after accepting early rounds of wage concessions at Chrysler and other small plants, the UAW found itself the object of membership ire as workers blamed the union and not corporations for the losses they were incurring. These divisions threatened to split the union and render it incapable of mobilizing support for any chosen course of collective political action.

This internal weakening of the UAW and the concerted attack on unions by governments and corporations led the UAW to search for a strategy which would effectively protect its members and defend the organizational integrity and strength of the union. The Canadian UAW ultimately returned to militant, mobilization-based politics. Canadian Autoworkers occupied plants scheduled for closure and undertook a campaign against concessions. On the political front, while the UAW continued with some lobbying, it put greater pressure on governments by engaging in massive demonstrations, alliance building with cross-sections of the Canadian public, and workplace action aimed at securing political victories (Yates, 1986). Finally, the Canadian UAW, represented by Robert White, entered the terrain of national politics in an attempt to put forth an alternative vision of Canadian society to that offered by business groups and their growing conservative political supporters.

Canadian Autoworkers were successful in their immediate struggles. They successfully resisted concessions demanded by corporations and set the stage for an alternate corporate strategy more dependent upon negotiation with unions, rather than their elimination. Moreover, the Canadian UAW preserved the key structures of collective bargaining, such as master and pattern bargaining, which in turn helped secure the organizational strength of the union. On the political front, the union also reaped rewards, largely due to its militant workplace strategies. For example, when policy advocacy failed to gain action by the Ontario government on the issue of plant closures, sit-down strikes were used, leading both to improved private severance settlements between the companies and workers and to provincial legislation governing severance packages and plant closures.

Beyond such immediate political gains, the Canadian UAW through its mobilization, forced the federal government to seek greater UAW involvement in decision-making that affected the auto industry, and the provincial government to maintain its more structured consultative relationship with the union. During and immediately following a number of successful no-concessions struggles, the UAW was invited to participate in the 1980 negotiation of the Chrysler loan and in provincial-federal government plans to aid financially the troubled American Motors Corporation. On the question of the Chrysler loan, Herb Gray, minister responsible for the loan, went so far as to fly all corporate and government officials to Winnipeg where Bob White was attending a CLC convention to ensure UAW approval of the terms of the loan.

Finally, the UAW was invited to participate on a number of task forces and policy advisory bodies on the Ontario economy and the auto industry in particular. The most important one was the 1983 federal task force on the auto industry. Since 1980, the UAW had identified rising Japanese auto imports as the key problem facing the auto industry and one on which government action was necessary. Yet, at the same time the federal government was abandoning its nationalist programme in favour of one of restraint and less state involvement in the economy. In the face of this government resistance to intervention in the auto industry and in anticipation that policy advocacy by the union alone would fail to push the government into action, the UAW adopted an alliance-building strategy to make more effective its demands. Beyond the solicitation of support from a vast number of other unions, the UAW secured alliances with the auto and parts companies and the Ontario and Québec governments, whose economies were most threatened by continued decline of the auto industry. At first the federal government undertook short-term measures in response to the growing political pressure. It negotiated with the Japanese a number of temporary agreements for voluntary restraint of imports. Then, in 1983, Edward Lumley, Minister of Industry, Trade and Commerce, established a task force to study and propose policy solutions for the auto industry. In an unprecedented move, Lumley asked Bob White to co-chair the task force with the President of the Automotive Parts Manufacturers' Association.

The report of this task force contained a number of victories for the union. The most important of these was the official endorsement by the corporate task force representatives of a trade agreement that would require off-shore vehicle producers who imported into Canada to meet minimum Canadian content requirements and in some cases establish assembly facilities in this country (Lavelle and White, 1983:Chaps. 7,8). Although the UAW followed up the release of the report with ongoing pressure on the government, just when it appeared that the union had garnered the support of Prime Minister Trudeau for the policy, Trudeau resigned, a federal election was called and the Conservative Party was elected. This party's successful negotiation of a free trade agreement with the US eliminated the possibility for such a trade proposal and once again confronted the UAW with uncertain political and economic fortunes.

Conclusion

This chapter has stressed that the understanding of labour-state relations must emerge from a broader examination of the evolution of capitalism. Elite pluralism and a predisposition to lobby are the product of specific social relations. As modes of interest representation, they form part of a specific regime of accumulation that dominated capitalist economies in the postwar period. The analysis of group-state relations must take account of broader structural properties of capitalist social formation. The regulation approach is particularly useful for these purposes.

When it comes to the Fordist mode of regulation in Canada, and in particular, the wage labour-capital relation, it is essential to note that it was primarily constituted in the private sphere. Because of its dependence on individual unions and corporations, this mode of regulation was fragmented and it remains quite fragile, subject to the strength of individual unions to bargain and defend both regulatory structures and wage and benefit packages for its membership. The private and fragmented nature of regulation also had its effect on the political structures of interest intermediation. Structured political relations with government became secondary to struggles in the workplace, therefore delaying the consolidation of labour-state relations. Moreover, these relations tended to be union specific. In the case of the UAW, these relations were not secured until the 1960s, and even then only at the federal level as they were initially articulated around problems in the auto industry.

Labour-state relations were stabilized through trade-union participation in a pressure pluralist policy network and labour's acceptance of a pluralist view of its role in society. This form of interest intermediation tended to reinforce fragmentation of the Canadian labour movement and encouraged unions to define their interests with those of corporations or with the industries in which they represented workers. A class-based discourse and politics, so pronounced in Western Europe, could not be sustained in Canada. For the UAW, policy advocacy brought few positive political results, but had potentially disastrous consequences, as seen in the demobilization of the union.

As Fordism reached its limits in the 1970s, the restructuring of labour-state relations along tripartite lines loomed as a real possibility. Although attempts at such restructuring failed at the federal level, they succeeded on the provincial front in Ontario. The newly formed tripartite structures, and the Ontario government's determination to gain trade-union cooperation in rebuilding the provincial economy, resulted in immediate and substantial political gains for the UAW and other unions. The economic crisis of the 1980s, however, interrupted the consolidation of this new relationship.

The UAW successfully mobilized its own membership to resist the worst effects of this crisis and forced a reformulation of its relations with the federal government such that the union became involved in government planning for the auto industry. These victories were soon snatched from the UAW when the Conservative Party was elected as the federal government in 1984 and began negotiating a free trade agreement with the US. While the UAW has not been weakened in the workplace, its political power, along with that of the rest of organized labour has waned. Moreover, attempts by the Canadian Autoworkers to restructure the labour movement to make it a more powerful national political force have foundered on jurisdictional squabbles with other unions and a general fear amongst the bulk of Canadian unions of rocking the political boat.

It seems that the legacy of fragmentation and union competition left by pressure politics and other elements of the Fordist regime, may undo the possibilities for organized labour to force its entry into the corridors of political power. Without concerted action by labour and an ideology that provides an alternative vision of the Canadian future to that offered by conservatives, unions may find themselves picked off one by one as the next economic recession gets underway. Labour has already lost its access to and influence over many governments and yet seems unable to remobilize in its own defence.

References

Aglietta, Michel (1976). *A Theory of Capitalist Regulation.* London: New Left Books.

Beigie, Carl (1970). *The Canada-U.S. Automotive Agreement: An Evaluation.* Washington: Canadian-American Committee.

Berger, Suzanne (1981). *Organizing Interests in Western Europe.* Cambridge: Cambridge University Press.

Bladen, V.W. (1961). *Report of Royal Commission on the Automotive Industry.* Ottawa: Queen's Printer.

Boyer, Robert (1989). "The Capital Labor Relations in OECD Countries: From the 'Golden Age' to the Uncertain Nineties." Paper prepared for the WIDER project on Capital-Labor Relations, March, Harvard, Mass.

Cuneo, Carl (1979). "State, Class and Reserve Labour: The Case of the 1941 Canadian Unemployment Insurance Act." *Canadian Journal of Sociology and Anthropology,* 16:147-70.

_____ **(1980).** "State Mediation of Class Contradictions in Canadian Unemployment Insurance, 1930-35." *Studies in Political Economy,* 3:37-63.

Davis, Mike (1980). "Why the U.S. Working Class is Different." *New Left Review,* 123:3-44.

Finkel, Alvin (1977). "Origins of the Welfare State in Canada." In L. Panitch, ed. *The Canadian State.* Toronto: University of Toronto Press: 344-70.

Fournier, Pierre (1986). "Consensus Building in Canada: Case Studies and Prospects." In K. Banting, ed. *The State and Economic Interests.* Toronto: University of Toronto Press: 291-336.

Giles, Anthony (1982). "The Canadian Labour Congress and Tripartism." *Relations Industrielles/Industrial Relations,* 37:93-125.

Jenson, Jane (1989a). "Different but not Exceptional: Canada's Permeable Fordism." *Canadian Journal of Sociology and Anthropology,* 26: 69-94.

_____ **(1989b)**. "Paradigms and Political Discourse: Policies to Protect Women and Children in the U.S.A. and France Before 1914." *Canadian Journal of Political Science*, 32: 235-58.

Kwavnick, D. (1972). *Organized Labour and Pressure Politics*. Montreal: McGill-Queen's University Press.

Lavelle, Pat and Robert White (1983). *An Automotive Strategy for Canada*. Report of the Federal Task Force on the Canadian Motor Vehicle and Automotive Parts Industries. Ottawa: Supply and Services Canada.

Lipietz, Alain (1987). *Mirages and Miracles*. London: Verso Books.

Martin, Andrew (1986). "The Politics of Employment and Welfare: National Policies and International Interdependence." In K. Banting, ed. *The State and Economic Interests*. Toronto: University of Toronto Press: 157-241.

Maslove, A. and G. Swimmer (1980). *Wage Controls in Canada, 1975-78*. Montreal: The Institute for Research on Public Policy.

McAllister, Heather (1984). "Labour's Direction in the Changing Political Economy." Paper presented to the annual meeting of the Canadian Political Science Association, Guelph, Ontario.

Panitch, Leo (1979). "Corporatism in Canada?" *Studies in Political Economy*, 1:43-92.

_____ **(1986)**. "Trade Unions and the Capitalist State." In Panitch, *Working Class In Politics in Crisis*. London: Verso Books.

Przeworski, Adam (1980). "Social Democracy as a Historical Phenomenon." *In New Left Review*, 122:27-58.

Wolfe, David (1984). "The Rise and Demise of the Keynesian Era in Canada." In M. Cross and G. Kealey, eds. *Modern Canada 1930-1980*. Toronto: McClelland and Stewart: 46-78.

Yates, C. (1986). "New Directions for the Canadian Labour Movement: The UAW and Beyond." Paper presented to Annual Meeting of the American Political Science Association, Washington.

_____ **(1988)**. *From Planting to Politics: The Canadian UAW, 1936-1984*. Unpublished Ph.D. dissertation, Carleton University, Ottawa.

Endnotes

*Some of the material presented in this text is based on interviews with Sam Gindin (Research Director UAW and Executive Assistant to President of CAW, 1984 and 1989) and with Robert White (Regional Director of UAW and President of CAW, undertaken in Dec. 1985).

1. Canadian UAW, "Win the Peace Plan," presented to C.D.Howe, Mar. 1945.

2. Canadian UAW Regional Director's Report to Canadian District Council, 19 & 20 June 1948, p.13; Minutes to Canadian District Council, 11 & 12 Dec. 1948, p.10.

3. Canada, Department of Labour, *Labour Gazette* vol. xliv, no.1, "Award on Issue of Union Security in Ford Dispute", Jan. 1946; Yates, 1988: Chap. 4.

4. The material which follows on the UAW's lobbying efforts is based on archival research of UAW archives deposited in the Walter Reuther Library in Detroit, Michigan and in the Public Archives of Canada (PAC), Ottawa. As this research was originally presented in my PhD dissertation and due to the need for brevity in footnotes, anyone wishing to refer to the particular documentation should see the dissertation. Only footnotes other than archival ones are cited in the following.

5. The term "tripartism" is used rather than "corporatism" as I prefer to reserve the use of the term corporatism as defined by L.Panitch who distinguishes corporatism as a "political structure in advanced capitalism" which involves a linkage between functional interest groups and the state wherein the state devolves certain decision-making capabilities onto the groups involved in this structure. As the cases discussed below do not include such devolution of decision-making, I prefer to refer to them as tripartite structures.

6. Letter from William Davis, Premier of Ontario, to D.McDermott, Canadian Director of UAW, 5 Feb. 1976.

CHAPTER TWELVE

BIASES IN THE SUPPLY OF PUBLIC POLICIES TO ORGANIZED INTERESTS:
SOME EMPIRICAL EVIDENCE

Réjean Laundry

P olicy decisions produce allocations of values. In a world of perfect information with no transaction costs, where the decisions are reached with the unanimity rule, the allocation of values would always generate Pareto optimal outcomes. This term means that the allocation of resources among alternative policy decisions would be such that no one could be made better off by a reallocation without making someone else worse off. Pareto efficiency is easy to state but difficult to achieve. In a decision-making environment in which information is not perfect, where transaction costs exist, and for which the decision rule is below unanimity, one has to pay attention to the redistribution of resources among the participants. As a result, policy analysis has always been concerned with two

---

See Glossary of Technical Terms at the end of this chapter.

fundamental questions: What are the benefits derived from the policy decisions? And who are their beneficiaries? These two questions have occupied a prominent place in those areas of policy analysis that stress the interrelations between policy decisions and organized interests.

The identification of the interconnections between policy decisions and organized interests has been inspired by four broad categories of conceptual frameworks. Political scientists have been mainly working with either party government models of policy-making, or pressure group models of policy-making (also labelled policy network models). Students of economics have been using either market failure models, or rent seeking models (also labelled transfer seeking models). With the exception of studies based on rent seeking models, most empirical investigations tend to rely on an inductive approach that is either atheoretical or that consists of loose hypotheses coupled with a small number of critical variables. As a result, findings tend to be valid for only specific countries or specific policy areas. Consequently, the inductive approach does not constitute an adequate research strategy if one wants to compare regularities across countries and policy areas. Furthermore, theoretical investigations that have stressed the interconnections between policy decisions and organized interests have produced deductive models and theoretical predictions that have not yet been empirically tested in a way that permits comparisons of regularities among countries and policy areas. Whether based on the inductive approach or on deductive theoretical models, most empirical accounts of the interactions between policy decisions and organized interests deal either with the history of a single group, or more often, small numbers of groups or associations of groups in a single policy area. There are no comprehensive analyses of the interactions between policy decisions and organized interests in Canada. The aim of this chapter is to draw upon previous studies in policy analysis and organized interests to develop a conceptual framework and to test its theoretical predictions against the policy decisions made through lawmaking in the Québec National Assembly from 1960 to 1985. Compared to the usual research designs that report a large number of facts in a single policy area, our research design aims to report a small number of facts on a large number of policy decisions. This research strategy calls first for a review of the main theoretical approaches regarding the interconnections between policy decisions and organized interests. The theoretical section of the chapter will provide the opportunities to derive theoretical predictions that will be tested against empirical data. The second part of the chapter will illustrate how data were collected and will present the evidence supporting the theoretical predictions.

Policy Decisions versus Organized Interests

Deriving the Wealth Transfer Bias

Policy decisions actually or potentially affect individual interests through allocations of values. In turn, these allocations of values create bundles of rights belonging to individuals. In this channelling process, political activities can be seen as investments in the maintenance and expansion of rights holdings. More specifically, investments in policy-making processes can take two forms: voting and lobbying. Lobbying can be carried out either by individuals or through organized groups. In most Western countries, lobbying activities usually take place between policy-makers and organized groups to which individuals belong in their capacity as workers, entrepreneurs, consumers, tax-payers, and so on.

Organized groups engaged in lobbying activities may be seen as entering into a kind of transaction with policy-makers. A market is created where organized groups offer votes and support to policy-makers in exchange for favourable policy decisions. However, when information and transaction costs exist, some organized groups will acquire information and organize their lobbying activities more cheaply than others. In turn, these differences in information and transaction costs will give rise to differences in the demands regarding the allocation of values to be made through policy decisions. The same argument holds for the policy-makers: in a world of perfect information and no transaction costs, all policy decisions would be Pareto-optimal, and only welfare-enhancing allocations of values would be adopted by elected representatives. Thus, the supply of policy decisions regulating the allocation of values is very sensitive to information and transaction costs.

Leaders of organized groups and policy-makers face two types of information costs: first, the cost of discovering the impacts of alternative policy decisions on their interests; and second, the cost of identifying other policy-makers or organized groups who could participate in a potential coalition on the policy issue at stake. If the policy-making environment is defined in terms of winners and losers, one can derive four different situations: *(1)* the costs of discovering the impacts of alternative policy decisions and the participants in a potential coalition are low for the winners and losers on the policy issue; *(2)* the costs of identifying the impacts of alternative policy decisions and the participants in a potential coalition are high for the winners and losers on the policy issue; (3) the identification costs are high for the winners but low for the losers; and conversely, (4) the identification costs are low for the winners but high for the losers. These last two cases might be seen as giving rise to a wealth transfer, but this deduction is incorrect for it does not take into account the incentive of organized groups or policy-makers to bear the information costs.

The transaction costs arising from the organization costs of lobbying activities must be considered. For groups, organization costs are like start-up costs (McCormick and Tollison, 1981:17): groups that have borne these start-up costs for purposes unrelated to lobbying activities will have a larger incentive to invest in the acquisition of information, and to lobby the policy-makers for the outcome most profitable to the interests of their groups. In other words, groups that are able to produce lobbying activities as a by-product of performing other activities do not have to bear start-up costs relative to their lobbying activities. As a result, these groups have a higher incentive to become involved in lobbying activities. Thus, policy-makers hear more frequently, if not exclusively, from them and the other groups will probably be ignorant of the benefits and costs of the policy decisions enacted. Therefore, the lobbying industry tends to be crowded by groups that do not have to bear start-up organization costs.

Olson (1965, 1982) has provided an analytical tool for distinguishing between groups that have high start-up costs and those that do not. Individuals concerned by policy decisions in their capacity as consumers or taxpayers have a low incentive to support the organizing costs required for the presentation of their policy demands to government because the costs of organizing such a large, diffuse group tend to exceed the benefits they can expect from the policy outcomes. In general, the transaction costs tend to exceed the expected benefits because taxes supported by taxpayers and expenses made by consumers concern a very large array of goods, each component of which often represents a small fraction in the overall basket of their expenses and taxes. Therefore, organized groups made up of individuals united in their capacity as consumers and taxpayers can be referred to as high cost coalitions. Conversely, individuals concerned by policy issues in their capacity as owners of production factors—workers, entrepreneurs, professionals—have a high incentive to support the organization costs required for the presentation of their policy demands to government. Policy decisions that impinge on their production factors exert a strong impact on their incomes. This follows because the largest part of the outcomes of the owners of production factors derives basically from the holding of one or two production factors. Thus, organized groups that reunite individuals in their capacity as owners of production factors can be referred to as low cost coalitions. These differences in the decision-making environment explain why groups representing owners of production factors have a higher incentive to invest resources in lobbying activities than groups representing consumers and taxpayers that face the free-rider problem.

Consequently, policy-makers tend to hear only from low cost coalitions, and the high cost coalitions will remain ignorant of costs and benefits, if not of the very existence of the policy decisions. Thus, the lobbying industry tends to be dominated by low cost coalitions, with very few representing the high cost coalitions.

This bias is coupled with an incentive structure that rewards wealth transfer activities of organized interests and policy-makers. Organized groups can maximize the benefits to their members by investing their resources either in the increase of the wealth produced by the society as a whole, or in obtaining a larger share of the wealth produced in the rest of the society. An organized group that invests its resources in order to increase the wealth of the society as a whole would actually be providing a public good for the whole society of which it is only a tiny part. In such circumstances, an organized group would support the total costs of a policy decision in exchange for a tiny fraction of the benefits. Thus, according to Olson (1982:44):

> the typical organization for collective action within a society will, at least if it represents only a narrow segment of the society, have little or no incentive to make any significant sacrifices in the interest of the society; it can best serve its members' interests by striving to seize a larger share of a society's production for them. This will be expedient, moreover, even if the social costs of the change in the distribution exceed the amount distributed by a large multiple; there is for practical purposes no constraint on the social cost such an organization will find it expedient to impose on the society in the course of obtaining a larger share of the social output for itself... The organizations for collective action within societies that we are considering are therefore overwhelmingly oriented to struggles over distribution of income and wealth rather than to the production of additional output—they are distributional coalitions, or organizations that engage in... rent seeking.

Because of the transaction costs and incentive structure prevailing in the world of organized groups, the incentive structure is biased against the promotion of the interests of high cost coalitions and toward promoting the interests of low cost coalitions. Moreover, organized interest groups have no incentive to pursue lobbying activities that would yield outcomes that are pure public goods, that is, goods available to everyone. Organized groups have an incentive to free ride at the expense of the rest of the society.

Policy-makers as well have no incentive to engage in the production of policy outcomes that are in the interest of high cost coalitions. Rather, they have an incentive to supply policy outcomes that benefit low cost coalitions at the expense of high cost coalitions. Benefits supplied to low cost coalitions tend to be like private goods, that is, goods that may be directed at some individuals only. Thus, policy-makers and organized groups have an incentive structure biased toward private goods and away from public goods.

This incentive structure holds because the driving force behind elected representatives, whether in groups or in governments, is the desire to be re-elected. The basic argument is as follows: elected representatives must serve their constituents in order to be re-elected. This purpose incites them to prefer policy outcomes that maximize the probability of their re-election. If a representative does not act like a vote maximizer, he or she can be defeated by a challenger who does. In the competition for elected positions, in organized groups and in governments, the surviving representatives—including the most altruistic ones—will be those who act like vote-maximizers.

In short, the commodity being exchanged between organized interests and policy-makers is a transfer of wealth. The motivations of the participants as well as the existence of information and transaction costs create a built-in bias toward transfer of wealth from high cost coalitions to low cost coalitions (Downs, 1957; Olson, 1965, 1982; Moe, 1980, 1981; Hayes, 1981; Frey, 1983).

The Calculus of Wealth Transfer

If elected policy-makers are fundamentally motivated by the desire to be re-elected, an heuristic theoretical framework must provide predictions about the benefits of wealth transfer and the organized groups benefiting from these transfers. Several economic and political theoretical frameworks attempt to explain how this process works.

- *The market failure approach*: a market failure occurs when the rules regulating the transactions on the private market prevent participants from capturing potential benefits that other rules might make available. These losses of potential gains are usually judged according to the criteria of efficiency and equity. For instance, positive externalities derived from private transactions may generate benefits that cannot be captured exclusively by entrepreneurs who have assumed the production costs. Conversely, negative externalities deriving from private transactions can impose inequitable costs on third parties. As a result, the market transactions generate an underproduction of positive externalities coupled with an overproduction of negative externalities. Governments are called upon to intervene in certain policy-specific ways to correct such market failures. In this approach, the role of the state is to recreate Pareto optimal outcomes through the production of public goods. Public goods produce indivisible benefits for which it is impossible to exclude anyone from consumption. But goods that are indivisible and non-excludable benefit everyone in the society.

Consequently, if a state was limiting itself to the production of public goods, the transfers of wealth that would take place would generate Pareto optimal outcomes. Wealth transfers giving rise to inefficient Pareto outcomes occur because governments produce goods that are not perfectly divisible and not perfectly excludable. Then, it becomes impossible to prevent certain special interest groups from receiving more benefits from wealth transfers than others. From the market failure approach, one can predict that wealth transfers benefit everyone if the state is engaged exclusively in the production of public goods. This postulate will be the first prediction to be tested.

Table 1

Four types of policy outcomes

	diffuse costs	concentrated costs
diffuse benefits	majoritarian* policies 3	client policies °4°
concentrated benefits	entrepreneurial policies 1°	adversarial policies 2°

* *The four labels are borrowed from Wilson (1980).*
Numbers in the quadrants indicate degree of probability of outcome. 1°
(entreprenurial policies) are most probable; 4°, least probable.

- *The wealth transfer approach*: contrary to the market failure approach which assumes that policy-makers are benevolent, the wealth transfer approach (Olson, 1965, 1982; Wilson, 1980; Mc-Cormick and Tollison, 1981) postulates that policy-makers prefer vote-winning policy outcomes to vote-losing alternatives. Well-known typologies concerning the supply of policy outcomes have focussed on the allocation of benefits (Lowi, 1972; Salisbury, 1968; Hayes, 1978). However, governmental interventions confer costs as well as benefits. Wilson (1980) explicitly considers the possibility that benefits and costs can be widely distributed, that is, diffused among individuals targeted in their capacity of taxpayers and consumers. Conversely, benefits and costs can be highly concentrated, that is shared among individuals targeted in their capacity of owners of production factors. These conceptual distinctions generate four categories of policy outcomes conveying different strategic considerations regarding voting (see Table 1). Since the seminal works of Downs (1957) and Olson (1965), the most debated strategy refers to policy outcomes providing concentrated benefits matched with diffuse costs. This strategy creates situations where gained votes exceed lost votes. Moreover, this wealth transfer strategy preserves consensus among individuals because high cost coalitions have an incentive to give up before fighting.

Conversely, policy outcomes conveying diffuse benefits and concentrated costs create situations where the votes gained are smaller than the votes wasted. This follows because high cost coalitions have a lower incentive to invest in lobbying activities than low cost coalitions.

The two other strategies constitute zero sum games in the sense that the number of votes gained is equal to the number lost. Policy outcomes producing concentrated benefits and concentrated costs refer to adversarial policies such as those arising from conflicts between business and labour. Finally, policy outcomes conveying diffuse benefits and diffuse costs are referred to as majoritarian policies and include decisions on matters like war, crime or improvement in the quality of education. The strategy of diffusing costs and benefits is more rewarding because it is more consensual than that of concentrating costs and benefits.

In short, and this is the second prediction to be tested, policy-makers maximize their probability of re-election if their basket of policy decisions is structured in such a way that: entrepreneurial policies>(are more vote-getting than) adversarial policies> majoritarian policies>client policies. The confirmation of this prediction would indicate that low cost coalitions made up of individuals reunited in their capacity as owners of production factors would benefit more than others from policy outcomes.

This second prediction assumes that costs and benefits are determined simultaneously in the same policy decisions and this may well be the case in some policy areas. However, the imposition of costs seems to occur separately from the conferral of benefits in most policy areas because they occur in different departments at different times and in different acts. Policy decisions regarding the improvement of educational services are typical of this disjoined phenomenon. This built-in trait of our political institutions calls for an analysis of benefits that is totally independent of the consideration of the costs. Such an analysis is possible if one considers the relations between benefits and costs in reference to diffusion, concentration and indeterminacy. The incorporation of this third dimension gives rise to nine exclusive strategies (Table 2).

Table 2*

The nine possible relations of benefits to costs

benefits	undetermined costs UC	diffuse costs DC	concentrated costs CC
undetermined UB	5°	6°	9°
diffuse DB	3°	4°	8°
concentrated CB	1°	2°	7°

*Numbers in the quadrants indicate probability of outcome:
1° policy outcomes are most probable; 9°, least probable.

Obscuring the relations between benefits and costs can be rewarding for policy-makers. It is easy to understand that supplying a policy outcome that combines concentrated benefits and undetermined costs is even more rewarding than offering concentrated benefits matched with diffuse costs. If the diffusion of costs incites high cost coalitions to give up before fighting, dissimulating totally the costs kills any incentive to fight against the conferring of benefits. Prediction 2 was about the biases advantaging owners of production factors at the expense of taxpayers and consumers. One is now paying attention to the rewarding aspects of policy outcomes based on illusions of costs. In theory, the policy outcomes based on illusions of costs will predominantly favour owners of production factors because they are usually parts of low cost coalitions compared to taxpayers and consumers whose high cost coalitions are faced with the free rider problem. Therefore, the third prediction to be tested is summarized in Table 2. Outcomes range from the most likely, that of concentrated benefits and undetermined costs, to the least likely, concentrated costs and undetermined benefits. As already noted, this prediction sees the owners of production factors to be the most advantaged.

- *The party government model of policy-making*: this model assumes that the election of a new party in government gives rise to a cycle of policy decisions based on the programme, ideology and electoral pledges of the incoming party. Therefore, one can expect that a newly elected conservative party would adopt public policies carrying benefits for entrepreneurs, as opposed to a newly elected social democrat party which would implement policies favourable to labour and citizens with below average incomes. The party government model reflects policy differences between political opponents. Prediction 2 states that policy outcomes will benefit owners of production factors at the expense of taxpayers and consumers whereas prediction 3 states that the policy-makers are incited to provide more benefits for the owners of production factors than for the taxpayers and consumers. The party government model provides assumptions and hypotheses about the categories of owners of production factors that are best placed ideologically to draw advantages from policy outcomes. Therefore, the fourth prediction to be tested is that a conservative government will favour organized interests representing individuals in their capacity as entrepreneurs whereas a social democrat government will favour organized interests grouping individuals in their capacity as workers.

The extent to which these theoretical predictions are supported by empirical evidence is examined after a short discussion of the methodology of data collection.

Data Collection Methodology

The analysis begins with a content analysis of all the public statutes adopted by the Québec National Assembly between 1960 and 1985. Data collection proceeded in four main steps: determination of the unit of analysis; selection of the documents to be analyzed; data recording; and data verification.

The unit of analysis chosen in this study was the proposition of governmental intervention. Such a proposition is made up of four basic components:

- who is responsible for the intervention? for example, *The Ministry of Social Services*.

- what is the connecting verb being used to describe the intervention? for example, *authorize*.

- what is the attribute of the intervention being provided? for example, *the receiving of benefits from the Québec Health Insurance Plan for a maximum four month period*.

- what are the individual groups or institutions being targeted by the intervention? for example, *a person who has moved from Québec to a province where a similar plan does not exist*.

From 1960 to 1985, the Québec National Assembly enacted 1662 public statutes, which adds up to about 8 feet of published paper (each act is published in French and English). Given this volume, and in order to make our study feasible, instead of studying the entire text of every act, we decided to study the abstracts of the acts. The average abstract has about 30 lines of length.

Data were recorded using a closed questionnaire. This approach to content analysis is somewhat analogous to an interview. The analysts ask questions of documents and answer a questionnaire developed for this purpose. The first task of the analyst was to identify the proposition of governmental intervention and to record it on the questionnaire. The second step was to analyze the content of the proposition. This task was facilitated by the use of a closed questionnaire made up of questions borrowed from various concepts of the theory of public goods relative to benefits and costs of governmental interventions. Let us illustrate the steps of the coding procedure with the concrete example reported in the presentation of the unit of analysis.

Step 1: Recording of the proposition:

/M/I/N/I/S/T/R/Y/ /O/F/ S/O/C/I/A/L/ /S/E/R/V/I/C/E/S/$/M/A/Y/ /A/U/T/H/O/R/I/Z/E///T/H/E/ /R/E/C/E/I/V/I/N/G/ /O/F/ /B/E/N/E/F/I/T/S/ /F/R/O/M/ /T/H/E/ Q/U/E/B/E/C/ /H/E/A/L/T/H/ /I/N/S/U/R/A/N/C/E/ /P/L/A/N/ /,/F/O/R/ /A/ M/A/X/I/M/U/M/ / 4/ /M/O/N/T/H/ /P/E/R/I/O/D///(/A/ /P/E/R/S/O/N/ /W/H/O/ /L/E/A/V/E/S/ /F/O/R/ /A/N/O/T/H/E/R/ /P/R/O/V/I/N/C/E/ / /W/H/E/R/E/ /S/U/C/H/ /P/L/A/N/ /D/O/E/S/ /N/O/T/ /E/X/I/S/T/)/ / / / / /

Step 2: Analysis of the proposition: are benefits offered to:

entrepreneurs?	1
workers?	2
other types of owners of production factors?	3
consumers?	4
undetermined targets?	9

The analyst enters the code 4 because the benefits are provided to consumers. The same question is asked with respect to costs. In the proposition under examination, the costs are coded as undetermined because there is no information about the imposition of costs. The analysts go through the whole questionnaire using the same procedure.

The questionnaires were administered by three research assistants who have worked on the research project on a full time basis. The completed questionnaires were then checked by a fourth person whose function was to increase the reliability and validity of the analysis. Once verified, questionnaires were then recorded on a computer tape, the validity of the analysis was checked by a computer program that was designed to detect illogical answers. These logical inconsistencies were checked manually. These operations of quality control led us to correct about 4 per cent of the completed questionnaires.

Measurement and Results

The data generated from the questionnaires allowed the testing of the four predictions.

Prediction 1: Wealth transfers benefit everyone if the state is engaged exclusively in the production of public goods.

A private good carries perfectly divisible and perfectly excludable benefits. Benefits are considered to be divisible if one can identify a finite amount that can be allotted among recipients. Otherwise, benefits are indivisible. In contrast, benefits are judged excludable if one can identify an eligibility criterion or a schedule of charges that recipients must satisfy before consuming the goods. Otherwise, benefits are considered to be nonexcludable. Reciprocally, a public good conveys benefits that are indivisible and nonexcludable. Moreover, these definitions generate two types of mixed goods: club goods carrying indivisible benefits from which exclusion is feasible and common pool goods conveying nonexcludable benefits that are divisible. Finally, when a proposition of governmental intervention does not provide sufficient information on divisibility and excludability, the goods are classified in the category of undetermined goods.

Here are some concrete examples for every type of goods:

1. *Private goods*:
   /The Water Pollution Act/establishes/grants for the construction of water purification plants/(for municipal corporations).

   /The Québec Farm Credit Corporation/increases/the maximum amount of authorized loans from 40,000 to 150,000 dollars/ (for individual farmers).

   /The Archives Act/establishes/a financial assistance programme/ (for services of private archives).

2. *Club goods*:
   /The Civil Code Act/reduces/to 18 the minimum age at which (a person) can make a testament/.

   /The Public Health Act/obliges/(every person operating a summer camp) to have a permit in conformity with the Act/.

/The Construction Act/establishes/a qualification scheme for construction builders/ (for construction builders).

/The Securities Commission Act/regulates/information regarding corporations going into the public domain for subscriptions/ (for stock holders).

3. *Common pool goods*:

/The Régie de la Place des arts de Montréal/may organize/shows/ (for general population).

/The Société d'habitation du Québec may subsidize/the operation of low cost housing/ (for municipalities).

/The Ministry of Social Services/guarantees/access to health services/ (for Québec population).

4. *Public goods*:

/The Official language Act/declares/French as the official language of Québec/.

/Regional Municipalities/are authorized to modify/their planning schemes/.

/The Ministry of Tourism/will diffuse/information regarding Tourist attraction sites/.

5. *Undetermined goods*:

/The Transportation Act/authorizes/the abolition of the Transport Commission/.

/The Agriculture Act/authorizes/(The Québec Farm Credit Corporation) /to conduct certain types of investigations and inspections/.

/The Civil Service Act/abolishes/the Ministry of Civil Service/.

Table 3 indicates that the supply of public goods amounts to 13.6 per cent of the goods provided, compared to 6.7 per cent for private goods and 62.2 per cent for club goods. These results are consistent with a recent study by Montmarquette (1988) who found that the production of public goods amounted to 15 per cent of the expenditures of the Canadian government. Thus, a very small fraction of the goods provided through legislation benefits everyone. This fraction rises from 13.6 per cent to 30 per cent if one assumes that undetermined goods can be assimilated to public goods on the ground that they are neither divisible nor excludable. The fact that 70 per cent of the goods provided are excludable means that the legislation enacted has produced benefits reserved for special interest groups. Who are the beneficiaries of the wealth transfers performed through governmental interventions?

Table 3

Types of goods supplied in the Legislation of the Québec National Assembly from 1960 up to 1985

Types	n	%
private goods	582	6.7
club goods	5388	62.2
common pool goods	104	1.2
public goods	1174	13.6
undetermined goods	1413	16.3
Total	8661	100.0

Prediction 2: Wealth transfers benefit owners of production factors at the expense of consumers and taxpayers.

The case of consumers and taxpayers speaks for itself. The owners of production factors have been subdivided into three subcategories: entrepreneurs, workers, and owners of other production factors. The figures presented in table 4 do not support prediction 2. On the contrary, they indicate that when the costs of governmental interventions are explicitly matched to benefits (slightly more than 25 per cent of the cases), the recipients of benefits have to support costs about 85 per cent of the time. Furthermore, it shows that the benefits provided to entrepreneurs very rarely impose costs on workers (3.0%) or consumers and taxpayers (1.5%). Similarly, the benefits conferred on workers rarely transfer costs to entrepreneurs (7.4%) or consumers and taxpayers (1.3%). In the same manner, benefits supplied to consumers and taxpayers do not impose significant costs on entrepreneurs (4.2%) or on workers (7.5%). Contrary to expectations, if one pays attention to the margins, entrepreneurs and workers assume more often than expected the costs of the benefits conferred to consumers and taxpayers. Furthermore, entrepreneurs, more often than workers, are supporting the production costs of the goods provided to consumers and taxpayers.

Prediction 3: Wealth transfers benefit owners of production factors through the diffusion of costs.

Referring back to Table 2, the pattern predicted only emerges in part. The cells with predicted order in parentheses occur as follows: CB/UC(1) = 2525 > UB/UC(5) = 2202 > CB/CC(7) = 1518 > DB/UC(3) = 1317 > DB/DC(4) = 340.[1] These cells account for 96 per cent of the 8251 goods provided. As predicted, the owners of production factors are the big winners with 2525 benefits matched to undetermined costs. But, the policy-makers did not produce as many vote-maximizing goods

Table 4

Distribution of benefits in relation to costs 1960-1985

BENEFITS	COSTS						
	Entre-preneurs	Workers	other owners of production	consumers and tax-payers	government & entre-preneurs	undeter-mined	Total
Entre-preneurs	85.0	3.0	2.2	1.5	95.2	17.7	2068 (25.1)
Workers	7.4	87.7	1.5	1.3	0.0	15.1	1354 (16.4)
Other owners of production factors	2.3	1.0	82.4	3.3	0.0	9.0	810 (9.8)
consumers and tax-payers	4.2	7.5	11.4	86.5	4.8	21.8	1766 (21.4)
undeter-mined	1.1	0.7	2.6	7.4	0.0	36.4	2253 (27.3)
Total	1122 (13.6)	398 (4.8)	273 (3.3)	393 (4.8)	21 (0.2)	6044 (73.2)	825 (100.0)

as expected. Providing governmental interventions carrying undetermined benefits matched to undetermined costs does not look like a good strategy for policy-makers who are expected to act in such a way as to increase their probability of re-election. Still, this is what they have offered voters 27 per cent of the time (2202). The next most used strategy—providing concentrated benefits matched to concentrated costs—creates, as indicated earlier, a kind of zero sum game in terms of electoral gains. The production of diffused benefits matched to undetermined costs comes in the fourth position with 1317 propositions. Such a supply does not have a high impact on electoral gains because diffuse benefits are more difficult to identify than concentrated benefits.

Wealth transfers benefit owners of production factors much more than they do consumers and taxpayers. Nevertheless, the wealth transfers do not benefit equally every group of owners of production factors. The data indicate that policy-makers prefer to provide owners of production factors with benefits while imposing undetermined rather than concentrated costs. Moreover, this ranking shows that entrepreneurs derive more advantages than workers, and that workers derive more benefits than other owners of production factors. The next question then is whether this ranking remains stable over time with the entry of new political parties to government office.

Prediction 4: Social democratic parties provide more benefits to workers than to entrepreneurs whereas conservative parties do the reverse.

The first issue to resolve is how to classify a party as social democratic or conservative. The Parti libéral du Québec (PLQ) of the 1960s and the Parti québécois (PQ) of the 1970s might be considered as social democratic. Both parties, especially the PQ, had claimed to hold a favourable predisposition toward workers. The Union nationale (UN) is usually defined as the party of small business. In the 1970s and 1980s, the PLQ has been identified more as the party of business. Finally, one may hypothesize that the PQ became much more sensitive to the cause of the entrepreneurs during the difficult economic situation of the province in the 1980s.

Table 5 indicates that entrepreneurs always receive a higher proportion of the benefits provided by governments, whatever the party in power. Therefore, the prediction does not seem to be confirmed by the data. An alternative test is to compare the difference between the proportion of benefits offered to entrepreneurs and workers with the average difference being 8.8 per cent. One might expect that a governing party favourable to workers will score below average whereas a governing party favourable to entrepreneurs will score

Table 5

Target groups of the benefits supplied by the Parties in government, 1960-1985 (Percentages)

Target groups	PLQ 60-62	PLQ 62-66	UN 66-70	PLQ 70-73	PLQ 73-76	PQ 76-81	PQ 81-85
entrepreneurs	19.0	30.1	22.2	26.6	30.1	21.6	23.7
workers	14.3	14.0	16.8	18.8	14.6	16.9	16.4
other owners of production factors	6.4	8.2	7.7	10.9	12.7	9.1	10.4
consumers and taxpayers	26.2	15.2	17.9	22.5	23.9	22.9	21.2
undetermined	33.2	32.5	35.4	21.2	18.8	29.5	28.3
Total %	100.0	100.0	100.0	100.0	100.0	100.0	100.0
n	(503)	(791)	(1089)	(1727)	(1178)	(1542)	(1403)
Difference between benefits conferred to entrepreneurs and workers (%)	4.7	16.1	5.4	7.8	15.5	4.7	7.3

above average. This kind of analysis indicates that the first PLQ government (1960-1962) and the first PQ government (1976-1981) were relatively more favourable to workers than the other five governments. On the other hand, the same figures show that the UN government (1966-1970), the third PLQ government (1970-1973), and the second PQ government (1981-1985) were less favourable to entrepreneurs than expected.

An alternative test is to hypothesize that the more a governing party favours a target group, the less it will impose costs on it. Table 6 indicates that the first PLQ government (1960-1962), the UN government (1966-1970), and the two PQ governments imposed costs on the entrepreneurs that were below the average (13.5%) of the seven governments formed in the 25 year period. These four governments, especially the two PQ governments, were the most favourable to entrepreneurs. With respect to the costs imposed on workers, the only governments above the average imposed cost (4.5%) are the PLQ government of 1970-1973 and the second PQ government of 1981-1985. These governments appear to have been less favourable to workers than the five other governments of the period.

Table 6

Imposition of costs by type of target groups and government, 1960-1985 (percentages)

Target groups	PLQ 60-62	PLQ 62-66	UN 66-70	PLQ 70-73	PLQ 73-76	PQ 76-81	PQ 81-85
Entrepreneurs	12.5	15.0	11.1	17.0	16.3	12.6	9.8
Workers	4.4	3.4	2.9	8.7	3.8	3.5	4.8
Other owners of production factors	2.8	2.0	3.0	3.6	5.3	2.9	2.9
Consumers and taxpayers	12.1	5.6	4.7	4.7	5.0	3.4	3.1
Government and entrepreneurs	0.2	0.1	0.2	0.3	0.4	0.4	0.0
Undetermined	68.0	73.8	78.1	65.6	69.1	77.2	79.4
TOTAL	503	791	1089	1727	1178	1542	1403

Conclusion

In a decision-making environment with perfect information and no transaction costs and where decisions are made utilizing the unanimity rule, every allocation of resources is Pareto efficient. However, these assumptions are never met in real life situations. As a result, one must pay attention to the transfers of wealth among members of the collectivity. The derivation of the biases inherent in wealth transfers has drawn upon three conceptual frameworks: market failure models; rent seeking models; and party government models of policy-making. The data used in this study do not support the market failure models: policy-makers produce 13.6 per cent of public goods as opposed to 6.7 per cent of private goods and 62.2 per cent of club goods. Clearly, the legislation enacted has produced benefits exclusively reserved for special interest groups. The data do not support the most significant prediction of the rent seeking theory either which states that policy-makers have an incentive to supply policies combining concentrated benefits and diffuse costs.

Third, the data support the prediction that the supply of policies carries a favourable bias toward the owners of production factors. Fourth, contrary to expectations, social democratic governing parties do not provide more benefits to workers than to entrepreneurs. As a result, entrepreneurs are the big winners in the policy-making game.

The significance of these findings must be recast in the larger institutional framework structuring the incentive structure of policy-makers and organized interests. In this respect, one must keep in mind that benefits and costs are difficult to match together, because they are not determined simultaneously in the same policy decisions. Despite this institutional trait, one can state that the more a group receives benefits from governmental interventions, the more it has to assume the costs of the conferred benefits.

Policy outcomes rarely correspond to pure public goods. Governmental interventions create incentives for special interest groups, especially for entrepreneurs and workers. Our data do not lead to the conclusion that the political market would be a substitute compensating for the inefficiencies and the inequities generated by the private market institutions. On the contrary, one is almost led to conclude that the political market feeds the private market by providing incentives rewarding owners of production factors. Consequently, one could have expected that the governing parties of a capitalist society provide more benefits to entrepreneurs than to workers. In any event, the benefits supplied to entrepreneurs through policy outcomes are so massive that one cannot associate the private market to a free market. It is a market regulated through governmental interventions. Given that this pattern of policy outcomes has not changed very much during the last 25 years, it is difficult to conclude that governing parties have become driven more and more by neo-liberal ideologies.

References

Coleman, William D. (1988). *Business and Politics. A Study of Collective Action.* Montreal: McGill-Queen's University Press.

Downs, Anthony (1957). *An Economic Theory of Democracy.* New York: Harper and Row.

Frey, Bruno S. (1983). *Democratic Economic Policy: A Theoretical Introduction.* Oxford: Martin Robertson.

Hayes, Michael T. (1978). "The Semi-Sovereign Pressure Groups: A Critique of Current Theory and an Alternative Typology." *Journal of Politics,* 40: 134-61.

_____ **(1981).** *Lobbyists and Legislators: A Theory of Political Markets.* New Brunswick: Rutgers University Press.

Lowi, Theodore H. (1972). "Four Systems of Policies, Politics and Choice." *Public Administration Review,* 32:298-310.

McCormick, Robert E., and Robert D. Tollison (1981). *Politicians, Legislation and the Economy. An Inquiry into the Interest-Group Theory of Government.* Boston: Martinus Nijhoff Publishing.

Moe, Terry M. (1980). *The Organization of Interests. Incentives and the Internal Dynamics of Political Interest Groups.* Chicago: The University of Chicago Press.

_____ **(1981).** "Toward a Broader View of Interest Groups." *The Journal of Politics,* 43: 531-43.

Montmarquette, Claude (1988). *Le marché politique: Qu'est-ce qui est produit? Qui y participe? Qui en profite?* Montréal: Cahier 1488, Département d'économique et C.R.D.E., Université de Montréal.

Olson, Mancur Jr. (1965). *The Logic of Collective Action: Public Goods and the Theory of Groups.* New York: Schoken Books.

_____ **(1982).** *The Rise and Decline of Nations: Economic Growth, Stagflation and Social Rigidities.* New Haven: Yale University Press.

Salisbury, Robert H. (1968). "The Analysis of Public Policy: A Search for Theories and Roles." In Austin Ranney, ed. *Political Science and Public Policy.* Chicago: Markham.

Thurow, Lester C. (1980). *The Zero Sum Society.* New York: Basic Books.

Wilson, James Q. (1980). *The Politics of Regulation.* New York: Basic Books.

Endnotes

*This paper draws on a research project supported by the Social Sciences and Humanities Research Council of Canada. I would like to thank Danile Gendreau and Dany Savard for research assistance; François Michaud for programming; William Coleman, Paule Duchesneau, Grace Skogstad, and Robert Young for their comments on the first draft of the paper.

1. These figures were obtained by abstracting from the data in Table 4. For example, the first figure, 2525, refers to "concentrated benefits and undetermined costs." Concentrated benefits are those that go to entrepreneurs, workers, or other owners of production factors; undetermined costs are those in the sixth column of Table 4. Hence the total of the cells in this column that refer to entrepreneurs, workers, or other owners of production factors comes to 2525.

Glossary of Technical Terms

Club goods:	goods from which benefits are indivisible and excludable.
Common pool goods:	goods conveying nonexcludable benefits that are divisible.
Concentrated benefits:	benefits offered to owners of production factors.
Concentrated costs:	costs assumed by owners of production factors.
Diffused benefits:	benefits provided to consumers or taxpayers.
Diffused costs:	costs supported by consumers or taxpayers.
Divisible benefits:	benefits for which one can identify a finite amount that can be allocated among recipients. Otherwise, benefits are indivisible.
Excludable benefits:	benefits for which one can identify an eligibility criterion or a schedule of charges that recipients must satisfy before consuming the goods. Otherwise, benefits are nonexcludable.
Free-ride:	the phenomenon whereby a group has an incentive to capture a benefit for which it can avoid assuming the production costs.
High cost coalitions:	groups made up of individuals concerned by an issue in their capacity as consumers or taxpayers.
Information costs:	the costs of acquiring and analyzing information required to make decisions.
Low cost coalitions:	groups composed of individuals concerned by an issue in their capacity as owners of a production factor.
Market failure:	a market situation in which the private market rules prevent the participants from capturing potential benefits that other rules might make appropriable.
Pareto optimal outcome:	such an outcome occurs when the allocation of resources among alternative policy decisions is such that no one could be made better off by a reallocation without making someone else worse off.
Private goods:	goods carrying divisible and perfectly excludable benefits.
Public goods:	goods conveying indivisible and nonexcludable benefits.
Transaction costs:	information costs; negotiation and decision-making costs assumed by participants in the decision-making process; and, finally, costs arising from the enforcement of the decisions made by the participants.
Wealth transfer:	this phenomenon occurs when interest groups or policy-makers work to redistribute income rather than working for the production of additional outputs of wealth.

CHAPTER THIRTEEN

CONCLUSION

William D. Coleman and Grace Skogstad

Public policy-making in Canada occurs within policy communities in which state actors and representatives of organized interests, primarily but not exclusively, interact to shape public policy in a given sector over time. Normally, the centre of the subgovernment are state actors, usually but not always the lead ministry responsible for the policy field. In proximal position are spokespersons for the organizations which claim to represent the dominant societal interests in the sector. Further removed from the central locus of decision-making, in the attentive public, are other state and private actors.

Policy communities, so defined, exist in most of the sectors examined in this volume. Let us take, for example, the British Columbia forest land use policy community identified by Wilson *(Chapter 6)*. He demonstrates that it included state authorities and industry associations linked together through a number of well-established mechanisms for the purpose of devising policies regarding the use of

BC's forest land. At the core of the sub-government are both state and private actors: the former, the Ministry of Forests as the lead agency, and two committees which separately draw together the deputy ministers and ministers of eight government departments; the latter, the Council of Forest Industries of British Columbia and individual forestry companies. Those actors on the periphery of the sub-government, who monitor and influence policy decisions but do not regularly participate in policy-making, are also identifiable: forest environment groups and the federal departments of forestry and environment, to cite three.

As this example illustrates, in mapping policy communities, the focus has been on understanding the relationships among public and private actors that form around particular issue areas within the policy community. These policy networks, as we have defined them, are importantly shaped by the structural characteristics of both state agencies and private interests. Attention has been directed to uncovering those organizational attributes which contribute to state autonomy and state capacity. The former refers to the degree to which state officials are able to define the problems confronting the sector and propose solutions to them quite independently of societal actors. The existence of professional bureaucracies, able to generate their own information and armoured with non-negotiable legal mandates and unambiguous regulations, appears to further state autonomy. The latter denotes the ability of state actors to draw on the requisite resources and policy instruments to translate their goals into policy outcomes. State capacity, though also enhanced by bureaucratic expertise, is importantly determined by the state's ability to coordinate and concentrate decision-making, through either single agency dominance or inter-departmental committees.

With regard to private societal interests, the significant structural characteristic is their degree of organizational development: that is, the degree to which representative, well-resourced, autonomous, and policy-capable associational systems exist to articulate the interests of private actors within the sector. Depending upon their level of organizational development, private actors are equipped to assume different roles in policy networks, interacting with state officials either as policy advocates or policy participants.

State-Society Interaction and Public Policy

Perceiving policy-making in terms of the relations between organized interests and state agencies differs from both societal-centred and state-centred views of public policy.[1] We reject the societal-centred argument that public policy is a function of the preferences and influence of social forces or interest groups, and that state officials or institutions have little autonomy to shape public policy in their own vision. Equally, we do not accept that characteristics of the state alone —its institutional structures and/or the capacities and goals of political officials within it—can explain policy outcomes. Rather, explanatory import is enhanced by examining closely the interaction between state and societal actors.

This interaction implies that the manner and the degree to which organized interests may exert influence can be critically shaped by state institutions. The state can encourage the mobilization of latent groups whose interests complement its own, as has occurred in the Nova Scotia fishery, and with respect to women's groups and official language minorities. Moreover, the institutional structure of the state shapes interest groups' ability to gain access to decision-making circles. Executive-centred institutions and executive federalism (Cairns, 1988), for example, often create barriers to entry for organized interests, while bureaucratic diffusion and shared jurisdiction may open up avenues and opportunities for influence. And finally, in its differential treatment of societal interests through public policies, the state may promote particular interests and undermine others, including the possibilities of a broader coalition of interests, as the example of agriculture attests.

Similarly, the ability of state actors to prevail in decision making may be importantly shaped by the goals and organizational development of societal interests. Public officials, whose objectives require the cooperation of sectoral interests, may find themselves powerless to act when these are not supported by key societal groups. Moreover, without the support of well-organized client interests, sectoral state actors may be unable to prevent interference in their policy community, and may find their own agenda usurped by central agencies or other departments. More generally, and a point discussed in greater detail below, political decisions made at one juncture create institutions that limit later options; a delegation of state authority by previous administrations has a lingering, constraining effect on the independence of future public officials.

The Impact of Macro Factors and Historical Residues

Although the focus in this collection is on group-state relations at the sectoral level, the chapters demonstrate that policy networks and policy communities are best understood when attention is paid to first, the broader political, economic, and ideological environment within which they function; and second, the legacy of history. Contemporary policy communities bear the brunt of yesterday's political decisions and function in an economy characterized by global interdependence and in a society whose boundaries are permeable.

The impacts of broader institutional and economic parameters on policy communities emerge in various chapters. Greater global economic interdependence can be a potent catalyst to the organizational development of societal interests. For example, the development of the Canadian Forest Industries Council was spurred by US trade protectionism *(Chapter 5)*; Ontario labour became more cohesive in the wake of the threat posed by the increasingly competitive Asian auto manufacturers in the late 1970s *(Chapter 11)*; and the Canadian Payments Association is a partial response to changes in telecommunications technology that furthered the globalization of capital markets *(Chapter 4)*.

Similarly, international economic threats and opportunities may induce state authorities to enhance their own policy capacities. Cases in point are the strengthening of the state to deal with the perceived crisis in the forestry *(Chapter 5,6)*, to the enhanced probability of instability in the financial sector *(Chapter 4)*, and to the perceived threat posed to domestic agricultural producers by the Canada-US Free Trade Agreement *(Chapter 3)*.

The broader institutional context also exerts an influence on state-group relations within sectors. A competitive party system may undermine the perceived need for collective action, and so deter organizational development, as the example of the Maritime fishery attests *(Chapter 2)*. The effects of federalism on organizational development may be more difficult to discern. In vesting important jurisdictional responsibilities at the provincial level, the federal system may undermine organizational development on a national plane. However, the perceived discriminatory exercise of jurisdiction at one level may be a catalyst to strong associational development at the other level, as demonstrated by the example of Québec agricultural producers *(Chapter 3)*. And finally, as social security policy in the 1960s shows *(Chapter 9)*, functional executive federalism strengthens the capacity of state officials and their ability to dominate a policy network.

Still another important macro-level factor is the normative, ideological order that pervades the whole political system, and conditions the norms and values of sectoral actors within the policy community. Such an order may strengthen the position of some actors (those with compatible values) and weaken others (those with incongruent values). Moreover, actors in policy communities whose principles are not in resonance with the prevailing order risk the possibility of central agencies "invading" the policy community and imposing their own point of view. Haddow *(Chapter 9)* alludes to such a scenario in social welfare policy during the 1980s. The second parameter that conditions the functioning of policy communities is the "weight of history". Contemporary policy communities and networks cannot be understood in isolation from the past. Past policies may limit later options of state officials by denying them the use of particular policy instruments. So may traditional mechanisms of processing claims (for example, by elaborate consultation) that outlive their rationale, but whose violation at a later date raises cries of illegitimate policy-making. Societal interests are also constrained by past policies; programs that treat particular interests within the sector differently, and so reduce common problems and interests, are likely to undermine collective action at a later date.

Policy Networks and Organizational Development

The studies in this book have demonstrated clearly that the policy communities, and the policy networks that form within these communities around particular issues, vary across policy sectors. Relatively stable and closed policy communities exist in banking and forestry, where a limited number of public and private actors routinely and consistently interact to formulate and/or implement public policy. In contrast, the fishery, social welfare, and day care policy communities display more openness and fluidity, with members being less well integrated. Across sectors, there are differences, as well, in the roles private actors play in the policy community. Organized interests are influential policy advocates in Ontario agriculture, active policy participants in agriculture and in the regulation of occupational health and safety standards in Quebéc, and neither on matters of poverty policy. These variations in the roles and policy efficacy of organized interests relate strongly to the level of organizational development of the associational systems in question. When coupled with differences in the autonomy and capacity of state officials from sector to sector, variations in organizational development give rise to a range of policy networks that embrace pressure pluralism, clientele pluralism, state direction, concertation, and corporatism. Table 1 summarizes the findings of the various chapters.

Table 1 indicates that pressure pluralist networks occur most frequently, and hence that organized interests interact with the state more often as policy advocates than as policy participants. Pressure pluralism best describes the networks within which most policies concerning labour, the fisheries, and Ontario farmers are made; it prevails, as well, in banking when it comes to financial institution deregulation, and in policy-making on day care, official language minority groups, and the disadvantaged.

Table 1

Political Issues and Policy Networks

Pressure Pluralism	Clientele Pluralism	Concertation	Corporatism	State Direction
*fisheries development			*fishing allocations	
	*payment system regulation (pre-1980)		*payment system regulation (post 1980)	
*forest planning		*forest management		
		*capital adequacy regulation		
*agricultural trade-Ontario		*agricultural trade-Quebec		
*occupational health and safety-overall framework			*occupational health and safety regulation-Quebec	
			*agricultural marketing	
*social welfare for the poor (1970s, 1980s)				*social welfare for the poor (prior to 1970)
*official language minorities promotion (1970-)				*official language minorities promotion (1960s)
*day care				
*automobile sector restructuring				

A review of these issue areas suggests several factors that favour the development of pressure pluralist networks. Distributive policies, that is, policies that allocate goods and services to individuals (day care, social welfare benefits, trade benefits), are common here. These policies demand less cooperation between state agencies and sectoral groups than regulatory policies, for example. Policies that strive to set out a planning framework for economic development of a sector will tend to be formulated in pressure pluralist networks in the presence of lowly developed organized interests (national forest associations) or bureaucratic competition (fisheries, forest industry, day care).

Table 1 also indicates that two of these pressure pluralist networks evolved from state-directed networks. In the absence of virtually any organizational development of societal actors, state actors were temporarily able in the 1960s to formulate and realize their own goals and objectives on the formulation of policies for the disadvantaged (the Canada Assistance Plan [CAP]), and activities surrounding the promotion of official language minorities. In addition, Burt *(Chapter 8)* suggests that the "women's issue" of maternity leave pay was addressed in a state-directed network. Skogstad *(Chapter 3)* notes that the creation of corporatist agricultural commodity marketing structures was preceded by a short period of state direction. Each of these state-directed networks was relatively short-lived and occurred in exceptional circumstances. Two represented a response to a crisis: a threatened breakdown in agricultural markets in Ontario and a regime crisis sparked by the rise of the independence movement in Québec. The maternity leave pay issue arose in the wake of the 1968 election and the Liberal agenda of a "Just Society". After this initial burst of energy, women's issues came to be addressed in the more usual pressure pluralist frameworks as interests became better organized. Finally, the design of the CAP in a state-directed network was the product of singular structural circumstances that allowed federal and provincial welfare officials to act on their own policy preferences. Subsequent social welfare policies moved into more pluralistic fora.

Concertation networks involving a capable and autonomous state actor and a policy capable, highly developed associational system occurred in British Columbia for the management of the forest resource, to address the issue of new standards of capital adequacy for chartered banks, and were rather common for addressing a number of issues relevant to Québec's farmers. Such networks appear to be more likely when regulatory policy instruments are the preferred means of state action. The design and implementation of regulatory regimes are more likely to require a close working relationship between state and sectoral actors, including the sharing of information and responsibility. When the state actor is a lesser partner in such a relationship, the network may lapse into clientele pluralism, the network that prevailed in the payments system prior to 1980 *(Chapter 4)*. Concertation networks also presume an interventionist state, a state that on its own initiative or at the behest of societal interests, is willing to shape and direct the dynamic of market activity. Maintaining a solvent and efficient financial system and overseeing the development of a key natural resource (forests in British Columbia) are two examples where the Canadian state has felt compelled to intervene.

Despite some structural similarities, corporatist networks arise in circumstances more akin to those of state direction than concertation. They represent an attempt by a relatively strong state actor (Schmitter, 1985) to mediate one kind of political crisis, a crisis involving intense social conflict between social groups. They differ from state direction in that the state tries to devolve responsibility for resolving the crisis to the societal actors in question and, to the extent that this devolution is successful, the networks are expected to endure into the medium and long term. Thus the nationalist goals of the PQ government—its desire to preserve a vulnerable political and cultural identity and to improve social cohesion prior to the Referendum—were an important factor in its promotion of corporatist structures for managing the divisive and bitter issues related to occupational health and safety. The federal Department of Finance, in partnership with the Bank of Canada, engineered the shift from clientele pluralism to corporatism in the banking payments system in the presence of growing friction among different sets of financial institutions. Such friction was a concern in an environment that was raising questions about the viability of the financial system in the wake of increased internationalization and competition in the financial services sector. Similarly, an economic crisis played a major role in forcing the federal government to take a leadership role in the East Coast fishery and to establish corporatist fishery sector management committees.

The fact that corporatism in the fishery was a fragile phenomenon reminds us that sectoral corporatism only becomes viable for resolving conflicts when associations exist to represent competing sectoral interests and have some capacity to participate in policy-making. Where interest associations are weakly developed or nonencompassing, state authorities can impose their own agenda in a state-directed network. Pross and McCorquodale *(Chapter 2)*stress that the associational systems in the fishing sector were not extensively developed. They were sufficiently capable to support the creation of the formal and continuing structures of the Atlantic Groundfish Advisory Committee and local sector management committees that involved fishery representatives, governmental staff, and processors associations in the preparation and implementation of an annual fishing plan. Yet the role of these committees remained advisory only; final decision-making authority was retained by the state.

In short, the weaker the level of organizational development of affected interests, the greater the likelihood that corporatism will dwindle into symbolic tripartite arrangements with policy continuing to be made in pressure pluralist networks. Yates' *(Chapter 11)* discussion of the Ontario Labour-Management Committee (which included government, business and labour representatives) and Tuohy's *(Chapter 10)* characterization of the broader framework for occupational health and safety policy-making in Québec illustrate this outcome. Both authors hesitate to characterize as corporatist the tripartite bodies they describe. Their lack of formal decision-making powers coupled with problems of a lack of representativeness, insufficient autonomy from members, and weak cohesion within both the labour and business communities all point to a corporatism that was stillborn. Yates and Tuohy both demonstrate that such symbolic structures are vulnerable to shifts in the partisan makeup of the government. We may need to speak at the sectoral level of scales of corporatism that range from the strong to the weak as Crouch (1983) and Lehmbruch (1984) have done at the macro-level.

These cases of very weak corporatism illustrate the importance of considering the level of organizational development of associational systems in analyzing the policy process. It is evident from the studies in this book that higher levels of organizational development increase the likelihood that specific societal interests will achieve their desired policy outcomes. Strong associational systems favour success in procuring public policy outputs or in gaining seats on advisory, possibly, governing councils. In the absence of a well developed associational system, organized interests are likely to succeed only with the support of other institutions or with the possession of purposive incentives that are deeply held. Thus the weakly developed systems of associations representing the Atlantic fishery became less of a hindrance once their issue became politicized at a regional level and entered the arena of partisan politics. Similarly, without exaggerating the success of BC's environmentalists, their purpose and the missionary zeal and intensive commitment that it generated, helped them to reach beyond their insecure and inadequate finances, and geographic and philosophical divisions. Yet that reach still was not far enough to break the hold on forest management policy of the highly developed foresty industry associational system in that province.

Changes in Policy Communities and Policy Networks

Stringer and Richardson (1982) comment that a major objective of actors within policy communities is to maintain the stable relationships that exist within the community and so to avoid abrupt policy change. The studies in this book reveal how difficult attaining this objective can be. The composition of policy communities changes— in the postwar period, these changes have almost always involved an expansion and not a contraction in the size of the community. New interests are added to the attentive public or to the sub-government and some interests seek to move from the attentive public to the sub-government. These changes in the policy community, in turn, spark changes in the policy networks—the structural arrangements between state and society for resolving issues of concern to a given community.

For the purposes of analysis, changes in policy communities can be treated as a summary variable reflecting broader changes in the political system and the society at large. Understanding the dynamics of changes in policy communities and of policy networks is a difficult task, and one that we can only begin to address here. What is clear at this stage is that the policy process in the postwar period has become more complex, more formalized, and less episodic. The increased presence of state actors in many aspects of society has invited a kind of organized pluralism. State actors, faced with devising rather complex policies and uncertain of the impacts of various instruments and strategies, invite affected interests to organize and to develop some minimum capacity to enter into a dialogue on policy. In some situations, societal interests organize to pre-empt state action or to defend against expected intervention. Consequently, the number of organized interest groups has grown rapidly in the postwar period in Canada (Coleman, 1988), as it has in other countries such as the United States (Walker, 1983). Discussions of organized pluralism began in the postwar period with Truman's (1951) classic work and grew into a major field of analysis in political science.

Despite the pluralism of these governing arrangements, as Stringer and Richardson imply, both state and societal actors sought to stabilize the arrangements. Such stability took several forms. Perhaps most common was a kind of regularized pressure pluralism involving state actors and several interested groups. In other instances, where only one societal interest was involved, the relationship congealed into clientele pluralism or concertation depending on the relative strength of the state and societal players. Whatever the particular form of the policy network, the membership in the policy community stabilized for a brief period of time with an understood division of labour among state actors and groups in the sub-government, and between the sub-government and the attentive public.

The studies in this book emphasize the importance of the degree to which these stabilized policy communities are open to change. Various factors, many of them interdependent, spark new arrangements in policy arenas. Socio-economic changes may be reflected in the policy community. For example, the tendency of farmers to specialize on specific commodities has fostered the creation and strengthening of commodity-based interest groups within agriculture at the expense of more encompassing associations like the Canadian Federation of Agriculture. The growth of deposit-taking by trust and loan companies in competition with the chartered banks has broadened the banking policy community. The expansion of women in the labour force, and their concentration in particular occupations, have altered the strategies of the trade union movement and expanded the community concerned with social policy.

Changes in values often associated with these socio-economic changes may bring additional changes to policy communities. Certainly the previous example of the expanded role of women in the labour force has spawned a new wave of feminism and a rapid rise of groups concerned with the "status of women" in society. As the demands of continued economic growth have created greater pressures on the environment, previously politically dormant societies of naturalists, anglers, and hunters as well as new groups espousing the ideology of environmentalism have entered policy communities dealing with resource management, urban planning, and industrial development. Well-established business groups, and new groups such as the Business Council on National Issues, reacting against the expanded state role, have begun to address policy areas related to social welfare where they previously had little or no interest. In short, both basic socio-economic changes and accompanying shifts in values quickly lead to alterations of policy communities in this complex regime of organized pluralism.

Changes in political institutions themselves foster changes in policy communities. The complexity of the task of governing has led to an increased formalization of policy-making, whether it be between ministers and public servants, within the public service itself, or within the cabinet. Groups have been forced to be more analytical in their approach to policy and the state has become more systematic in trying to assess the impact of policy. A rationalized, formalized policy process may lead a department of the environment to seek out environmentalists' perspectives as well as those of industry, or the Department of Health and Welfare to investigate the impact of policy on recipients of social welfare and not only on those paying for new services.

The addition of new state institutions increases the size of a policy community and possibly leads to the creation of new communities. We speak here not only of new departments and agencies, but also of changes in basic constitutional arrangements. Thus the introduction of the Charter of Rights and Freedoms has brought significant changes to policy communities dealing with linguistic minorities, the equality of women, the rights of trade unions, and the physically handicapped. The plurality of political authorities has reinforced the pluralism of the policy networks within these communities.

Patterns of Network Change
The studies in this book have suggested several possible shifts that take place in policy networks in response to changes in the policy community. At this stage in theory building, we can only point to these and hope that future research will be able to identify better the general conditions favouring such changes.

1. pressure pluralism > state direction > pressure pluralism

Variations in this pattern occurred in policy areas related to the promotion of official language minorities, maternity leave provisions, and social welfare benefits targetted to the poor. Other studies on the National Energy Program (Doern and Toner, 1985) and on the development of a space satellite prime contractor capacity (Atkinson and Coleman, 1989) have also traced this pattern. The circumstances prompting political authorities to depart from the standard pluralist pattern vary, but normally tend to be extraordinary and short-lived; government leaders and bureaucratic officials work to foster new interest associations or to repair relations with existing groups in order to return to a pressure pluralist mode of operation.

2. concertation > pressure pluralism

Some of the most enduring relationships between societal actors and the state in the postwar period took the form of partnerships between particular state agencies and a highly developed interest association. Wilson's *(Chapter 6)* description of the relationship between the Ministry of Forests in British Columbia and the forest companies provides a ready example of this phenomenon. His analysis of the challenges to this policy network both from within the state (environmental and parks authorities) and in society (naturalist societies, environmentalists) showed the strength of the partnership in the face of change. Nonetheless, it does appear that this network is moving slowly toward a pressure pluralist system. Another example of a concertation relationship undergoing change comes from the banking sector. Briefly alluded to by Coleman *(Chapter 4)*, the network for discussing the regulation of institutions engaged in deposit-taking has expanded from one limited to the Canadian Bankers Association and the Department of Finance to a pressure pluralist network involving the addition of numerous interest groups on the societal side and provincial governments on the state side. Skogstad *(Chapter 3)* describes the creation of a concertation network in Québec agriculture but finds little evidence that this relationship between farmers and the Department of Agriculture and Food is under any stress. Critical to the challenge to any concertation network appears to be a well-developed associational system (competing financial institutions), an ability to influence votes (environmentalists in BC), or an ideological shift by government leaders.

3.   pressure pluralism > corporatism

This kind of change arises in times of crisis when conflict among major societal groups has led to a breakdown in the policy process. Corporatism becomes a feasible response to such a crisis, providing that the state is relatively capable and autonomous from both sides, and that associational systems exist which are sufficiently developed to exercise some control over members in exchange for a share in state authority. Perhaps the most successful example of this kind of shift in policy networks occurs in agricultural marketing at the provincial level. Skogstad *(Chapter 3)* shows how the resolution worked itself out in Ontario with the restructuring of marketing boards, a story repeated in most other provinces. Atkinson and Coleman (1985, 1989) relate a similar tale for the dairy processing sector on the national plane. Pross and McCorquodale *(Chapter 2)* trace the installation of a limited corporatism in the management of the Atlantic fishery. The contrast between these examples and that provided by Tuohy *(Chapter 10)* suggests some conditions for this kind of network change. Associational systems must be at a significant level of organizational development and there must be some commitment by Parliament or the legislature to place the corporatist network in a non-partisan arena. When both of these conditions are lacking, the corporatist solution quickly begins to unravel as Tuohy indicates so well.

These patterns of network change were the most evident from the studies in this book. There is no reason to expect that they are the only ones that will occur. For example, the particular choice of sectors in this book ended up providing few examples of clientele pluralist networks. Yet there is good reason to suspect that these are particularly vulnerable to change. Coleman *(Chapter 4)* shows how such a network was transformed into a corporatist arrangement when other financial institutions challenged the chartered banks' domination of the national payments system. Similarly, the regulation of the over-the-counter securities business in Canada has shifted from a clientele pluralist network to a concertation arrangement as pressure has increased on the state to increase its own policy capacity (Coleman, 1989). Finally,

Young (1990) traces the breakdown of clientele pluralism in the US dairy sector and its replacement with a pressure pluralist network. We expect that further research will improve our understanding of these changes as well as of the three patterns that emerged clearly from this book.

Policy Networks and Policy Innovation

Students of public policy remain very interested in why particular policy outcomes emerge and how policy innovation and change might be brought about. The analysis of the evolution of policy communities and policy networks appears to be particularly helpful for the first of these tasks; the evidence is more sketchy for the second. None the less, several concluding points do emerge from the studies in this book that may prove fruitful for future research. First, concertation networks embracing a strong sectoral interest association and specialized, capable and autonomous state agencies can provide a particularly stout defence against changes demanded by other societal interests or state actors. Innovation appears to be much more incremental in these kinds of networks. Three cases in this book illustrate this finding. Wilson *(Chapter 6)* describes the frontal assault on a business-dominated forest policy mounted by a host of interests with environmental concerns in British Columbia, an assault that has not been able yet to break the fortress-like policy network composed of the Ministry of Forests, the Council of Forest Industries of British Columbia, and the large forestry companies. Similarly, Coleman *(Chapter 4)* notes a series of changes in the financial sector that allowed such near-banks as trust and loan companies and financial cooperatives to enter the banking field by the early 1960s. Yet it has taken three decades to bring about full recognition of these changes in legislation. Slowing the pace of change has been the entrenched relationship that has existed between the Department of Finance and the chartered banks through the Inspector General of Banks (later the Supervisor of Financial Institutions). Even as late as 1988, when a new system for the regulation of bank capital was being developed, near banks were virtually excluded from the policy network. And finally, Skogstad *(Chapter 3)* notes that the concertation network in Québec agriculture proved more formidable than pressure pluralism in Ontario in warding off potentially deleterious effects of the Free Trade Agreement.

In contrast, state-directed networks, where state agencies are autonomous and possess considerable policy expertise, can be important sources of innovation. Haddow *(Chapter 9)* argues that the initial set of postwar policies directed toward the disadvantaged emerged from such a network. Similar points are made by Pal *(Chapter 7)* in his assessment of policy promoting official language minorities, by Burt *(Chapter 8)* in her analysis of the initial governmental responses to the postwar feminist movement, by Yates *(Chapter 11)* in her discussion of the Autopact, and by Pross and McCorquodale *(Chapter 2)* in their description of changes in fisheries policy in the late 1970s. The absence of highly developed organized interests focussing specifically on a sector appears to free the hand of the state somewhat, given supportive political leaders.

Finally, a government bent on a significant change in policy direction is likely to be more successful if faced by a pressure pluralist network rather than a closed network such as concertation or corporatism. Haddow *(Chapter 9)* shows that the Conservative government elected at the federal level in 1984 was not stymied significantly by the weakly organized poverty associational system it faced when it sought to cut back on welfare state provisions. Burt *(Chapter 8)* indicates that the Conservatives were able to play upon the competition in the women's associational system to promote their particular approach to child care policy and to weaken the position of the dominant association, the National Action Committee on the Status of Women. Yet the same government has had much more difficulty implementing its blueprint for financial system reform in part because of the entrenched networks that exist between particular interest associations and specialized parts of the state apparatus at both levels of government. In an argument consistent with these observations, Tuohy (Chapter 10) suggests that the lingering pressure pluralist elements in the associational systems of business and labour permitted the Liberal government to tinker significantly with the corporatist apparatus for administering occupational health and safety law put in place by its PQ predecessor.

These conclusions are preliminary. Yet they do indicate one possible future direction for the study of public policy and policy outcomes in particular. The authors of the studies in this volume believe that the organizational capacities of *both* state and societal actors must be assessed in the study of policy and that the *structural* linkages between these sets of actors are crucial to the kind of outcome that emerges. The policy network and policy community concepts central to virtually all the chapters provide a beginning point for a more refined theoretical understanding of the policy process and, we hope, some better answers to Lasswell's question: "who gets what, when, and how?"

References

Atkinson, M.M. and W.D. Coleman (1985). "Corporatism and Industrial Policy." In Alan Cawson, ed. *Organized Interests and the State: Studies in Meso-Corporatism.* London: Sage.

_____ (1989). *The State, Business and Industrial Change in Canada*. Toronto: University of Toronto Press.

Cairns, Alan (1988). "Citizens (Outsiders) and Governments (Insiders) in Constitution-Making: The Case of Meech Lake." *Canadian Public Policy*, XIV Supplement: 121-45.

Coleman, William D. (1988). *Business and Politics: A Study of Collective Action*. Montreal: McGill-Queen's University Press.

Crouch, Colin (1983). "Pluralism and the New Corporatism: A Rejoinder." *Political Studies*, 31:452-60.

Doern, G. Bruce and Glen Toner (1985). *The Politics of Energy: The Development and Implementation of the NEP*. Toronto: Methuen.

Hall, Peter A. (1986). *Governing the Economy*. New York: Oxford University Press.

Ikenberry, G. John, David A. Lake, and Michael Mastanduno (1988). "Introduction: approaches to explaining American foreign economic policy." *International Organization*, 42: 1-14.

Lehmbruch, G. (1984). "The Logic and Structural Conditions of Neo-Corporatist Concertation." In John Goldthorpe, ed. *Order and Conflict in Contemporary Capitalism*. Oxford: Oxford University Press.

Schmitter, Philippe C. (1985). "Neo-corporatism and the State." In Wyn Grant, ed. *The Political Economy of Corporatism*. London: Macmillan.

Stringer, J. and J. Richardson (1982). "Policy Stability and Policy Change: Industrial Training 1964-82." *Public Administration Bulletin*, 39: 22-39.

Truman, David B. (1951). *The Governmental Process*. New York: Knopf.

Walker, Jack L. (1983). "The Origins and Maintenance of Interest Groups in America." *American Political Science Review*, 77: 390-406.

Young, Brigitte (1990). "Does the American Dairy Industry Fit a Meso-Corporatism Model." *Political Studies*, forthcoming.

Endnotes

1. A good overview of these two approaches can be found in Ikenberry, Lake, and Mastanduno (1988: 7-14).

Acronyms

ABCPF	Association of BC Professional Foresters
AC	Agriculture Canada
ACOA	Atlantic Canada Opportunites Agency
ACGIH	American Conference of Governmental Industrial Hygienists
ADCO	Association of Day Care Operators of Ontario
AECQ	Association des entrepreneurs en construction du Québec
AFA	Atlantic Fishermen's Association
AGAC	Atlantic Groundfish Advisory Committee
APSA	American Political Science Association
ARIO	Agricultural Research Institute of Ontario
B & PW	Business and Professional Women
BCWF	BC Wildlife Federation
BIS	Bank for International Settlements
BNA Act	British North America Act
CACSW	Canadian Advisory Committee on the Status of Women
CAP	Canada Assistance Plan
CASW	Canadian Association of Social Workers
CAT	Commission des accidents du travail
CAW	Canadian Auto Workers
CBA	Canadian Bankers Association
CBRT and GW	Canadian Brotherhood of Railway, Transport, and General Workers
CCB	Canadian Council of the Blind
CCCS	Canadian Co-operative Credit Society
CCF/NDP	Co-operative Commonwealth Federation/New Democratic Party
CCFM	Canadian Council of Forest Ministers
CCLOW	Canadian Congress on Learning Opportunities for Women
CCMA	Canadian Childcare Management Association
CCSD	Canadian Council on Social Development
CDCAA	Canadian Day Care Advocacy Association
CDE	Centre des Dirigeants d'Entreprise
CDIC	Canada Deposit Insurance Corporation
CEIC	Canadian Employment and Immigration Commission
CEO	Chief executive officer
CEQ	Centrale de l'Enseignement du Québec

CFA	Canadian Federation of Agriculture (Chapter 2)
CFA	Canadian Forestry Association (Chapter 5)
CFAWU	Canadian Food and Allied Workers Union
CFFO	Christian Farmers Federation of Ontario
CFIC	Canadian Forest Industries Council
CFS	Canadian Forestry Service
CIF	Canadian Institute of Forestry
CLC	Canadian Labour Congress
CLHIA	Canadian Life and Health Insurance Association
CMA	Canadian Manufacturers Association
CNIB	Canadian National Institute for the Blind
COFI	Council of Forest Industries of British Columbia
CPA	Canadian Payments Association
CPPA	Canadian Pulp and Paper Association
CPQ	Conseil du Patronat du Québec
CRCD	Canadian Rehabilitation Council for the Disabled
CSAWU	Canadian Seafood and Allied Workers Union
CSD	Centrale des syndicats démocratiques
CSN	Confédération des syndicats nationaux
CSST	Commission de la Santé et de la Securité du Travail
CUPE	Canadian Union of Public Employees
CWC	Canada Welfare Council (Chapter 9)
CWC	Canadian Wood Council (Chapter 5)
CWF	Canadian Wildlife Federation
DEA	Department of External Affairs
Desjardins group	Confédération des Caisses Populaires et d'Economie Desjardins
DFO	Department of Fisheries and Oceans
DIST	Department of Industry, Science and Technology
DOE	Department of Environment
DRIE	Department of Regional Industrial Expansion
E and I	Department of Employment and Immigration
EDI	Electronic Data Interchange
EFT/POS	Electronic funds transfer at the point of sale
ELUC	Environment and Land Use Committee
ELUTC	Environment and Land Use Technical Committee
FBCN	Federation of BC Naturalists

FCC	Fisheries Council of Canada
FER	Friends of Ecological Reserves
FFGL	Forest Forum Group Leaders
FFHQ	la Fédération des francophones hors Québec
FIMTF	Forest Industry Machinery Task Force
FMCBC	Federation of Mountain Clubs of BC
FPAT	Farm Products Appeal Tribunal
FPI	Fisheries Products International
FPMA	Farm Products Marketing Act
FPMB	Farm Products Marketing Board
FPMC	Farm Products Marketing Commission
FRACC	Forest Research Advisory Council of Canada
FSAC	Forest Sector Advisory Council
FTA	Canada-US Free Trade Agreement
FTQ	Fédération des Travailleurs et Travailleuses du Québec
G-7	Group of Seven
G-10	Group of Ten
GAI	Guaranteed Annual Income
GATT	General Agreement on Tariffs and Trade
GDP	Gross Domestic Product
GFO	General Farm Organization
GM	General Motors
HWC	Health and Welfare Canada
ICNAF	International Commission on the North Atlantic Fishery
IDAC	Investment Dealers Association of Canada
IRSST	Institute de recherche en santé et en securité du travail du Québec
ISIC	International Standard Industrial Classification
ITA (US)	International Trade Administration
IWA	International Woodworkers of America
LDC	Less developed country
M and I	Department of Manpower and Immigration
MAI	Ministry of International Affairs of Québec
MAPAQ	Ministry of Agriculture, Fisheries and Food of Québec
MCCR	Ministry of Consumer and Commercial Relations (Ontario)
MFU	Maritime Fishermen's Union

MIC	Ministry of Industry and Commerce (Québec)
MITT	Ministry of Industry, Trade, and Technology (Ontario)
MNA	Member of the National Assembly
MOE	Ministry of the Environment
MOF	Ministry of Forests
MOP	Ministry of Parks
MSY	Maximum sustainable yield
NAC	National Action Committee on the Status of Women
NACCU	National Association of Canadian Credit Unions
NAFEL	Newfoundland Association of Fish Exporters Limited
NAPO	National Anti-Poverty Organization
NCW	National Council of Welfare
NDP	New Democratic Party
NFFAWU	Newfoundland Fish, Food and Allied Workers' Union
NFPMC	National Farm Products Marketing Council
NFSS	National Forest Sector Strategy Task Force
NFU	National Farmers Union
NPC	National Planning Committee
NPSCF	National Pensioners and Senior Citizens Federation
NSFA	Nova Scotia Fishermen's Association
NSP	National Sea Products
OCA	Ontario Cattlemen's Association
OECD	Organization for Economic Co-operation and Development
OFA	Ontario Federation of Agriculture
OFU	Ontario Farmers Union
OHSA	Occupational Health and Safety Administration (US)
OLC	Official Language Communities
OLMGs	Official language minority groups
OMAF	Ontario Ministry of Agriculture and Food
ORC	Outdoor Recreation Council
OSFI	Office of the Superintendent of Financial Institutions
OSPS	Okanagan Similkameen Parks Society
PAC	Public Archives of Canada
PCO	Privy Council Office
PELs	Permissible Exposure Levels
PLQ	Parti libéral du Québec

POL	Promotion of Official Languages
PQ	Parti Québécois
PWD	Public Welfare Division
QWL	Quality of Working Life
RCBB	Royal Commission on Bilingualism and Biculturalism
REAL Women	Realistic Equal Active for Life
Régie	Québec Régie des marchés agricoles
RWDSU	Retail, Wholesale, Department Store Union
SFPQ	Syndicat des Fonctionnaires Provinciaux du Québec
SICMC	Securities Industry Capital Markets Committee
SPANS	Seafood Producers' Association of Nova Scotia
SPGQ	Syndicat des Professionels du Gouvernement du Québec
SPRG	Social Policy Reform Group
SSC	Secretary of State of Canada
TAB	Transitional Assistance Benefit Programme
TAC	Total allowable catch
TCAC	Trust Companies Association of Canada
TFLs	Tree Farm Licences
TMAC	Treasury Management Association of Canada
TSAs	Timber Supply Areas
TLV	Threshold Limit Values
UAW	United Auto Workers
UCC	Union des Cultivateurs Catholiques
UIC	Unemployment Insurance Commission
UMF	United Maritime Fishermen
UN	Union nationale
UPA	Union des Producteurs Agricoles
WAC	Wilderness Advisory Committee
WCWC	Western Canada Wilderness Committee

Index